D0921595

The Ukraine
within the USSR

edited by
I. S. Koropeckyj

The Praeger Special Studies program—utilizing the most modern and efficient book production techniques and a selective worldwide distribution network—makes available to the academic, government, and business communities significant, timely research in U.S. and international economic, social, and political development.

The Ukraine within the USSR

An Economic Balance Sheet

PRAEGER SPECIAL STUDIES IN INTERNATIONAL ECONOMICS AND DEVELOPMENT

Praeger Publishers   New York   London

Library of Congress Cataloging in Publication Data
Main entry under title:

The Ukraine within the USSR.

(Praeger special studies in international economics
and development)
    Includes bibliographical references and index.
    1. Ukraine—Economic policy—Addresses,
essays, lectures. 2. Ukraine—Economic conditions
—1945-   —Addresses, essays, lectures.
3. Ukraine—Commerce—Addresses, essays, lectures.
I. Koropeckyj, I. S.
HC337.U5U477   1977   330.9'47'71085   77-7817
ISBN 0-03-022356-3

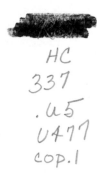

HC
337
.U5
U477
cop.1

PRAEGER SPECIAL STUDIES
200 Park Avenue, New York, N.Y., 10017, U.S.A.

Published in the United States of America in 1977
by Praeger Publishers,
A Division of Holt, Rinehart and Winston, CBS, Inc.

THE CHICAGO PUBLIC LIBRARY

BUSINESS SCIENCE/TECHNOLOGY

789   038   987654321

© 1977 by Praeger Publishers

JUL 6 15.   JUL 6 1978

All rights reserved

Printed in the United States of America

R03129 54365

Although I have been absent these . . . years, with little regret, from that native land which I own in common with yourselves, and whose agreeable climate attracts many foreigners from the most distant quarters of the world, yet it would be in no degree pleasing or desirable to me dwell in a region from which the truth of God, pure religion, and the doctrine of eternal salvation are banished, and the very kingdom of Christ laid prostrate! Hence I have no desire to return to it; yet it would be neither in accordance with human nor divine obligation to forget the people from which I am sprung, and to put away all regard for their welfare.

John Calvin

FOREWORD
Abram Bergson

Among the 15 republics constituting the Soviet Union, the Ukrainian is one of two (the other being the Belorussian) that are members of the United Nations. That, of course, is a legacy of Yalta, and testifies to Stalin's bargaining skill at that historic conference rather than to any approach of those two republics to the status of sovereign countries. Yet it is fitting that the Ukrainian Soviet Socialist Republic, at least, should have some special status within the USSR. True, the so-called Russian Republic by almost any standard overshadows all of its fellows, but the fact remains that the Ukrainian SSR is generally second only to that entity. Indeed, with a territory of 603,000 square kilometers, a population (on January 1, 1974) of 48.5 million, and a gross national product of perhaps $160 billion, the Ukrainian SSR has dimensions fully comparable to those of many of the larger countries of the world.

Although the republic's inhabitants almost inevitably have in the course of time become rather mixed heritage, 75 percent of its total population still designated themselves as "Ukrainian" in the Soviet census returns for 1970. Such persons have a history, language, and culture of their own.

In short, the Ukrainian SSR merits the attention of Western scholars simply for its own sake, but this volume, setting forth the proceedings of a conference held in Cambridge, Massachusetts, on September 26–27, 1975, represents one of the relatively few Western studies thus far to explore systematically the economy of a major political and cultural entity of the Soviet Union. It necessarily gains much in interest on that account.

Thus, we find here careful and detailed inquiries into such intriguing questions as the comparative growth of the Ukraine within the USSR; the corresponding trends in population, labor force, and consumption; the financial and commodity relations of the Ukraine with the balance of the USSR that underlie those developments; and the relative status in the USSR of Ukrainian mineral resources. The policies that have shaped the Ukrainian economy and the role of Ukrainian political and economic agencies in formulating and executing those policies are, at least implicitly, themes throughout the volume, but they are also singled out for special attention. At the conference, all the principal papers were the subject of evaluative comments.

The volume deepens understanding of the economy not only of the Ukraine but also of the USSR generally. It also provides essential background information on the recurring question concerning the import for politics in the Soviet Union of the notable diversity of peoples constituting that country. The conference at which the volume originated was sponsored by the Committee on Research and Development of the American Association for the Advancement of Slavic Studies, and was held at the Harvard Ukrainian Research Institute.

Students of the Ukraine and of the USSR have thus been put in debt to those organizations, and also to Professor I. S. Koropeckyj, who so skillfully organized the conference and edited the proceedings for publication.

This volume focuses attention on the economy of one of the largest Soviet republics—the Ukraine—and attempts to answer an important question: How has the Ukraine fared as a part of the USSR? Obviously, the answer to such a complex problem cannot be given in the form of a few numbers or unequivocal statements. Nevertheless, it is believed that the reader can reach but one conclusion: that the political status of the Ukraine has inhibited the growth of its economy and of the welfare of its citizens. An analysis of ideological and political advantages or disadvantages to the Ukraine resulting from this situation is beyond the scope of this book.

In view of the considerable progress that has been made in the study of Soviet economy, a single author can hardly treat the many aspects of the problem at hand. Therefore, this volume draws on the expertise of specialists. Their contributions to this symposium are based on papers—substantially revised since then—presented at the conference on the Ukrainian economy held at Harvard University on September 26 and 27, 1975. The chapters by Holland Hunter and Peter Wiles were added later, in order to round out the volume.

The authors could not be expected to exhaust all aspects of their particular topics. The reasons for this were limitations of space and, more important, the lack or inadequacy of statistical data and other pertinent material. It was hoped that the participation at the conference of specialists from Kiev and Moscow would help to overcome this deficiency. Unfortunately, invitations to these economists remained unanswered. It might be hoped that after the appearance of this volume Soviet scholars will contribute in their own publications, on a professional level, to the clarification of the issues raised.

A few remarks of an editorial nature are in order. The term "the Ukraine" is often used in the volume to designate "the Ukrainian SSR." In Soviet literature the abbreviation for the latter in Ukrainian is "UR(adians'ka)SR" and in Russian "US(ovetskaia)SR." To avoid confusion with the English abbreviation for the Soviet Union, the terms "UkRSR" and "UkSSR," respectively, are used. For the sake of simplicity, the constitutional status of the Ukraine is referred to as "republic" (and not "union-republic") and various central organs as "union" (and not "all-union"). The term "republic" is used as a noun and as an adjective. Finally, the transliteration of Ukrainian and Russian geographic and personal names is from the Ukrainian (with a few exceptions that are well known in the West) and Russian, respectively, according to the modified Library of Congress system.

The Harvard conference was sponsored by the Committee on Research and Development of the American Association for the Advancement of Slavic Studies. Additional and substantial aid in various forms was provided by the

School of Business Administration, Temple University, and the Harvard Ukrainian Research Institute, on whose premises the conference took place. I am very grateful to these institutions for their aid. I wish also to thank George W. Hoffman, chairman of the Committee on Research and Development, and Omeljan Pritsak, director of the Ukrainian Research Institute, for their personal interest in the project and their kind cooperation, and especially Seymour L. Wolfbein, dean of my school, and Louis T. Harms, chairman of my department, for their continuous help and encouragement. I am very grateful to Abram Bergson for his thoughtful remarks at the conference dinner; to Aron Katsenelinboigen, Michael J. Lavelle, S.J., Stephen Rapawy, Theodore Shabad, and Carl B. Turner for their perceptive comments at the conference; and to Holland Hunter, Herbert S. Levine, and Peter Wiles for their skillful chairing of conference sessions. In addition, Holland Hunter was very helpful in preparing the manuscript for publication, for which I am especially thankful. But most of all, I wish to thank my colleague V. N. Bandera for his constant good counsel and help during the preparation of the conference and during the editing of the papers for publication.

CONTENTS

LIST OF TABLES, FIGURES, AND MAPS

LIST OF ABBREVIATIONS

BOD	biological oxygen demand
CMEA	Council of Mutual Economic Assistance
CPSU	Communist Party of the Soviet Union
EEC	European Economic Community
EHV	extra-high voltage
ENDI	Economic Scientific Research Institute
FTM	foreign trade monopoly
GDP	gross domestic product
GNP	gross national product
GVO	gross value of output
kcal	kilocalorie
km^3	cubic kilometer
KMA	Kursk Magnetic Anomaly
kv	kilovolt
kw	kilowatt
kwh	kilowatt-hour
mw	milliwatt
NMP	net material product
RSFSR	"Russian Republic"
SSR	Soviet Socialist Republic
TsEMI	Central Economic-Mathematical Institute
TsSu	Central Statistical Administration
USSR	Soviet Union
VAT	value-added tax
VNDIVO	All-Union Scientific Research Institute for the Protection of Waters

LIST OF PUBLICATION ABBREVIATIONS

CDSP	Current Digest of the Soviet Press
DSUP	Digest of the Soviet Ukrainian Press
EDCC	Economic Development and Cultural Change
EG	Ekonomicheskaia gazeta
EiMM	Ekonomika i matematicheskie metody
EN	Ekonomicheskie nauki
ERU	Ekonomika Radians'koi Ukrainy
ESU	Ekonomika Sovetskoi Ukrainy
I	Izvestia
KU	Komunist Ukrainy
KUr	Kommunist Ukrainy
Narhosp	Narodne hospodarstvo Ukrains'koi RSR
Narkhoz	Narodnoe khoziaistvo SSSR
OiPONKh	Organizatsiia i planirovanie otraslei narodnogo khoziaistva
P	Pravda
PKh	Planovoe khoziaistvo
PoC	Problems of Communism
PP	Problemy pravoznavstva
PPE	Problemy politychnoi ekonomii
PU	Pravda Ukrainy
RES	Review of Economics and Statistics
RP	Radians'ke pravo
RU	Radians'ka Ukraina
S	Survey
SGiP	Sovetskoe gosudarstvo i pravo
SGRaT	Soviet Geography: Review and Translations
SR	Slavic Review
SS	Soviet Studies
VE	Voprosy ekonomiki
VS	Vestnik statistiki
VT	Vneshnaia torgovlia SSSR
VVR	Visti Verkhovnoi Rady Ukrains'koi RSR

PART

I

AN INTRODUCTORY
FRAMEWORK

1

OVERVIEW
Holland Hunter

The Union of Soviet Socialist Republics is not a single, undifferentiated unit whose purposes and experience can be analyzed in homogeneous terms. Politically, ethnically, geographically, and economically it is a large, sprawling collection of territories with distinct features. This book focuses on the most interesting and important subregion of the USSR—the Ukraine. The RSFSR is of course much larger, but it must be seen as a cluster of diverse parts. The Kazakh SSR is twice as large as the Ukraine but has only 30 percent as many people. In most of the significant demographic and economic dimensions of Soviet life, the Ukraine accounts for about 20 percent of the national total; and since the October Revolution it has had more than its share of the turbulent experiences that make up the Soviet record. It thus deserves its own analysis. Western scholarship on the USSR has understandably tended to give priority to obtaining an overall national assessment, focused on Moscow and the Kremlin's management of the whole structure; but this is no longer either necessary or sufficient for a sensitive appreciation of the full complexity of the forces at work in the Soviet Union today.

In Western economic analysis, attention to interregional issues steadily increases. The spatial dimension was slighted for half a century or so in neo-classical economic theory, but modern analysis draws on new tools and finer evidence to enlarge the scope of our understanding. Here too it is no longer either necessary or sufficient to confine oneself to national aggregates in reviewing the experience of a large economy. The theory and practice of economic development throughout the Third World gives significant attention to locational aspects of development problems. In this context the experience of major regions within the USSR provides case-study material that can contribute importantly to comparative analysis across a variety of political and institutional frameworks.

3

One way of setting the stage for an evaluation of the Ukraine's place in the Soviet economy is to remind the reader of four overlapping facets of "the economic problem" in its regional dimension so that Ukrainian experience can be analyzed in universal terms. The short-run questions are Whose interests shape economic activity (that is, by whom and where shall output be consumed)? By whom and where shall production be carried on? In the longer-run perspective, a third question is By whom and where should development be stimulated? In this connection one may also ask, What is the weight of infant-industry considerations? It is usually necessary also to ask how national defense considerations affect economic location policy. These questions have played decisive roles in the economic history of all the major developed economies, and they are burning issues among the developing economies today. Though hard to unravel, they are easy to state.

Perhaps the most fundamental issue involved in evaluating a territory's economic experience concerns whose interests shape its economic activity. In each economic community, contending interests share in both production and consumption. What determines who produces and who consumes, and the interregional aspects of redistribution? In addition to this internal question, there is the vital question of how far the boundaries of the community reach. In 1946 Gunnar Myrdal built his *An International Economy*[1] around the thesis that a nation-state is defined by a legislated willingness to consider all its citizens as legitimate participants in its output and income. He admired the way U.S. citizens of relatively wealthy states like Connecticut paid taxes that in part benefited citizens of relatively poor states like Mississippi, and held up a vision of how this willingness could increasingly extend from the high-income, developed nation-states of North America and Western Europe to less fortunate parts of the world. For a decade or two, international development programs seemed to move in this direction, though the movement has clearly lost momentum.

In the mid 1960s, Vsevolod Holubnychy noted an assertion in certain Soviet publications that it was the "international duty" of the member countries of Comecon to join forces in a common effort to help the Soviet Union "build Communism"—that is, to catch up with and surpass the United States in economic development for the benefit of the entire socialist camp.[2] This inversion of the Myrdal vision, demanding that the periphery build up the center, was a lingering reflection of the Stalinist era and is no longer the explicit ground for Soviet policy. The two visions, one noble and the other selfish, represent two extremes for specifying policies on how to increase and share the goods and services that are produced in a large economy. Defining the boundaries of the economy is, however, a basic political question—one that economists usually assume has been settled before their analysis begins.

The Soviet government has made the same assumption for more than 50 years, perhaps without full justification. Myrdal argued that "the citizens of the country must have such a strong feeling of belonging to the nation that they are prepared to bear their share of common sacrifices when these are decided upon by due political process."[3] This is not an easy provision to fulfill, as the history of many countries attests. Aron Katsenelinboigen observed in his comments at the conference that if a whole country is ethnically homogeneous, or if its ethnic groups are thoroughly intermingled, interregional transfers of income will be "less painfully received." Perhaps the massive migrations of U.S. citizens from one part of the United States to another have tended to reduce the regional animosities that at times ran strong in earlier stages of the nation's development. From this point of view, the conscious Bolshevik policy of establishing ethnically based territorial components in the USSR might be said to have courted bad feelings. Certainly it has produced resentment among some ethnic groups who have seen their territory taxed in order to provide benefits for other ethnic groups, primarily Russians, in other parts of the USSR. The issue receives detailed attention in several of the papers in this volume.

The postwar literature in economic development contains searching analyses of the question of where development efforts should be concentrated. One well-established precept, noted by Father Michael Lavelle in his comments at the conference, says that increments of capital investment and other development resources should go to the regions and sectors where they will generate the highest increments in national income and output. If this means that further gains come to groups and regions already above the national average, the apparent inequity is defended on the ground that rapid growth will permit larger resource increments to flow to backward parts of the nation than if feeble efforts are scattered throughout the country. The issue is thus not only one of location but also one of timing: how long should the underdeveloped parts of a large territory be asked to wait for participation in the development process?

Still another theme in considering national policies relates to national defense. In his inquiry into the nature and sources of the wealth of nations, whose bicentennial has just been celebrated by economists, Adam Smith asserted with great force that defense was more vital than opulence. He was quite prepared to qualify his advocacy of free trade in order to assure the survival of the nation. In like manner, national development programs have everywhere been modified to meet the requirements of national defense as perceived by the nation's leaders. For at least the first three decades of Soviet experience, this precept had strong implications for the Ukraine. It was exposed to invasion from the west, and Soviet authorities gave high priority to establishing an interior industrial base. Under present international conditions, however, does this consideration retain its force?

A fourth powerful principle has shaped national policies toward trade and development: the "infant industry" argument for protecting an industry or region while it is getting established. During the nineteenth century, both the United States and Germany deliberately thwarted the canons of free trade, as enunciated by Great Britain, in order to protect U.S. and German infant industries while their competitive strength developed. Tariff protection against low-cost imports from well-established foreign producers has been a classic device in international trade. Within the nation-state, subsidies in the form of land grants, promotion of social-overhead capital, special freight rates, and tax concessions have been employed to give new regions and activities a boost. In the United States, for example, this meant that industry in western Pennsylvania and northern Ohio, and later in the Chicago area, was able to expand rapidly and, eventually, to surpass the initial manufacturing centers along the eastern seaboard.

Stanley Cohn suggests that in its resource endowment and other respects, the Ukraine bears a general resemblance to the north-central regions of the United States. In this historical respect, however, the nineteenth-century experience of the Ukraine was very different from that of the American Midwest. The iron and steel industry that grew up in the eastern Ukraine, together with associated manufacturing branches, made up the first large center of heavy industry in tsarist Russia. Such industry as developed around St. Petersburg and Moscow lacked an adequate resource base. When Soviet authorities came to consider policies of special support for new industrial centers, the Ukraine was already an established region, competing with more glamorous prospective centers farther east.

Even these sketchy remarks suggest, therefore, that the place of the Ukraine in the Soviet economy involves a number of analytically interesting issues. Before pursuing them in greater detail, it will help to provide a little perspective on the Ukraine's resource background and growth experience. How richly endowed is the Ukraine? What are its resource strengths and weaknesses? How has its growth compared with that of the rest of the USSR?

The Ukraine has long enjoyed a well-rounded resource base combining fertile soil and usually adequate rainfall with ample deposits of iron ore and coking coal. As Leslie Dienes points out, its industrial resources were especially appropriate for the age of steam and have been heavily exploited for over a century, supporting the growth of neighboring regions as well as that of the Ukraine itself. Long-standing deficiencies in forest products have been made up by imports from the north and east. The Ukraine's modest reserves of petroleum and natural gas are not expected to last for more than another decade or so.

Long-continued exploitation of Ukrainian resources, without much attention to replacement or concern for environmental damage, has created a serious situation. The republic's water resources, for example, have been fairly adequate in the past but seem increasingly inadequate today, as shown by Craig Zum-Brunnen. Many parts of the Ukrainian republic suffer occasional water shortages, and the growth of heavy industry has taxed the water capacities even of well-favored districts. The major efforts that were made in the mid-1950s to establish new grain-growing regions east of the Volga Valley arose directly from the serious droughts that periodically cause drastic crop losses in the Ukraine.

The republic is only precariously self-sufficient in water; it is one of the regions that may conceivably benefit if grandiose schemes for diverting water south and west from major rivers lying to the north and east ever become operational.

Though its water resources are less than ample in relation to developing needs, the Ukraine is sure to remain a major agricultural region because Soviet alternatives are even less favorable. To the north the growing season is increasingly restricted; to the east annual rainfall steadily shrinks. The "breadbasket of the Ukraine" that so attracted Hitler is still a reality, though a North American should realize that the Ukraine resembles Minnesota rather than Iowa.

The adequacy of Ukrainian agricultural, energy, and raw material resources must be judged in relation to the demands placed on them. The Ukraine has been serving far more than its own needs for more than a century; and trends in technology appear to be increasing the demand for resources it needs but lacks, while simultaneously laying claim to remaining Ukrainian supplies for use outside the republic.

The population of the Ukraine (75 percent Ukrainian, 19 percent Russian, 6 percent other) fits the resource base well, without either the overcrowding that hampers growth in some parts of the world or the underpopulation that hinders expansion in other places. The proportion who live in rural areas and engage in agriculture is higher than in most other parts of the USSR, since agricultural conditions are so favorable; but agricultural output per person is low by Western standards, and the Ukraine lags behind in the general shift toward urban areas and nonagricultural occupations. As David Bronson and Douglas Whitehouse show, there has recently been a tendency for skilled labor to be siphoned off from the Ukraine to other parts of the USSR, leaving an agricultural labor force that is significantly undereducated and overage. A counterflow of Russians and others into the Ukraine has involved relatively well-educated people who enter urban occupations.

Interaction between land, labor, and capital in the Ukraine has led to money and real wage rates close to the national average; money wage rates are somewhat lower, but so is the cost of living. As Gertrude Schroeder shows in detail, the agricultural population has fared less well (especially the collective farm members); their incomes are substantially below those of farm families in the Baltic republics and also below those of farm families in many of the Central Asian and Transcaucasian republics. Overall, while real incomes per capita have been rising throughout the USSR, the Ukraine has not quite kept up and is falling increasingly below the national average.

Comparing input and output growth trends for the USSR and for the Ukraine, Stanley Cohn finds that the Ukraine is close to, but somewhat below, the national average, and that recent developments are less favorable for the Ukraine than the situation that prevailed in the 1950s. The Ukraine's share of agricultural output is above its share of population and employment, while its share of industrial output is slightly below. In recent years construction activity has shifted increasingly away from the Ukraine and toward the east and north, so that the Ukraine's share is decreasing. Nevertheless, total factor productivity in the Ukraine is above the national average, thus indicating that resources invested in the Ukraine would be more productive than elsewhere in the USSR.

Returning to the Ukrainian experience in relation to the questions posed earlier, we can recognize many familiar forces at work. When Soviet industrialization began in the late 1920s, industrial development in the Ukraine was recommended as promising the quickest and highest returns, although some argued the vulnerability of a base so close to the western frontier. The actual decision was to use the Ukraine and the Leningrad and Moscow regions as springboards from which to launch construction of the "Ural-Kuznetsk Kombinat," a new heavy industrial base east of the Urals. Massive investments in the European part of the USSR yielded prompt increments of output that went into the new eastern base, safe from Nazi invasion. The process involved heavy taxation of the people in developed territory, from which they derived no direct benefit. Much of the springboard industry was destroyed during World War II; ex post, one can see that its construction was a necessary but calculated risk. Perhaps defeat of the Nazi invaders was a form of recompense for the previous taxation.

The heavy damage suffered by the Ukraine and other occupied regions of the USSR was repaired after the war; but in subsequent economic growth the Ukraine's share of the national capital stock declined at the expense of previously undeveloped regions, mainly in the east. As shown in V. N. Bandera's paper, the Ukraine was increasingly called on to supply large flows of raw material exports to Eastern European members of Comecon, without receiving an equivalent inflow of imports in return. In this new era of unrequited outflows it is not clear what potential return can provide a rationale comparable with the national defense argument of the 1930s. We come, therefore, to the issue of economic exploitation as a major feature of recent relations between the Ukraine and central decision makers of the USSR.

Several of the papers in this volume address the complex issue of regional economic exploitation. Careful reading of the arguments advanced leads to a number of valuable insights that move the discussion to a higher level. At the beginning one notes that, since the Ukraine makes up about 20 percent of the USSR in most economic data, it should be compared not with the whole USSR, but with the national total minus the Ukrainian figure. This elementary point is often overlooked. It leads easily, as pointed out by Father Lavelle, to the observation that one should disaggregate the rest of the USSR, at least down to the level of the other constituent republics. If one's vantage point shifts to that of another republic, the Ukraine joins the "rest of the USSR" that may well seem exploitative to another ethnic group. Peter Wiles suggests that in fact the Baltic republics may be more exploited than the Ukraine.

We are thus led to consider a range of regional situations lying above and below the national average. A neutral analyst might think of subdividing the

RSFSR into 10 or 15 regions, and perhaps dividing the Ukraine into two or three, comparable with other SSRs, so that units of roughly similar population and economic size could be ranked from high to low for a variety of significant measures. In certain respects such subdivisions are already available in Soviet statistical handbooks. Detailed research along these lines has not yet gone very far, but the present volume will gain in impact as such studies are put along-side it.

It may eventually be possible, for example, to estimate regional contributions to, and receipts from, the central national budget, to see which regions are net gainers and which are net losers. Experience with similar efforts for the United States suggests that allocating "benefits" will be a difficult problem. Even in advance of a comprehensive, disaggregated effort, it seems clear that official Soviet policy has been directed toward raising output in regions that lie far below the national average, using net contributions from developed regions like (most of) the Ukraine. It is this trend that leads Peter Wiles to observe that "poor countries should get themselves annexed to the USSR." Further evidence demonstrating this tendency was assembled in an unpublished report by Donald R. Green and Herbert S. Levine.

There is, however, something of a counter trend in the way industrial output per capita has moved since the 1950s. As one moves from the Baltic republics east and south, observed growth rates for industrial output fall from very high to high to modest, while growth rates in population change from very low to quite high. In respect to the quotient of industrial output growth relative to population growth, therefore, regional inequalities have been growing wider. The Ukraine falls about midway in this spectrum. As V. N. Bandera points out, "Inasmuch as the USSR as a whole is making progress, the loss to the Ukraine cannot be measured in absolute terms but is observed as being relative to the metropolis, relative to other regions within the union, and relative to neighboring countries."

In a long view of economic development on Soviet territory, perhaps one can see the early development of heavy industry in the eastern Ukraine as a logical start where conditions were most favorable, followed by efforts that spread to the Ural region, the Volga Valley, and other scattered parts of European Russia and the Caucasus. What remains to be developed, unfortunately, is a very large and forbidding territory where costs are extraordinarily high because of permafrost impediments to extraction, harsh living conditions that require premium wages as an offset, and extremely long distances for delivering energy and raw materials to major population centers. Technological progress has reduced extraction and processing costs, and further gains can be achieved, no doubt; but raising the outlying parts of the USSR to parity with the center seems sure to be a slow and expensive process.

Contemplation of these interregional alternatives and trends brings us to several of the issues in resource management that are analyzed in this volume.

I. S. Koropeckyj makes it very clear, for example, that under the nominally federal structure of Soviet political organization, regional investment and allocation decisions are made in Moscow, not in the republics. During 1957-64, when Khrushchev's form of modest decentralization prevailed, some very interesting beginnings of regionalized decision making occurred, but since 1965 Moscow's preferences have dominated. The republics are mere administrative units for carrying out centrally determined policies.

Soviet republics are not, however, coterminous with the boundaries of resource clusters or industrial regions. This is a problem for the Ukraine, since its eastern coal fields spread over into the neighboring districts of the RSFSR, the upper reaches of its major rivers lie outside the Ukraine, and its heavy industry is closely linked with that around Rostov-on-Don. Thus, though "the republics are basic subdivisions for regional economics," they are not ideally bounded in terms of resource management. If "nodes in the management structure" could be designed from the beginning, many republic boundaries would be shifted. This, however, would tend to disturb their ethnic and historical rationale.

The chapters by Z. L. Melnyk and V. N. Bandera analyze the current and capital flows that link the Ukrainian economy with the rest of the USSR and with the external world; here the multiple meanings of words like "capital" can cause confusion in an already intricate set of relationships. If part of the annual income generated in the Ukraine is taxed away and used for capital formation elsewhere in the USSR, that is a current transaction and, as Peter Wiles points out, it should not be called "capital." The effect may well be to reduce current Ukrainian consumption rather than capital formation. Measuring the extent of the loss is a matter of some intricacy, involving comparisons with unobserved alternatives that might have occurred under other conditions; Part IV of this volume breaks new ground in examining the issue. At least four forms of loss can be argued: current income is invested in capital formation outside the Ukraine rather than within its borders; neither dividend income nor interest is paid to Ukrainian lenders (whether private or public); the principal sums involved in such transfers are never returned; and neither permission nor consent is obtained from those in the Ukraine who provide the funds. The reader must decide for himself whether these losses, or any part of them, would have been smaller under other political auspices, or whether there is a sense in which they were inevitable. Peter Wiles wryly suggests, for example, that "a capitalist Ukraine in a modernized Tsarist Russia might find itself mulcted of about the same sum. . . ."

Underlying these financial flows on current and capital account are real trade flows between the Ukraine and other parts of the USSR, as well as flows between the Ukraine and other countries. Here James Gillula's paper provides much interesting detail in an input-output framework. The fact that on balance the Ukraine is a net exporter of commodity output measured in rubles does not in itself demonstrate a net loss for the Ukraine; inflows on capital account for 1966 might have been involved. Bandera's balance-of-payments estimates for

1960 give no sign of such an inflow, however; and the estimates for 1959-70 in Melnyk's paper show that, on the contrary, there has been a considerable financial outflow from the Ukraine to Moscow.

The siphoning off of current income from the Ukraine for use elsewhere in the USSR is a basic feature of Ukrainian economic history. It resembles the experience of other economies in which some regions enjoyed a head start in economic development, only to see outlying areas catch up with them as development spread. However, the apparent similarity in this case masks a profound contrast in the terms on which Ukrainian resources have been taken. Melnyk's findings need to be placed in a larger analytical framework of regional, historical, national accounts, for cliometric reconstruction of regional flows and trends, before we can obtain a completely clear picture of what has been happening. Similar analysis for other large economies is only beginning to appear. Nevertheless, the available clues suggest that in recent decades the people of the Ukraine have suffered unrequited interregional outflows of resources and income that go well beyond the experience of comparable groups in other countries. Had the Ukraine been an independent nation, as conjectured in some of Wiles's scenarios, its "external investments" would no doubt have been smaller and more geographically diversified. In any case, they would have yielded a return commensurate with their internal opportunity costs.

The Ukraine's role in Soviet foreign trade involves a further form of distortion. Soviet foreign trade organizations purchase Ukrainian output at arbitrary domestic prices and sell imported goods to Ukrainian firms at similarly fixed prices, without allowing any decision-making voice to Ukrainian sellers and buyers and without Ukrainian participation in any trading gains. In the postwar period Ukrainian exports have greatly exceeded imports, yielding "unrequited export balances." Though these balances have tended to decline, both in absolute terms and relative to the gross national product, Bandera argues forcefully that Ukrainian imports should be raised and/or Ukrainian exports should be reduced, through some combination of higher prices and lower quantities for exports, and higher quantities and lower prices for imports. As he ruefully points out, however, the Ukraine's "action capability" is not equal to that of Moscow, so it is not clear how these changes in the terms of Ukrainian trade can be accomplished.

Larger forces may be at work. The energy and raw material needs of all of the European part of the USSR—including the Ukraine—and of Eastern Europe will increasingly have to come from farther east, and at higher costs. Moreover, they will have to compete against the claims of the outside world market, where the possibility of large hard-currency earnings already raise the opportunity costs of supplies sent to the Ukraine. At the same time, as Theodore Shabad noted in the conference discussion, the Ukraine is attracting people from the north by its relatively pleasant climate and drawing various kinds of industry to its ports by new forms of trade with the West. These factors may sustain or even raise the relative standing of the Ukraine among Soviet republics, if high labor productivity and continued technological progress outweigh the real increases in resource costs.

This overview is not so much a careful summary of the papers that follow as a series of reflections on the experience of an old, developed region in a growing economy. The reflections may seem overly broad, but they are designed to show the relevance and importance of the detailed material in these studies. Since analogies are elusive, comparisons between the Ukrainian experience and that of other countries may be misleading; they should not deflect the reader from the solid evidence and analysis in the rest of this volume.[4] For an informed, wide-ranging study of the Ukraine in the Soviet economy, therefore, read on.

NOTES

1. Gunnar Myrdal, *An International Economy: Problems and Prospects* (New York: Harper, 1946), esp. chs. 3, 4.

2. See his introduction to Z. Lew Melnyk, *Soviet Capital Formation: Ukraine, 1928/29-1932* (Munich: Ukrainian Free University Press, 1965), p. xii.

3. Myrdal, op. cit., p. 29.

4. Further research on the Ukrainian economy will be greatly facilitated by the thorough bibliography of sources in Ukrainian and Russian, prepared by Stephen Rapawy, and in other languages, prepared by Joseph Danko, in *Annals of the Ukrainian Academy of Arts and Sciences in the U.S.* 13 (1977).

2

ECONOMIC PREROGATIVES
I. S. Koropeckyj

INTRODUCTION

Aside from the historical, there is also economic justification for the existence of the Ukrainian SSR as an administrative and political entity within the USSR. In the context of this paper, the Ukraine, through its government, should be considered as a territorial node in the management structure of the Soviet economy. The purpose of this government is to serve as one of the intermediaries between the central leadership of the USSR in Moscow and the republic's productive system. Specifically, the Kiev authorities are expected to assist the Moscow leadership in imposing its preferences regarding resource allocation on the Ukrainian productive system, whose preferences may be different.[1] This function cannot be exercised as effectively by Moscow directly, because of political and efficiency limitations.

In order to perform this function, the republic receives targets from the central planners, disaggregates them, and assigns specific goals to individual enterprises directly or, more likely, through subordinated intermediate bodies. By the same token, the republic is required to aggregate production plans and input requirements for all its enterprises and to submit them to the top level of the hierarchy. Other very important functions of the republic authorities are to utilize all propaganda media for the achievement of plan goals, to render necessary assistance, and to control plan implementation. Since the efficient discharge of these responsibilities requires the republic authorities to make choices, they

I am grateful to V. N. Bandera, Yaroslav Bilinsky, and Holland Hunter for reading this paper and for giving helpful comments.

have some discretionary powers vested in them by the top leadership. (The terms "powers," "decision making," "rights," "competences," and "prerogatives" will be used interchangeably in this paper.) Consistent with bureaucratic behavior, these republic authorities may strive to expand their decision-making powers. On the other hand, the union leadership may be reluctant to countenance this beyond a certain point, for fear that the republic may substitute its own preferences for those of the leaders at the center.

The study of decision making at the intermediate levels of the Soviet management system, including that of the republics, has been neglected by Western scholars, who emphasize the two extremes: the union and enterprise levels.[2] This omission is regrettable, not only because there is a lack of understanding of the economic role of the republics but also because the entire area of regional economics, for which the republics are basic subdivisions,[3] has not yet been adequately explored. The purpose of this study is to partly fill this gap by analyzing the changing prerogatives of the Ukraine during the postwar period, specifically after 1950, when immediate postwar reconstruction was completed. The emphasis will be on the division of and relationship between the decision-making powers of the Ukraine's Council of Ministers—the republic's highest executive body—and the central organs in Moscow. The extent of the council's economic prerogatives has, as Aron Katsenelinboigen convincingly argued at the conference, an important implication for political, social, and cultural conditions in the republic. However, the discussion of this aspect is largely beyond the scope of this paper.

In addition to the introductory remarks, this paper consists of four parts. The first outlines the legal status of the Ukraine and describes the attempts of some Ukrainian officials and economists to broaden the republic's competences in the macroeconomic sphere; in the second part, the changes in microeconomic decision making by the Ukrainian government during the period under review are presented; the third part is devoted to a description of present-day prerogatives of the Ukrainian government, primarily in the planning area; and the last part offers some conclusions.

In order to facilitate subsequent discussion, the structure of Ukrainian economic administration, which, in essence, parallels that of the USSR, needs to be briefly described.[4] The highest legislative body, the Supreme Soviet, in addition to passing various laws pertaining to the economy, is responsible for appointing and dismissing the chief economic administrators.[5] The Council of Ministers, directly or through subordinate bodies, plans and manages the republic's economy. It consists of two categories of ministries and two categories of such central organs as committees and administrations: branch and functional. Branch ministries are responsible for enterprises belonging to an economic sector or to an industrial branch. Functional ministries are responsible for economic activities that extend across the entire economy.

The ministries (also committees and administrations) of the republic Council of Ministers can legally be of two types. Those over which the Council of Ministers has exclusive jurisdiction are referred to as "republic-subordinated ministries." The ministries that are under the dual subordination—of the Council of Ministers and of the ministry of the same name in Moscow—are "union-republic ministries." For example, the (republic) union-republic Ministry of Food Industry of the Ukrainian SSR is subordinated to the Ukrainian Council of Ministers and, at the same time, to the (union) union-republic Ministry of Food Industry of the USSR. However, some enterprises (usually of unionwide importance), while located and operating in a republic and belonging to such ministries, may be subordinated directly to a union-republic ministry of the USSR in Moscow. There are also enterprises in a republic that are subordinated to a "union ministry" in Moscow. The republic Council of Ministers has no jurisdiction over enterprises in the latter two cases. Within individual ministries there will be a number of departments (*glavks*) responsible for specific functions or subbranches.

The size of the Council of Ministers has varied according to Moscow's general approach to the planning and management of the national economy. The number of ministries was relatively large during the branch system—before 1957 and after 1965—when individual industrial branches were represented in the Council of Ministers by their ministries. During the period of the territorial system (1957-65), industrial and construction ministries were liquidated and their enterprises were subordinated to the regional Councils of National Economy (*sovnarkhoz*), which were responsible to the Council of Ministers.

LEGAL FRAMEWORK

Constitutional Prerogatives

A number of prerogatives usually exercised by independent states, including economic prerogatives, are not within the jurisdiction of Ukrainian authorities but of the authorities of the USSR. Yet the Ukrainian Constitution proclaims that the republic ". . . exercises its power independently, maintaining its full sovereign rights."[6] But, since the USSR itself is a sovereign state, we have a case where both the union and its constituent republics are said to have sovereignty.*

---

*Noteworthy is the fact that the term "independent" is rarely used for the description of the legal status of republics, although it is synonymous with "sovereign."

Various Soviet authors have tried to reconcile this apparent contradiction. Indeed, the extensive literature on the subject indicates the importance of this issue to the Soviet leadership in its policy toward the non-Russian nationalities.

Despite minor differences in interpretation, Soviet authors argue that the transfer of certain prerogatives by republics to the union does not reduce their sovereignty. According to them, sovereignty is inherent in the status of republics and cannot be decreased or increased. It can be strengthened over a period of time, a process that is supposedly taking place in the USSR.[7] The number of competences exercised by a republic can change over time, depending on the level of economic development, external and internal conditions, and other factors.[8] The change in a republic's competences, however, allegedly does not influence its sovereignty for the following reasons:[9] distribution of competences between union and republic governments is preceded by mutual consultation and has beneficial results for both sides; certain competences are exclusive to republics and cannot be taken away by the union;[10] republics, through their participation in union organs, share in the exercise of functions that are under union jurisdiction; and, in the case of dissatisfaction, the republics have the right to secede from the union according to Article 17 of the USSR Constitution.*

Such an interpretation of the relationship between sovereignty and prerogatives may be acceptable, in view of international experience. For example, member countries of the European Economic Community delegate some of their economic prerogatives to the authorities of that economic union. However, this interpretation is not entirely applicable to the USSR and its republics because, in practice, the prerogatives usually enjoyed by independent countries are concentrated in Moscow to such an extent that the republics are left with very few, and mainly unessential, prerogatives. (All the states of the United States, not claiming any sovereignty, have far greater powers and are far more independent from the federal government than are the Soviet republics.) Any change in the division of competences between the union and the republic takes place at the initiative of the former. Finally, there is no practical mechanism by which a republic can, on its own initiative, regain any of the prerogatives from the central authorities.†

---

*How seriously the right of republics to secede is taken by the present Soviet leaders can be seen from the following episode. In 1961 seven Ukrainian professionals, mostly jurists, were tried in L'viv because they attempted to organize a society whose purpose was to be the propagation of secession of the Ukraine from the USSR. They proposed that secession take place only subject to approval by the Supreme Soviet of the Ukraine or by referendum of the republic's population, and that it should be accomplished in a peaceful manner. Although the activities of these men did not conflict with any existing criminal or constitutional laws of the USSR, the participants were severely punished. The leader of the group, a lawyer named L. H. Luk'ianenko, was sentenced to death (later commuted to 15 years in jail), and others to long jail terms. See reprint of samizdat material, *Ukrains'ki iurysty pid sudom KGB* (Munich: Suchasnist', 1968), pp. 29 ff.

†I am grateful to Professor V. Markus' for clarifying these points for me.

It is no wonder that objective scholars do not take "the sovereignty" of Soviet republics seriously.[11] Even Soviet authors are forced to admit that this sovereignty is of a special, socialist kind.[12] According to former Justice of the World Court V. Korets'kyi and Academician B. Babii: "Bourgeois ideology and its lackeys . . . are unable to comprehend and evaluate fairly the state relations among Soviet Republics."[13]

Soviet authors argue that the division of competences between the USSR and its republics is based on the principle of democratic centralism, as advanced by Lenin. With respect to republics, this concept is defined as ". . . the combination of a single leadership, exercised from one center over the public life of all our country, with the broad initiative, independence, and free activity of union republics."[14] More specifically, according to A. I. Lepeshkin, the following factors should be taken into account in deciding which competences should be exercised by the union and which by the republic government:[15] the objectives for which the USSR was created (economic and cultural development of the people, defense of the country, and free development of all nationalities); the importance to the union of individual economic sectors and industrial branches; and the equality and strengthening of the sovereignty of each nationality on the basis of reconciling the interests of the USSR and the interests of a particular republic. Other writers assign equal importance to such factors as the level of economic development, the internal and external situation, the availability of skilled personnel in individual republics, and differential technological progress of individual branches located in the republic.[16]

The problem with these formulations is that they are incomplete and imprecise. For example, should the economic competences of republics be increased or decreased, in view of their unquestionable economic progress? Or what effect do such external factors as periodic cold wars and detentes have on the extent of republic competences? Soviet jurists fail to discuss these relationships in specific terms; they simply list them. The study of the past zigzag distribution of decision-making powers between union and republics also fails to provide a clue to the relationship between this distribution and internal and external factors.

The pragmatic approach that a given economic function should be performed by whichever authority can perform it most efficiently is thought to be most reasonable.[17] But here some technical and political problems arise. How does one evaluate efficiency in practice? Unfortunately, economic science cannot reliably calculate the cost and benefit of the transfer of decision making from one level of government to another. Nor is it easy to reconcile the conflicts of interest between the union and a republic. The answer of Soviet authors to this problem is that the interest of the union takes precedence over that of the republic. Should the republic try to insist on priority for its own interests, the union, which is effectively dominated by Russians, has the power to enforce its will. In other words, we have here ". . . [a] relationship of effective domination or control, political or economic, direct or indirect, of one nation over another."[18] This is nothing less than a general definition of imperialism that accurately describes the prevailing relations between Russia, on the one hand, and the Ukraine and other non-Russian republics of the USSR, on the other.

Given this two-tiered structure of the USSR, economic competences within a republic can be exercised, according to Soviet writers, in three ways:[19] in areas of unionwide importance, decision making is exclusively in the hands of union organs; a republic exercises functions in those areas that are strictly of republic importance or that are specific to a given republic because of its level of economic development, its geographic and natural conditions, and its historical and national characteristics; in spheres in which the union and the republics have common interest, decision making is exercised jointly by organs of both (union-republic organs).

The USSR Constitution reserves the following economic responsibilities for the union government:[20] foreign trade, on the basis of state monopoly; determination of economic plans of the USSR; approval of a single state budget for the USSR and reporting on its implementation; determination of taxes and receipts for union, republic, and local budgets; management of banks and industrial and agricultural establishments and enterprises, as well as of commercial enterprises of union subordination; general guidance of industry and construction of union-republic subordination; management of transportation and communication of union subordination; guidance of the monetary and credit system; organization of state insurance; state loans; formulation of basic principles of utilization of land, mineral wealth, forests, and water; formulation of basic principles in education and health care; organization of a single system of economic accounting; formulation of principles of labor legislation. These responsibilities of the USSR government are intended to assure the unity of state policy in the enumerated areas for the entire country.[21]

On the other hand, the Constitution of the Ukraine enumerates the following areas of responsibility in economic affairs for the republic's government:[22] approval of the republic's economic plan; approval of the republic's budget and reporting on its implementation; determination, according to the laws of the USSR, of state and local taxes, assessments, and receipts other than taxes; guidance in the implementation of local budgets of oblasts; guidance in insurance and savings areas; management of industry and construction of union-republic subordination; management of banks and industrial, agricultural, and commercial enterprises and organizations of republic subordination; guidance of local industry; control and supervision of the management of enterprises of union subordination; formulation of rules for the exploitation of land, mineral wealth, forests, and water; guidance of housing and municipal enterprises, housing construction, and planning of cities and other inhabited localities; construction of roads, guidance of transportation and communication of republic and local importance; labor legislation; guidance of social security matters; guidance of cultural-educational and scientific organizations and establishments in the Ukraine, and management of cultural-educational and scientific organizations and establishments of republic importance; guidance of health care and management of health care establishments of republic importance.

Such a delineation of decision making between the USSR and the Ukraine is much too general and does not provide a clear guidance in practice. Moreover, the present constitution was introduced in 1936 and now requires amendments to accommodate important changes in the economic system since then.[23] The ad hoc resolutions of the Council of Ministers and laws passed by the Supreme Soviet of the USSR have not always resolved jurisdictional problems. For example, various functions that are now constitutionally under the jurisdiction of republic organs are exercised, in practice, by union organs and vice versa.[24] As will be discussed in Part III, the overlapping of decision-making powers between the union and the republic is particularly confusing in economic activities under joint jurisdiction (union-republic ministries).

In 1967, to deal with the increasing confusion, the USSR Council of Ministers requested a legal commission to work out, in cooperation with various union organs and republic Councils of Ministers, a proposal streamlining, eliminating duplications, and codifying existing legislation.[25] To the best knowledge of this writer, no such document has been published. Apparently the ambiguity and vagueness regarding the delineation of prerogatives is perpetuated intentionally. A similar view in the realm of criminal law is expressed by Leszek Kolakowski, a recognized authority on socialist regimes.[26] The lack of legal clarity in economics, civil rights, and other areas makes all human activity in socialist countries amenable to the manipulation and arbitrary decisions of the Communist party.

Tendencies to Expand Prerogatives

Decision making in the areas of production, distribution, and, to a lesser extent, consumption is exercised in the USSR by the state. Such decision making can be split into the following elements (in Russian): *partiinoe rukovodstvo, planirovanie,* and *rukovodstvo* or *upravlenie.* Following Stanislaw Wellisz, they can be translated as "guidance," "planning," and "management," respectively.[27] While there is agreement among Soviet authors that the function of *partiinoe rukovodstvo* includes both ideological guidance of economic development and basic macroeconomic decisions,[28] there is definitional ambiguity with respect to the other two concepts. Planning is sometimes considered to be a separate function and sometimes a part of management, particularly at the lower levels of the hierarchy.[29] The function of plan execution is often called, interchangeably, guidance or management.* For the purpose of the present discussion it is sufficient to make a distinction between guidance, as defined, and planning and management, the latter corresponding to microeconomic decision making.

A closer look at these functions should help us to understand the distribution of economic decision making between the authorities in Moscow and Kiev. The Communist party of the USSR considers its ultimate objective to be the construction of full-fledged Communism in the entire world. The more immediate goal is the construction of Communism in one country, the USSR. Its achievement depends, above all, on the strengthening and expanding of the power of the party, which rests on a strong economy.[30] For this reason, the maximization of economic growth within an intermediate time horizon is of overriding importance, superseding the objectives valued by the consumers, such as improvement in the standard of living, full employment, and economic equality.[31]

In view of the eschatological nature of the listed objectives, the party determines for the society the more immediate and specific goals and makes, for this purpose, the necessary macroeconomic decisions (distribution of national income between consumption and saving and between labor and capital, incomes of various labor groups, consumer products mix, sectoral and regional distribution of investment, organizational structure). The function of translating these general party directives into comprehensive, consistent, and specific plans of action can be called planning in the strict sense. The implementation of plans is the responsibility of managers. In other words, the planners and managers at all levels of the economic hierarchy are responsible for microeconomic decision making.[32]

It is obvious from the record that macroeconomic decision making has been exercised in the USSR by none but the top party leadership in Moscow. Even so, this guidance cannot be so complete as the leadership would like it to be. In many instances it is technically impossible to reach all levels of life. In other cases, the leadership may be indifferent as to whose preferences prevail. Or the costs of imposing its preferences can sometimes be higher to the leadership than are the benefits derived.[33] Thus, in some small measure other levels of government and party in the USSR, including the leadership of the Ukraine, as well as individual consumers, can pursue their own economic objectives.

Sometimes, however, Ukrainian authorities are dissatisfied with the macroeconomic decisions made in Moscow and would like to change them in their favor, or expand their own competences. Investment allocation, which is

---

*Some Soviet economists suggest that in respect to state-owned enterprises both terms should be used—that is, these enterprises are both guided and managed by the state, while cooperative enterprises are only guided by the state. See I. F. Pankratov, *Gosudarstvennoe rukovodstvo sel'skim khoziaistvom* (Moscow, 1969), pp. 59-60.

of obvious importance, is a case in point. According to *samizdat* (unofficial, unpublished) sources:[34]

> There is no doubt that the officials of the USSR Gosplan encounter major difficulties during the reconciliation of capital construction plans with the Gosplan and the Council of Ministers of the Ukrainian SSR. Ukrainian officials always persistently ask for the increase in allocation of investable funds basing these demands on the level of output which the Ukraine contributes to the all-union fund. They bluntly say that they are being robbed.

Among the reasons for such attempts on the part of the republic's officials are the following:

A well-known practice of Soviet managers at all levels is to try to obtain maximum inputs, chiefly capital, in order to fulfill the assigned plans more easily.

Every bureaucrat in any hierarchy is more comfortable with a larger budget.

According to law, a small portion of allocated investment can be utilized by republics at their discretion.

Republic leaders may be genuinely interested in increased employment and a higher standard of living for their countrymen, goals that can be achieved mainly through larger investment. In fact, according to the statements of recent emigrants from the USSR, nationalism is particularly strong among the Ukrainian planners and managers who have an intimate knowledge of the economic discrimination against their republic by Moscow.

Whatever the underlying reasons may have been, the following is a sample of demands for larger investments by Ukrainian leaders and economists. Immediately after World War II, at the session of the Supreme Soviet of the USSR in 1946, Ukrainian representatives were quite vocal in their demands for funds to reconstruct their devastated country.[35] In more recent times, they have been preoccupied with the shortage of fuels and energy that can endanger any further growth of the Ukrainian economy. Demands for investment in this area were strongly expressed in 1966 by V. V. Shcherbyts'kyi, at that time the chairman of the Council of Ministers and now the first secretary of the Communist party of the Ukraine.[36] They were echoed in 1971 by the former first secretary, P. Iu. Shelest.[37] Economists have explicitly supported these requests and argued that since the output of coal, the main source of energy in the Ukraine, is not growing, its export to other republics and foreign countries will have to decrease and the supply of substitutes in the Ukraine, mainly natural gas and oil, will have to be developed.[38] It is claimed that not enough funds are being allocated to exploration for oil, although exploratory drilling in the Ukraine is relatively cheap. Inadequacy of refining capacities has been particularly deplored.[39]

Another reason for the demand for greater investment in the Ukraine is unemployment and underemployment of the labor force, mainly in the western regions.* The Ukrainians hope, unofficially, that greater development of industry in these regions will prevent migration of young people to other republics and, thus, their eventual denationalization there.[40]

Ukrainian economists support this demand by three efficiency arguments. In the first place, inadequate utilization of labor in less-developed regions that are well-endowed with mineral resources means the country will fail to reach maximum production capability.[41] Second, the existing branch structure of Ukrainian industry is inefficient. Its capital-intensive branches, usually with large-scale plants, are well developed and located chiefly in the eastern regions, while labor-intensive branches are relatively weaker. The faster development of the latter would allow the dispersion of their usually small-scale plants throughout the Ukraine and, thus, the absorption of unemployed labor.[42] But even some capital-intensive branches, for which appropriate conditions (labor, materials, and market) exist in the Ukraine, are inadequately developed. This applies primarily to the machine-building industry and, within it, to automobile industry.[43] Finally, Ukrainian economists argue that the comparative productivity of capital is not taken into account in the distribution of investment among regions, especially between the Asiatic and European parts of the country. The Ukraine should receive more than at present because, if all costs are accounted for and a time horizon shorter than infinity is considered, investment is more productive in this republic than in other parts of the USSR.[44]

Ukrainian leaders and economists have also pressed for larger allocations of industrial inputs to the Ukraine by USSR authorities. For example, Shcherbyts'kyi asked the USSR Supreme Soviet for more of various inputs so that plan targets could be met by the Ukraine.[45] In this respect, one economist warned that if additional lumber is not allocated to the Ukraine, further irresponsible cutting of the Carpathian forests will result in ecological disaster.[46] Voices were also raised against too much export from the Ukraine of various commodities and investable funds. Shelest seems to have been particularly determined in his fight for better treatment of the Ukraine. (This was probably one of the reasons for his demotion in 1972.)[47] He protested against squeezing grain out of the Ukraine in 1964, when Nikita Khrushchev demanded that this republic deliver 1 billion *puds* (16 million metric tons). (What Khrushchev was not able to achieve in 1964, Leonid Brezhnev achieved in 1973.) Shelest complained that the 1964 action lead to bread lines in the Ukraine.[48] Also during Shelest's era, to show the drain of capital from the Ukraine, economists calculated very

---

*For example, 23.7 percent of the labor force in Zakarpattia, 20.3 percent in Ivano-Frankivs'k, and 15.8 percent in Chernivtsi oblasts were not, in recent years, part of the socialized labor force. In other words, they were unemployed or underemployed. See L. M. Mushketik, *Kompleksnyi territorial'nyi plan v usloviiakh otraslevogo upravleniia* (Kiev, 1974), p. 34.

carefully the budgetary relationship between the Ukraine and the USSR for 1959-61 and convincingly demonstrated the sizable and persistent excess of payments from the Ukraine to the USSR budget over Ukrainian receipts from Moscow.[49]

With respect to the institutional framework, Shelest had the courage in 1965, at the demise of the sovnarkhoz system (under which the competences of the Ukraine were somewhat increased), to praise that system for, in his opinion, its success in improving interbranch coordination, material and technical supply, and equipment maintenance. He even explicitly criticized the post-Khrushchev leadership for the wholesale condemnation of this period: "Some comrades are wrong when they excessively criticize sovnarkhozes. We should objectively evaluate phenomena in our life."[50] In this, Shelest was joined by economists. For example, F. Khyliuk claimed that during the sovnarkhoz period, Ukrainian planning had been comprehensive and balanced, and had promoted the rapid growth of the republic's economy.[51] S. Iampol's'kyi argued that the improved interbranch specialization of production during this period facilitated wide application of the most modern technology and advanced methods of management.[52]

The centralization that followed the 1965 reforms evoked protests among Ukrainian officials and economists. For example, the Ukrainian minister of light industry claimed that it would be more efficient if he were given the right to make all decisions, except those relating to budget payments and product mix. Specifically, the powers of the union ministry of the same name to change the quarterly output plans for final output and the output plans for semifabricated products, and to determine the prices should be turned over to him.[53] With respect to price determination in general, a demand was made that this function in the Ukraine should be exercised by the Ukrainian State Committee on Prices.[54]

Ukrainian officials also protested the take-over of certain industrial branches (such as oil drilling) by Moscow organs.* They also demanded the return of others (such as gas processing) to Kiev authorities.[55] In the case of the machine-building industry, which has been completely under Moscow's jurisdiction since 1965, it was claimed that its various plants, mostly those producing consumer goods, are not working efficiently under new arrangements.[56] Furthermore, it was argued that this branch, as well as some others, whose products serve to a great extent as inputs for the entire industry, should properly be subordinated to republic authorities rather than organized as union ministries. According to this proposal, the products of interbranch importance would be manufactured on a large scale in specialized republic ministries and wasteful,

---

*An irritated official called such a take-over "'. . . a very grave mistake . . .'" that ". . . should not have been allowed in the socialist economy." See *DSUP* (March 1967): 13-14.

small-scale production of these inputs by individual branches for their use only would be prevented.[57] It is interesting to note that several Ukrainian economists and high officials (including two vice-chairmen of the Council of Ministers) spoke on this issue, that they used very similar arguments, and that they published their articles within a relatively short period of time (around 1968). These articles were published not only in Kiev but also in Moscow journals, apparently to exert greater pressure on central authorities. One gets a distinct impression that this discussion represented a concerted effort by Ukrainians to regain control over at least part of the machine-building industry.

Such open defense of the economic interests of the Ukraine, and of other republics,[58] is only the tip of the iceberg. Most likely, much greater and more intensive struggle goes on within Gosplan and other offices, hidden from the general public. "Enterprises and organizations [and, as this writer was told, also republics] often send special representatives to Moscow and wherever is necessary, to argue, lobby, press, cajole, and bribe in order to get desired plans and supplies."[59] This bargaining process usually results in a compromise. But the influence of even the highest republic authorities on Moscow bureaucrats should not be overrated.*

To implement its objectives, the leadership in Moscow would like to centralize both macroeconomic and microeconomic powers—that is, planning and management. However, economic and technical expediency forces the center to delegate some management powers in the microeconomic area to lower levels of the hierarchy. Through decentralization, the leadership also hopes to eliminate bureaucratic inefficiency and to simulate at all levels the initiative that is dulled under the existing overcentralization. However, substantive decentralization would require the admission of a market for goods and resources. But since the market would interfere with the leadership's ideological and political objectives, such a reform is unlikely and, hence, the hope for less bureaucracy and more local initiative is not realistic.[60]

It is argued that the need for decentralization of macroeconomic and microeconomic decision making is particularly great when the economy is sufficiently developed, production structure is complicated, structural changes

---

*The following episode was told to this writer by a reliable source. In the early 1970s a building was constructed in L'viv for the Western Division of the Academy of Sciences of the Ukraine. Scholars wanted to have a slightly higher ceiling than is prescribed by the union norms. They asked the first secretary of the Ukraine Communist party and a member of the Politbureau of the CPSU, Shelest, to intervene on their behalf. When Shelest went to Moscow and asked for this alteration, he was refused. Morover, the Gosstroy bureaucrats later bragged that they had put Shelest in his place. One wonders how much influence Shelest's predecessors had on Moscow, or how much his successor now enjoys (who seems to have less personality than he).

are not radical, and further growth depends more on intensive than on extensive use of resources.[61] Regardless of how ripe these conditions may be in the USSR, a shift of macroeconomic decision making from Moscow to republics can hardly be expected. On the other hand, there has been a continuous shift in microeconomic prerogatives between Moscow and Kiev. The next part of this paper will trace these shifts during the postwar period.

CHANGES IN THE SCOPE
OF ECONOMIC DECISION MAKING

The Period Before 1957

There are basically three possible ways in which economic decision-making powers can be transferred from union to republic levels:

Individual ministries can be changed from union to union-republic or from union-republic to republic-subordinated status

Certain specific economic competences can be transferred from the Council of Ministers of the USSR to the Council of Ministers of republics

The planning and management system of industry and construction can be changed from branch to regional.

Of course these changes can also be made in the opposite direction. Since these three aspects of transfer of economic prerogatives between hierarchical levels are interrelated, they will be discussed in the order in which they were introduced during the review. This historical investigation can serve as a basis for presenting the relations between the center and a republic with the help of a formal mathematical model. as was suggested by Aron Katsenelinboigen at the conference.

All three kinds of changes in the Ukraine were an integral part of the reforms in the USSR. The reasons for the reforms were largely the same in the Ukraine as in the entire country. They were widely discussed in the West and, hence, references to reasons for unionwide reforms will be made here only to provide a background for the reforms in the Ukraine.[62]

The economic prerogatives of the Ukraine, like those of the other Soviet republics, were severely restricted during Stalin's rule. The union government directly planned and managed the most important sectors and industrial branches—all heavy industry, enterprises of light industry and the food industry of union importance, as well as special construction enterprises, most of transportation, communication, commerce, part of the municipal economy, and some parts of agriculture. Under the Ukraine's jurisdiction were local industry, industrial cooperatives, the remaining part of agriculture, motor vehicle transport, and social and cultural establishments.[63] The ministerial system of economic planning and management contributed considerably to the weakness of republic governments and thus facilitated rigid centralization in Moscow. Under it ". . . the republican authorities were totally by-passed, the line of subordination stretching straight from the enterprise to the glavk of the appropriate ministry in Moscow, regardless of the republic in which the enterprise was located."[64] As a result, no comprehensive plans for the Ukrainian economy were even prepared for the Fourth (1946-50) and Fifth (1951-55) Five-Year Plans.[65]

The disadvantages of the ministerial system are well-known to specialists in the USSR and in the West: the tendency toward empire building by individual ministries and the centralization of decision making at the top of the hierarchy, the lack of cooperation among ministries, unnecessary long hauls and cross hauls of transport system, and the lack of complex development of regions, to mention just a few.[66] Soviet authors add that branch administration does not allow party organs at various levels of territorial government to participate effectively in the mobilization and better utilization of resources.[67] Centralized administration is inflexible, its decisions are often delayed, and local initiative is dampened. After Stalin's death, the new leaders decided to deal with the latter problem; they started to loosen the grip of central planners on the economy by transferring some of the economic power from Moscow to republic governments.

As a first step, a change in the status of various ministries was undertaken. The following union ministries were converted to union-republic subordination in the Ukraine between 1954 and 1956: ferrous metals, coal, communication, and paper and wood processing.[68] Also most of the enterprises of such union-republic ministries as food, meat and dairy, fishing, procurements, light industry, textiles, construction materials, paper and wood processing, highway transport and highways, internal shipping, and public health were transferred to republic subordination. At the same time, the retail trade network and public catering enterprises were transferred to republics.[69] Altogether, the Ukraine took over almost 15,000 enterprises between 1954 and 1956.[70] As a result, at the beginning of 1957 almost all Ukrainian industry was planned and managed by 25 economic ministries in Kiev.[71]

Of considerable importance for the increase in the republics' planning and management competence was a 1955 resolution of the USSR Council of Ministers.[72] The document is rather long (it contains 112 separate provisions with several subprovisions), and because of space limitation cannot be reproduced or summarized here. Its most important features, which are still in force, as well as those of similar resolutions in other years, are included in the description of competences of republic governments in Part III. This resolution presents an astonishing picture of lack of any power on the part of republics until that time. It alleviated the situation somewhat in such areas as planning, investment, budget, labor and wages, and agriculture.

The Sovnarkhoz Period, 1957-65

In 1957 a radical reform, replacing the ministerial system with a regional system, was introduced by Khrushchev.[73] There is a consensus among Western scholars that his purpose was not only to eliminate the previously mentioned inefficiencies but also to weaken the influence of other contenders for power in the central organs in Moscow and, at the same time, to strengthen his supporters in the republics.[74] The reform dissolved existing union, union-republic, and republic-subordinated ministries in charge of industry and construction. Six union ministries (aviation, defense, radio, ship construction, chemical, and electric power) were retained, but made responsible for research only. All the enterprises of liquidated ministries and industrial enterprises of noneconomic ministries were transferred to the jurisdiction of 104 sovnarkhozes created to manage industry and construction.

As a result of this reform, 11 union-republic ministries (construction of enterprises of coal industry, construction of enterprises of metallurgical and chemical industries, coal, light industry, timber, urban and rural construction, paper and wood processing, meat and dairy products, food, fishing, and ferrous metallurgy) and two republic-subordinated ministries (local and fuel, and municipal services) were liquidated in the Ukraine. Construction and construction materials ministries were converted from union-republic to republic-subordinated status. In the place of liquidated ministries 11 sovnarkhozes—subordinated to the Council of Ministers—were organized in the Ukraine.[75] Their number was increased to 14 in 1960.[76] Outside the sovnarkhozes and subordinated directly to the Ukrainian Council of Ministers were all sectors other than industry; local and cooperative industry (including some enterprises previously of republic subordination), under the jurisdiction of oblasts; and the ministries of medium machine building (nuclear energy); gas industry; international trade; sea, rail, and air transport; and transport construction, all directly under the USSR Council of Ministers.[77]

Three agencies were attached to the Ukrainian Council of Ministers: Gosplan (Central Planning Committee), the State Scientific-Technical Committee, and TsSU (Central Statistical Administration). It is necessary to stress that these agencies were of republic subordination—that is, the corresponding union agencies could communicate with them, at least in theory, only through the USSR Council of Ministers and then through the Ukrainian Council of Ministers. The Ukrainian Gosplan became a particularly important body. It was made responsible for long-term and short-term planning, coordination of the work of the republic's sovnarkhozes, determination of their production structure, and control of plan fulfillment. It also was in charge of supply and sales planning, and the supervision of relevant enterprises. Technological research and geographic distribution of industry for individual industrial branches were under the jurisdiction of the respective branch departments of the USSR Gosplan.[78] As a result of these broadened competences, the Ukrainian Gosplan was able to prepare, for the first time, comprehensive plans for the Ukrainian economy (excepting union-subordinated sectors and branches) for 1957 and 1958.[79] The increase in importance of republic planning organs can be seen also from the fact that the number of indicators in the union plan (indicators assigned specifically to individual republics) decreased from 9,490 to 1,780 between 1953 and 1958.[80]

The 1957 reforms made the Ukrainian Council of Ministers a powerful organ. It could create sovnarkhozes; appoint their chairmen, deputy chairmen, council members; and determine their administrative structure. The council supervised and controlled the work of sovnarkhozes, the decisions of which it could change and suspend. Finally, the chairman of the Ukrainian Council of Ministers became an ex-officio member of the USSR Council of Ministers.

Republic Gosplans were successful, to a degree, in handling their increased reponsibilities. According to M. Urinson, they were able to reconcile central planning and local initiative and also to prepare plans formulated successively from the bottom to the top.[81] But they were less successful in coordinating and controlling the work of the sovnarkhozes. Therefore, even before the next round of reforms at the end of 1962, administrative changes were introduced in the Ukraine. The functions of coordination and control of the sovnarkhozes, and to some extent also of current planning, were taken over by the newly created Ukrainian Sovnarkhoz in 1960.[82] Within it were established 15 branch subdivisions with the task of coordinating the work of individual industrial and construction branches of the sovnarkhozes, particularly research and development. The chairman of the Ukrainian Sovnarkhoz became a member of the Ukrainian Council of Ministers. This reform put the Ukrainian sovnarkhozes in dual subordination, to the Ukrainian Sovnarkhoz and to the Ukrainian Council of Ministers, the former being the more important.

Considerable change was also introduced into the management of construction and of local industry before 1962. As mentioned earlier, at the time of the reform the Ministry of Construction and the Ministry of Construction Materials were converted from union-republic to republic-subordinated status. The former was made responsible for projects of republic and inter-sovnarkhoz importance, and the latter for research in this field. The State Committee for Construction and Architecture, until then responsible for research, was liquidated. Soon the Ministry of Construction Materials was also liquidated (in 1958). Its research function was transferred to the newly created Gosstroy (State Construction Committee) of the Ukraine and its productive enterprises to the sovnarkhozes.[83] In order to provide some leadership in construction sector, 3 of the 15 subdivisions of the Ukrainian Sovnarkhoz were charged with this responsibility. The management of construction enterprises was taken completely away from the sovnarkhozes in 1963. Sovnarkhozes became the customers of the Main Administration of Construction established in each enlarged sovnarkhoz in order to supervise construction enterprises. The administrations were subordinated to the newly created Ministry of Construction of the Ukraine. The previously existing Ministry of Construction was converted into the Ministry of Installation and Special Construction Work.[84]

Some changes were also introduced in local industry. Before 1957 the work of local industry was supervised jointly by the republic-subordinated Ministry of Local Industry and the oblasts. After the reform, supervision rested with the oblast authorities. In 1960 the industrial cooperatives were included in local industry. In order to coordinate the work of these enterprises, the Main Administration of Local Industry and Consumer Services of the Council of Ministers of the Ukraine was organized.[85] in the same year the Ministry of Municipal Services was resurrected.[86] In 1963 the enterprises of local industry were transferred under the management of the sovnarkhozes, while those of consumer services remained under the management of oblasts. To supervise the former, the Main Administration of Production of Cultural and Everyday Products of the Ukrainian Sovnarkhoz was organized, while consumer services were planned by the Main Administration of Consumer Services of the Ukrainian Council of Ministers.[87]

In 1957 and 1959, two further resolutions significantly increased the competence of republic governments in various areas of economic life.[88] These changes in the role of the republics required changes in the budgetary laws.[89] Their codification took place in 1959 and, together with the provisions of these resolutions, the changes will be summarized in Part III.[90]

As a result of these resolutions, laws, and reforms, the economic prerogatives of the Ukraine reached a peak in 1960-62. Chart 1 indicates that the Ukrainian government planned and managed its largest share of the national economy at that time, as compared with other postwar years. Also, as can be seen from Figure 2.2, the shares of the Ukraine in the USSR budget with respect to three main expenditure categories in the total investment of the USSR, and the share of the gross industrial output under the Council of Ministers' jurisdiction in the total output in the Ukraine, were largest during this period. (Unfortunately, no other quantitative indicators of the role of the Council in national economy can be found.)

The enlarged economic prerogatives of the Ukrainian government have had wider implications.* The Ukrainian SSR was increasingly functioning as an economic entity within the USSR economy. Shortly after the 1957 reforms, an

---

*It is convincingly argued that economic decentralization in the USSR would most likely be followed by political decentralization. See R. V. Burks, "The Political Implications of Economic Reform," in Morris Bornstein, ed., *Plan and Market: Economic Reform in Eastern Europe* (New Haven: Yale University Press, 1973), pp. 390-92, 400-01.

FIGURE 2.1

Ministries, State Committees, and Main Administrations of the Council of Ministers of the UkSSR (1950-75)

	1950	51	52	53	54	55

1 COUNCIL OF MINISTERS
2 REPUBLIC COMMITTEE FOR AGRICULTURE
3 UKRAINIAN COUNCIL OF NATIONAL ECONOMY

MINISTRIES
4 POWER AND ELECTRIFICATION
5 CHEMICAL INDUSTRY
6 GEOLOGY
7 COAL INDUSTRY
8 FERROUS METALLURGY
9 AIRCRAFT INDUSTRY*
10 DEFENSE INDUSTRY*
11 SHIPBUILDING INDUSTRY*
12 CONSTRUCTION, HIGHWAY, AND MUNICIPAL MACHINE BUILDING*
13 HEAVY, POWER, AND TRANSPORT MACHINE BUILDING*
14 CHEMICAL AND PETROLEUM MACHINE BUILDING*
15 MACHINE TOOL AND TOOL BUILDING INDUSTRY*
16 MOTOR VEHICLE INDUSTRY*
17 TRACTOR AND AGRICULTURAL MACHINE BUILDING*
18 PRECISION INSTRUMENTS, AUTOMATION EQUIPMENT AND CONTROL SYSTEM*
19 MACHINE BUILDING*
20 GENERAL MACHINE BUILDING*
21 RADIO INDUSTRY*
22 MACHINE BUILDING FOR LIGHT AND FOOD INDUSTRY AND FOR HOUSEHOLD
    APPLIANCES*
23 ELECTRICAL EQUIPMENT INDUSTRY*
24 ELECTRONICS INDUSTRY*
25 NONFERROUS METALLURGY*
26 PETROLEUM EXTRACTION INDUSTRY*
27 FORESTRY
28 PAPER AND WOOD PROCESSING
29 LIGHT INDUSTRY
30 FOOD INDUSTRY
31 FISHING INDUSTRY
32 MEAT AND DAIRY INDUSTRY
33 CONSTRUCTION MATERIALS INDUSTRY
34 CONSTRUCTION
35 INDUSTRIAL CONSTRUCTION
36 RURAL CONSTRUCTION
37 CONSTRUCTION OF HEAVY INDUSTRY ENTERPRISES
38 AGRICULTURE
39 LAND RECLAMATION AND WATER RESOURCES
40 STATE FARMS
41 AGRICULTURAL PROCUREMENTS
42 COMMERCE
43 COMMUNICATION
44 FINANCE
45 LOCAL INDUSTRY
46 LOCAL FUELS INDUSTRY
47 MOTOR TRANSPORT
48 CONSTRUCTION AND UTILIZATION OF HIGHWAYS
49 MUNICIPAL SERVICES
50 CONSUMER SERVICES
51 SOCIAL SECURITY
52 HOUSING AND CIVIL CONSTRUCTION

STATE COMMITTEES OF THE COUNCIL OF MINISTERS
53 STATE PLANNING COMMISSION
54 STATE COMMITTEE FOR CONSTRUCTION AFFAIRS
55 STATE COMMITTEE ON PRICES
56 STATE COMMITTEE FOR UTILIZATION OF LABOR RESOURCES**
57 STATE COMMITTEE FOR SUPERVISION OF SAFE WORKING PRACTICES IN IN-
    DUSTRY AND FOR MINE SUPERVISION** +
58 STATE COMMITTEE FOR SCIENCE AND TECHNOLOGY
MAIN ADMINISTRATIONS OF THE COUNCIL OF MINISTERS
59 UKRAINIAN ASSOCIATION FOR SALE OF AGRICULTURAL EQUIPMENT AND
    ORGANIZATION OF MACHINERY REPAIRS AND UTILIZATION
60 MAIN ADMINISTRATION FOR PETROLEUM REFINING AND PETROLEUM PRODUCTS
    SUPPLIES +
61 MAIN ADMINISTRATION OF MATERIAL AND TECHNICAL SUPPLY
62 MAIN ADMINISTRATION OF HORTICULTURE, VITICULTURE AND WINE
    PROCESSING
63 CENTRAL STATISTICAL ADMINISTRATION
64 MAIN ADMINISTRATION OF PRODUCTION OF CULTURAL AND EVERYDAY
    PRODUCTS

REPUBLIC MINISTRY   UNION – REPUBLIC MINISTRY

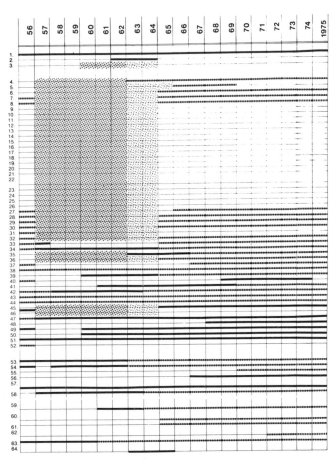

	56	57	58	59	60	61	62	63	64	65	66	67	68	69	70	71	72	73	74	1975

SOVNARKHOZ (REPUBLIC)   SOVNARKHOZ (UNION-REPUBLIC)

Notes:

*The names of USSR ministries after the 1965 reform.

**Legal subordination not clear.

+The date of organization not determined.

Sources: Various issues of *RU* and *VVR*. Changes in the management structure are shown for the entire year, although in most cases they took place sometimes during and not at the beginning of the particular year.

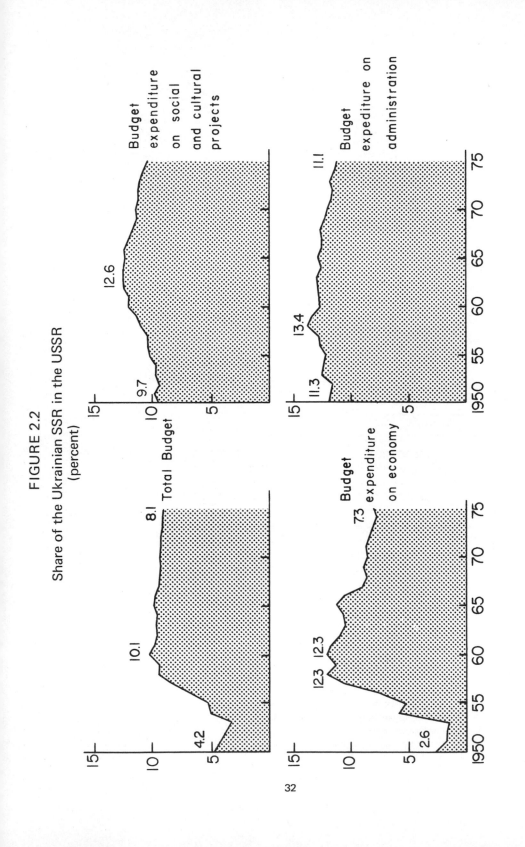

FIGURE 2.2

Share of the Ukrainian SSR in the USSR
(percent)

Total Budget

Budget expenditure on economy

Budget expenditure on social and cultural projects

Budget expediture on administration

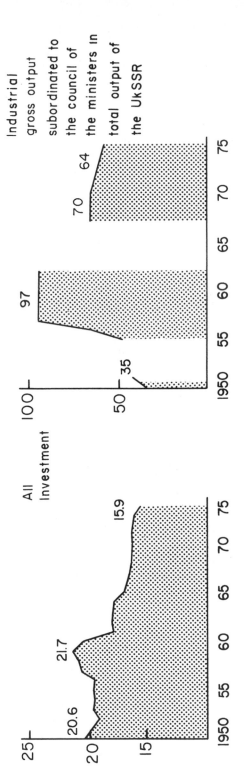

Industrial
gross output
subordinated to
the council of
the ministers in
total output of
the UkSSR

All
Investment

Note: In view of the lack of data for all years, the total budget expenditures of the Ukraine do not include the repayment of government loans and the category called "other expenditures," both of which account for slightly more than 1 percent of the total.

Sources: Panels 1-4 (from the top)—Ministerstvo Finansov SSR, *Gosudarstvennye biudzhety soiuznykh respublik v piatoi piatiletke* (Moscow, 1957), pp. 7, 16-18, 36-38; *Gosudarstvennyi biudzhet SSSR i biudzhety soiuznykh respublik* (Moscow, 1962), pp. 18-19, 109-10; *Gosudarstvennyi* (1966), pp. 20-21, 111-12; *Gosudarstvennyi* (1972), pp. 25, 118-19; *Narodnoe khoziaistvo SSSR* (Moscow, 1974) (*Narkhoz*) 1973, p. 778; *Narodne-hospodarstvo Ukrains'koi RSR* (Kiev 1974) (*Narhosp*) 1973, p. 559; *Pravda* (*P*), Nov. 20, 1976; *Radians'ka Ukraina* (*RU*), Nov. 28, 1976. Panel 5—*Narkhoz 1960*, p. 591; *Narkhoz 1973*, p. 554; *Narhosp 1964*, p. 421; *Narhosp 1973*, p. 349; *P*, Dec. 21, 1974, and Jan. 25, 1975; *RU*, Dec. 26, 1974, and Jan. 25, 1975. Panel 6—*Narhosp 1961*, p. 116; F. Khyliuk, "Voprosy sovershenstvovaniia planirovaniia v respublike," *Planovoe khoziaistvo* (*PKh*) (1967): no. 5, 24; L. M. Mushketik, *Kompleksnyi territorial'nyi plan v usloviiakh otraslevogo upravleniia* (Kiev, 1974), p. 10.

editorial in the official journal of the Communist party of the Ukraine called on the Ukrainian Gosplan to prepare comprehensive current and perspective plans for the entire Ukrainian economy, approaching it from a regional perspective, something that had not been done before.[91] It was suggested that such plans take into better account the needs and possibilities of the republic than had the previous plans, which were based on development plans of the individual branches.[92] To do this planning effectively, estimates of national income for the Ukraine were needed. As a result there appeared a competent monograph dealing with the national income of the Ukraine for 1959-61.[93] Economists started to stress the importance of the Ukraine in the international trade of the USSR.[94] In addition, officials heading the international department of the Ukrainian Gosplan were identified for the first time.[95] The Ukraine was visited by several economic delegations from foreign countries.[96] Finally, the republic began to participate separately from the USSR in various international fairs.[97]

The greater assertiveness of the Ukraine during this period was also felt outside the economic sphere, particularly with respect to foreign relations, science, and the arts. Although the Ukraine was a founding member of the United Nations, it did not appoint its first permanent delegate to that body until 1958.[98] The first secretary of the Communist party of the Ukraine, M. V. Pidhornyi, represented the country in 1960 at the general session of the United Nations, where he delivered his speech in Ukrainian.[99] In general, the foreign relations of the Ukraine with other countries increased considerably during this period.[100] Internally, the Ukraine witnessed a renaissance of its sciences and arts, particularly literature. Scholars and writers stressed the separateness and the historical continuity of their nation.[101] These developments were not simply the result of greater economic prerogatives of the Ukraine but followed the decisions of Soviet leaders at the Twentieth Congress of the CPSU in 1956 to relax the Stalinist system and to meet, though only to a small degree, the aspirations of non-Russian nations. Enlargement of the economic prerogatives of the Ukrainian government and the assertivenesss of the population in other spheres of national life reinforced each other.

However, this picture of considerable economic prerogatives for the Ukrainian government was clouded by old centralizing tendencies. The USSR Council of Ministers, according to the sovnarkhoz law, was only supposed to suspend the decisions of sovnarkhozes, but actually it issued orders directly to them.[102] The plans prepared by USSR Gosplan were too detailed for republics and thus limited the latter's flexibility.[103] Instead of using the route through the USSR Council of Ministers, the republic Council of Ministers, the republic Gosplan, and the sovnarkhoz, the USSR Gosplan often issued orders directly to the sovnarkhoz or even to an enterprise within the sovnarkhoz, if the enterprise was of unionwide importance.[104] The Central Administration of Intersovnarkhoz Material and Technical Supplies, an organ of the USSR Gosplan, was most guilty of centralizing tendencies.[105] Ukrainian officials complained, and demanded that this organ yield to sovnarkhozes the marketing, for example, of such important inputs as ferrous-metal products and timber.[106] They also demanded that in all dealings concerning the Ukraine the Central Administration should communicate only with the republic's government.[107] However, despite the advice of Ukrainian officials and economists, more power was increasingly concentrated in the hands of this intersovnarkhoz administration.[108]

The results of the 1957 reforms were mixed.[109] On the positive side, they resulted in greater utilization of enterprises with a social overhead character;[110] they led to a decrease in transportation costs;* they encouraged merging of small neighboring enterprises into larger ones, with resulting economies of scale;† and they facilitated greater interbranch cooperation in research, development, and solution of multibranch problems.

The disadvantages of the sovnarkhoz system (in Moscow's eyes) were several. Sovnarkhozes modified central investment plans to accord with their own interests. Some of the Ukrainian sovnarkhozes were responsive to the desires of the population, and allocated more funds to residential and municipal construction and, incidentally, paid higher wages than the central planners would have liked to see.[111] As might be expected, the accusation of "localism" was often heard. It found its expression in the severing of long-established supply connections between enterprises located in different sovnarkhozes, and in using the output primarily for the sovnarkhoz's own needs. The reluctance of Ukrainian sovnarkhozes to ship their output outside the borders of their republic appears to have been strong.‡ Sometimes they decreased the output of commodities that were to be exported to other parts of the country.[112] Sovnarkhozes did not cooperate in research and development, and this resulted in duplication of these activities on a small scale. Finally, as the Polish economist Pawlik observed, the sovnarkhoz system had nother very important deficiency. It was not conducive to the transfer of investable funds from the western regions of the country, in which they were largely accumulated, to the Asiatic regions that the leaders wanted to develop.[113]

As indicated earlier, the creation of Sovnarkhozes in the republics that had several sovnarkhozes in 1960 was intended primarily to improve the coordination

---

*According to the chairman of the Ukrainian Sovnarkhoz, transportation costs before 1957 often were greater than the benefits from large-scale production. See A. Kuz'mych, "Chotyry roky roboty radnarhospiv," *ERU*, no. 4, 20.

†During this time—in 1961, to be precise—the first Soviet firm "Progress," comprising a number of small shoe-producing enterprises, was created in L'viv. See *P*, June 13, 1963. This was the beginning of the present movement toward creation of production and industrial associations.

‡For example, during one month there was a complaint that the Kiev sovnarkhoz failed to deliver certain goods to Memel (Lithuania) and Minsk (Belorussia), and the Kharkiv sovnarkhoz, to the Bashkir republic. See *DSUP* (March 1958): 13.

of the latter. Another measure with a similar objective was the 1961 division of the country into 17 (later 18) large economic regions. In the Ukraine three such regions were created: Donets'k-Dnieper, South Western, and Southern.[114] In each of these a Coordination and Planning Committee was organized with the responsibilities implied by the name but without any implementing apparatus. Still another measure, which had already led to the recentralization of decision making in Moscow, was the increase in the number of branch committees with primary responsibility for research and development in individual branches. There were no corresponding organs in the republics. The official route of communication of the branch committee was through the USSR Council of Ministers, the Ukrainian Council of Ministers, the sovnarkhozes, and individual enterprises. But in practice, as in the case of other union bodies, they often circumvented these channels and issued orders directly to enterprises.[115]

The disadvantages of the sovnarkhoz system proved to be more significant than the advantages. Since most of these disadvantages were associated with the relatively small economic potential of individual sovnarkhozes, the purpose of the reforms in 1962-63 was the elimination of this deficiency through the enlargement of sovnarkhozes in the RSFSR, Kazakhstan, and the Ukraine, and through the transfer of powers from sovnarkhozes to republics, and from republics to union authorities. One can speculate that these three republics, which are relatively large and have well-developed and diversified economies, could have handled these problems within their borders, without losing some of their economic prerogatives.[116] However, the situation in the remaining 12 republics was different. Here the borders of sovnarkhozes coincided with the borders of republics. One possible solution could have been the merger of a few sovnarkhoz-republics into a larger sovnarkhoz. This was attempted in the case of four Central Asian republics and three Transcaucasian republics. But in view of political complications, this attempt was halfhearted.[117] Another solution, actually implemented, was recentralizing some decision making in the hands of union authorities. But since all the republics are legally equal, the decrease in powers of smaller republics had to be accompanied by the decrease in powers of the three largest republics.

At any rate, the reforms of 1962-63 considerably changed the economic prerogatives of the Ukraine.[118] Its 14 sovnarkhozes decreased by half. The Ukrainian Sovnarkhoz gained in power, mainly at the cost of the republic Gosplan, which retained only its responsibility for current and perspective planning. The Ukrainian Sovnarkhoz was supposed to coordinate and control the sovnarkhozes. Its competence with respect to coordination was extended not only to industry but also to such economic sectors as the supply of material and technical resources, trade, transportation, communication, and consumer services. The responsibility of Coordination and Planning Committees of large regions was now limited to long-term planning under the Ukrainian Gosplan.

But the real effect of these reforms was the weakening of prerogatives of republic organs in the Ukraine and in other republics. The USSR Sovnarkhoz, which was required to coordinate the work of sovnarkhozes supposedly through the republic Sovnarkhozes, was organized in Moscow.[119] The republic Sovnarkhozes became union-republic bodies as did the republic Gosplans, Gosstroys, and, in 1964, the republic State Committees for Coordination of Scientific and Research Work. The Ukrainian Academy of Sciences was also put under the supervision of the USSR Academy of Sciences and admonished to do a better job.[120] Now the union authorities could communicate directly with their Kiev counterparts without going even as a formality through the Council of Ministers, obviously a considerable decrease in the power of the Ukrainian Council of Ministers. The increase in the number and responsibilities of branch committees at the union level was also of considerable importance. They were made responsible for establishing norms and standards, for the distribution of material and financial resources among enterprises in their branch, and for checking on the work of their enterprises. For this reason, the Ukrainian sovnarkhoz and sovnarkhozes transferred construction and research establishments, experimentation bureaus, and specialized organizations for the introduction of new projects to the branch committees.[121]

The system performed even less well as a result of these new reforms. According to Alexei Kosygin, it had several deficiencies.[122] First, a complicated and multilevel structure of decision making resulted in unclearly defined and overlapping competences of various planning and management organs.[123] (This was particularly true in the case of the relations between union and republics.)[124] Second, there was a lack of unity in the guidance of production, technological research and development, and economic decisions in individual branches of industry.[125] Third, investment activity was not coordinated. One can add that the enlarged sovnarkhozes were completely divorced from administrative and Communist party organs, in order, according to Nikita Khrushchev, to combat localism.[126] But it seems that the Soviet economy cannot function properly without "day-to-day-care" or, rather, prodding from these organs. The situation was aggravated by the split of Communist party at all levels into industrial and agricultural sectors.[127] Finally, the continuous reforms, so much favored by Khrushchev, kept the entire economy in a state of uncertainty and instability.

The Period After 1965

After the downfall of Khrushchev his successors, not surprisingly, introduced a new reform in 1965. This amounted largely to a return to pre-1957 conditions. Sovnarkhozes and union and republic Sovnarkhozes, the Supreme Council of National Economy, and state branch committees were liquidated, and

30 industrial ministries (17 union and 13 union-republic) were resurrected. The main idea of the reform was not only to transfer the decision-making powers from sovnarkhozes to these ministries, but also to assign these powers either upward to the ministries or downward to individual enterprises.

In the Ukraine many changes took place.[128] Six union-republic ministries were already in existence (power and electrification, agriculture, installation and special construction work, commerce, communication, and finance), and 11 were added (ferrous metals; coal industry; chemical industry; geology; lumber, celluloid, paper, and woodworking industry; building materials industry; and land reclamation and water resources). The ministry of local industry joined four existing republic-subordinated ministries (motor vehicle transport and highways; construction; municipal services; and social security). Also, the Main Administration for Material and Technical Supply (Glavsnab) was added to the existing state committees. The union-republic State Committee for Coordination of Scientific and Research Work was liquidated.

Since 1965, further administrative changes have taken place in the management structure of the Ukrainian economy, excluding the agricultural sector. In 1966 the union-republic Ministry of Forestry and the republic-subordinated Ministry of Consumer Services were established.[129] In 1967 the republic Ministry of Construction was split into two union-republic ministries: construction of heavy industry enterprises and industrial construction, and the republic State Committee of Utilization of Labor Reserves was established.[130] In 1968 the union-republic Ministry of Timber, Celluloid, Paper, and Wood Processing retained union-republic status but was renamed Ministry of Timber and Wood Processing, while the other two product groups were transferred to union subordination.[131] In the same year the republic-subordinated Ministry of Motor Vehicle Transport and Highways was divided into two ministries of the same status: motor transport and construction and utilization of highways.[132] In 1970 the union-republic State Committee for Prices was organized and the union-republic Ministry of Chemical Industry was liquidated, its enterprises becoming a part of the union ministry.[133] In 1971 the Administration of the Petroleum Refining and Petrochemical Industry became the Main Administration, and in 1972 the Main Administration of Horticulture, Viticulture, and Wine Processing was established.[134]

The preceding discussion concerned organizational changes in Ukrainian industry and construction. Changes in agriculture also took place during the postwar period, though to a smaller degree. An early post-Stalin resolution called for greater decentralization in the planning of agricultural deliveries.[135] Instead of assigning production targets down to the raion (county) level, the USSR Gosplan was now required to assign only delivery targets to republics, and the latter had to disaggregate these plans. The republic Council of Ministers was also made responsible for aggregation of agriculture production plans and for presenting the result to the USSR Gosplan. Through various resolutions of the USSR

Council of Ministers, the republic Council of Ministers obtained certain powers with respect to agriculture.

According to the 1957 reforms, the Ministry of Agriculture and the Ministry of Sovkhozes merged into the union-republic Ministry of Agriculture, with very limited responsibilities. The planning and supervision of these sectors was shifted to the Ukrainian Gosplan.[136] This ministry lost further powers in 1961, retaining only the responsibility for research. The distribution of inputs went to the Ukrainian Association for Sale of Agricultural Equipment and the Organization of Machinery Repairs and Utilization (Ukrsel'khoztakhnika), procurement to the Ministry of Agricultural Procurement, and the control over sovkhozes to the Main Administration of Sovkhozes, all of republic subordination.[137] According to V. M. Marchuk, this framework did not provide leadership in agriculture.[138] Therefore, in 1962 the Ministry of Agricultural Procurement and the Main Administration of Sovkhozes were merged into the republic-subordinated Ministry of Production and Procurement of Agricultural Products, which was made responsible for the supervision of the work of 190 (in 1963 increased to 250)[139] newly created territorial production kolkhoz-sovkhoz associations. This agricultural structure was to be controlled by the Republic Committee for Agriculture, headed by the first secretary of the Communist party of the Ukraine.[140]

In agriculture, as in industry, the 1965 reforms meant basically a return to the pre-1957 system. The Republic Committee for Agriculture was disbanded, as were the territorial production associations. The lowest administrative unit for agriculture again became the raion.[141] The Ministry of Production and Procurement of Agricultural Products was incorporated into the union-republic Ministry of Agriculture, which was made responsible for planning and control of this sector.[142] The procurement function of the former was taken over by the republic-subordinated State Committee on Grain and Fodder Products. In 1969 the name was changed to the Ministry of Grain Products, and in 1970 it became a union-republic ministry.[143] To supervise the work of sovkhozes in the Ukraine, the republic-subordinated Ministry of Sovkhozes was organized in 1969; in 1973 it acquired union-republic status.[144]

While the 1965 reforms curtailed the decision-making powers of republics, the stated objective of two resolutions issued in 1965 and 1967 was to expand these powers.[145] But the significance of these resolutions on the issue of union versus republics should not be overestimated. Of much greater importance in Soviet life than any law is the "general'naia liniia" of the Communist party, the direction really preferred by the party leadership. And each official who has to make decisions knows perfectly well that the emphasis is now on the union, to the detriment of the republics.

The reforms of 1965 have not solved all the ills of the Soviet economy. For example, according to Leon Smolinski, a Western specialist of Soviet reforms, three problems have become particularly acute in industry.[146] First, despite the explicit intention to delegate more decision-making powers to individual enterprises, these powers are again centralized in the reconstituted ministries.[147] Second, each ministry again began to strive to become self-sufficient, and consequently became involved in production of commodities outside its own branch. The resulting inefficient production on a small scale was unavoidable. Third, since ministries—and their administrative subdivisions—are not constrained by any explicit optimizing criteria, they often give incorrect orders from the point of view of the entire economy.

The neglect of regional planning, as implied in the second problem, seems to be particularly important to Ukrainian officials and economists. In discussions of the 1965 reforms, they repeatedly stress[148] Kosygin's statement, which accompanied the introduction of these reforms. He said that ". . . the industrial branch principle of management must be combined with the territorial principle, with the interbranch tasks of the integral development of the national economy as a whole and of the economies of the country's republics and regions, with expansion of the economic powers of the republics."[149]

It required little time, however, to show that the coexistence of these two planning approaches is hardly possible in the Soviet system. Branch planning immediately became dominant, as it had been before the sovnarkhoz system. According to the chairman of the USSR Gosplan, ". . . [post-1965] territorial planning largely amounts to a mechanical compilation of more important targets for a republic or an economic region, derived in the process of preparation of plans for ministries."[150] At the same time the chairman of the Ukrainian Gosplan called for simultaneous preparation of branch and republic plans and greater cooperation between the USSR and republic Gosplans.[151] The latter have experienced difficulties in preparing balanced plans for their republics, because plants located in their territory are subordinated to several central authorities that have proved not to be cooperative and that are not subject to jurisdiction of republics.* In general, Soviet specialists argue, the neglect of territorial planning is quite harmful to the performance of the entire economy.[152]

To cope with these new—or, rather, revived—difficulties, still another reform was introduced in 1973 requiring the grouping of a few enterprises into production associations.[153] The associations acquired some powers previously

---

*For example, "Industrial enterprises, sovkhozes, construction, transportation, geological and other state and cooperative enterprises located on the Ukraine's territory, are subordinated to 26 union, 60 union-republic, 24 republic-subordinated ministries and departments and also to executive committees of republic subordination of 24 oblasts and two cities. Planning of industrial development on the republic's territory is performed by 72 ministries and departments, and investment by 97 ministries and departments, and executive committees of 24 oblasts and of Kiev and Sevastopil'." I. Bezuhlov, "Udoskonalyty narodnohospodars'ke planuvannia," *ERU* (1968): no. 2, 6.

held by enterprises and ministries, or by their glavks, which were to disappear by 1973.[154] Associations within union and USSR union-republic ministries are directly subordinated to these ministries, and associations within the republic union-republic and republic-subordinated ministries are subordinated to their ministries. Associations within republic union-republic ministries are under the operative leadership of the republic, while the USSR union-republic ministries should be responsible for such general problems as the development of the branch, technological progress, improvement in administration, and the study of demand.[155] In certain cases there is an additional management level above the production associations called an industrial association.

It has been emphasized by I. Raznatovs'kyi, a Soviet jurist, that associations should include enterprises located in different administrative units (presumably also republics), should efficiency require it.[156] On the other hand, V. F. Pavlenko, an economist, argues that since the cooperation and coordination between state and economic administrations is of vital importance for efficiency, associations would be most effective, under Soviet conditions, if organized within an oblast or, at most, a republic.[157] Therefore, it seems that no decrease in republic prerogatives is likely to take place on this account. On the contrary, associations may eventually lead to the decentralization of decision making from ministries to regional authorities. If an association comprises enterprises that previously belonged to more than one ministry, then the respective ministries will lose their power over these enterprises. Since under Soviet conditions some organ has to supervise associations, it is likely that such power may be vested in governments of oblasts and republics.[158] No such interministry associations yet exist in the Ukraine, but the Soviet economist M. D. Horbovyati favors their organization and proposes that they be supervised by a special glavk subordinated to the Ukrainian Council of Ministers.[159]

Prognosis

This brings us to reflections on the future distribution of decision making between Kiev and Moscow. One important factor may be the greater use of computers in Soviet planning. Their net impact is, however, not obvious. According to a recent study, computerization initially leads to greater centralization in decision making but, as Western experience shows, ". . . the optimal satiation point for information hunger may be reached at the center, and decentralization may follow as with the law of diminishing returns."[160] Since the USSR is not yet advanced in computer technology, one can assume that this point has not yet been reached; consequently, a trend toward greater centralization of the Soviet economy, at least for this reason, can be anticipated for some time to come.

The future of economic prerogatives of the Ukraine and, for that matter, of any other problem in the USSR, is much more related to history—and especially to politics—than to economics and technology. Over the last three centuries a struggle has been going on between Russia and the Ukraine. Russia has sought to russify the Ukraine, as well as other non-Russian nationalities under its rule, and to integrate them permanently into the Russian empire. The Ukrainians, with the growth of their national consciousness, desired of course, the creation of a sovereign state of their own. This struggle has carried into the twentieth century. Since neither of these two forces was strong enough to win decisively during the 1917-20 Revolution, the result was a compromise in the form of the Ukrainian SSR, which in theory is a sovereign state but in practice is effectively dominated by Moscow.[161]

This compromise is explained by the Soviet dialecticians, for the Ukraine as well as for other non-Russian nations, in the following terms. It is claimed that two tendencies exist among nations of the USSR. On the one hand, they "flourish" under the Soviet system by acquiring better features of culture from other nationalities. On the other, there is "rapprochement" among nations, the developing of common characteristics.[162] In practice the latter tendency is equivalent to the russification of non-Russian nationalities. Since ethnic assimilation is an express objective of the regime, it has tried in the past to speed up this process through various centralizing policies. State intervention depended in the past on internal and external developments. It was strong during Stalin's period, but relatively weak in the 1920s and the second part of the 1950s. Since the announcement of the Party Program in 1961, the centralizing forces have again been in the ascendancy,[163] though during most of the 1960s this tendency was rather subdued. It gained strength at the end of the 1960s and has been explicit since 1972. In his speech on the occasion of the fiftieth anniversary of the creation of the USSR, Leonid Brezhnev announced the existence of a new historical community of people, the Soviet people; urged the use of the Russian language by all; encouraged ethnically mixed marriages; and praised population migration as a means of achieving ethnically mixed regions.[164] At the present time, an intensive russification campaign, under the euphemism of internationalization, is taking place in the non-Russian republics in all aspects of life.

The reforms of 1965 were an economic reflection of this trend. According to K. Diablo, a Soviet jurist, ". . . they became a kind of catalyst for the expansion of competences of the organs of the USSR based on the principle of democratic centralism not only in the sector of industry, but also in the administrative-political and sociocultural sectors."[165] Good examples of this attitude are two articles by M. Urinson, a Soviet specialist in republic planning. In one article, written a few months before the reforms, he speaks of the need for the improvement in planning the comprehensive development of the economies of individual republics.[166] In the other, written shortly after the introduction of the reforms, he stresses the need to subordinate republic economies to the objectives of the USSR economy as an integrated economic complex, and does not refer any more to republics as economic entities.[167]

In view of such a changed attitude toward the economies of the republics, an article by V. Kistanov, a well-known regional economist, sounds ominous.[168] In it he argues, using an appropriate quotation from Lenin, that the ethnic principle is not the only and most important criterion for division of administration and of economic management in the USSR. He believes that, in terms of efficiency, new regions with administrative and economic powers can be organized within republics, or that the existing borders of republics can be modified regardless of the ethnic distribution of the population. If such reforms were to be introduced, some republics would cease to exist and the survival of their nationalities would be in jeopardy. Despite this potential threat, competent observers in the West believe that no such radical changes can be expected in the foreseeable future.[169]

PREROGATIVES OF THE UKRAINIAN GOVERNMENT

Specific Powers

The economic prerogatives of the Ukraine's Council of Ministers are defined in the Ukrainian Constitution as follows.[170] The Council of Ministers, subordinated to the Supreme Soviet of the Ukrainian SSR, issues resolutions and orders within the laws of the USSR and the Ukraine and within the resolutions of the USSR Council of Ministers. It controls the implementation of these resolutions and orders. Other functions of the Council of Ministers are coordination and guidance of the work of Ukrainian ministries and other organs subordinated to it; coordination and control of work done by representatives of union ministries and other union organs in the Ukraine; implementation of economic plans and of republic and local budgets; and, when necessary, the organization of special committees and main administrations.

This formulation is not of much assistance for understanding the true prerogatives of the Ukrainian Council of Ministers. It is as vague as was the formulation of legal rights of the Ukraine in general, discussed in Part I. To understand what the Ukrainian government can and what it cannot do in economic matters it is necessary to study, in the context of Soviet conditions, various powers explicitly assigned to it in the resolutions of the USSR Council of Ministers, and also its role in the planning process. Let us start with the former problem.

The powers of a republic's government over each of three legal types of enterprises (union, union-republic, and republic-subordinated) vary. The republic Council of Ministers can review the output plans of union ministries' enterprises located in its territory (1965, 1) and the development, location, and construction plans of enterprises subordinated to union industrial ministries (1965, 2).* On the basis of these plans, the council can make proposals to the relevant union authorities. These proposals should be helpful in the preparation of annual and perspective plans. The Council of Ministers can also allow, in consultation with the union authorities, the combining of investment funds of union ministries and republic ministries for construction of housing and establishments for preschool children (1967, 2).

As noted, the Ukrainian Constitution also requires the republic Council of Ministers to control the work of union-subordinated enterprises, the success of which is important to a republic for three reasons. First, a part of the turnover taxes on products produced by any enterprise goes to the republic budget. (See the discussion of budget rights below.) Second, according to the law, up to 50 percent of the above-plan output of all enterprises located in a republic remains at the disposal of the republic. The exact percentage depends on the relationship between plans and performance and applies to the products on a list determined by the USSR Council of Ministers (1965, 3). Third, republic authorities are praised for the successful operation of union enterprises on their territory. However, all these competences of republic over union enterprises are rather academic, since no laws regulate the relationship between union ministries and a republic.[171] The union ministry may simply ignore suggestions beneficial to the republic, and the republic has no legal means to press its point further.

Republic-subordinated industry theoretically is entirely under the jurisdiction of republic authorities. This includes planning, material-technical supply, investments, labor and wages, control, and other matters. With respect to planning, the following are some of the most important prerogatives specified in the official documents: to change, in response to changes in demand during the duration of a plan, the composition and volume of consumer goods, excluding products to be exported to other republics, provided that there are no changes in payments to the budget (1959, 1); to approve plans for industrial output consumed entirely within a republic and to determine its product mix, while the USSR Gosplan ensures the necessary inputs (1965, 4); to allow ministries to change the output mix, planned by republics, with the agreement of users of this output (1967, 8). Republic organs have the right to determine technological norms and standards for production of processed food and other industrial consumer goods produced by republic-subordinated and union-republic ministries of a republic.[172] They are also responsible for organization of the material-technical supply for republic-subordinated ministries.

---

*The subsequent discussion is based on resolutions of the USSR Council of Ministers cited in notes 72, 88, and 145, and the law of the USSR Supreme Soviet cited in note 90. They will be referred to in the text according to the year of publication and the original number of a particular provision.

The situation with regard to the prerogatives of republics over their union-republic ministry is particularly complicated, even for Soviet legal conditions. The laws have very little to say about the division of powers in this case between the republic Council of Ministers and the USSR ministry of the same name. According to the USSR Constitution, Article 76, a USSR union-republic ministry guides a given branch, as a rule, through the republic ministry of the same name and directly manages only a limited number of enterprises, a list of which must be approved by the Presidium of the USSR Supreme Soviet. The Ukrainian Constitution, Article 51, states that a Ukrainian union-republic ministry guides a certain branch in subordination to the Ukrainian Council of Ministers and to the USSR ministry of the same name. Not much more explicit is the General Charter of the USSR Ministries of 1967.[173] Article 6 repeats the provision of the Constitution in this regard; Article 7 adds that individual USSR and republic union-republic ministries jointly represent a system of the respective ministry; and Article 17 states that within the existing legislation a USSR minister issues orders and instructions to the republic union-republic ministry of the same name and supervises their implementation.

Obviously, such regulations are too general to provide adequate guidelines in practice. Soviet writers are of not much help, either. I. Raznatovs'kyi, who tries to be more specific but offers no legal justification, argues that the responsibility of the USSR union-republic ministry to the republic ministry of the same name is limited to providing targets for perspective and annual plans, technological progress, and organization of labor; determination of norms of the use of raw materials and other resources; and control over the implementation of these plans. Remaining powers should be within the jurisdiction of the republic union-republic ministry.[174] K. E. Kolibab, another writer, believes that the powers of the USSR union-republic ministries over their republic counterparts are quite extensive, but should not go so far as to change the financial relation of the latter to the republic budget.[175] However, most of the writers are satisfied simply with repeating the general statement that a USSR union-republic ministry provides general guidance for a particular industrial branch, while its republic union-republic ministry has direct operative production and economic functions.[176]

In view of the lack of a general law that would regulate the republic union-republic ministries, their legal status varies from one ministry to another. For example, out of 28 Ukrainian union-republic ministries in 1971, 19 had individual charters issued to them by the Ukrainian Council of Ministers, while the rest operated without any legal document.[177] Not surprisingly, the division of decision making between the union and the republic was quite different among these ministries.[178] In general, it seems that the powers of USSR union-republic ministries over republic union-republic ministries are greater in heavy industry than in light industry.[179]

Soviet economists and officials are dissatisfied with this situation. More-over, they fear that the lack of legal clarity may lead to the complete centrali-zation of decision-making powers in Moscow-based ministries, as was the case before 1954.[180] Therefore they urge the passing of legislation that would delineate ". . . with legal precision (without declarative, diffuse formulations) . . ." the extent of the rights of republic union-republic ministries.[181] Another jurist, speaking about a similar lack of such legislation in the early 1960s, demands that such delineation of powers between the union and local manage-ment levels should be clear and ". . . not dodge the decision of this question under the cover of general phrases 'jointly', 'in cooperation', 'in close contact', etc."[182] That officials are also concerned about the uncertainty of their powers is reflected in the following passage from an interview with the minister of the Ukrainian union-republic Ministry of Light Industry: ". . . on the subject of ministerial rights and duties, it is high time to have this defined within the legal framework . . . we find ourselves in a situation similar to that which existed prior to 1957."[183]

More recently another, more radical proposal has been advanced. It is being suggested, although only implicitly, that union-republic ministries of heavy industry be reorganized into union ministries and union-republic ministries of light industries into republic-subordinated industries.[184] In other words, union-republic ministries should be liquidated. The proposal is based on administrative experience as it has evolved during the postreform period. Various authors claim that now, in certain union-republic ministries of heavy industry, all decision-making power lies anyhow in the hands of USSR union-republic ministries that use their republic counterparts simply as a mailing address and often ignore them in the most important matters. On the other hand, in various union-republic ministries of light industry the competences of republic governments are not much different from those over republic-subordinated ministries.[185]

However, as the situation stands, the division of competences over union-republic ministries between union and republic is not clear and varies signifi-cantly from ministry to ministry. Very often these competences overlap. But if a USSR union-republic ministry wanted to take over a certain decision-making power under its jurisdiction, the republic would be unable to resist and would have to surrender this power. Finally, should there be a difference of opinion between the two levels of Soviet bureaucracy, there is no doubt that the Moscow side would win.*

---

*In general, the regional manager is in a weaker position than the branch manager if there is a disagreement because ". . . the latter has the advantage of national perspective, greater technical knowledge, and more intimate access to the central leaders." See Jerry F. Hough, *The Soviet Prefects: The Local Party Organs in Industrial Decision-making* (Cam-bridge, Mass.: Harvard University Press, 1969), p. 204.

Let us now consider republic competences in investment, labor and wages, agriculture, and budget because these areas have a functional and specific (agriculture) importance for the entire economic life of the Ukraine.

According to one study, the competences of a republic in investment are the following:[186] to approve investment plans within the framework of the plans for the republic's national economy (these plans comprise all sources of funds, including those of kolkhozes); to determine the order of approval of regional and city construction plans; to approve investment projects up to 2.5 million rubles and to determine their costs and the prices of construction and installation works if such union data are unavailable; to determine the order of approval of productive and nonproductive projects if the investment funds for them were to be allocated to the republic; to determine the price lists for housing and sociocultural construction; to determine the order of organization, reorganization, and liquidation of republic construction organizations; to approve plans for the supply of enterprises, regardless of subordination, with local construction materials; to determine the order of contracts for construction works in kolkhozes; to determine the order of receiving all finished sociocultural projects and, in the case of productive projects, up to 3 million rubles. All these republic powers are also applicable to union enterprises in a given republic.[187]

In addition, official documents mention the following investment competences of republics with respect to the economic activity subordinated to the republic: to retain 5 percent of the total investment in the republic-subordinated economy as a reserve (1955, 16); to redistribute investment funds among productive objects (up to 5 percent) without change in construction plans (1965, 8); to allow the use of investment funds allocated for a project without regard to quarterly distribution of these funds (1967, 1); to allow the combining of funds of republic-subordinated and local enterprises for construction of housing and municipal projects (1967, 3); to use up to 2.5 percent of funds of productive investment for housing, subject to fulfillment of productive investment plans (1967, 4); to transfer up to 10 percent of investment funds from projects underfulfilling their construction plans to projects overfulfilling the plans (1967, 5).

Although decision making on wages and working conditions is essentially in the hands of union organs, the republics possess some limited powers over the republic-subordinated economy in this area. The most important such powers are the following: to determine employment distribution of graduates of institutions of higher education within a republic (1955, 4) (most likely, excluding the graduates from institutes maintained by union ministries); to retain 2 percent of the overall labor and wage fund allocated to the republic-subordinated economy as a reserve (1955, 7); to determine the structure of administrative personnel of republic-subordinated ministries, oblasts, and other units (1957, 14); to determine the wage rates of faculty members and deans of institutions of higher education (1957, 33); to change the number of workers in a republic-subordinated economy without change in wage fund and labor productivity plans (1959, 11); to change the quarterly wage fund up to 2 percent (1959, 12); in case of change in output of a given enterprise, to change the wage category of workers (1959, 15), managers, engineer-technical, and clerical personnel (1967, 20); to determine the labor plans for construction-projecting organizations within the overall labor plan of the republic (1965, 29); to determine the wage and bonus structure for new enterprises, taking into account similar existing enterprises (1965, 32); to raise institutions of higher education from one wage group to another (1965, 35); to increase the planned wage fund of workers of certain repair and consumer services (1967, 21).

As in the other cases, the competences assigned to republics in agriculture and forestry are very limited. The republic Council of Ministers has the power to ease financial obligations of kolkhozes (1955, 36, 37, 38); to allow organization, reorganization, and liquidation of sovkhozes (1955, 57); to change the boundaries between neighboring kolkhozes (1955, 60); to settle questions connected with the use of land held by kolkhozes, sovkhozes, and the state (1957, 23); to allow agricultural enterprises to sell up to 3 percent of an increase in livestock to rural teachers, clerical personnel, and others (1967, 38).

The rights of republics in budgetary matters are the following:[188] the budget of the republic is approved by its Supreme Soviet (Constitution, Article 80); in the case of change in USSR laws, any resulting deficit in the current budget of a republic will be covered and any surplus absorbed by the USSR budget (34); the receipts of republic budgets consist of a share of the profits of state enterprises, forest tax, income tax of kolkhozes, income tax of cooperative enterprises and social organizations, agricultural tax, 50 percent of the income tax on the republic's population, various smaller taxes in accordance with USSR legislation, a part of social security contributions needed for payment of pensions, a part of the turnover tax, and a part of other state incomes in accordance with the USSR legislation (35, 36); budget expenditures are divided into national economy, social and cultural measures, administration, and others (37); the republic is responsible for delineation of republic and local budgets (38); additional budget receipts must be used for the national economy and for social and cultural measures (41); the republic Supreme Soviet can increase the receipts and expenditures of the republic budget without changes in relation to the USSR budget (39); any budget surplus resulting from efficient management remains at the disposal of the republic Council of Ministers (42).

Other decision making powers include retention of 5 percent of the total credit allocated to the republic as a reserve (1959, 3); allocation of credits from one republic-subordinated ministry to another;[189] permission for ministries to combine the above-plan profits of their enterprises for housing construction

(1959, 8); permission to transfer certain fixed assets from one enterprise to another (1965, 25); and determination of many local prices.*

The competences of the republic Councils of Ministers listed above are the most important among those that appeared in resolutions of the USSR government after Stalin's death.† Since during his rule the republics did not have any rights to speak of, these are the only ones they now possess. Numerous other prerogatives, which are not listed here but are usually exercised by other socialist states, are in the hands of union organs in Moscow.

Obviously, it is rather difficult to give a complete picture of the decision-making powers of the republics on the basis of the preceding list. However, certain conclusions are justified. A republic Council of Ministers does not have any power over the substantial segment of the economy that is directly subordinated to Moscow. This fact has an important implication: enterprises and officials subordinated to Moscow enjoy extraterritorial status that doubtless weakens the power of the republic Council of Ministers. The competences of republics over their union-republic ministries are imprecise and vague, and seemingly can be overruled at any time by Moscow officials. Finally, the rights over a republic-subordinated economy are very detailed, so that there is very little room left for independent decisions by republics. But even these decisions can be made, in most cases, only "in consultation," "in agreement," "in coordination," or "jointly" with union authorities. What this means to the republic government needs no further elaboration. Moreover, these prerogatives can be taken away from a republic at any time, because the power to give and to claim such prerogatives is exclusively in the hands of the USSR government.

One power of republic authorities is real: the power to use all necessary propaganda, persuasion, and publicity to improve the performance of the republic's economy and to fulfill—or, better yet, to overfulfill—the plans. One need only to look at the Kiev newspapers to see all the resolutions passed by the Ukrainian government and Communist party, and the speeches made by Ukrainian leaders to exhort their countrymen to greater effort. No detail is too small

---

*According to the vice-chairman of the USSR Price Committee, republics determine prices of 40 percent of all consumer goods, 20 percent of all producer goods, local transport, a significant part of consumer services, and many procurement, purchase, delivery, and wholesale prices of various raw materials and forestry products. See *EG* (1967): no. 2, 8.

†The prerogatives to allow traveling construction crews to rent rooms in private houses, and construction enterprises to reimburse up to 3 rubles per month (1955, 30), or to allow residents of regions without forests to work on construction projects in regions with forests and take home the cut timber (1967, 37), and such similar "powers" of the republic government were not listed.

for their attention. A further analysis of this function of the Ukrainian government would take us too far from economics.

Planning Powers

The USSR and its republics prepare current (one-year), intermediate (five-year), and long-term economic plans.* Only the latter two are of importance for territorial planning. The annual plans are the tools for the implementation of the other two types of plans. Therefore, the methodology and the included indicators of all these plans are almost identical. The following description, which deals primarily with annual planning, is thus applicable to intermediate and long-term plans.

A republic prepares two types of annual plans: state plans for the development of the national economy and basic indicators of complex development. State plans include the economy subordinated to the republic Council of Ministers (the economy of republic-subordinated ministries and of republic union-republic ministries). They have the power of law. Basic indicators refer to the entire economy located within a given republic, but they have no legal power.

The state plans for the development of the national economy of a republic are prepared in the following manner. The USSR Gosplan annually prepares output plans (control figures), identifies the amounts of available resources (limits), and then disaggregates them among republics and union ministries.[190] For republics these targets are divided into ten groups. The output targets and resource limits are disaggregated by republics among their ministries, intermediate organs, and, ultimately, enterprises. On the basis of the targets and limits, enterprises prepare their output plans and input requirements for the coming year. These are aggregated by the successively higher bodies. The republic Gosplan aggregates the plans for the republic and submits them to the USSR Gosplan. The USSR Gosplan reconciles these plans and presents them for the review before the USSR Council of Ministers. The final stage is approval of the plans by the USSR Supreme Soviet, which gives them the status of law. A few days later the plans for individual republics are approved by their Supreme Soviets. The formulation of plans by different levels of the economic hierarchy

---

*Unfortunately, this writer was unable to find any definite description of the planning by republics at the present time. Although the official text on planning, Gosplan SSSR, *Metodicheskie ukazaniia k razrabotke gosudarstvennykh planov razvitiia narodnoto khoziaistva SSSR* (Moscow, 1974), contains a separate chapter on the planning by union republics, it was of little use for the understanding of this problem. Therefore, the present description is based on a not very precise account given by Pavlenko, *Territorial'noe*, pp. 162-77.

does not take place in isolation but in constant consultation, bargaining, and reconciliation of targets and inputs between higher and lower bodies.

The majority of the ten targets enumerated below are not assigned to republics by union authorities as single indicators, but as a large number of sub-targets that vary from year to year. The most important among them are the following:

1. Industry—the volume of finished and marketed production in wholesale prices of enterprises and, in the case of important products, also in physical units for each union-republic ministry separately and for republic-subordinated ministries combined (in 1975 there were 65 indicators in physical units for union-republic and 218 for republic-subordinated ministries).

2. Agriculture—the volume of sales of agricultural products and raw materials; the volume of deliveries of agricultural products and livestock feed to the state fund (or receipts from this fund); various indicators for soil improvement.

3. Forestry—improvement in forests.

4. Transportation and communication—river transport; truck transport; bus passengers; value and various indicators in physical units of communication services.

5. Capital construction (centralized and decentralized sources)—introduction of production facilities, in physical units; value of introduced facilities; capital investment in 1969 prices.

6. Geological prospecting—by individual ministries and individual minerals.

7. Scientific-research and utilization of achievements of science and technology in national economy—various indicators with respect to the republic-subordinated economy only.

8. Labor—wage fund; growth of labor productivity in local industry and agriculture; training and distribution of professional-technical personnel within the republic.

9. Finance—profits for republic-subordinated ministries, consumer services, and sovkhozes.

10. Increase in standard of living—the following seven groups, with several subgroups: trade, consumer services, education, culture, health, housing, and municipal construction.

The targets for industrial and construction union-republic ministries and for the Ministry of Geology, State Committee for Forestry, and the Ministry of Procurements are allocated simultaneously to the republic Council of Ministers (for enterprises under their jurisdiction) and to the USSR union ministries in question. The targets for enterprises under republic jurisdiction of other economic and noneconomic union-republic ministries and, of course, of republic-subordinated ministries are allocated only to the republic Council of Ministers.

These instructions serve the republic authorities as a basis for the preparation of summary plans for the republic, administrative, and economic bodies, and for individual enterprises. They have the power of law.

Enterprises subordinated to union ministries do not submit their plans to republic organs but, through the intermediate bodies, to the ministries in Moscow. The latter, with the exception of defense industries, are required to inform the republic Council of Ministers about the output, location, and development plans for their enterprises located in the republic. These plans are reviewed by republic organs, and the relevant proposals are submitted to the Council of Ministers and the Gosplan of the USSR. After final approval, the plans for union-subordinated plants in a republic are communicated to the republic's Council of Ministers. On the basis of these plans and plans for the economy under republic jurisdiction, the republic Gosplan prepares basic indicators of complex development.* These are comprehensive plans that comprise the entire economy of the republic, but they have no legal power. Their objective is to counterpose variables within the republic: for instance, incomes and supply of consumer goods, investment and supply of construction materials, and so on. Because they can reveal the gaps between such variables, these plans are supposed to serve as a basis for the improvement of future state plans and plans of longer term.

Because basic indicators are applicable to the entire economy located on the republic's territory, the targets for the economic sectors in which there are union-subordinated enterprises—industry, capital construction, labor, and housing—differ from the targets for these sectors in the state plans for republic. The targets for all other sectors are the same under both types of plans.

It is obvious that preparation of the latter plans by the republic Gosplan depends on the availability of information on the union-subordinated economy. But according to Soviet officials and writers, union ministries sometimes fail to supply such data, or supply them late and incompletely.[191] Therefore, in the absence of adequate data, the work of republic planning organs can hardly be effective and the basic indicators generated by them probably are not very important in Soviet planning.

This rather general description of planning in the Ukraine should help us to answer two questions: What share of a republic's economy is planned by its own government? What freedom of action does a republic government have in planning?

As indicated, the real importance lies with the state plans for the development of the national economy, in which only the entreprises for republic-subordinated and republic union-republic ministries are included, while the

---

*Such a plan was prepared for the first time in the Ukraine for the year 1968. See V. Prykhod'ko and V. Korobko, *ERU* (1967): no. 7, p. 33.

union-subordinated enterprises are excluded. The rough estimate of this writer is that the authorities of the Ukraine plan, in the sense described in this paper, between 75 and 80 percent of its gross national product (Western methodology) at the present time.*

The specific competences of the Ukraine in the planning area can be discussed from the standpoint of preparation, approval, and changes of plans. Let us consider each of them in turn.

The republic, being a level in the hierarchical structure of Soviet management, receives a number of targets from the central planners and then disaggregates and addresses them to subordinated bodies for implementation. The extent of received targets, or, alternatively, the extent of decisions a republic can make on its own, could be regarded as an indicator of the republic's autonomy. Although precise quantification of such indicators is not feasible, the preceding discussion suggests that a republic receives indeed a very large number of them and that they are very detailed.[192] Moreover, the targets assigned for most of the union-republic economy are simultaneously assigned to the respective USSR ministries, so that the authority of republics is shared with Moscow.

But even in the case of the republic-subordinated sector, the responsibility of the republic is lessening. Several Soviet writers have recently claimed that, in view of the greater economic integration of the USSR, the planning of this segment of a republic's economy involves close cooperation between union and republic organs.[193] This cooperation undoubtedly means the erosion of the remaining exclusive decision-making powers of republics. In a broader sense, this trend has very important political and constitutional implications. According to one author, the existence of exclusive competences of republics is an attribute of the federative structure of the USSR, and "If one assumes that union republics do not possess exclusive competences in the Soviet union state then the latter loses its federative character and becomes the usual unitary state, and union republics lose their status with the sovereignty inherent in it."[194]

It seems that even if certain competences of republics are explicit under the letter of the law, this does not necessarily mean that they actually exercise these competences in practice. How, otherwise, can the following two statements, one by a competent jurist and the other by a competent economist, be interpreted?

> The provision about the management of banks of republic importance by their [republic] organs should be excluded from the Constitutions of union republics because there are no such banks at present.[195]

---

*This estimate was derived on the assumption that the output share of sectors under republic jurisdiction is proportional to their employment share in total Ukrainian employment.

The Gosstroy of the Ukrainian SSR planned [according to a law] the subordinated activity of construction establishments, but in reality it did not perform these functions.[196]

Certainly, with respect to the approval of plans, the claim of republic sovereignty is meaningless. The republic Council of Ministers approves the plans for the republic; but it has to submit them for reconciliation to Moscow, where, in the process of integration into the plans for the entire country, they can be, and are, changed. The approval of final plans by the republic Supreme Soviet is nothing but a rubber stamp of the approval of these plans by the USSR Supreme Soviet a few days earlier. The same is true for the approval of the republic's budget. Furthermore, although the plans of a republic have been approved by its highest legislative and executive bodies, they are often changed by Moscow while they are in effect.[197] It follows that the powers of republic organs in the preparation, approval, and change of plans are, to say the least, rather limited, even for the part of the republic economy for which these organs are legally responsible.

CONCLUSIONS

The previous discussion justifies the following conclusions.* Present prerogatives of the Ukraine are greater than during Stalin's rule. However, the progress this represents cannot be described as a straight line, but as a zigzag one. Furthermore, the disparity between the Ukraine's constitutional rights and its practical domination by Moscow, as well as between the economic powers as specified by law and those actually exercised by the Ukrainian government, is so great that Western observers are often unable to perceive it. This is another attempt to perpetrate traditional Russian fraud (*ochkovteratel'stvo*) upon public opinion in the West.

Anticipating the future is not easy. The need for greater economic efficiency may lead to some form of decentralization, including the transfer of certain decision-making powers from Moscow to Kiev. But as with anything else in the USSR, this issue will be decided more on political than on economic grounds. On the one hand, the tradition of the Russian state and the nature of the Soviet system will press toward further centralization. On the other hand, there are sufficient indications that various Ukrainian leaders have resisted this

---

*In view of the almost complete uniformity of economic laws and practice for all republics, only minute changes would be required to apply the findings and conclusions of this paper to the remaining constituent republics of the USSR.

trend in the past and have attempted to expand their economic powers. There is no reason to believe that some of them would not continue to do so in the future, particularly if they could sense the support of the population. This can be explained not only by the usual bureaucratic behavior but also, no doubt, by the awareness of Ukrainian leaders that future political and cultural progress—or, indeed, the survival—of their nation will depend decisively on economic autonomy.

The fact that the economic prerogatives of the Ukraine have been severely restricted has had an effect on the economic efficiency and welfare of the republic itself, as shown in other papers in this volume, and on the rest of the USSR as well. It is hardly possible to speak of present planning and management in the Ukraine as being conducive to the full utilization of its resources. There exist unemployment and underemployment, which force young people to migrate to other regions of the USSR. Available mineral resources are not efficiently exploited. There is no provision made for the future supply of the Ukrainian economy with energy and fuels. Foreign trade takes place not according to the principle of comparative advantage but in order to satisfy the needs of other regions of the USSR. Finally, some investable funds generated in the Ukraine are not utilized there but are transmitted, without any compensation, to other regions—where, moreover, they are less productive. It is true that the Ukraine has enjoyed a high rate of growth that brought it to a high level of economic development. But there is also no doubt that the Ukrainian growth rate, as a result of these factors, has not been the maximum possible under the Soviet type of economic system. Consequently, the welfare of the population in the Ukraine has also not been advanced at the maximum possible rate.

Since the Ukraine is a significant part of the USSR, the failure to reach its maximum production level lowered the production level of the USSR. The same reasoning applies to welfare. The lower-than-maximum possible welfare in the Ukraine decreased the average for the USSR. But there is one qualification: certain regions of the USSR, which were developed on the basis of defense or political considerations, substantially at the expense of Ukrainian resources, have benefited from this lower-than-possible productivity and welfare in the Ukraine. Thus the Soviet leadership has benefited in terms of greater political and military power.

Finally, the effect of the existence of the Ukrainian SSR and of other republics on planning and management of the Soviet economy per se should be considered. Since the complete centralization of all decision making in Moscow is not feasible, some division of the country into more or less similar subunits is absolutely necessary. The present division must be a real nuisance for planning and management when such dissimilar units—with respect to the size of population, territory, and economic activity—as, for example, the RSFSR and Estonia or Turkmenia have to be treated equally. The use of regions of similar economic size, such as the 18 large economic regions, would be much more appropriate for this purpose.[198] But we know that economic decision making cannot function in the USSR without a parallel political and administrative apparatus. To construct it for these regions would require the prior liquidation of such apparatuses in the republics. It seems that the Moscow leadership is not yet prepared to undertake this step because it fears reaction from the Ukraine and other non-Russian republics to the removal of the last vestiges of their political identity. Here also, politics seems to prevail over economics. Yet, forced to live with the Ukrainian republic, the leadership utilizes the Kiev authorities for its purposes. Because these authorities are of the same nationality as the people, are able to use the same language, and are close to the people, it appears that the primary justification for their existence, in the opinion of the Mowcow leadership, is their usefulness as an additional tool for plan fulfillment and, thus, for making the Soviet regime stronger.

NOTES

1. See Robert Campbell, "On the Theory of Economic Administration," in Henry Rosovsky, ed., *Industrialization in Two Systems: Essays in Honor of Alexander Gerschenkron* (New York: Wiley, 1966), p. 191.

2. Exceptions are Alec Nove, *The Soviet Economy* (2nd rev. ed.; New York: Praeger, 1969), ch. 2; S. A. Billon, "Centralization of Authority and Regional Management," in V. N. Bandera and Z. L. Melnyk, eds., *The Soviet Economy in Regional Perspective* (New York: Praeger, 1973).

3. V. F. Pavlenko, *Territorial'noe i otraslevoe planirovanie* (Moscow, 1971), p. 19.

4. For a discussion of the structure of Soviet economic administration, see Nove, loc. cit.

5. The importance of the Supreme Soviet in economic life is emphasized by I. M. Raznatovs'kyi, *Upravlinnia promyslovistiu Ukrains'koi RSR* (Kiev, 1970), pp. 54 ff., and dismissed by H. V. Prons'ka, *Kompetentsiia hospodars'kykh ministerstv Ukrains'koe RSR* (Kiev, 1973), p. 47. Most Western observers would undoubtedly agree with the latter's viewpoint.

6. *Konstytutsiia (osnovnyi zakon) Ukrains'koi Radians'koi Sotsialistychnoi Respubliky* (Kiev, 1972), Art. 13.

7. B. L. Manelis, "Protiv burzhuaznoi fal'sifikatsii natsional'no-gosudarstvennogo ustroistva SSSR," *Sovetskoe gosudarstvo i pravo* (*SGiP*) (1968): no. 3, 63.

8. B. L. Manelis, "Iedinstvo suvereniteta Soiuza SSR i suvereniteta soiuznykh respublik v period razvernutogo stroitel'stva kommunizma," *SGiP* (1964): no. 7, 21.

9. A. I. Lepeshkin, "O Razmezhevanii kompetentsii mezhdu organami Soiuza SSR i soiuznykh respublik v oblasti rukovodstva narodnym zhoziaistvom," *SGiP* (1966): no. 6, 4-5; Prons'ka, op. cit., pp. 11-12.

10. According to an editorial, "Velyka zhovtneva sotsialistychna revoliutsiia i utvorennia Ukrains'koi radians'koi derzhavy," *Radians'ke pravo* (*RP*) (1962): nos. 9-10, 6-7, such basic rights are the voting of a republic's population for its constitution, in conformity with the USSR constitution but not subject to approval by the USSR Supreme Soviet; establishment of supreme organs; territorial supremacy; relations with foreign countries; equality with other republics; conferring of citizenship of the Ukrainian SSR; legislation within the framework of the constitutions of the USSR and the Ukrainian SSR; right to secede.

11. See Samuel Bloembergen, "The Union Republics: How Much Autonomy?" *Problems of Communism (PoC)* (September-October 1967).

12. Manelis, "Iedinstvo suvereniteta," p. 21.

13. V. Korets'kyi and B. Babii, "Radians'ka bahatonatsional'na derzhava-uosoblennia iednosti i druzhby bratnikh respublik," *RP* (1967): no. 10, 14.

14. Prons'ka, op. cit., p. 10.

15. Lepeshkin, op. cit., pp. 7-11.

16. P. I. Romanov, "Demokraticheskii tsentralism v upravlenii sovetskim obshche-narodnym gosudartsvom," *SGiP* (1963): no. 5, 41; S. N. Dosymbekov, *Problemy gosudarstvennogo upravleniia promyshlennostiu v soiuznoi respublike* (Moscow, 1974), pp. 36-39.

17. Prons'ka, op. cit., p. 9.

18. Benjamin J. Cohen, *The Question of Imperialism* (New York: Basic Books, 1973), p. 16.

19. Prons'ka, op. cit., pp. 14-15.

20. *Konstytutsiia (osnovnyi zakon) Soiuzu Radians'kykh Sotsialistychnykh Respublik* (Kiev, 1972), Art. 14.

21. Raznatovs'kyi, op. cit., p. 50.

22. *Konstytutsiia (osnovnyi zakon) Soiuzu Radians'kykh Sotsialistychnykh Respublik*, Art. 19.

23. For discussion of such cases, see Martha B. Trofimenko, "Legal Aspects of Economic Centralization," in Bandera and Melnyk, op. cit., pp. 332-33.

24. A. M. Shafir, *Kompetentsiia SSSR i soiuznoi respubliki* (Moscow, 1968), pp. 45-46.

25. *Resheniia partii i pravitel'stva po khoziaistvennym voprosam (Resheniia)*, VI (Moscow, 1968), p. 525.

26. Leszek Kolakowski, "Hope and Hopelessness," *Survey (S)* (1971): no. 3, 41.

27. Stanislaw Wellisz, *The Economics of the Soviet Bloc* (New York: McGraw-Hill, 1964), pp. 24 ff. The third function is called "administration" by Wellisz. Since this term is usually applied to the activity of the state in all spheres of public life, state activity in economic life will be referred to here as "management."

28. V. M. Marchuk, *Organy gosudarstvennogo upravleniia UkSSR na sovremennon etape* (Kiev, 1964), pp. 35-36; O. Kozlova, "Nekotorye voprosy teorii upravleniia proizvodstvom," *Voprosy ekonomiki (VE)* (1967): no. 1, 4.

29. A. Rumiantsev and A. Ieremin, "K voprosu o nauke upravleniia sotsialisticheskoi ekonomikoi," *VE* (1967): no. 1, 12.

30. W. Keizer, *The Soviet Quest for Economic Rationality* (Rotterdam: Rotterdam University Press, 1971), p. 24.

31. Wellisz, op. cit., pp. 14 ff.

32. A. Rumiantsev, "Ekonomicheskaia nauka i upravlenie narodnym khoziaistvom," *Kommunist* (1966): no. 1, 46.

33. Keizer, op. cit., p. 184.

34. *Politicheskii dnevnik* (June 1965) (Arkhiv Samizdata no. 1002). I wish to thank Professor Yaroslav Bilinsky for providing me with this source and also with those in notes 36 and 48.

35. See the speeches by the well-known poet M. P. Bazhan and Communist party official L. R. Korniets' at the session of the USSR Supreme Soviet in *Zasedaniia Verkhovnogo Soveta SSR pervaia sessiia* (Moscow, 1946), pp. 117-23 and 261-68, respectively.

36. *Pravda Ukrainy (PU)*, April 7, 1966. For ramification and interpretation of these and related problems, see Yaroslav Bilinsky, "The Communist Party of Ukraine After 1966," in Peter J. Potichnyj, ed., *Ukraine in the Seventies* (Oakville, Ontario: Mosaic Press, 1975).

37. *Digest of the Soviet Ukrainian Press (DSUP)* (May 1971): 2. I am grateful to the publishers, Prolog Associates, for providing me with the back issues of this publication.

38. M. Zurabov, "Pytannia formuvannia palyvno-enerhetychnoho balansu Ukrains'koi RSR," *Ekonomika Radians'koi Ukrainy (ERU)* (1970): no. 10, 12-13.

39. T. Gonta, "Nekotorye problemy razvitiia neftianoi i gazovoi promyshlennosti Ukrainy," *Kommunist Ukrainy (KUr)* (1967): no. 1, 80.

40. Zev Katz, "Insights from Emigres and Sociological Studies on the Soviet Union," in Joint Economic Committee, *Soviet Economic Progress for the Seventies* (Washington, D.C.: U.S. Government Printing Office, 1973), p. 93; also see translation of the samizdat document by Ivan Dzyuba, *Internationalism or Russification?* (New York: Monad Press, 1974), p. 108. At the same time, Dzyuba, pp. 110-11, points out the migration of Russians, usually for more important positions, to the Ukraine.

41. P. Pershyn and M. Palamarchuk, "Udoskonalyty rozmishchennia produktyvnykh syl respubliky," *KU* (1964): no. 8, 26.

42. I. Velychko, "Osnovni napriamy polipshennia rozmishchennia promyslovosti Ukrains'koi RSR," *ERU* (1970): no. 10, 69-71.

43. V. Demydion and I. Kuhukalo, "Problemy rozvytku i rozmishchennia mashy-nobuduvannia i metaloobrobky v Ukrains'kii RSR," *ERU* (1970), no. 12, 13; M. Kovalenko et al., "Deiaki pytannia rozvytku avtomobil'noi promyslovosti na Ukraini," *ERU* (1967): no. 10, 51-52.

44. For analysis of this discussion, see Vsevolod Holubnychy, "Some Economic Aspects of Relations Among the Soviet Republics," in Erich Goldhagen, ed., *Ethnic Minorities in the Soviet Union* (New York: Praeger, 1968), pp. 86-88.

45. *DSUP* (November 1967): 7.

46. S. Hensiruk, "problema defitsytu derevyny v sviti," *ERU* (1968): no. 11, 81.

47. P. Iu. Shelest, in *Ukraino nasha Radians'ka* (Kiev, 1970), was accused, in the description of the development of the Ukrainian economy, of not paying enough attention to help from Russia and other republics; also, "elements of economic autarchy are obvious in the book." See editorial, "Pro seriozni nedoliky ta pomylky odniei knyhy," *KU* (1973): no. 11, 80.

48. *Plenum Tsentral'nogo Komiteta Kommunisticheskoi Partii Sovetskogo Soiuza, 24-26 Marta 1965g.* (Moscow, 1965), pp. 37, 38.

49. Akademiia Nauk UkRSR, *Natsional'nyi dokhod Ukrains'koi RSR v period rozhornutoho budivnytstva komunizmu* (Kiev, 1963), Ch. 7.

50. *DSUP* (December 1965): 3.

51. F. Khyliuk, "Rozvytok derzhavnoho planuvannia v. Ukrains'kii RSR," *ERU* (1966): no. 8, 18.

52. S. Iampol's'kyi, "O nekotorykh problemakh razvitiia ekonomicheskoi nauki," *KUr* (1966): no. 3, 58.

53. *DSUP* (April 1967): 4-6.

54. D. Nedashkivs'kyi, "Zmitsniuvaty derzhavnu dystsyplinu tsin," *ERU* (1970): no. 8, 63.

55. *DSUP* (July 1966): 5-6.

56. *DSUP* (February 1969): 8-9.

57. For example, F. Khyliuk, "Voprosy sovershenstvovaniia planirovaniia v respub-like," *Planovoe Khoziaistvo (PKh)* (1967): no. 5; Iu. Lebedyns'kyi, "Udoskonaliuvaty upravlinnia protsesamy spetsializatsii vyrobnytstva," *ERU* (1968): no. 5; V. Honcharenko et al., "Spetsializatsiia mizhhaluzevykh vyrobnytstv—vazhlyvyi napriam pidvyshchennia efektyvnosti mashynobuduvannia," *ERU* (1969): no. 5.

58. For cases of economic defense in the Baltic republics, see Yaroslav Bilinsky, "The Background of Contemporary Politics in the Baltic Republics and the Ukraine, Comparisons

and Contrasts," in Arvids Ziedonis, Jr., ed., *Problems of Mininations: Baltic Perspectives* (San Jose, Calif.: Association for the Advancement of Baltic Studies, 1973), pp. 96-98; in Kazakhstan, see *Khrushchev Remembers*, translated by Strobe Talbott (New York: Little, Brown, 1974), pp. 120-21; and in Georgia and Belorussia, see V. V. Kistanov, *Kompleksnoe razvitie i spetsializatsiia ekonomicheskikh raionov SSSR* (Moscow, 1968), p. 192.

59. Katz, op. cit., pp. 93-94. Each republic maintains a permanent representative at the USSR Council of Ministers in Moscow whose official responsibility is to coordinate the work between the union and his republic, but certainly also to lobby for the interests of the latter before the union organs.

60. P. J. D. Wiles, *The Political Economy of Communism* (Cambridge, Mass.: Harvard University Press, 1962), p. 138.

61. Keizer, op. cit., p. 187.

62. For a recent and comprehensive discussion of Soviet reforms, including non-Soviet bibliography, see George R. Feiwel, *The Soviet Quest for Economic Efficiency: Issues, Controversies, and Reforms* (2nd ed.; New York: Praeger, 1972).

63. Khyliuk, "Rozvytok derzhavnoho," p. 17.

64. Nove, op. cit., p. 69.

65. M. S. Urinson, *Planirovanie narodnogo khoziaistva v soiuznykh respublikakh* (Moscow, 1963), p. 83.

66. *Zasidannia Verkhovnoi Rady Ukrains'koi RSR, chetverta sesiia* (Kiev, 1957), pp. 150-57.

67. Marchuk, op. cit., p. 52.

68. Ibid., p. 43.

69. *Pravda (P)*, June 3, 1956.

70. M. D. Horbovatyi, *Rozvytok i vdoskonalennia orhanizatsiinykh form upravlinnia sotsialistychnoiu promyslovistiu* (Kiev, 1975), p. 84.

71. *Zasidannia Verkhovnoi Rady*, pp. 292-93.

72. Resolution of May 4, 1955, "Ob izmenenii poriadka gosudarstvennogo planirovaniia i finansirovaniia khoziaistva soiuznykh respublik," in *Resheniia*, IV, 200-17.

73. "Zakon o dal'neishem sovershenstvovanii organizatsii upravleniia promyshlennostiu i stroitel'stvom," of May 10, 1957, in *Resheniia*, IV, 343-47.

74. For instance, Nove, op. cit., p. 73; John A. Armstrong, *The Politics of Totalitarianism* (New York: Random House, 1961), ch. 23.

75. *Radians'ka Ukraina (RU)*, May 11, 1957.

76. *RU*, May 19, 1960.

77. J. Pawlik, *Gasiziowy i terytorialny system zarzadzania przemyslem i budownictwem w ZSRR* (Cracow, 1968), pp. 44, 47.

78. A. Iefimov, *Perestroika upravleniia promyshlennostiu i stroitel'stvom v SSSR* (Moscow, 1957), p. 77.

79. Urinson, op. cit., pp. 85-86.

80. Ibid., p. 86.

81. M. Urinson, "Vozrosshaia rol' soiuznykh respublik v planirovanii narodnogo khoziaistva," *PKh* (1961): no. 2, 32.

82. *RU*, August 8, 1960. Following Soviet usage, the republic Sovnarkhoz will be written with the uppercase *S*, in contrast with the original sovnarkhoz, written with the lowercase *s*.

83. *RU*, April 9, 1958.

84. *DSUP* (July 1963): p. 1; Marchuk, op. cit., pp. 64-66.

85. Marchuk, op. cit., pp. 66-67.

86. *RU*, July 22, 1960.

87. Marchuk, op. cit., pp. 70-71.

88. Resolution of August 29, 1957, "O dopolnitel'noi peredache nekotorykh vopro-sov khoziaistvennogo i kul'turnogo stroitel'stva na reshenie sovetov ministrov soiuznykh respublik," in *Resheniia*, IV, 370-75; *Sobranie postanovlenii pravitel'stva SSSR*, 13/81/1959.

89. N. G. Berdichevskii, "Biudzhetnye prava Soiuza SSR i soiuznykh respublik,"*SGiP* (1960): no. 1, 25.

90. "Zakon o biudzhetnykh pravakh Soiuza SSR i soiuznykh respublik," of October 30, 1959, in *Resheniia*, IV, 616-25.

91. "Povnishe vykorystovuvaty perevahy novoi formy upravlinnia promyslovistiu i budivnytstvom," *KU* (1958): no. 3, 14.

92. Urinson, "Vozrosshaia rol'," p. 29.

93. Akademiia Nauk, op. cit.

94. See the discussion by the chairman of the Ukrainian Gosplan, *DSUP* (May 1962): 8-11; or by the foreign minister of the Ukraine, "Ukraina na mizhnarodnii areni," *KU* (1963): no. 3, 49-51.

95. *DSUP* (March 1970): 15.

96. *DSUP* (July 1960): 7-8; *DSUP* (October 1960): 20-21, esp. on relations with countries in Asia and Africa.

97. *DSUP* (June 1958): 5; *DSUP* (February 1961): 24; *DSUP* (December 1961): 20-21.

98. *DSUP* (July 1958): 24.

99. *DSUP* (November 1960): 1-2.

100. For one description of these relations, see *DSUP* (February 1963): 23-24.

101. For a description and analysis of these processes, see Yaroslav Bilinsky, "Assimi-lation and Ethnic Assertiveness Among Ukrainians in the Soviet Union," in Goldhagen, op. cit.

102. I. Magid, "Pravovoe polozhenie soveta narodnogo khoziaistva" in a collection edited by N. Tolstoi (Leningrad, 1959), p. 30, as quoted in Pawlik, op. cit., p. 52.

103. M. Urinson, "Nekotorye voprosy planirovaniia v soiuznykh respublikakh," *PKh* (1965): no. 7, 29-30.

104. Pawlik, op. cit., pp. 55, 93-94.

105. P. Furduev and I. Burnshtein, "Puti uluchsheniia material'no-tekhnicheskogo snabzheniia," *PKh* (1962): no. 1, 44.

106. *DSUP* (June 1958): 10.

107. *DSUP* (June 1960): 14.

108. According to Pawlik, op. cit., p. 81, the number of centrally funded commodities increased from 10,000 in 1957 to 12,800 in 1960, to 14,000 in 1961, and to 18,000 in 1965.

109. For an excellent discussion of these problems, see Pawlik, op. cit., ch. 4.

110. For an account of the increase in interbranch specialization and cooperation in the Ukraine, see A. Kochubei, "Dva roky roboty promyslovosti respubliky v novykh umovakh," *ERU* (1959): no. 3, 4-7.

111. For complaints about the diversion of investment to housing by Dnipropetrovs'k and Luhans'k (now Voroshylovhrad) sovnarkhozes and overpayment of wages by Dnipro-petrovs'k, Kharkiv, and Luhans'k sovnarkhozes, see *DSUP* (June, August, and September 1958).

112. For example, Dnipropetrovs'k (pig iron), Donets'k (coal), and Luhans'k (coal) sovnarkhozes, cited in F. Khyliuk, "Pidvyshchyty riven' ekonomichnoho obhruntuvannia planiv," *ERU* (1963): no. 6, 64.

113. Pawlik, op. cit., pp. 66-67, 138-39. A Kiev economist, P. Horodens'kyi, "Vyrivni-annia ekonomiky respublik—sakonomirnist' nashoho rozvytku," *ERU* (1965): no. 11, admits that investment in Kazakhstan and Turkmenia had to be financed largely by funds

accumulated in the Ukraine (p. 75) and that the regional system of management led to the development of a harmful tendency—localism (p. 76). In this context, the author meant that the system was not a good mechanism for the territorial transfer of investment funds.

114. *DSUP* (October 1961): 14-16.

115. Pawlik, op. cit., p. 99. At the end of 1962 there were five such committees for defense industries and six for other industrial branches.

116. According to Marchuk, op. cit., p. 69, "The five-year experience of sovnarkhoz work showed that large sovnarkhozes manage industrial branches better, possess extensive possibilities for manoeuvering material and technical resources, and provide better conditions for concentration, specialization, and cooperation of production."

117. Committee on the Judiciary, *The Soviet Empire* (Washington, D.C.: U.S. Government Printing Office, 1965), pp. 102-04.

118. *RU*, December 27, 1962.

119. Resolution of January 11, 1963, "O dal'neishom uluchshenii organizatsii planirovaniia razvitiia narodnogo khoziaistva," in *Resheniia*, V, 272-76.

120. See resolution of April 11, 1963, "O merakh po uluchsheniiu deiatel'nosti Akademii Nauk SSR i Akademii Nauk soiuznykh respublik," in *Resheniia*, V, 304-09.

121. Resolution of January 11, 1963, "O povyshenii roli gosudarstvennykh komitetov i ikh otvestvennosti za razvitie otraslei promyshlennosti," in *Resheniia*, V, 267-71.

122. See his speech, *P*, September 28, 1965.

123. For a vivid description of planning problems encountered by a chemical enterprise in the Ukraine under the multitude of planning organs, see V. Kalechyts' and V. Boholiubov, "Sprostyty systemu planuvannia v promyslovosti," *ERU* (1965): nos. 1-2.

124. V. G. Vishniakov, "Ob opyte perestroiki apparata upravleniia ekonomikoi," *SGiP* (1963): no. 10, 52-54.

125. According to Raznatovs'kyi, op. cit., pp. 14-15, the Ukrainian industry in 1964 was subordinated to the following union authorities—VSNKh, Gosplan, Sovnarkhoz, three state production committees, 11 state committees, and 12 state branch committees—as well as to the following republic authorities—Sovnarkhoz, Gosplan, Ministry of Electric Power, and seven sovnarkhozes.

126. See his speech at the November plenum of the Central Committee of the Soviet Communist party, *P*, November 20, 1962.

127. *P*, November 24, 1962.

128. *RU*, October 24, 1965.

129. *DSUP* (June 1966): 29; *DSUP* (November 1966): 27.

130. *Visti Verkhovnoi Rady Ukrains'koi RSR (VVR)*, 11/91/1967; *VVR*, 18/165/1967.

131. *VVR*, 36/232/1968.

132. *VVR*, 49/330/1968.

133. *VVR*, 5/32/1970; *VVR*, 29/206/1970.

134. *VVR*, 35/269/1971; *VVR*, 35/302/1972.

135. See resolution of March 9, 1955, "Ob izmenenii praktiki planirovaniia sel'skogo khoziaistva," in *Resheniia*, IV, 192-97.

136. *RU*, May 11, 1957.

137. *DSUP* (April 1961): 22, 23.

138. Marchuk, op. cit., p. 84.

139. *DSUP* (January 1963): 5.

140. *DSUP* (May 1962): 12-13, 23.

141. *RU*, November 21, 1964.

142. *DSUP* (May 1965): 28.

143. *VVR*, 7/58/1969; *VVR*, 1/6/1970.

144. *VVR*, 11/84/1969; *VVR*, 10/72/1973.

145. See resolutions of October 4, 1965, and July 10, 1967, respectively, "O pere-dache dopolnitel'no na resheniie sovetov ministrov soiuznykh respublik voprosov khoziaist-vennogo i kul'turnogo stroitsel'stva,' in *Resheniia*, V, 685-90, and VI, 517-25.

146. See Leon Smolinski, "Towards a Socialist Corporation: Soviet Industrial Reor-ganization of 1973," *S* (Winter 1974): 29-30.

147. According to Michael Keren, "The New Economic System in the GDR, an Obituary," *Soviet Studies (SS)* (April 1973), the recentralization of decision making under the conditions of taut planning is unavoidable. In view of the consistent excess of demand over supply, central planners must have the authority to distribute inputs in short supply, allocate targets, and arbitrate among enterprises.

148. See, for example, articles by two important officials of the Ukrainian Gosplan, F. Khyliuk, "Vdoskonalennia upravlinnia promyslovistiu i planuvannia narodnoho hospodarstva," *ERU* (1965): no. 12; S. Ostrovs'kyi, "Pro poiednannia tsentralizovanoho haluzevoho upravlinnia z terytorial'nym planuvanniam," *ERU* (1966): no. 12.

149. *P*, September 28, 1965.

150. *P*, October 1, 1968.

151. *Ekonomicheskaia gazeta (EG)* (1968): no. 22, 11-12.

152. A. Shul'man, "Problemy tsentralizovanogo i territorial'nogo planirovaniia," *PKh* (1967): no. 5, 18.

153. For the text of the resolution on associations, see *P*, April 3, 1973. At the begin-ning of 1974, there were 288 associations in the Ukraine, of which 45 were within union ministries, 216 within union-republic ministries, and 27 within republic-subordinated minis-tries. See Horbovatyi, op. cit., p. 135.

154. For the description and evaluation of this new management form, see Smolinski, op. cit., and Alice C. Gorlin, "Socialist Corporations: The Wave of the Future in the USSR?," in Morris Bornstein and Daniel R. Fusfeld, eds., *The Soviet Economy: A Book of Readings* (4th ed.; Homewood, Ill.: Richard D. Irwin, 1974).

155. N. Drogichinskii, "Upravlenie promyshlennostiu na sovremennon etape," *PKh* (1973): no. 12, 8-9, 16.

156. I. Raznatovs'kyi, "Udoskonalennia upravlinnia promyslovistiu," *RP* (1973): no. 9, 58.

157. V. F. Pavlenko, *Territorial'noe planirovanie v SSSR* (Moscow, 1975), p. 232. Despite this, there are some associations—for example, in the automobile industry—that cross republic borders (p. 233).

158. See the remarks of Aron Katsenelinboigen in Potichnyj, op. cit., p. 100.

159. Horbovatyi, op. cit., pp. 138-39.

160. Vsevolod Holubnychy, "The Present State of Cybernetics and Republic-Level Economic Planning," in Potichnyj, op. cit., pp. 85-86.

161. For a well-argued review of this problem, see Ivan L. Rudnytsky, "The Soviet Ukraine in Historical Perspective," *Canadian Slavonic Papers* (1972): no. 2.

162. See V. Stanley Vardys, "Modernization and Baltic Nationalism," *PoC* (Septem-ber-October 1975): 33-34.

163. *P*, November 2, 1961.

164. *P*, December 22, 1972.

165. K. Diablo, "Rozvytok spivvidnoshennia kompetentsii Soiuzu RSR i soiuznykh respublik ta dal'she zmitsnennia radians'koi sotsialistychnoi federatsii," *Problemy pravoz-navstva (PP)* (1973): no. 24, 67. Such a knowledgeable observer of the USSR as Alec Nove comes to the same conclusion, though by a different route. He believes that ". . . in all those circumstances the changes in republican powers may have been intended for tidying up rather than diminution. However, it is worth observing that the logic of the present wave of

reforms, which strengthens enterprises, ministries, and obyedinenia, is broadly inconsistent with territorial administrative powers over the economy. Therefore republican powers have declined and complaints are being published to this effect." Op. cit., p. 87.

166. Urinson, "Nekotorye voprosy" (published in July 1965).

167. M. Urinson, "Planirovanie narodnogo khoziaistva soiuznykh respublik v novykh usloviiakh," *PKh* (1966): no. 2, 29, 31.

168. V. Kistanov, "Leninskaia natsional'naia politika i ekonomicheskoe raionirovanie v SSSR," *VE* (1972): no. 12, 64.

169. Teresa Rakowska-Harmstone, "The Dialectics of Nationalism in the USSR," *PoC* (May-June 1974): 19-21; John N. Hazard, "The Status of the Ukrainian Republic Under the Soviet Federation," in Potichnyj, op. cit., pp. 229-30.

170. Arts. 39-43.

171. Dosymbekov, op. cit., pp. 68-69.

172. Ibid., p. 286.

173. See "Obshchee polozhenie o ministerstvakh SSSR," of July 10, 1967, in *Resheniia*, VI, 494-507.

174. Raznatovs'kyi, *Upravlinnia promyslovistiu*, p. 130.

175. K. E. Kolibab, "O pravovom polozhenii ministerstv SSSR," *SGiP* (1968): no. 1, 18-19.

176. M. T. Malyshko, "Pytannia koordynatsii diial'nosti respublikans'kykh ministerstv z orhanamy Soiuzu RSR," *PP* (1973): no. 24, 115; A. Sh. Tuganbaev, "Upravlenie promyshlennostiu soiuznoi respubliki," *SGiP* (1969): no. 6, 60.

177. V. Andzhyievs'kyi and O. Kostiuchenko, "Zakonodavche vyznachennia pravovoho statutu ministerstv," *RP* (1971): no. 1, 58-59.

178. For the great variety of activities of Ukrainian ministries, see D. Iakuba and V. Kas'ianov, "Vporiadkuvaty normotvorchu diial'nist' ministerstv soiuznoi respubliky," *RP* (1973): no. 4. Some authors (Raznatovs'kyi, *Upravlinnia promyslovistiu*, p. 128; Horbovatyi, op. cit., p. 107) claim that there is almost no difference between competences of republic-subordinated and union-republic ministries in the Ukraine, while others (*DSUP* [August 1967]: 13) show, using the example of the Ukrainian Ministry of Chemical Industry when it still was of union-republic subordination, that even the operative powers were concentrated in the ministry of the same name in Moscow. Also, Dosymbekov, op. cit., pp. 101-05, shows that in the case of the union-republic Ministry of Nonferrous Metallurgy in Kazakhstan, the decision-making powers were concentrated to a larger degree in the hands of the corresponding ministry in Moscow than in the case of the union-republic Ministry of Light Industry.

179. S. B. Baisalov and V. M. Levchenko, "Kompetentsiia otraslevykh organov upravleniia promyshlennostiu," *SGiP* (1969): no. 3, 72.

180. Ibid., p. 73.

181. V. I. Shabailov, "K sovershenstvovaniu pravovogo polozheniia ministerstv soiuznykh respublik," *SGiP* (1968): no. 2, 66; for similar demands in the area of planning, see Shafir, op. cit., pp. 127-28.

182. Vishniakov, op. cit., p. 52.

183. *DSUP* (April 1967): 5.

184. Pavlenko, *Territorial'noe*, pp. 197-98.

185. Ibid.; Baisalov and Levchenko, op. cit., 71; Tuganbaev, op. cit., p. 62.

186. O. N. Sadikov, ed., *Pravovoe regulirovanie kapital'nogo stroitel'stva v SSSR* (Moscow, 1972), pp. 18-19.

187. Ibid., p. 20.

188. See the law cited in note 90. The numbers in parentheses are those of original provisions.

189. Dosymbekov, op. cit., p. 293.

190. For a description of the preparation of such plans for the USSR, see Nove, op. cit., pp. 66 ff.

191. See, for example, the complaints of the chairman of the Ukrainian Gosplan, *EG* (1971): no. 2; Dosymbekov, op. cit., pp. 56-57.

192. According to Pavlenko, *Territorial'noe*, p. 170, the number is much too large.

193. See I. O. Bisher, "Ministerstva soiuznykh respublik: nazrevshie problemy," *SGiP* (1973): no. 5, 30; Malyshko, op. cit., p. 116.

194. Lepeshkin, op. cit., p. 5.

195. Shafir, op. cit., p. 113.

196. Khyliuk, "Rozvytok dershavnoho," p. 18. The statement refers to the situation in the early 1960s.

197. For example, Baisalov and Levchenko, op. cit., pp. 74-75.

198. See Kistanov, *Kompleksnoe razvitie*, pp. 198-99.

3

ECONOMIC GROWTH
Stanley H. Cohn

THE UKRAINE IN THE SOVIET NATIONAL ECONOMY

In economic terms the Ukrainian SSR may be thought of as 20 percent of a nation. Its population proportion in 1974 was just under 20 percent, and its share of net material product (NMP) about 18.5 percent.* Per capita national product is just under, or equal to, the national average, depending upon the measurement concept employed. The Ukraine's share of gross industrial output was slightly below its NMP share, but its share of agricultural output was considerably higher. As might be expected from the republic's relatively compact distribution of economic activity, if one compares it with the USSR as a whole, the Ukraine generated less than its proportionate share of transportation services. The construction share of the Ukraine is also below its NMP share, as would logically follow from its relatively favored position in terms of climate and provision of infrastructure, as well as a lower growth rate than the country's eastern regions. As indicated by employment estimates, the Ukraine generates about its expected proportion of services, except for science. (See Table 3.1.)

The economic specialization of the Ukraine can be seen more clearly by comparing its output of particular industrial and agricultural products with those

---

*Its proportion of GNP would be about 1 percent higher, the difference explained by imputation of returns to capital. See I. S. Koropeckyj, "National Income of the Soviet Union Republics in 1970: Revision and Some Applications," in Zbigniew M. Fallenbuchl, ed., *Economic Development in the Soviet Union and Eastern Europe*, I (New York: Praeger, 1975). Koropeckyj's estimates of gross national product (GNP) by sector of origin also indicate that in the Ukraine a larger-than-union-average share originates in agriculture, and correspondingly smaller shares in manufacturing and other sectors (Table 11.8).

TABLE 3.1

Ukraine Economy as a Percentage of the Soviet Economy, Selected Years, 1950-74

	1950	1960	1965	1974
Population	20.5	20.0	19.6	19.3
Net material product	18.2	18.6	19.9	18.3
Industry (net output)	16.4	17.2	18.2	17.4
Electric power	16.1	18.5	18.7	18.5
Steel	30.6	40.1	40.6	38.5
Coal	29.9	33.8	33.6	31.2
Gas	25.0	30.3	30.8	26.2
Mineral fertilizers	28.0	27.8	23.4	20.3
Cement	19.7	17.8	17.0	18.7
Window glass	32.1	26.9	25.2	22.5
Tractors	20.8	36.9	33.4	25.7
Diesel locomotives	100.0	87.9	96.7	93.8
Turbines	15.0	27.6	30.1	30.0
Power transformers	6.2	50.5	46.6	45.4
Passenger autos	n.a.	0.4	20.2	8.4
Metal-cutting tools	14.9	13.1	13.4	15.0
Bulldozers	47.7	34.6	42.0	43.9
Paper	3.0	6.1	5.1	4.4
Cotton cloth	0.5	1.5	2.6	4.6
Meat	19.8	20.7	21.1	22.5
Margarine	22.2	28.3	31.5	33.7
Sugar	71.6	60.9	60.6	57.5
Agriculture (net output)	24.6	23.6	25.5	23.5
Plant crops	n.a.	23.6	26.6	25.7
Animal products	n.a.	22.8	22.4	22.2
Grains	25.1	18.0	26.1	23.5
Potatoes	22.9	23.0	21.2	25.8
Sugar beets	70.2	55.0	60.5	62.0
Vegetables	24.8	29.9	30.4	28.6
Meat	21.6	23.8	22.3	23.3
Milk	19.3	22.7	22.9	23.4
Transportation	16.1	15.6	16.7	16.3
Construction	19.1	18.6	17.9	15.9
Retail trade	15.9	17.0	17.7	17.5
Employment				
Workers and employees	17.1	17.2	17.4	17.9
Workers and employees plus kolkhozniks	19.9	20.4	20.3	20.5
Kolkhozniks	24.0	29.4	31.1	31.4
Services and trade	16.0	15.9	17.1	18.1

n.a. = data not available.

Sources: USSR—*Narodnoe Khoziaistvo SSSR 1960* (Moscow, 1961) (*Narkhoz*), *1963, 1965, 1974.* Ukraine—*Narodne hospodarstvo Ukrains'koe RSR 1961* (Kiev, 1962) (*Narhosp*), *1972, 1974.*

of the USSR as a whole. The Ukraine is the country's foremost producer of ferrous metals and solid fuels, with more than 33 percent of the total. Within machinery production it specializes in farm machinery, electrical machinery, railroad equipment, and construction machinery. It is also a major food processing region. Within agriculture it produces the bulk of the country's sugar beets and a large proportion of its fats and oils, as well as a higher than proportionate share of meat and dairy products. Its preeminence in ferrous metallurgy and in agriculture gives the Ukraine a close resemblance to the status of the Great Lakes states in the U.S. economy. This analogy will be considered further in an evaluation of the Ukraine's growth relative to that of the union as a whole and to that of the eastern regions.

The industrial sectors in which the Ukraine is highly dependent on other regions of the USSR are textiles and forest products. Natural-resource endowments largely explain these dependencies. Within the machinery sectors the Ukraine imports most of its machine tools and motor vehicles. Nevertheless, on balance it appears to be one of the more self-sufficient regions of the country.[1]

If employment is restricted to the worker and employee concept, the Ukrainian proportion is slightly below its NMP proportion; but if those employed on collective farms (*kolkhozniks*) is included, the Ukrainian share is considerably higher. This difference is explained by the higher-than-average prevalence of collective farms in the republic. Approximately 33 percent of all collective farmers are Ukrainians. The distribution of industrial employment by sectors reflects Ukrainian and national differences in the structure of industrial production.

UKRAINIAN ECONOMIC GROWTH TRENDS

Any analysis that seeks to explain growth trends in the Ukrainian economy in comparison with those in the Soviet economy as a whole since World War II must disentangle cyclical and secular aspects. Such a division of explanatory factors closely parallels the distinction between exogenous influences and explicit policy decisions. Analytically, it would also be worthwhile to begin with aggregate indicators and progressively use finer degrees of disaggregation in order to understand the republic's changing role in the postwar Soviet economy.

In terms of the most aggregative official indicator, NMP, the position of the Ukraine has changed little in two decades (Table 3.1), but within that time frame there have been distinct cyclical fluctuations (Table 3.2). During the 1950s Ukrainian NMP growth closely matched that of the national economy, with a higher growth rate in industrial production likely reflecting the delayed impact of reconstruction. If the Ukraine's proportions of output of major industrial products are examined (Table 3.1), it would appear that this recovery thesis is confirmed by rises in the output share in such traditional industries as steel, coal, and electric power. At the same time, the Ukraine's growth of agricultural

TABLE 3.2

Economic Growth Indicators: Ukraine and USSR, Selected Periods
(annual average rates)

	1950-60	1960-65	1965-74
Net Material Product			
USSR	10.3	6.6	6.9 (5.9)
Ukraine	10.5	6.9	6.1 (5.3)
Net industrial output			
USSR	n.a.	8.8	8.4 (7.4)
Ukraine	n.a.	10.1	8.4 (7.6)
Net agricultural product			
USSR	n.a.	1.6	1.2 (0.2)
Ukraine	n.a.	3.2	0.3 (-0.5)
Gross industrial production			
USSR	11.7	8.6	8.0 (7.0)
Ukraine	12.2	8.9	7.9 (7.1)
Gross agricultural output			
USSR	4.9	2.4	3.3 (2.3)
Ukraine	4.5	3.4	3.0 (2.2)
Employment in services and trade			
USSR	3.9	5.6	3.9
Ukraine	3.9	4.0	4.1
Capital stock (fixed)			
USSR	9.5	8.6	7.6
Ukraine	n.a.	7.9	6.1

Note: Figures in parentheses are per capita growth rates.
n.a. = data not available.
Sources: USSR—*Narkhoz 1960, 1963, 1965, 1974.* Ukraine—*Narhosp 1961, 1972, 1974.*

production lagged behind that of the national economy. This performance reflected the rapid output increases in the New Lands in Siberia and Kazakhstan.

During the first half of the 1960s (Seventh Five-Year Plan), Ukrainian national product continued to advance more rapidly than the national average. Industrial growth proceeded at a faster rate. This was a period in which the leadership chose to concentrate output increases in traditional industrial regions, such as the Ukraine. It is difficult to detect this policy in the output sample presented in Table 3.1; but if official gross production indexes of industrial sectors are compared, Ukrainian indistry grew more rapidly than that of the USSR as a whole in such new sectors as chemical and machinery. The superior performance of Ukrainian agriculture, evaluated below, also sustained higher-than-average output expansions in the food and light-industry sectors. Apparently these gains more than offset slower growth performance in the republic's traditional sectors of specialization—ferrous metals and coal mining. Ukrainian performance was particularly impressive in agriculture, especially in grain crops. This superior record reflects the greater reliability of Ukrainian agricultural weather conditions, compared with the newer farm areas in the east.

Since 1965 there has been a reversal in the Ukraine's position. Its aggregate growth has been somewhat below the national average, and this slower growth has prevailed in most of the economy's major sectors. Since the Ukraine's production share of most indicator industrial products, as well as of the gross total, has declined, it seems apparent that the renewed investment emphasis in the eastern industrial regions has borne fruit. Within a declining share of total industrial output, the structure of Ukrainian production has been trending toward the "progressive" sectors. The most conspicuous loss of position has been in the "traditional" steel and coal sectors. Within machinery production, the picture has been mixed. Among the indicators selected, there have been declines in the shares of tractor, locomotive, and passenger auto production; there have been increases in the shares of turbine and machine-tools production. Ukrainian shares of output of processed foods, particularly in the high-quality products of livestock, has been rising steadily.

The slower growth in agricultural production is explained by a combination of improved weather conditions in the newer farming areas, as indicated by the Ukraine's loss of position in grain production, and of more intensive agricultural investment in other regions. However, the republic is emerging as a specialized producer of labor-intensive, high-quality animal products, the "progressive" branches of agriculture. The most glaring losses of position in terms of material product have been in the transportation and construction sectors. Both of these sectors are sensitive indicators of concentration of economic development in the newer industrial regions. Although most services are excluded from the Soviet material product concept, it is possible to approximate output generated in these highly labor-intensive sectors through the proxy of employment. By this criterion, Ukrainian service output has been increasing at a rate in excess of the national average.

Population growth in the Ukraine, as in most of European USSR, has been below the national average. Even if this differential is considered, Ukrainian growth has still been below the national average since 1965, but the differential has been reduced by approximately 50 percent (Table 3.2).

ANATOMY OF GROWTH—FACTOR INPUTS, PRODUCTIVITY, AND ECONOMIC STRUCTURE

The Ukraine has grown more slowly than the national economy since the mid-1960s. To what extent is this trend explained by relative increases in

TABLE 3.3

Increases in Primary Factor Inputs, 1960-65 and 1965-74
(average annual rates)

	Employment		Fixed Capital Stock	
	1960-65	1965-74	1960-65	1965-74
Economy				
USSR	2.7	2.1	8.6	7.6
Ukraine	2.7	1.9	7.9	6.9
Industry				
USSR	4.5	2.2	11.1	8.6
Ukraine	4.5	2.8	10.4	8.1
Agriculture				
USSR	-1.0	-0.6	7.4	8.4
Ukraine	-0.5	-1.3	7.4	7.3

Sources: USSR–*Narkhoz 1960, 1963, 1965, 1974.* Ukraine–*Narhosp 1961, 1972, 1974.*

productive inputs, by productivity increases in these factors of production, and by the republic's particular economic structure?

In terms of employment increases, the Ukraine has closely matched national rates for the economy as a whole. In industry the growth rate has been somewhat higher than the national average since 1965. In agriculture the decrements were below the national rate in the early 1960s and have been higher since 1965. The Ukraine has a disproportionately high share of kolkhozniks, so the latter trend is not unexpected. Since the Ukraine's population growth has been below that of the USSR, equal rates of growth in employment imply a rising participation ratio (ratio of employment to population). Since a lower population growth rate results in a population of older average age, it becomes feasible to sustain a higher participation ratio.

It is in investment policy that significant differences emerge. Particularly after 1965, the gap between Ukrainian and national Soviet rates of increase in fixed capital stock widened appreciably. The growing lag of Ukrainian capital increments was especially dramatic in agriculture, although it was also substantial in industry (Table 3.3). The share of total investment accruing to the Ukraine declined appreciably after 1965 in agriculture, transportation, and housing (Table 3.4). The apparent inconsistency between the lagging Ukrainian growth rate for industrial capital stock and a nearly constant investment share for the period 1965-74 may be explained by the higher average age of Ukrainian industrial plant and equipment, with a concomitant higher rate of asset retirement. As a first approximation, it may be concluded that relatively lower Ukrainian economic growth after 1965 may be explained by lower rates of net investment. However, declining Ukrainian investment shares lie outside of industry. The declining agricultural share is probably explained by developmental emphasis on the more humid regions in the northwestern USSR. The sharply reduced transportation and housing shares directly reflect the necessity for high infrastructure outlays in the developing eastern regions.

The declining share of the Ukraine in the Soviet investment effort does not imply stagnation, since the coastal region of the republic is the special beneficiary of the increasing involvement of the Soviet economy in international technological exchange. According to Theodore Shabad, nearly 50 percent of the nation's maritime traffic uses Ukrainian ports. The Black Sea littoral has become the site of many of the new industrial facilities being constructed as essential elements in the so-called compensation deals in which Western companies finance Soviet projects and are paid with the outputs of these particular installations.

Might the cause of lower Ukrainian growth lie in lower rates of productivity advance rather than in lower investment priorities? The procedure used to test this hypothesis will be the familiar Cobb-Douglas production function with two factors of production, employment and fixed capital stock: $Y = a\Delta E + b\Delta K + \Delta R$, assuming $a + b = 1$, where y = net material output, E = employment input, K = fixed capital input, R = output per unit of input (or joint factor productivity), a = elasticity of output with respect to employment, and b = elasticity of output with respect to capital. Separate coefficients have been computed for the USSR and the Ukraine. The output elasticities are computed from incomes accruing to the two factors for the entire economy, exclusive of services, and for the industrial and agricultural sectors.[2]

TABLE 3.4

Ukrainian Investment as a Proportion of the National Total, 1950-74

Sector	1950-60	1960-65	1965-74
Industry	17.2	17.5	17.3
Agriculture	18.4	18.5	17.1
Transportation	14.2	19.5	17.6
Housing	16.4	15.6	14.5
Total	16.8	17.0	16.3

Sources: USSR—Narkhoz 1960, 1963, 1965, 1974. Ukraine—Narhosp 1961, 1972, 1974.

The productivity column in Table 3.5 indicates that in the early 1960s, compared with the USSR as a whole, the Ukraine made more efficient use of its available productive factors in the two principal sectors, as well as in overall production. Since 1965 it has managed more or less to match national productivity improvement rates for the economy as a whole, to lag insignificantly in industry, and to exceed in agriculture because of the reduction in labor-intensive *kolkhoz* employment. In terms of efficiency the republic has maintained its relative standing in the Soviet national economy. Other explanations must be sought to explain its low growth rate in recent years.

A third possible explanation of the Ukraine's relative economic performance may lie in its particular economic structure. As noted earlier, the Ukraine is more heavily oriented toward agriculture than the Soviet economy as a whole,

TABLE 3.5

Sources of Growth: Ukraine and the USSR, 1960-65 and 1965-74
(average annual rates)

		Combined Factor Inputs (1)	Productivity (2)	Output (3)
Net material product				
USSR	1960-65	4.9	1.6	6.6
	1965-74	4.1	2.2	6.4
Ukraine	1960-65	4.6	2.1	6.9
	1975-74	3.8	2.2	6.1
Industry (net output)				
USSR	1960-65	7.4	1.3	8.8
	1965-74	5.0	3.3	8.4
Ukraine	1960-65	7.1	2.8	10.1
	1965-74	5.2	3.1	8.4
Agriculture (net output)				
USSR	1960-65	1.7	−0.1	1.6
	1965-74	2.2	−1.0	1.2
Ukraine	1960-65	1.6	1.6	3.2
	1965-74	0.9	−0.6	0.3

Sources:

Column 1: See Table 3.3 for growth rates for employment and capital stock separately. For derivation of coefficients, see Appendix A, "Derivation of Factor Income Shares."

Column 2: Output per unit of combined factor inputs.

Column 3: See Table 3.2 for estimates of net material product.

TABLE 3.6

Economic Structure and Ukrainian NMP Growth, 1965-74

Sector	Percentage of Income Originating[a]		Index of Ukrainian Net Sector Output[b] (1965 = 100)
	USSR	Ukraine	
Industry	52.7	50.1	206
Agriculture	18.4	23.6	103
Transportation	6.1	5.4	195
Construction	11.0	9.6	167
Trade	11.8	11.3	185
Computed NMP 1965-74	USSR	6.7 percent	
(average annual rate)	Ukraine	6.4 percent	

[a]1974 distribution.
[b]Index for 1974.
Sources: USSR—*Narkhos 1960, 1963, 1965, 1974.* Ukraine—*Narhosp 1961, 1972, 1974.*

somewhat less toward industry, and considerably less toward transportation and construction. To what extent does this structuring toward slow-growing sectors influence the republic's overall growth?

If Ukrainian net output indexes for the five component NMP sectors are weighted by their shares of income origin for the USSR economy as a whole, and for the Ukraine, the computed aggregate growth rate is only slightly lower for the Ukrainian structure of output. A difference of 0.3 percent is so small as to rule out economic structure as a clear explanation of a lower rate of growth. The difference is not likely to widen in the future, because the nonagricultural portion of total output is increasing as rapidly in the Ukraine as in the overall Soviet economy.

Another possible structural explanation lies within the industrial sector. The Ukraine, with its coal and steel specialization, at first approximation appears to be highly concentrated in "older" industrial technology, with less than the national average representation in the "newer" and more rapidly growing industries (Table 3.7).

If the USSR and Ukrainian industrial branch output indexes for the 1965-74 period are weighted, respectively, by USSR and Ukrainian branch value-added proportions, slightly lower aggregate growth rates are yielded by the Ukrainian value-added weights. For the USSR output indexes, the Ukrainian value-added weights yield an aggregate growth rate that is reduced by 0.2 percent per annum; for the Ukrainian output indexes the reduction is also 0.2

TABLE 3.7

Structural Composition of Net Industrial Output, 1974

Industrial Branch	Value Added Proportion (1970)		Gross Output Index (1965 = 100)	
	USSR	Ukraine	USSR	Ukraine
Electric power	6.2	4.8	205	204
Petroleum and gas	6.7	2.1	165	138
Coal	3.0	7.8		
Ferrous metals	6.1	11.9	160	148
Forest products	7.2	4.2	160	178
Construction materials	5.8	6.6	199	198
Chemicals	5.9	4.6	266	288
Machinery				
and metalworking	31.7	31.0	271	278
Light industry	12.4	10.8	179	219
Other branches	5.1	4.8	n.a.	n.a.
Food processing	9.8	11.3	163	157
Total	100.0	100.0	200	198

n.a. = data not available.

Sources: USSR–*Narkhos 1960, 1963, 1965, 1974.* Ukraine–*Narhosp 1961, 1972, 1974,* and Appendix B.

percent (Table 3.8).* Since these differences closely match that obtained by comparing the official indicators of USSR and Ukrainian industrial output (Table 3.2), it appears that the Ukrainian industrial structure may well explain the republic's slightly below-average gross industrial growth since 1965. In turn, the Ukraine's structural features reflect developmental policies, as well as natural resource endowments.

---

*In symbols the comparisons are as shown below.

Columns

$\Sigma P_{su} V_{su} = 8.7$ $\Sigma P_{su} V_{uk} = 8.5$

$\Sigma P_{uk} V_{su} = 9.0$ $\Sigma P_{uk} V_{uk} = 8.8$

Rows

$\Sigma V_{su} P_{su} = 8.7$ $\Sigma V_{su} P_{uk} = 9.0$

$\Sigma V_{uk} P_{su} = 8.5$ $\Sigma V_{uk} P_{uk} = 8.8$

where P = production index for sector, V = value-added weight for sector, subscript "su" refers to Soviet Union, and subscript "uk" refers to Ukraine.

TABLE 3.8

Synthesized Aggregate Industrial Output Indexes, 1965-74
(average annual rate)

	Gross Output Index	
Value-Added Weights	USSR	Ukraine
USSR	8.7	9.0
Ukraine	8.5	8.8

Source: Table 3.1.

In terms of direction of industrial growth, the Ukraine has been slightly less traditional than the Soviet economy as a whole since 1965. The synthesized aggregate industrial growth rates for the Ukraine that are obtained by weighting, respectively, USSR and Ukrainian branch value-added proportions by the USSR and Ukrainian branch gross output indexes are about 0.3 percent higher than the USSR aggregate rates with both sets of value-added weights (Table 3.8). Thus, the course of industrial development since 1965 has been relatively favorable to the Ukraine, but has been overshadowed by the Ukraine's less favorable production structure in terms of the impact on aggregate industrial growth (Table 3.8).

FIVE-YEAR-PLAN PROGNOSTICATION

As Table 3.9 indicates, the Tenth Five-Year Plan (1976-80) basically represents a continuation of the Ninth Five-Year Plan's trends.[3] This is

TABLE 3.9

Projected Increases in Selected Indicators
During the Tenth Five-Year Plan
(percent)

	USSR	Ukraine
National income	26	27
Industrial output	36	33
Labor productivity in industry	31	29
Agricultural output	16	13
Labor productivity in agriculture	28	28
Investment	19	17

Sources: Pravda (P), October 30, 1976; *Radians'ka Ukraina (RU)*, November 20, 1976.

confirmed by the economy's performance during the first four years of the Ninth plan period (Tables 3.1, 3.2, and 3.8). The growth of Ukrainian industry, agriculture, investment, and other areas is projected at a lower rate than for the USSR. With respect to other republics, the Ukraine is scheduled to grow more slowly than, for example, the RSFSR or such fast-growing republic as Kazakhstan. However, the plan foresees a slightly faster growth of the Ukraine's industry, though not of agriculture, than would be the case in a more mature republic, such as Latvia.* The deemphasis on the significance of the Ukraine in the future economy of the USSR is quite evident.

A U.S. ANALOGUE

The evolving economic position of the Ukraine within the Soviet economy is not unique. There is a close analogue in U.S. economic history of an industrially and agriculturally rich region whose proportional contribution to national output has gradually declined as the regional development gap has narrowed. Yet this region continues to rank high by most absolute economic indicators.

The U.S. analogue is the nation's primary heavy industrial producer and its leading agricultural area—the East North Central or Great Lakes region.† As a contributor to national manufacturing output, the region reached its maximum share in the early 1950s. Since then its share has declined somewhat with the more rapid development of manufacturing in the southern and far western states. Many of these regional shifts have been accompanied by structural changes. The Great Lakes states, with their primary emphasis on steel, motor vehicle, and machinery production, have not been major participants in the more rapidly growing manufacturing branches—electronics, computers, and aircraft.

While the region has suffered a quantitative loss of position, it has maintained its standing in terms of productivity. Relative to the national average,

---

*Projected growth rates (percentage) under the Tenth Five-Year Plan for the RSFSR, Kazakhstan, and Latvia are shown below.

	Increase in Industrial Output	Average Annual Growth in Agriculture
RSFSR	36	16
Kazakhstan	40	15
Latvia	27	16

Source: Izvestia, October 30, 1976.

†This region includes Ohio, Michigan, Indiana, Illinois, and Wisconsin. See Bureau of the Census, Long Term Economic Growth, 1860-1965; Annual Survey of Manufactures, 1971; 1967 Census of Manufactures.

it has retained its peak ratio of value added per employee in manufacturing. In this respect it is also analogous to the Ukraine.

THE UKRAINE IN A SOVIET ECONOMIC PERSPECTIVE

The postwar trends in the Ukrainian economy are consistent with the usual expectations for a more mature region within a national economic context. Economic historians who have investigated regional economic trends in an international comparative perspective have formulated a theory of regional income differentials that trace out a reverse U-shaped curve, with regional disparity on the vertical axis and time on the horizontal axis.[4] In the initial stages of industrialization, regional disparities tend to widen, as development is concentrated in regions of superior natural resource and human endowments. Later a peak of income disparities is reached and the process begins to reverse itself as the industrialization process encompasses the less favored regions. In the United States there were widening regional income differentials from 1840 to 1880, relative stabilization and reversal from 1880 to 1920, then a narrowing of differentials since 1920. Similar tendencies have been observed in other market economies.

The Ukraine was a region in which industrialization took early root in Tsarist times and expanded greatly in the early (prewar) period of Soviet industrialization, along with development of the central (Moscow) and northwest (Leningrad) areas. Advanced development also took place in the Baltic republics. Commencing with a forced eastward industrial relocation during World War II and proceeding at a slower and irregular pace since 1945, there has been a progressive shift toward the east. The Ukraine and other older industrial regions have suffered a relative loss of position in production. In absolute terms the Ukraine has continued to experience rapid development by any international standard. It has maintained productivity advances on the level of the economy as a whole and has not been disadvantaged by its particular economic structure. Rather, its reduced position is explained by national developmental policies.

Since the Ukraine's investment share has been progressively below its share of national income produced (Tables 3.1 and 3.4), there has been a transfer of capital (saving) to the newer industrial regions. Such a resource transfer should be expected in the normal course of interregional development. What is missing is any tangible return to the Ukraine on its investment contribution outside the republic. The United States analogue for this tendency is not the interregional flow of capital in response to market mechanisms, but policies of the U.S. government in the nineteenth century to develop the western territory through heavy subsidies to road and rail transportation. Presumably in both the Ukrainian and U.S. examples, the returns to the capital-exporting regions are indirect, in the form of expanded trade with the developing industrial regions.

In this respect the Ukraine, within the context of a Soviet national entity, is not being "exploited" any more than the northeastern or midwestern regions of the United States are being "exploited" to provide the saving necessary for development of less industrialized regions in the south and west. If the Ukraine were a sovereign economic entity instead of a component of a large state, it would still very probably be an exporter of capital, as are highly industrialized regions in the United States, the United Kingdom, Germany, France, and Japan. The degree of its capital exports under Soviet control may be determined by centralized policy, but the direction is a function of the republic's advanced stage of development.

APPENDIX A

Derivation of Factor Income Shares, 1970

USSR factor income shares, which are assumed to be equivalent to output elasticities of employment and fixed capital stock in the production functions for Soviet NMP, industry, and agriculture for 1970, are obtained from estimates in the working papers for the Soviet GNP growth estimates, published by the C.I.A., appearing in *The Soviet Economy: 1974 Results and 1975 Prospects* A (ER) 75-62 (Washington, D.C.: March 1975). Factor payments and other charges against appropriate components of GNP have been distributed to employment (labor) or to capital, depending upon whether they are labor incomes or property-type incomes. Specific estimates are shown below.

Net Material Product (million rubles)

Wages	95,505	Fixed capital charges	39,974
Other money income	34,230	Working capital charges	18,907
Imputed income	18,873	Rent	9,924
Social insurance		Depreciation	15,161
contributions	7,136	Profits	11,763
		Investment in kind	1,104
Total labor income	155,744	Total return to capital	96,833
	Total factor payments	252,577	
	Employment share	61.7 percent	
	Capital share	38.3 percent	

Note: NMP is defined as comprising the following sectors: industry, agriculture, construction, freight transportation, productive communications, and domestic trade.

Industry (million rubles)

Wages	50,549	Fixed capital charges	19,250
Other money income	5,131	Working capital charges	6,644
Social insurance		Depreciation	9,005
contributions	3,639	Profits	11,763
Total labor income	59,319	Total return to capital	46,662

Total factor payments   105,981
Employment share   56.0 percent
Capital share   44.0 percent

Agriculture (million rubles)

Wages	10,404	Fixed capital charges	8,676
Other money income	25,695	Working capital charges	2,135
Imputed income	18,300	Rent	9,924
Social insurance		Depreciation	2,964
contributions	1,608	Investment in kind	1,104
Total labor income	56,007	Total return to capital	24,803

Total factor payments   80,810
Employment share   69.3 percent
Capital share   30.7 percent

The factor income shares for the Ukraine are obtained by comparing returns to labor and capital for the USSR and the Ukraine, as estimated by I. S. Koropeckyj for 1970.[5] The differences that he obtained in the shares for the two geographical entities are then applied to my previously computed shares for the USSR to obtain the shares for the Ukraine. The purpose of this indirect procedure is to preserve similarity in methodology of estimation for both entities.

Koropeckyj's labor and capital incomes shares are shown below.

Sector	USSR	Ukraine
NMP		
Labor	65.9	66.8
Capital	34.1	33.2
Industry		
Labor	58.2	57.4
Capital	41.8	42.6
Agriculture		
Labor	71.6	76.2
Capital	28.4	23.8

If the ratios of Ukrainian to USSR shares, as computed by Koropeckyj, are multiplied by my computed shares for the USSR, Ukrainian income shares are derived as shown below.

Sector	USSR	Ukraine
NMP		
Labor	61.7	62.7
Capital	38.3	37.3
Industry		
Labor	56.0	55.2
Capital	44.0	44.8
Agriculture		
Labor	69.3	73.7
Capital	30.7	26.3

APPENDIX B

Derivation of Value Added in Ukrainian Industrial Branches

Estimates of value added in Ukrainian industrial branches are obtained from 1970 employment-distribution data and from analogues of overall Soviet ratios of wage cost to total value added, by branch of industry. Also for 1970, such analogues assume similar production functions, by branch, between the Ukraine and the Soviet Union as a whole. Given the high degree of decision making in technological matters, such an assumption should closely approximate reality.

Branch	Wages as Percentage of Value Added for USSR (1)	Distribution of Ukrainian Industrial Employment (2)	Derived Distribution of Ukrainian Value Added in Industry (3)
Electric power	19.3	1.6	4.8
Petroleum and gas	11.1	0.4	2.1
Coal	60.8	8.2	7.8
Ferrous metals	39.1	8.0	11.9
Forest products	68.5	5.0	4.2
Construction materials	62.6	7.1	6.6
Chemicals	48.2	3.8	4.6
Machinery	70.5	37.6	31.0
Light industry	71.2	13.2	10.8
Food processing	52.2	10.2	11.3

Sources: Col. 1–Working papers for Central Intelligence Agency, *The Soviet Economy: 1974 Results and 1975 Prospects*, A (ER) 75-62 (Washington, D.C.: 1975), Table A-5; Col. 2–*Narhosp 1972*, pp. 104, 112, 114; Col. 3–col. 1 × col. 2 ÷ 100.

The Ukrainian value-added proportions are obtained by multiplying the Soviet wage/value-added ratio for each branch by that branch's share of total Ukrainian industrial employment. The derived Ukrainian value-added proportions are then divided by the sum of derived proportions to reduce them to a basis of 100 percent.

The only significant differences in income shares appear in the agricultural sector. This result is consistent with earlier findings as to the unusually labor-intensive character of Ukrainian agriculture, with the prominence of the kolkhoz institutional form.

NOTES

1. A. G. Granberg, *Opitimizatsiia territorial'nykh proportsii narodnogo khoziaistva* (Moscow, 1973), pp. 159-60.

2. Central Intelligence Agency, *Research Aid–The Soviet Economy in 1973: Performance, Plans, and Implications* (Washington, D.C., 1974).

3. *State Five-Year Plan for the Development of the USSR National Economy for the Period 1971-1975*, Pt. II (Arlington, Va.: Joint Publications Research Service, 1975).

4. Jeffrey Williamson, "Regional Inequality and the Process of National Development: A Description of the Patterns," *Economic Development and Cultural Change* (July 1968): Pt. II.

5. I. S. Koropeckyj, "National Income of the Soviet Union Republics in 1970: Revision and Some Applications," in Zbigniew M. Fallenbuchl, ed., *Economic Development in the Soviet Union and Eastern Europe*, I (New York: Praeger, 1975), Tables 11.3, 11.6.

4

CONSUMPTION AND
PERSONAL INCOMES
Gertrude E. Schroeder

INTRODUCTION

By dint of Herculean effort, Western research has produced indexes of total and per capita money incomes and consumption for the USSR as a whole in the postwar period.[1] These measures have been painstakingly put together from detailed data for major population groups and categories of consumption. In considering how the Ukraine has fared in terms of personal incomes and consumption, one would like to obtain similar measures for that republic. Unfortunately aggregate indexes could not be constructed, because of the paucity and unassessable reliability of available data for the Ukraine. Nonetheless, the measures of trends in personal incomes given in this chapter are quite complete, since they cover nearly all incomes from work; the most important missing items are money transfer payments and incomes from nonagricultural private activities. With respect to consumption, various indicators could be assembled for major components. These measures, together with the data on incomes, permit a good assessment of recent levels and trends in the economic well-being of people in the Ukraine relative to other republics and to some other countries. The focus is on the period since 1960, in the main, since few of the needed data are available for the Ukraine before that year.

A word is required about the reliability of data for the Ukraine. Of necessity, use had to be made of officially published statistics, supplemented with information provided in research studies by Soviet economists. Western scholars have carefully assessed the quality of official statistics on the USSR as a whole: many published value aggregates and indexes have been found to be seriously defective.[2] The objective of Western studies of incomes and consumption has therefore been to produce measures that are independent of the published indexes and value aggregates for the USSR, particularly of official price indexes.

Whether official statistics for the republics suffer equally from these deficiencies has yet to be determined.*

This chapter first considers relative levels and trends in wages and salaries of the state labor force, earnings of collective farmers, and total money incomes of the population as a whole. Next, levels and trends in household consumption of food, clothing, and consumer durables are described, followed by consideration of housing and communal consumption (mainly state-provided health and education services). Finally, an overall assessment is made of personal incomes and levels of living in the Ukraine, compared with other Soviet republics and other countries in the postwar period. Data will be presented for each republic as a whole, even though in the Ukraine and the RSFSR, in particular, there are sizable differences in levels of income and consumption among constituent regions. Neither republic publishes wage and consumption statistics for its regions, and the few fragmentary data available from other sources preclude reliable assessment of intrarepublic differentials and trends.

PERSONAL INCOMES

This section considers levels and trends in money incomes of major groups of employed workers in the Ukraine, compared with averages for the USSR as a whole and for other republics. Available data are marshaled to indicate the extent to which earnings from employment are supplemented by transfer payments and services financed by "social consumption funds." Finally, we consider the extent to which conclusions about the position of workers in the Ukraine, as reflected in nominal incomes, are modified when account is taken of trends in consumer prices and differences in the cost of living among regions of the USSR.

As is true for the USSR as a whole, the volume of published data on personal incomes in the Ukraine is scanty indeed, by comparison with the statistics available for most Western countries and for many Communist countries of Eastern Europe. The statistical handbooks published annually by the Ukraine provide data since 1960 on the average monthly wages of the state labor force (workers and employees) for the republic economy as a whole and for 12 of its major sectors. Secondary sources occasionally give data for scattered years for some branches of industry. Data on average earnings by occupations, regions, and sex are not published, except in fragmentary form. Information about incomes of collective farmers is particularly scarce. The handbooks provide data

---

*Such a test has been made in respect to the industrial production index published for the Ukraine. The official index for the Ukraine was found to differ more from an independently calculated index than in the case of the index for the USSR. See Roman Senkiw, "Industrial Production in Ukraine" (Ph.D. diss., University of Virginia, 1974).

only since 1960 on total wages in money and in kind paid to members of collective farms for work on the farms and on payments per man-day. For information about incomes from private-plot activities, recourse must be had to calculations of percentage changes and index number relatives provided in studies published by Soviet researchers. The reliability of these data cannot be determined independently; the studies may distort differences in levels of family incomes among the republics and trends over time, since they are based on information from sample surveys of family budgets. These surveys have been faulted by both Soviet and Western economists on many counts.[3]

With respect to trends and relative levels of real income, neither the Ukraine nor the USSR publishes overall indexes of the cost of living. The indexes of state retail prices that are published are methodologically faulty and biased downward.[4] Only fragmentary data are available on regional differences in prices of consumer goods and services. To assess changes in real incomes over time, the Ukraine, like the USSR, publishes a single index—real per capita income of the population as a whole for the period since 1960, an index whose meaning and method of construction is not explained.

Data on average money wages of the state labor force may be considered quite reliable; such wages account for the bulk of nominal incomes in the Ukraine, as well as in the USSR as a whole. The reliability of available data on incomes of collective farmers and incomes of all citizens from private agricultural activities probably are not grossly in error, although their quality cannot be assessed independently. Information on incomes from other kinds of private activities is totally absent. Data on incomes from transfer payments (pensions and welfare benefits) may be considered reliable, albeit pitifully small in quantity. All price data must be used with the caveat that they probably understate price increases to a significant but undeterminable extent.

Earnings of the State Labor Force

In 1974, the state employed 17.9 million workers and employees in the Ukraine and paid them an average monthly wage of 128.5 rubles. The largest share of the state labor force (36 percent) was employed in industry, at an average monthly wage of 144.8 rubles. The remainder were employed in 11 other major sectors of the economy, only the construction industry having as many as 10 percent of the total. In 1974, the latter paid the highest monthly wage (150.5 rubes); the lowest average wage (90.4 rubles) was paid in public health. The ruble data are shown in Table 4.1. During the period 1960-74, average wages increased by 64 percent, somewhat more slowly than state employment (68 percent). Among the sectors, increases in average wages ranged from 46 percent in state administration to 125 percent in state agriculture. With the exception of the latter, the relative positions of the sectors did not change greatly during the

TABLE 4.1

Average Monthly Wages of Workers and Employees in the Ukraine, by Sector of the Economy, 1960-74
(rubles)

Sector	1960	1965	1970	1974
Industry	93.2	106.5	130.1	144.8
State agriculture	51.4	71.5	95.7	115.9
Transport	78.3	95.6	120.9	140.7
Communication	59.7	69.9	92.3	102.8
Construction	85.6	103.3	135.0	150.5
Trade	54.1	70.7	88.0	95.3
Housing-communal economy	52.5	66.2	87.5	96.3
Health	55.6	74.2	85.0	90.4
Education and culture	68.9	92.1	102.2	116.5
Science	83.5	102.3	121.9	136.4
Credit and insurance	66.6	79.9	103.7	115.7
State administration	78.8	98.7	111.8	114.7
Total USSR	80.6	96.5	122.0	141.1
Ukraine	78.3	93.9	115.2	128.5

Sources: *Narodne khoziaistvo SSSR 1974* (Moscow 1975) (*Narkhoz*), p. 562; *Narodne hospodarstvo Ukrains'koi RSR 1974* (Kiev, 1973) (*Narhosp*), p. 389; *Narkhoz Ukraine 1974*, p. 408.

period. Trade, housing, and communal economy and health were low-wage sectors throughout, with industry, construction, and transportation retaining their position as relatively high-wage sectors.

Table 4.2 compares average annual money wages in the Ukraine as index number relatives with those for the USSR as a whole and for the other 14 republics in 1960, 1965, and 1970. Wages in the Ukraine were somewhat below the national average in all three years, with the relative level being a little lower in 1970 than in 1960. In 1970 the Ukraine ranked ninth among the republics, compared with its ranking of seventh in 1965 and 1960. Since wage and salary scales and wage policies are set centrally and tend to apply uniformly throughout the USSR, the change in the relative position of the Ukraine probably is to be explained in terms of a more rapid industrial development in some of the smaller republics, where special regional wage differentials apply in some cases. Throughout the period, however, wages in the Ukraine were lower than in the RSFSR, Estonia, Latvia, and Kazakhstan, but exceeded those in Georgia, Moldavia, and Belorussia. In individual sectors the Ukraine's relative position tends to be the same as or near its position with respect to average wages for all sectors.

TABLE 4.2

Indexes of Relative Levels of Average Annual Wages in the State Sector of the USSR, by Republic, 1960-70

	Average Annual Money Wages		
	1960	1965	1970
USSR	100.0	100.0	100.0
RSFSR	103.1	102.6	103.4
Ukraine	97.1	97.3	94.4
Belorussia	78.4	83.8	87.2
Uzbekistan	87.0	92.4	94.0
Kazakhstan	101.7	101.6	101.6
Georgia	92.8	89.9	87.5
Azerbaidzhan	93.3	93.4	90.0
Lithuania	89.8	92.8	97.5
Moldavia	83.6	84.9	84.3
Latvia	97.4	98.4	103.0
Kirgizia	92.3	92.3	90.5
Tadzhikistan	97.1	99.5	96.4
Armenia	93.5	95.2	100.0
Turkmenia	103.6	103.6	104.9
Estonia	101.6	103.5	110.9

Estimates for Azerbaidzhan, Kirgizia, and Turkmenia for 1960 and 1965 are subject to a wider margin of error than those for 1970.

Sources: The data on which these indexes are based were taken directly or derived from the statistical handbooks published by the republics or from their official reports on annual plan fulfillment. Money wages for Azerbaidzhan, Kirgizia, and Turkmenia in 1965 were derived from V. Zlatin and V. Rutgaizer, "Sopostavlenie urovnei ekonomicheskogo razvitiia soiuznykh respublik i bol'shykh raionov," *Ekonomicheskie nauki (EN)* (1968): no. 8, 32.

The high-priority sectors—industry, construction, and transportation—tend to pay high wages in all republics; and the relatively less favored, such as trade and housing-communal economy, tend to be low-wage sectors. Although Soviet policy has favored the development of public health, the persistent low-wage position of the sector may reflect the fact that women make up the vast bulk of those employed. In the Ukraine they accounted for 84 percent of the total in 1970. Wage differentials tend to be quite narrow among the various sectors in the Ukraine, as well as in the other republics for which data are available. In 1970, the differentials ranged from 17.2 percent above the overall average (construction) to 26.2 percent below the average (public health). The range was somewhat wide in 1960, reflecting the fact that in the Ukraine, as elsewhere in the USSR, there has been a slight narrowing of intersector differences in average earnings. The main reason is the Soviet policy of raising the uniform minimum wage without corresponding adjustments in the wage scale generally.

Neither the Ukraine nor the USSR publishes indexes of real wages—that is, money wages corrected for changes in consumer prices. Both, however, publish indexes of state retail prices for various postwar years in comparison with 1940. According to both indexes, the average level of retail prices was the same in 1970 as in 1960, with a small increase in food prices being offset by decreases in prices of nonfood goods. For many individual commodities, however, the indexes for the Ukraine differ considerably from those published by the USSR. So far as is known, the Ukrainian TsSU uses the same methodology to compute its price indexes as does the TsSU of the USSR. If this index were used to deflate money wages, one would conclude that the changes in real wages and money wages have been almost identical since 1960. However, the Soviet (and presumably the Ukrainian) retail price index is not a reliable measure of changes in the cost of living for consumers. First of all, it excludes prices on collective farm markets and all unofficial markets, as well as prices of services. Prices have been rising in both types of markets, although the extent cannot be measured with available data. The Ukraine ceased publishing an index of collective-farm market prices in 1969. Second, the method of construction of the official index of state retail prices fails to record price changes on new products and increases in prices actually paid by consumers because of the disappearance of cheaper grades of some goods and higher prices for allegedly better-quality goods, whose quality in fact has not changed.

These phenomena occur in the Ukraine as elsewhere in the USSR, but whether they are more common in the Ukraine cannot be determined. The data needed to construct independent price indexes are not available either for the USSR or the Ukraine. All of the anecdotal evidence, however, points to a rising level of retail prices since 1960. Also, collective-farm market prices in the Ukraine rose 31 percent during 1960-69.[5] Thus, real wages have been rising less rapidly than money wages to an unknown, but probably moderate, degree. One Western study concludes that consumer prices in the USSR actually rose by a minimum of 24 percent during 1960-75, compared with an increase of less than 1 percent given by official indexes.[6]

As noted above, the Ukraine tends to rank near the middle among the republics in level of average money earnings of the state labor force. In 1974, the Ukrainian level was below the national average by 9 percent and below the RSFSR average by 13 percent. Wages in all major sectors of the economy were below levels prevailing in both the USSR and the RSFSR. The reasons for this relatively low position are many, but the data required to explore most of them are not at hand. First, wages in the Ukraine are not influenced by regional wage coefficients, which are applicable to many parts of the RSFSR, the Baltic republics, and Central Asia. Second, wages in some sectors are affected by the extent of urbanization; the Ukraine ranks fifth on this measure, behind the average in the USSR and the RSFSR. Third, differences in employment structure affect average wage levels among the republics. Here, however, the Ukrainian distribution is much like that for the USSR and the RSFSR, as is the distribution of employment among branches of industry. Therefore, part of the cause for relatively lower wages must be sought in the nature of the goods produced in the branches of industry and their relative wages, a task beyond the available data.

Differences in supplies of manpower may also be important, along with relative levels of labor productivity, especially in view of the widespread use of output-related wage systems. Finally, in state agriculture, wages depend on the nature of the products, growing conditions, and various specific agricultural factors.

For the Ukraine, however the absence of regional wage coefficients probably is an especially important explanatory factor. These coefficients are added to basic wages and salaries in specified geographic areas and industries, both to compensate workers for higher retail price levels and extra living expenses due to climatic conditions, and to attract workers to labor-deficit regions. The Ukraine does not qualify for wage increments on any of these grounds. With respect to consumer prices, the Ukraine falls in Zone 1 (the lowest) for food products having zonal prices. Information on regional price levels is not published officially; recourse must be had to a few studies made by individual researchers at different times.

The most comprehensive of these studies is a comparison of average levels of 1963 state retail prices in Moscow, for all consumer goods and for food, with levels in the republics.[7] According to this study, price levels in the Ukraine were among the lowest. For all goods, prices in the Ukraine averaged 93.5 percent of the level in the USSR as a whole; for food the ratio was 87.4 percent. Only Moldavia and Turkmenia had lower relative price levels. Although data are not available for later years, relative price levels among regions would have been significantly affected by the 1966 abolition of the surcharges on prices of many goods sold in rural areas. Additional scattered information supports the evidence provided here that prices in the Ukraine are low relative to most other republics and that interrepublic price differences are not large.[8]

A more recent study provides estimates of cost-of-living differences among several republics and regions of the RSFSR in 1968.[9] The study takes into account price differences as well as differences in the composition of purchases resulting from location factors. According to this study, the cost of a "rational" standard basket of goods and services for a single worker in the Ukraine (including taxes) was 92.1 percent of that for a worker in the Central Region of the RSFSR; compared with the Urals and Siberia, the difference was much larger. For a family of four the comparable figure was 93.9. Besides several regions and oblasts in the RSFSR, the study included Central Asia and Kazakhstan. The cost

of living in the Ukraine was somewhat above the former and considerably below
the latter. These estimates, together with the sketchy information on prices
previously cited, suggest strongly that the relatively low level of average wages
in the Ukraine is associated with a relatively lower cost of living.

Earnings of Collective Farmers

In 1970, there were 9,141 collective farms in the Ukraine, with 5.1 million
households; the average annual number of farmers participating in collective
farm activity was 5.4 million. In contrast, there were 1,605 state farms, with a
total average annual employment of 1.0 million workers who were paid an average annual wage of 1,148 rubles. Collective farms dominate the agricultural
sector in the Ukraine to a much greater extent than in the USSR as a whole.
Neither of the employment figures cited includes employment in private-plot
activity, in which both groups of workers engage extensively, as do many urban
workers. Private-plot employment can be roughly estimated at about 3.5 million
in 1970.* Approximately 40 percent of the total labor force in the Ukraine is
engaged in agricultural activity, of which more than 75 percent are collective
farmers and members of their families. Thus, income of this group is a major
determinant of average levels of personal income in the Ukraine. The only official data on earnings of collective farmers are total payments by the farms to
members for work on the farms and the average pay per man-day. To estimate
total collective farmer incomes and private-plot incomes for all workers, recourse
must be had to a few studies by Soviet economists, to fragmentary data published here and there, and to assumptions to fill in gaps. The most comprehensive of the Soviet studies—those published by M. I. Sidorova in 1969 and
1972—provide estimates of collective farmer incomes from various sources in the
15 republics during 1960-70, expressed as percentages of the USSR average.[10]

Using these percentages and ruble figures for the USSR from officially
published data, one can get estimates of earned incomes of collective farmers for
1960, 1965, and 1970 in each republic. Table 4.3 gives the results in the form of
index number relatives, along with other measures of relative levels of collective
farmer incomes given by Sidorova. The relatives for total incomes shown in
Table 4.3 include earned incomes and state expenditures from social consumption funds. Earned incomes refer to incomes in money and in kind from work on
the collective farms and from private plots.

---

*Total employment on private plots in the Ukraine was estimated by the author in
connection with the estimates of earned incomes given in Table 4.4. The methodology is
explained in the second note to that table.

TABLE 4.3

Indexes of Relative Levels of Collective Farmer Incomes in the USSR, by Republic, 1960-70

	Total Income per Collective Farm Family			Total Income per Collective Farm Family Member			Earned Incomes per Collective Farm Family		
	1960	1965	1970	1960	1965	1970	1960	1965	1970
USSR	100	100	100	100	100	100	100	100	100
RSFSR	102	102	102	106	104	109	101	100	100
Ukraine	83	84	80	93	95	92	89	93	88
Belorussia	87	84	84	92	89	94	96	94	93
Uzbekistan	142	112	118	97	74	69	146	122	133
Kazakhstan	120	140	148	98	109	110	116	114	125
Georgia	112	95	105	103	85	94	122	108	122
Azerbaidzhan	94	82	92	68	52	58	100	87	101
Lithuania	124	131	122	140	153	150	136	150	134
Moldavia	73	87	85	70	82	84	79	99	97
Latvia	135	120	115	188	168	162	151	129	134
Kirgizia	95	104	93	74	79	68	98	110	104
Tadzhikistan	85	97	95	56	62	55	89	107	107
Armenia	112	108	117	78	74	76	118	113	122
Turkmenia	120	130	153	120	86	90	125	144	178
Estonia	132	120	122	165	200	205	135	123	124

Sources: Total collective farmer incomes—M. I. Sidorova, *Vozmeshchenie neobkhodimykh zatrat i formirovanie fonda vosproizvodstva rabochei sily v kolkhozakh* (Moscow, 1972), pp. 109, 123; earned incomes per family—derived from percentage distributions and income relatives in ibid., pp. 100, 107-09, and ruble data for the USSR as a whole given in *Narkhoz 1922-72*, 263 (the ruble data give the total payments in money and in kind made by collective farms to their members for work on the farms); number of collective farm households needed in these calculations—*Sel'skoe khoziaistvo SSR* (Moscow, 1971), p. 488.

In assessing these data, it must be kept in mind that incomes from agricultural activity fluctuate greatly from year to year with the weather, and that the impact of weather varies greatly among regions. Hence, conclusions about trends in relative positions of a region cannot legitimately be made from data for only three years. Moreover, the factors that explain differences in farm incomes among the 15 republics, and thereby the relative position of the Ukraine, are many and complex; to sort them out requires a detailed analysis of the agricultural sector in each republic, including product structure, prices, climatic and growing conditions, productivity, characteristics of the labor force, relative importance of various sources of family income. Obviously, such a task cannot be undertaken here. The estimates rely heavily on Sidorova's figures, evidently derived from the results of family budget surveys, which may distort interrepublic differentials in unknown ways.

The Ukraine ranks low on all measures presented in Table 4.3, and its position seems to have changed little over the decade. The Ukraine's relatively less favorable standing in respect to income per family than in respect to income per collective farm member is due largely to the fact that family size is small—3.1 members in 1970, compared with 3.5 for the USSR as a whole; only in the Baltic republics are families smaller than in the Ukraine.[11] The most important component of total income is wages from work for the collective farm. According to Sidorova, this source provided 42 percent of total family income in the Ukraine in 1970, compared with 40.7 for the USSR and 44.2 percent for the RSFSR.[12] The Ukraine tends to rank low in respect to both average pay per man-day and average number of man-days worked per year. In 1970 average pay per man-day was 3.58 rubles, and only Belorussia had a lower rate.[13] The average number of man-days worked was 203, putting the Ukraine in seventh place and below the USSR average of 207. During 1960-70, average pay per man-day tripled, somewhat more than in the USSR as a whole.[14]

The second largest source of income comes from private-plot activity, including consumption in kind as well as sales in collective-farm markets. This source provided 36 percent of total family income in the Ukraine in 1970, compared with 29.8 percent for the USSR and 25.8 percent for the RSFSR. In 1965, the Ukraine ranked seventh in respect to the share of private activity in family incomes, but ranked eleventh (in 1969) in respect to the level of family income from such activity.[15] The remaining sources of family income are wages earned by family members for work in state enterprises; miscellaneous incomes from interest, state lottery winnings, gifts and the like; and income from social consumption funds. The latter, mainly health and education services and transfer payments, accounted for 13.1 percent of total family income in the Ukraine in 1970.

In the Ukraine, average annual pay per collective farmer rose 182 percent during 1960-70. Average annual wages of state farm workers increased 85 percent, and average earnings of industrial workers rose only 38 percent. Even though these figures omit earnings from private plots, it is evident that a dramatic reduction in income differentials between agricultural and nonagricultural workers took place in the Ukraine. In the USSR as a whole, where trends were similar, average annual incomes in agriculture were 54 percent of those in nonagricultural activities in 1960 and 74 percent in 1970.[16] For the Ukraine in the latter year this relationship was also about 74 percent.

A large reduction in the income gap between collective farmers and state agricultural workers has also occurred in the Ukraine, as elsewhere. In 1960, the average annual income of collective farmers from work in the socialized sector in the Ukraine was 45.7 percent of that in state agriculture, whereas in 1970 the figure was 69.6 percent. The large reductions in rural-urban income differentials have resulted primarily from increases in farm prices paid by the government and changes in the compensation system for collective farmers, designed to make it like that used on state farms, both in nature and in level of wages. Wage differentials continued to narrow during 1971-74, when man-day earnings of collective farmers rose 5.4 percent and wages of workers and employees rose 11.6 percent.

Total Personal Incomes

Using income relatives provided by Sidorova for collective farmer incomes in the republics, official data on wages of the state labor force, and various other data, it is possible to estimate total earned incomes in each republic for 1960, 1965, and 1970.[17] These totals can then be expressed per capita and per worker to provide an assessment of changes in republic income differences during the decade. Table 4.4 gives the estimates of earned income per worker in rubles and as index number relatives.* These estimates cover the vast bulk of earned incomes, the principal omissions being military pay and incomes from private nonagricultural activities.

As shown in Table 4.4, earned income per worker in the Ukraine was about 10 percent below the national average in 1970 and about 15 percent below the average for the RSFSR. The Ukraine ranked twelfth in 1970 and tenth in 1960. The rate of change over the decade was only slightly below that of the RSFSR and the USSR as a whole. When incomes are expressed per capita, however, the Ukraine's relative position is much better, with a ranking of fifth in 1970 and sixth in 1960, and a relative level only slightly below the national

---

*Total incomes from private plots of workers in state agriculture may have been underestimated in deriving the ruble values shown in Table 4.4. The relative would not change, but ruble values would rise slightly.

TABLE 4.4

Relative Levels of Earned Income per Worker in the USSR, by Republic, 1960-70

	Index Numbers			Rubles		
	1960	1965	1970	1960	1965	1970
USSR	100	100	100	887	1,087	1,387
RSFSR	106	105	106	941	1,139	1,470
Ukraine	91	93	90	806	1,006	1,250
Belorussia	79	81	83	701	883	1,155
Uzbekistan	100	97	94	886	1,052	1,304
Kazakhstan	112	112	111	992	1,222	1,544
Georgia	96	90	86	853	974	1,195
Azerbaidzhan	90	95	94	798	1,037	1,300
Lithuania	88	91	94	781	991	1,307
Moldavia	74	83	79	660	898	1,094
Latvia	101	100	106	896	1,082	1,471
Kirgizia	97	97	93	858	1,058	1,284
Tadzikistan	85	95	94	751	1,029	1,301
Armenia	104	104	107	919	1,128	1,483
Turkmenia	97	105	109	862	1,145	1,511
Estonia	109	106	115	967	1,153	1,589

Notes: Earned incomes include incomes from wages and salaries of the state and collective-farm labor force and incomes of farmers from private agricultural activities.

The totals for the USSR given in Feshbach and Rapawy were distributed by republic on the assumption that the share of each one in total employment was the same as its share in total income from private farming activity. The latter was obtained as a component in the estimates of incomes earned by farmers.

Sources: The estimates of earned income were derived as explained in the sources of Tables 4.2 and 4.3 with respect to wages and salaries and incomes of collective farmers. Also included are estimates of incomes of state-farm workers from private plots. For details of the derivation of this small component, as well as more detail on the methodology in general, see Gertrude E. Schroeder, "Regional Differences in Incomes and Levels of Living in the USSR," in V. N. Bandera and Z. L. Melnyk, eds., *The Soviet Economy in Regional Perspective* (New York: Praeger, 1973), pp. 192-93. Employment includes workers and employees and collective farmers given in *Narkhoz 1970*, pp. 405, 517. Employment in private farming activities for the USSR was taken from Murray Feshbach and Stephen Rapawy, "Labor Constraints in the Five-year Plan," in Joint Economic Committee, *Soviet Economic Prospects for the Seventies* (Washington, D.C.: U.S. Government Printing Office, 1973), pp. 520-21.

average. Population in the Ukraine increased only 10.5 percent during the decade, one of the lowest rates in the USSR. The rapid increase of populations in Central Asia, Armenia, Azerbaidzhan, and Kazakhstan caused their relative positions, when measured per capita, to change dramatically. Thus, while earned income levels per worker are relatively quite low in the Ukraine, families are small and the dependency ratio is low.

The relative levels of income in the republics, measured by earned incomes, may be contrasted with the results obtained when the Soviet concept of national income (net material product) is used as a measure. In the case of the Ukraine the two measures give closely similar results—level of income per worker about 10 percent below the national average and a level of income per capita only slightly below the national average. For most other republics, however, the two measures give quite different results.[18] In any event, national income is a poor measure of personal income and consumption levels in the republics, since it omits many incomes and fails to reflect interrepublic income transfers carried out by the Soviet government through tax and expenditure policies.

HOUSEHOLD CONSUMPTION

The best overall measure of trends in household consumption of goods and services would be an index in real terms of household purchases in all markets, plus household consumption in kind of food products. As a substitute for such a comprehensive measure for the Ukraine, Table 4.5 assembles various published data concerning the volume of retail trade and personal services and the availabilities of trade and service facilities during 1960-74. As a measure of changes in real consumption of goods over time, the official index of retail trade in constant prices is subject to doubts about the validity of the price index used to deflate current ruble sales. Moreover, retail sales include some sales to producers. In the Ukraine such sales accounted for somewhat over 5.5 percent of the total in 1965.[19] Retail sales data also include various so-called "productive services," mainly repair services; in 1970 such services were 2 percent of total retail trade in the USSR;[20] similar data are not available for the Ukraine. In respect to interrepublic comparisons, retail sales data for a given republic include some purchases by nonresidents and similarly, urban sales include purchases made by rural residents, who must buy most clothing and durables in cities. Nonetheless, the relative levels of retail sales in the republics correspond fairly well with levels of personal incomes.

In 1974, total retail sales per capita in the Ukraine were 710 rubles, 9 percent below the national level and 17 percent below the level for the RSFSR. The Ukraine ranked sixth among the republics on this measure, closely in line with its ranking on earned income per capita and share of urban population in the total. Sales were fairly evenly divided between food and nonfood goods, a

TABLE 4.5

Indicators of Retail Trade and Services in the Ukraine, 1960-74

Indicator	1960	1965	1970	1974
1. Retail trade (rubles per capita)	312	409	582	710
Food	159	218	306	365
Nonfood	153	191	276	345
2. Retail trade (per capita, in constant prices)	100	132	188	230
Food	100	133	194	217
Nonfood	100	132	183	246
3. Retail trade (rubles per resident)				
Urban	521	630	827	968
Rural	124	179	284	347
4. Personal services (rubles per capita)	4	7	17	25
5. Retail stores (per 10,000 people)	28	31	31	30
6. Service establishments (per 10,000 people)	7.4	8.8	10.4	11.4
7. Seats in restaurants (per 10,000 people)	187	287	430	545

Sources: 1–*Narhosp 1972*, 460; *Narkhoz Ukraine 1974*, 466; 2–ibid.; 3–*Narhosp 1972*, 7, 456; *Narkhoz Ukraine 1974*, 7, 463; 4–calculated from data in *Narkhoz 1973*, 9, 697; *Narkhoz 1974*, 673; 5–*Narkhoz 1922-72*, 609; *Narkhoz 1974*, 660; 6–calculated from data in *Narkhoz 1922-72*, 620; *Narkhoz 1974*, 9, 670; 7–*Narkhoz 1922-72*, 610; *Narkhoz 1974*, 661.

typical pattern. Expressed in constant prices, retail sales per capita rose 30 percent in the Ukraine during 1960-74, somewhat faster than the national average but in line with a slightly faster rate of urbanization. Sales in urban areas per urban resident in 1974 were nearly three times higher than rural sales per rural resident, but the gap was much larger in 1960. In respect to retail facilities, the Ukraine, with its 30 retail stores and 11 restaurants per 10,000 population, is somewhat better off than most of other republics; but decades of neglect in development of a retail services infrastructure leave the Ukraine well behind both Eastern and Western Europe in this regard.

An even more neglected consumer sector is personal services, such as repair services, barber and beauty shops, laundries and dry-cleaning shops, tailoring, and the like. The total value of such services provided by state enterprises in the Ukraine amounted to a mere 25 rubles per capita in 1974—nearly a sixfold increase over 1960. In 1974, there were only 11.4 such service establishments per 10,000 population. Here, too, however, the Ukraine was better off than most other republics except the Baltic states. The scarcity and poor quality of state-provided everyday services are perennially aired in the press. To fill the pressing and growing demand for such services as incomes rise, a flourishing private sector has developed, especially in rural areas, where shortages are most acute. Unfortunately, its size cannot be gauged with any degree of accuracy, either for the USSR or for the Ukraine.

Food Consumption

The Ukraine publishes data on consumption of various food products in kilograms per capita per year. In general, the food consumption pattern in the Ukraine is similar to that in the RSFSR and, therefore, to the USSR average. In 1974, the peoples of the USSR's two largest republics consumed about the same amount of meat and sugar. Citizens of the Ukraine ate less milk, eggs, and fish than those in the RSFSR, but more potatoes, vegetables, and grain products. Thus, the starch-staple ratio would be higher in the Ukraine, making the diet of lower quality overall by this measure. This relationship is in line with the Ukraine's more rural character. Peasants in the Ukraine, as elsewhere, probably eat substantially more potatoes and grain products than do urban dwellers. Although no published data are at hand for the Ukraine, in the USSR in 1968, the latest year for which such data have been published, peasants consumed less than 75 percent as much meat and fish as did workers and employees (largely urban) and more than 20 percent more grain products and potatoes.[21]

The dietary pattern in the Ukraine differs considerably from that of the high-income Baltic republics, whose people eat 50 percent again as much meat and about 33 percent less grain products than Ukrainians. Comparable data on consumption of foods are not available for other republics. Although there are significant differences in some items, overall the food consumption pattern in the Ukraine tends to resemble that in Italy, whereas the pattern in the Baltic republics is more like that in the wealthier countries of northern Europe. The Ukraine, like most other Soviet republics, has a long way to go before its food consumption pattern matches the "rational consumption norms," which the Soviet planners seem to regard as optimal. Only for sugar and vegetable oil are the norms now met in the Ukraine. Meat consumption, for example was 71 percent of the norm in 1974, whereas consumption of grain products exceeded the norm by 25 percent and potatoes by 54 percent. Nonetheless, considerable progress was made in the desired direction during 1960-74, when consumption of meat and milk rose by 33 percent or more, with a concomitant sizable drop in consumption of potatoes and grain products.

Soft Goods

Available data permit comparison of consumption of cloth and leather shoes per capita in the Ukraine with the USSR and the RSFSR and with the "rational" consumption norms. Per capita consumption in the Ukraine in 1974 (29.3 square meters of cloth and 3.07 pairs of shoes)[22] was below the national average and also that of the RSFSR. The rational norms established for these products are 59.6 square meters of cloth and 3.3 pairs of shoes. During 1960-74, per capita consumption in the Ukraine rose 21 percent for cloth and 75 percent for shoes, about the same as for the USSR as a whole. The low quality of Soviet domestic production of both these goods has been a perennial complaint of consumers, but whether quality in the Ukraine tends to be worse or better than elsewhere cannot be judged from available evidence.

Durable Goods

One of the hallmarks of modern consumerism as it has developed in the West is the widespread household ownership of a variety of consumer durables. Table 4.6 presents data on household stocks of various kinds of durables in the Ukraine, together with some comparative data. Household stocks of common durables in the Ukraine, measured per 100 families, are behind those in the USSR as a whole in most categories, and even further behind the RSFSR. Ownership of durables is strongly correlated with the degree of urbanization. At the end of 1974, 59 percent of the total population in the Ukraine was urban, somewhat less than the USSR average of 60 percent and well below the RSFSR figure of 67 percent. During the 1960s, household ownership of consumer durables rose considerably more rapidly in the Ukraine than in the USSR generally, as did the rate of urbanization. Possession of consumer durables is also related to levels of personal incomes. As shown above, average money incomes in the Ukraine are somewhat below the USSR average and much farther below levels in the RSFSR. Although data on stocks of durables are not available for other republics, Ukrainians evidently have shared rather equitably in the distribution of the rapidly growing output of consumer durables in the USSR in recent years. However, consumers in the Ukraine, like the rest of the people in the USSR, have also suffered from the long-delayed development of production capabilities for such goods, a hallmark of Soviet investment policy. Quality is often poor and repair facilities minuscule.

Soviet specialists have worked out rational norms for household stocks of durables. For all items, except watches and washing machines, actual stocks in 1974 were far below these norms in the Ukraine and in the RSFSR. For two items for which international comparisons can be made—radios and television sets—even 1974 stocks in the RSFSR were far below those in the United States and the major countries of Western Europe, and even well behind stocks in Italy and Japan, countries nearest to the USSR in per capita consumption.[23] The comparisons in Table 4.6 do not include passenger cars, because data on personal ownership of cars are not available for the republics. Only in the past few years

TABLE 4.6

Household Stocks of Consumer Durables in the Ukraine, USSR, and RSFSR, 1960-74
(number per 100 families)

	Ukraine				USSR	RSFSR	Rational
	1960	1965	1970	1974	1974	1974	Stocks
Watches	233	278	397	451	438	456	416
Radios and phonographs	36	50	59	67	77	84	127
Television sets	6	21	52	75	71	76	106
Cameras		15	23	25	27	29	67
Refrigerators	2	8	26	53	55	56	90
Washing machines	4	19	45	62	62	67	47
Vacuum cleaners	2	4	10	17	16	17	45
Sewing machines		39	49	52	60	63	98
Individual transport*	47	60	62	67	62	62	83

Note: Ukraine data given in units per 1,000 population were converted to stocks per 100 families on the basis of 2.9 persons per family, the coefficient used by the Soviets to convert data for the USSR and RSFSR.

*Bicycles, mopeds, motorcycles, scooters.

Sources: Ukraine—*Narhosp 1972*, 387; *Narkhoz Ukraine 1974*, 439; USSR—*Narkhoz1974*, 604; RSFSR—*Narkhoz RSFSR 1974*, 403; Rational stocks—Phillip Weitzman, "Soviet Long-Term Consumption Planning: Distribution According to Rational Needs," *Soviet Studies* (July 1974): 308.

has Soviet policy permitted production of passenger cars for sale to the public on a significant scale. Private ownership of cars in 1974 was minuscule by Western standards. How well Ukrainians have fared in the distribution of the cars available for sale to the public is not known.

HOUSING

In respect to urban housing, the Ukraine is somewhat better off relative to other republics than it is on other counts; but its relative superiority has decreased somewhat since 1960.[24] In 1974, the Ukraine ranked fourth among the republics in square meters of urban housing space per urban resident, a ranking it had in 1960 by a slightly smaller margin. During 1960-74, urban housing space per capita in the Ukraine increased from 9.8 square meters to 12.8 square meters of total (useful) space. The average for the USSR in 1974 was 11.9 square meters. By this measure, only Estonia, Latvia, and Georgia were better off than the Ukraine. Information about the quantity of rural housing per capita in the Ukraine is not available, but for the USSR as a whole it is about the same as urban housing. In the Ukraine, as elsewhere in the USSR, most urban residents live in small, crowded apartments owned by the state and managed by housing bureaus of cities or enterprises. In 1974, 61 percent of the total urban housing stock was state-owned, compared with 46 percent in 1960. The poor quality of Soviet housing is notorious, as evidenced by extensive anecdotal information given in the press. Since working arrangements in housing construction are essentially uniform throughout the Soviet Union, the quality of housing in the Ukraine probably is no better than elsewhere. Electricity is now available in nearly all housing, however, and gas is coming increasingly into use in urban housing.

In the postwar period, the Ukraine has made a sizable effort to improve housing for its people. Housing construction has absorbed 16 percent of total investment during the entire period 1946-74, but the share has been declining steadily since 1960. In 1974, housing accounted for 13 percent of total investment, compared with 15 percent for the USSR. The total amount of housing constructed has increased in each successive five-year plan since 1950. Since 1960, the annual amounts have ranged between 17.6 and 19.9 million square meters of total space. Between 1.7 and 2.0 million persons obtained housing in newly constructed buildings each year. Despite this large-scale program, progress remains slow and investment plans for housing are rarely met, evidence of its generally low priority. Better housing, both in quantity and in quality, clearly is urgently desired by the population. Present per capita living space available in the Ukraine (8.5 square meters) is still below the 9.0 square meters of living space established by the Soviety government as the minimum standard for health and decency. Per capita living space in Ukrainian cities also compares unfavorably with that of most European countries, both East and West.

COMMUNAL CONSUMPTION

In addition to direct purchase of goods and services out of personal incomes, households in the Ukraine receive supplemental incomes and benefits from the government, financed mainly out of general tax revenues and provided without direct charge. "Payments and benefits from social consumption funds" is a Soviet statistical category that includes public-sector expenditures on health, education, and culture (excluding investment), pensions, disability and sickness benefits, maternity and child allowances, and similar welfare payments; paid leave; the state housing subsidy and subsidies for vacation and health resorts; and other minor payments and benefits. The social consumption fund in the Ukraine was 14.9 billion rubles in 1974, equal to 18.0 percent of the total for the USSR; the Ukraine's population was 19.3 percent of the total. In 1974, 53 percent of the total fund represented cash payments, and the rest represented government current expenditures for health and education and subsidies for housing and recreation.[25] On a per capita basis, social consumption funds in the Ukraine increased somewhat faster than in the USSR during 1960-74, reflecting, at least in part, a somewhat faster growth of urban population. In 1974, the Ukraine ranked fifth among the republics, as it did in respect to percent of the urban population in total population. Its ranking on both measures has been fairly stable. Numerous factors determine a republic's relative position with respect to per capita payments and benefits and their relative growth. Among the most important is the relative degree of urbanization, which particularly affects the size of the housing subsidy and state expenditures on health and education. Other important factors are the age-sex structure and rate of growth of the population and the level of industrialization; these variables, in particular, affect levels of pension and welfare payments.

Payments and benefits from social consumption funds are calculated separately for workers and employees and for collective farmers. Stated Soviet policy is to increase the share in the total consumption of each group that is supplied by social consumption funds, as opposed to private consumption. In 1974, payments and benefits added 558 rubles per year, or 36.2 percent, to average money wages of the 17.917 million workers and employees in the Ukraine. The combined "wage" may be thought of as the "social wage." Although data are not published on payments and benefits for collective farmers, they can be roughly estimated at about 550 rubles per year for each of the 5.190 million collective farm members reported as participating in collective farm work. This estimate, however, overstates the average amount per worker, because it does not take into account the large number of collective farm family members who work only on private plots.

Social consumption funds finance a wide array of pension and welfare programs that apply uniformly throughout the USSR. These programs pre-empted 37 percent of the total funds in 1974. The amount of data published on the results of these programs is minuscule for the USSR and no breakdowns are provided by republic, so one cannot gauge the extent of regional differences in levels of benefits and number of beneficiaries. Similar lacunae exist in respect to the several kinds of state subsidies that are financed from these funds. The housing subsidy results from the fact that rents for state housing are set far below the cost of maintenance—rents reportedly cover only about 33 percent of such costs in the USSR as a whole.[26] Since rents are uniform, the size of this subsidy presumably would differ among republics according to the amount of state-owned housing. Subsidies to health and recreation come about because the government requires workers to pay only a small part of the cost of stays at vacation and health resorts, which are run mainly by the state-dominated trade unions.

In the USSR as a whole in 1974, expenditures on education, culture, and health accounted for 44 percent of total expenditures from social consumption funds.[27] Recent data on outlays by republic are not available. These expenditures are financed mainly (about 70 percent in 1970) from the state budget, but also from funds of enterprises, collective farms, and trade unions.[28] Total outlays for education, culture, and health from the republic budget in the Ukraine totaled 4.4 billion rubles in 1974, or 92 rubles per capita. Of this total, 2.8 billion was allocated to education and culture, and the rest to health and physical culture. On a per capita basis, such expenditures in the Ukraine are among the lowest among the republics. The Ukraine's low ranking in respect to expenditures on education is associated with a similarly low ranking in respect to number of students in elementary and secondary schools per 1,000 population, which in turn reflects its low rate of population growth and increasingly urban character. In 1970, for example, the Ukraine had 178 students per 1,000 population, compared with 202 for the USSR. When expenditures (from republic budgets) are expressed per student, the Ukraine, with an outlay of 145 rubles per student, exceeded the average for all republics of 141 rubles per student. In respect to educational attainment, moreover, the Ukraine scores well.[29] At the beginning of 1975, 559 persons per 1,000 aged 10 and over had some higher and secondary specialized education. The average for the USSR was 554, and the Ukraine was exceeded only by the RSFSR and Georgia on this measure. When educational attainment is expressed per 1,000 persons employed, the figure for the Ukraine is 762, compared with a national average of 751, and is exceeded by only four republics.

Expenditures on health and physical culture financed from the budget of the Ukraine amounted to 1.9 billion rubles in 1974, or 39 rubles per capita, compared with 44 rubles per capita for all republics. Expenditures rose nearly 85 percent during the 1960s, a little more slowly than during the 1950s. The Ukraine's relative position in respect to provision of health care can also be assessed from data on medical personnel and hospital beds. In 1974, the Ukraine had 30.9 doctors per 10,000 population, somewhat below the national average (31.5), and ranked seventh among the republics, a rank it also had in 1960.[30] In addition, the Ukraine had 96.4 middle medical personnel (semiprofessionals) per capita, a measure on which it has consistently ranked fifth among the republics.[31] The Ukraine had 115.7 hospital beds per 10,000 people in 1974, about the same as the national average.[32] Its ranking has moved from seventh to fourth since 1960. Although Soviet-published comparisons are exaggerated, the Ukraine and the USSR as a whole are well ahead of most other countries, including Eastern Europe, in regard to numbers of medical personnel and hospital beds. The quality of the health services provided is another matter, but one on which international comparisons are elusive. Soviet policy apparently has aimed at providing a minimum level of basic health care without direct charge to recipients, but at minimum cost to the state. The success of this policy in the Ukraine may be judged by the fact that death rates are moderately low by modern standards (9.3 per 1,000 population in 1973-74).[33] The higher death rate in the Ukraine than in the USSR as a whole accords with the larger share of persons age 60 and over in its population.

AN OVERALL VIEW

Lacking the data with which to develop reliable aggregate indexes of personal incomes and standards of living in the Ukraine during the postwar period, this chapter instead has assembled bits of partial evidence, focusing on the period 1960-74. Wages of state employees rose by nearly 67 percent during the period, somewhat more slowly than in the USSR as a whole. The Ukraine ranks almost 10 percent below the national average in respect to money wages, and its position deteriorated a little during the period. In real terms, however, the relative position of Ukrainian workers is better, since the cost of living is also lower.

In respect to agricultural incomes, the Ukraine ranks even lower—for managers and skilled workers as well as for ordinary farmhands.[34] Its ranking changed little during the period studied. The reasons for the Ukraine's relatively low position are numerous and complex. On the one hand, the Ukraine is a region of in-migration and relative labor surplus, with women and nonable-bodied workers accounting for relatively larger shares in the total labor force.[35] On the other hand, crop yields are high for nearly all products, and costs are low relative to those in other republics. Neverthelsss, the ruble value of agricultural output in the Ukraine tends to be lower when measured per hectare or per center, a direct result of the fact that state procurement prices paid in the Ukraine are also low. These prices are set by the Soviet government and differ widely among regions for a given crop. The fragmentary regional price data available indicate that the Ukraine's price position is highly unfavorable.

Average incomes for workers and peasants combined in the Ukraine were nearly 10 percent below the national average in 1970, giving it a ranking among the lowest of the republics and a somewhat less favorable position than in 1960. Because of low population growth, however, per capita income in the Ukraine is relatively much higher. The Ukraine ranks fifth among the republics, behind the RSFSR and the Baltic republics; its relative level is only slightly below the national average and has improved somewhat over the period. On a per capita basis, the Ukraine's position in respect to earned money incomes corresponds to its position in respect to level of economic development (as measured by national income produced, Soviet concept) and the degree of urbanization. Because of serious reservations about the validity of official price indexes, the measures of incomes have not been presented in real terms. Both the USSR and the Ukraine publish official indexes of "real income per capita" that purportedly include all money and in-kind incomes plus the value of services financed from public funds. According to this measure, real income per capita in the Ukraine increased 93 percent during 1960-74, compared with 84 percent in the USSR as a whole.

The available data on levels and trends in consumption in the Ukraine give essentially the same picture as data on personal incomes. The Ukraine does not publish ruble figures on total consumption or national income used, as the USSR does. However, a Ukrainian source states that the share of consumption in total national income used in 1973 was 72 percent, compared with a reported 71 percent for the USSR.[36] According to a Ukrainian study, the share was 71 percent in 1960.[37] In respect to structure of the consumption fund, another Ukrainian source provides the following percentage distribution for an unspecified year (probably 1968):[38]

Total fund	100.0
Private consumption	90.5
Retail purchases	71.1
Collective-farm market sales	4.9
Consumption in kind	8.9
Housing depreciation	4.1
Payments for utilities	1.1
Other	0.4
Public consumption	9.5
Material expenditures of institutions serving the population	7.4
Material expenditures in science administration	2.1

The share of private consumption in the total fund in the Ukraine is somewhat higher than that in the USSR as a whole. The official indexes of growth of national income pertain to income produced rather than income used, the latter being net of losses and income transfers. Total income produced in the Ukraine rose 136 percent during 1960-74 and 108 percent on a per capita basis, approximately the same figures as in the USSR.

Similar results are given by evidence concerning various kinds of consumption. Per capita retail sales in the Ukraine rose at about the same rate as earned incomes. Per capita payments and benefits from social consumption funds increased more rapidly than per capita retail sales, suggesting a continuation of the relative shift toward communal consumption, which has been a hallmark of Soviet policy. The Ukraine tends to rank fifth or sixth among the republics on most measures of personal and communal consumption when expressed per capita, a position in line with its ranking in respect to incomes. Not much change has taken place since 1960 in this regard. The food consumption pattern in the Ukraine and consumer stocks of durables are more or less in line with its position in respect to urbanization but, like the pattern for the USSR as a whole, remain backward when compared with most countries of both Eastern and Western Europe. Broadly speaking, on most measures the Ukraine tends to rank behind the RSFSR and the Baltic republics, and ahead of the other republics.

On balance, the evidence assembled suggests that consumers in the Ukraine improved their lot substantially during 1960-74. Judging from indirect evidence, the level of living in the Ukraine must have risen even more rapidly during the 1950s. Industrial production, agricultural output, and retail trade increased more rapidly during the 1950s than during 1961-74. In the USSR as a whole, where trends were similar, per capita consumption increased somewhat faster during 1951-60 than during 1961-74.[39] On the whole, the weight of the evidence indicates that, at least for the latter period, the Ukraine has not been able to improve its relative standing among the republics; if anything, its position may have deteriorated slightly. Finally, despite notable quantitative progress, consumers in the Ukraine, as in all republics, continue to suffer from poor-quality consumer goods, sporadic shortages of desired products, a deplorably low level of everyday service facilities, inadequate and poorly built housing, and limited ability to influence consumption pattern. These phenomena are familiar consequences of Soviet investment policy and working arrangements in the economy.

NOTES

1. Janet G. Chapman, "Consumption," in Abram Bergson and Simon Kuznets, eds., *Economic Trends in the Soviet Union* (Cambridge, Mass.: Harvard University Press, 1963), pp. 235-82; Gertrude E. Schroeder and Barbara S. Severin, "Soviet Consumption and Income Policies in Perspective," in Joint Economic Committee, *Soviet Economy in a New Perspective* (Washington, D.C.: U.S. Government Printing Office, 1976), pp. 620-60.

2. Vladimir G. Treml and John P. Hardt, eds., *Soviet Economic Statistics* (Durham, N. C.: Duke University Press, 1972).

3. Marshall I Goldman, "Consumption Statistics," in Treml and Hardt, op. cit., pp. 321-35.

4. Gertrude E. Schroeder, "An Appraisal of Soviet Wage and Income Statistics," in ibid., pp. 307-12; Morris Bornstein, "Soviet Price Statistics," in ibid., pp. 370-83.

5. *Narodne hospodarstvo Ukrains'skoi RSR (Narhosp) 1969* (Kiev, 1970), p. 504.

6. Schroeder and Severin, op. cit., p. 631.

7. L. Bauman and V. Tolkushin, "Ob uchete territorial'nykh razlichii gosudarstvennykh roznichnykh tsen," *Vestnik statistiki (VS)* (1965): no. 4, 32-29.

8. For a summary of the available information on regional price differences, see Gertrude E. Schroeder, "Regional Differences in Incomes and Levels of Living in the USSR," in V. N. Bandera and Z. L. Melnyk, eds., *The Soviet Economy in Regional Perspective* (New York: Praeger, 1973), pp. 175-76.

9. Ie. Kapustin and N. Kuznetsova, "Regional'nye osobennosti povysheniia zhiznennogo urovnia naseleniia," *Ekonomicheskie nauki (EN)* (1972): no. 1, 49-58.

10. M. I. Sidorova, *Obshchestvennye fondy potrebleniia i dokhodov kolkhoznikov* (Moscow, 1969); and *Vozmeshchenie neobkhodimykh zatrat i formirovanie fonda vosproizvodstva rabochei sily v kolkhozakh* (Moscow, 1972).

11. Ibid., p. 136.

12. Ibid., pp. 100, 102. For unknown reasons, the percentages of income from various sources given here for the USSR differ somewhat from those given in *Narodnoe khoziaistvo SSSR (Narkhoz) 1973* (Moscow, 1974), p. 633.

13. Sidorova, *Vozmeshchenie*, p. 136.

14. *Narhosp 1972*, p. 285; *Narkhoz 1922-72*, p. 263.

15. Sidorova, *Vozmeshchenie*, p. 115.

16. Gertrude E. Schroeder, "Consumer Goods Availability and Repressed Inflation in the Soviet Union," in NATO, Directorate for Economic Affairs, *Economic Aspects of Life in the USSR* (Brussels: NATO, 1975), p. 40.

17. Gertrude E. Schroeder, "Soviet Wage and Income Policies in Regional Perspective," *ACES Bulletin* (Fall 1974): 3-20.

18. See Schroeder, "Soviet Wage and Income Policies," pp. 14, 17.

19. A. Zaitseva and G. Moroz, "Izuchenie vyborotnym metodom pokupok tovarov organizatsiiami, uchrezhdeniiami i predpriiatiiami v roznichnom rinke," *VS* (1971): no. 5, 34.

20. V. I. Nikitin, *Planirovanie roznichnogo tovarooborota* (Moscow, 1972), p. 52.

21. *Narkhoz 1968*, p. 595.

22. *Narkhoz Ukraine 1974*, p. 438.

23. Comparisons for the USSR and Western countries are cited in Abram Bergson, *Soviet Post-war Economic Development* (Stockholm: Almgvist and Wiksell, 1974), p. 75.

24. All figures pertaining to housing were obtained or derived from the annual statistical handbooks of the USSR and the Ukraine.

25. *Narkhoz Ukraine 1974*, p. 416.

26. V. Komarov, "Sfera uslug i ee struktura," *VE* (1973): no. 2, 41.

27. *Narkhoz 1974*, p. 575.

28. Ibid., p. 759; *Gosudarstvennyi biudzhet i biudzhety soiuznykh respublik, 1966-1970 gg.* (Moscow, 1972), pp. 36, 62.

29. *Narkhoz 1974*, pp. 42-43.

30. Ibid., p. 728.

31. Ibid., p. 730.

32. Ibid., p. 731.

33. *Narkhoz Ukraine 1974*, p. 20.

34. V. N. Zhurikov and V. I. Solomakhin, *Spravochnik po oplate truda v kolkhozakh* (Moscow, 1973), p. 9.

35. L. Ia. Gorelik, *Problemy ekonomiki truda v sel'skom khoziaistve* (Moscow, 1971), p. 60.

36. *Narhosp 1973*, p. 398; *Narkhoz 1973*, p. 605.

37. Akademiia Nauk UkRSR, *Natsional'nyi dokhod Ukrains'koi RSR* (Kiev, 1963), p. 251.

38. N. Grebenchenko, "Nekotorye voprosy sovershenstvovaniia planirovaniia fonda neproizvodstvennogo potrebleniia v soiuznoi respublike," *Ekonomika Sovetskoi Ukrainy* (1969): no. 4, 74.

39. Schroeder and Severin, op. cit., p. 646.

5

WATER POLLUTION
Craig ZumBrunnen

INTRODUCTION

Long before the industrialization drive during the Soviet era, the eastern Ukraine had become a major center of heavy industry: coal, ferrous metallurgy, and inorganic chemicals. As a result of the rapid industrialization of the Ukraine since 1928, these industries have expanded prodigiously. Concomitantly, new branches of Ukrainian industry have been developed and urbanization has been rapid. All of these activities potentially generate water-pollution problems of varying qualitative and quantitative degree. Although the industrial and urban development of the Ukraine has necessarily been ecologically detrimental to the vegetation, wildlife, soils, air, and waters of the Ukraine, space permits only an attempt to assess the negative impact of Ukrainian economic development upon one crucial natural resource: fresh water.

The international scholarly community has focused considerable effort on a search for political, economic, and technological explanations and solutions for such "externality problems" as air and water pollution. Although any explanatory model of resource and environmental management problems and decision making must take appropriate cognizance of political, social, and economic inputs, the very fact that the existence of environmental pollution cuts across ideological, political, social, and economic boundaries strongly supports the

The support of the Ford Foundation; the Institute of Comparative Studies at the University of Washington, Seattle; the U.S. Environmental Protection Agency; and the employees of VNDIVO at Kharkiv is gratefully acknowledged.

hypothesis that environmental pollution of air and water resources in more explicable in terms of the common evolution of industrial-technological processes than it is in terms of political or economic ideology. Air resources, especially, are mobile and "dynamically" resist efforts to impose ownership rights, regardless of the ideological or economic institutions of the landscape over which they move.

Even surface waters —our major concern here—because of their fluidity and linkages with the global hydrologic cycle, are difficult to "own" except in the case of relatively small lakes, where an individual, group, organization, or government may effectively assume ownership of the lake water by owning the surrounding land. In England, fishing rights constitute a surrogate form of water ownership and function with some degree of success in controlling water-pollution levels.[1] In some sense, the Soviet use of more stringent water-quality standards for lakes and stretches of rivers having sport or commercial fishing importance is implicitly at least a weak form of a water property right. Nonetheless, by its very physical nature, water exemplifies a "free good." Accordingly, both Western market and Soviet command economies have serious difficulties in trying to institutionally "internalize" the costs of water pollution. By themselves, differences in ideology and legal, political, and economic institutions are far more efficacious in explaining differences between American and Soviet resource management practices and problems for land, timber, mineral, and fossil-fuel resources than they are for the "free good" resources: air and water. Nevertheless, some Ukrainian-Soviet institutional shortcomings in water resource management will be noted.

Partially because of the seemingly international polemical debate over which social order is "least worst," only a comparatively modest amount of research has attempted to treat Soviet ecological problems from a both spatial and a quantitative perspective. This paper has two primary objectives. The first is to evaluate the surface-water endowment of the Ukraine. The second is to present an operational procedure for regionally (oblast level) and quantitatively estimating the water pollution potential* of the Ukraine and to compare the mapped results of three estimated water-quality parameters both within the Ukraine and between the Ukraine and other regions of the USSR.[2] Unfortunately, the obligatory use of regional rather than point-source raw data in the analyses obscures many serious Soviet water-quality problems that exist on a smaller or local scale. Contaminated zones along the Dnister, Dnieper, Sivers'kyi Donets', and other Ukrainian rivers and the Black Sea and Azov Sea coastal areas are hardly visible at the regional scale used here. Thus, in order to become

---

*The word "potential" is used here because the estimating procedure estimates only the quantity of effluent being generated, and not that actually being discharged.

acquainted with some of the details of actual Ukrainian water-pollution problems, the interested reader is referred to two articles that present a number of empirical case studies of water-pollution problems within the combined Black Sea-Azov Sea drainage basins.[3] A secondary task is to cite briefly some of the critical institutional shortcomings of water-quality management in the Ukraine.[4]

Before beginning the discussion of the pollution-estimating procedure, we must take note of the surface-water endowment of the Ukraine, since the severity of pollution problems depends on the relationship between the volume (and qualitative composition) of effluent discharged, on the one hand, and the assimilative capacity of the receiving water body, on the other. Although temperature and turbulence influence the latter, river discharge (or the volume of water in a given lake or reservoir) is the chief determinant of assimilative capacity.

THE SURFACE-WATER ENDOWMENT OF THE UKRAINE

The Soviet Union ranks first in the world in terms of the total volume of surface and underground river flow ($4,412$ km^3/year).[5] Nevertheless, the Soviet Union, with 17 percent of the earth's land surface, has only 11 percent of the earth's fresh water.[6] To make matters worse, the freshwater resources of the country are very unevenly distributed. Approximately 80 percent of total water resources are located in the sparsely populated northern and eastern portions of the country. For example, the Urals, western Siberia, eastern Siberia, and the Far East contain 73 percent of the country's freshwater supplies, but represent only 60 percent of total land area and have only 11 percent of the total population. The Ukraine, on the other hand, with 4.7 percent of the freshwater resources of the country (including the Danube), represents a relatively modest 2.7 percent of the territory but serves as a home for 19 percent of the USSR's total population. Thus, while on average the Ukraine has a higher total river discharge per unit area (3.46×10^5 m^3/km^2) than the national average (2.10×10^5 m^3/km^2), only four economic regions of the country have lower figures on total river discharge per capita. The respective values for the Ukrainian SSR, the Central European region, the Moldavian SSR, the Armenian SSR, and the Central-Chernozem region are 4,420, 4,250, 3,160, 3,160, and 2,790 m^3/person/year. Surprisingly, the availability of water in per capita terms in the five arid Central Asian republics ranges from 9,310 m^3 in Kazakh SSR to 31,200 m^3 in the Turkmen SSR. The national average is 19,300 m^3/person/year (34,500 m^3/urban resident/year), with the highest figure being for the sparsely settled Soviet Far East (307,500 m^3/person/year).[7] Hence, in terms of total runoff per capita, the Ukraine has only 23 percent of the national average.

Within the Ukraine the relatively poor overall freshwater endowment with respect to human population is further exacerbated by a pronounced skewness in the geographical distribution of water supplies. For example, except for the Dnieper River, which transects the Ukraine, the republic is practically without large rivers of national consequence. Only the Dnieper, the lower Desna, and short stretches of the Southern Buh and Dnister are navigable. Furthermore, of the total average flow of fresh water in the Ukraine (209.0 km^3/year), only 23.9 percent (or 49.9 km^3/year) originates within the republic, while the remaining 76.1 percent (159.0 km^3/year) originates beyond the republic's boundaries.[8]

For present purposes we are more concerned with total runoff per urban resident, as urban wasteloads constitute the major point sources of water pollution. The annual Ukrainian average is 8,000 m^3 of total river discharge per urban resident. However, the regional values of this index are not normally distributed. First, three of the most intensively industrialized oblasts of the Ukraine—and, for that matter of the whole union—Kharkiv, Donets'k, and Voroshylovhrad oblasts, have very low freshwater supplies in relation to their population, area, and demands for municipal and industrial water supplies. Second, with the exception of Chernivtsi Oblast, the Dnieper River flows through all the regions with high values. These two observations should be kept in mind when interpreting the results of the regional pollution-potential estimates.

In summary, then, by either Soviet or world standards the Ukraine is only modestly endowed with surface freshwater supplies. Moreover, at the regional level within the republic, the Ukraine suffers from the same geographical malady as the USSR as a whole does. In essence, there exists nearly an inverse relationship between the geographical distribution of freshwater supplies and the loci of municpal, industrial, and agricultural demands for clean, fresh water. This unfortunate culmination of physiographic and cultural evolution constitutes a very serious current and long-term problem for Soviet planners.[9] This problem, in turn, appears to serve as a convincing rationale for the gigantic river basin diversion schemes so long debated within the USSR. The fundamental implication of this adverse relationship is that the areas most in need of nature's "self-purifying" resource—fresh water—tend to be located in regions with low freshwater assimilative capacities.

METHODOLOGY FOR ESTIMATING
THE WATER-POLLUTION POTENTIAL
OF THE UKRAINE

Initial Limitations and Simplifications

Ideally, in order to assess the magnitude of the present Ukrainian water-pollution problems and the damage inflicted on the environment in physical and economic terms, one needs at least four types of data:

1. Quantitative and qualitative records from all municipalities and indus-trial enterprises discharging effluents into the republic's waterways

2. Water-quality data from the hundreds of hydrological monitoring points throughout the republic.

3. Hydrological data giving information about such parameters as average annual flow (in m^3/year or km^3/year) and seasonal fluctuations in discharge (m^3/sec.) for specific locations and/or regions

4. Relatively complete information pertaining to fish kills, outbreaks of water-borne infectious diseases, and capital investments in water purification and sewage purification facilities.

This ideal state of affairs, however, is not attainable for two major reasons. One is, of course, the paucity of published Soviet data. Of the four categories of data enumerated above, only the third—location-specific and regional river flow data—are published in a kind of comprehensive manner.[10] The other published data are scattered throughout a vast number of books, journals, and press releases. But even if quantitative and qualitative data of all Ukrainian municipal and industrial effluent loads were monitored, recorded, and available, the analysis of such quantities of data would pose a formidable human task. For example, during the Eighth Five-Year Plan (1966-70) alone, about 2,000 large industrial enterprises were put into operation—a sizable fraction of them in the Ukraine.[11] Hence, some limitations and simplifications are imposed on the study.

Water-pollution problems arise from at least four major sources: industrial effluents; domestic sewage; agricultural runoff from fields and livestock yards that contain pesticide residues, fertilizers, and fecal materials; and natural decomposition processes.

Agricultural and irrigational runoff are considered beyond the scope of this study, even though they probably constitute the major area sources of water pollution. Although unfortunate, this restriction has been necessary because no method seemed feasible for incorporating estimated agricultural and irrigational water runoff. Then, too, because of their small relative significance, natural decomposition processes have also been excluded. Although pollution can affect both surface water and groundwater, only surface-water pollution is considered here.

Other major simplifications are required because of the large number of measurable water-quality characteristics. The U.S. Geological Survey's data sheet for a water analysis lists nearly 100 different water-quality parameters.[12] There is no single characteristic that can provide a simple quantitative index of water pollution levels. Probably the best single measure of pollution is dissolved oxy-gen (DO), although biochemical oxygen demand (BOD) is a better measure of the waste load. Consequently, in addition to figures on the total effluent volume and thermal pollution, BOD loads have been estimated.

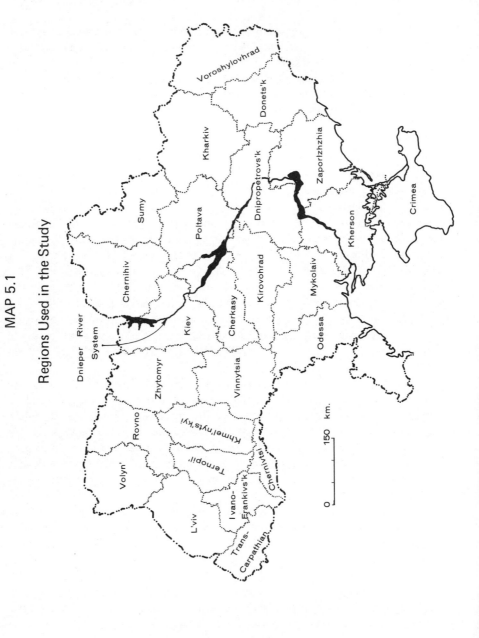

MAP 5.1

Regions Used in the Study

Dnieper River System

Voroshylovhrad
Donets'k
Kharkiv
Zaporizhzhia
Sumy
Poltava
Dnipropetrovs'k
Crimea
Kherson
Chernihiv
Cherkasy
Kirovohrad
Mykolaiv
Kiev
Vinnytsia
Odessa
Zhytomyr
Rovno
Khmel'nyts'kyi
Volyn'
Ternopil'
Chernivtsi
Ivano-Frankivs'k
L'viv
Trans-Carpathian

0   150   km.

Data Collection Units and Raw Data

Since neither point-source effluent data nor point-source industrial production data are available, the 25 Ukrainian oblasts (see Map 5.1) were adopted as the regions for data collection. These regions were imposed externally because they represent the smallest Ukrainian regions for which demographic, economic, and hydrologic data are available. Table 5.1 lists the original 28 variables and their respective units, which were collected and keypunched for each of the 25 regions for 1970. The data are for 1970 because, unfortunately, aggregation problems for key industrial sectors have increased significantly since then. More current data would necessitate the use of tenuous extrapolations for a number of regional production figures.

Two criteria were utilized to select the raw data variables. First, and most important, industrial commodities were selected that contribute the largest volume and most harmful effluent. Accordingly, metallurgy, oil refining, the pulp-and-paper industry, food industries, chemical industries, and domestic sewage were selected.[13] The second criterion is externally imposed—the variables selected are also those for which the most reliable, detailed, and disaggregated data are available. An earlier study included some synthetic chemical fiber and plastics industries.[14] However, these data were very crude and made only minor contributions to total effluent and BOD loads; consequently these industries have been excluded from the present study. Obviously, data for all of the 28 variables are not systematically published at the oblast level of aggregation. For a discussion of the details of the data-allocation problems and of certain regional data-estimating procedures, the reader is referred to two earlier works.[15]

Fortunately, there is a great deal of overlap between industrial activities that generate by far the largest proportion of potential water pollutants and those industries for which Soviet data are available. The notable exceptions are some branches of the chemical industry. On the other hand, inclusion of these activities because of their spatial distribution would serve only to highlight those regions that are most polluted, and would not substantially alter the overall regional patterns of potential pollution intensity that emergy from the pollution-estimating procedure.

Limitations of the Methodology

Although the objective is to arrive at a spatial and quantitative estimate of the volume of the industrial and domestic sewage effluent being discharged into the surface waterways of the Ukraine, the procedure employed here really produces only an estimate of the quantity of effluent being generated, rather than that actually being discharged. This is true because data (should they exist)

TABLE 5.1

Raw Data Variables and Units of Measurement

Variable Number	Variable	Unit
1	Area	km^2
2	Total runoff	m^3/yr
3	Local surface flow	m^3/yr
4	Urban population	1,000's
5	Paper production	m.t.
6	Cardboard	m.t.
7	Granulated sugar	m.t.
8	Meat	m.t.
9	Vegetable oil	m.t.
10	Butter	m.t.
11	Conserves	1,000 cans
12	Pig iron	1,000 m.t.
13	Steel	1,000 m.t.
14	Refined oil	1,000 m.t.
15	Potash fertilizer	1,000 m.t.
16	Thermal power	1,000 kw
17	Coal production	1,000 m.t.
18	Aluminum	1,000 m.t.
19	Cotton fabric	1,000 l.m.
20	Woolen fabric	1,000 l.m.
21	Linen fabric	1,000 l.m.
22	Silk fabric	1,000 l.m.
23	Lead smelting	1,000 m.t.
24	Zinc smelting	1,000 m.t.
25	Sulfuric acid	1,000 m.t.
26	Phosphate fertilizer	1,000 m.t.
27	Nitrogen fertilizer	1,000 m.t.
28	Synthetic rubber	1,000 m.t.

Note: m.t. = metric tons.
    l.m. = linear meters.
    kw = kilowatts.
    Data, data sources, and details of certain regional data-estimating procedures are available from the author.

concerning the actual discharge of waste water, waste-water recycling, and the percentage of the various contaminants intercepted and removed by sewage-purification installations, on either a location-specific or an oblast basis, are not obtainable. Despite this limitation, it is believed that the procedure yields results that represent fairly accurately both the relative and the absolute magnitudes of the potential pollution intensity of the Ukraine.

A second unfortunate and unavoidable limitation is that the procedure considers only the potential pollution load generated within a given region; that is, no account is taken of the contribution an "upstream" region makes to the "downstream" neighboring region(s). This limitation cannot be avoided because the data-collection units or regions do not conform to drainage basin boundaries. The estimated pollution levels within regions near the outlet of major rivers (such as Kherson and Odessa oblasts) may be biased downward because the pollutants that pass through them from upstream sources are not included. This limitation is lessened by the fact that thermal and BOD loads are degradable.

The procedure assumes constant effluent norms (discussed below) for any given pollution-generating activity. In reality, varying sizes and technologies of manufacturing plants may result in different effluent quantities and qualities per unit of production for any given commodity. Moreover, the norms represented in Table 5.2 are not all derived from Soviet sources. Because of this, the estimates of the total effluent and BOD indexes may be more reliable than the thermal ones. In any case, the use of non-Soviet norms may bias the polluting estimates downward rather than upward.

Finally, the limitations cited above, together with those arising from the need to estimate certain regional production figures, make necessary one major qualification in the interpretation of the results of the analysis. Although the legends on the regional water-quality maps (Maps 5.2-5.5) have the ranges of their respective water-pollution intensity indexes expressed in ratio form, these values should be interpreted with caution. In other words, the actual values may be used only to indicate the relative order of magnitude of the respective pollution indexes and an ordinal scale of intensity.

The Estimating Procedure

The method employed in the study is straightforward and uncomplicated. Industrial production output data and population data were multiplied by their appropriate effluent norms. "Industrial production output data" refer to the annual regional production figures of various industries measured in physical units (metric tons/yr). "Population data" simply refer to census data for the number of urban inhabitants of any given territorial unit (see Table 5.1). An industrial "effluent norm" is defined as the average volume of waste water

TABLE 5.2

Waste Water Effluent Coefficients Used in the Analysis

Variable	Total Effluent (m^3/ton)	Thermal Effluent (°C)	BOD (gm/m^3)
Urban population	73*	0	250
Paper	350	9	345
Cardboard	400	9	345
Sugar	12.7	5	2,300
Meat	7.9	5	1,780
Vegetable oil	15 (est.)	5	3,048
Butter	54.2	5	136
Conserves	0.284 m^3/case	5	1,120
Pig iron	200	5.55	41
Steel	200	5.55	41
Refined oil	50	5.55	100
Potash fertilizer	250 (est.)	2.24	0
Thermal power	0	1,290 m^3/kw/yr at 7.2 °C.	0
Coal	1.4	0	600
Aluminum	1,400	5.55 (est.)	41
Cotton	275	10	600
Wool	583	10	3,748
Linen	250 (est.)	10	600
Silk	250 (est.)	10	400
Lead smelting	1,000 (est.)	5.55	41
Zinc smelting	1,000 (est.)	5.55	41
Sulfuric acid	123	2.24	480
Phosphate fertilizer	250 (est.)	2.24	50
Nitrogen fertilizer	250 (est.)	2.24	480
Synthetic rubber	2,050	2.24	78

Note: Underlining represents coefficients taken from Soviet sources.

*Cubic meters/person/year.

Sources: Urban population—I. A. Ivanov, "Vodosnabzhenie i kanalizatsiia gorodov SSSR," *Vodosnabzhenie i sanitarnaia tekhnika* (April 1970): 18; B. S. Levine, ed. and trans., *USSR Literature on Water Supply and Pollution Control,* VI (Washington, D.C.: U.S. Public Health Service, 1964), 29, 42-43, 146, 199; Iu. V. Voronov and T. A. Kariakhina, "Novye issledovaniia v oblasti biologicheskoi ochistki stochnykh vod," *Gorodskoe khoziaistvo Moskvy* (October 1966): 47.

Paper—Levine, loc. cit.; U.S. Environmental Protection Agency, *The River Basin Model: An Overview* (Washington, D.C.: U.S. Government Printing Office, 1971), pp. 63, 106-07; U.S. Department of the Interior, *Industrial Waste Profile (IWP),* no. 3 (Washington, D.C.: U.S. Government Printing Office, 1967), p. 26.

Cardboard—Levine, loc. cit.; U.S. Environmental Protection Agency, loc. cit.; *IWP,* loc. cit.

Sugar—Nelson L. Nemerov, *Liquid Waste of Industry: Theories, Practices, and Treatments* (Reading, Mass.: Addison-Wesley, 1961), pp. 91, 264, 351-52, 436, 438, 442-45,

454-55, 477, 494, 497, 503; U.S. Environmental Protection Agency, loc. cit.; Levine, loc. cit.

Meat—Levine, loc. cit.; U.S. Environmental Protection Agency, loc. cit.; *IWP* (1967): no. 8, 2-5.

Vegetable oil—U.S. Environmental Protection Agency, loc. cit.; Nemerov, loc. cit.

Butter—*IWP* (1967): no. 9, 17; U.S. Environmental Protection Agency, loc. cit.

Conserves—*IWP* (1967): no. 6, 33; U.S. Environmental Protection Agency, loc. cit.

Pig iron—V. Fomin, "By Way of Raising the Question: Bodies of Water Are not Bottomless," *Current Digest of the Soviet Press* (*CDSP*) (Feb. 7, 1968): 27; *IWP* (1967): no. 1, 17, 20-22, 55; U.S. Environmental Protection Agency, loc. cit.

Steel—Vasili Parfenov, "How Much Does a Gallon of Water Cost?" *Soviet Life* (August 1966): 7; D. Armand, *Nam i vnukam* (Moscow, 1966), p. 61; M. Loiter, "Economic Measures in the Rational Utilization of Water Resources," *Problems of Economics* (July 1968): 43; *IWP* (1967): no. 1, 17, 20-22, 44; U.S. Environmental Protection Agency, loc. cit.

Refined oil—Levine, loc. cit.; N. T. Kuznetsov and M. I. L'vovich, "Multiple Use and Conservation of Water Resources," in W. A. D. Jackson, ed., *Natural Resources of the Soviet Union: Their Use and Renewal* (San Francisco: Freeman, 1971), p. 22; Levine, op. cit., III, p. 238; I. V. Komar, "The Exchange of Matter 'Nature-Society-Nature' and Some Problems of Optimization," *Soviet Geography: Review and Translations* (*SGRaT*) (November 1970): 718; *IWP* (1967): no. 1, 17, 20-22, 55; Nemerov, loc. cit.

Potash fertilizer—U.S. Environmental Protection Agency, loc. cit.; and *Inorganic Fertilizer and Phosphate Mining Industries—Water Pollution Control* (Washington, D.C.: U.S. Government Printing Office, 1971), pp. 94-95, 99.

Thermal power—Armand, loc. cit.; N. G. Ovsiannikov, *Vodnye resursy—nashe bogatstvo* (Moscow, 1968), pp. 6, 9; A. G. Bannikov and N. A. Gladkov, "Okhrana prirody—delo vsego naroda," *Priroda* (February 1961): 5; U.S. Department of the Interior, *The Cost of Clean Water*, I, *Summary Report* (Washington, D.C.: U.S. Government Printing Office, 1968), p. 31.

Coal—Komar, loc. cit.; Levine, VI, loc. cit.

Aluminum—B. S. Abramov, "Skrytye istochniki zhizni," *Priroda* (July 1963): 26; Ia. Grushko, "Life and Problems of Science: Mismanagement According to Rules," *CDSP* (Oct. 12, 1966): 33; *IWP* (1967): no. 1, 17, 20-22, 55; U.S. Environmental Protection Agency, *The River Basin Model*, loc. cit.

Cotton—Kuznetsov and L'vovich, loc. cit.; U.S. Environmental Protection Agency, *The River Basin Model*, loc cit.; Levine, VI, loc. cit.; Voronov and Kariakhina, loc. cit.

Wool—Nemerov, loc. cit.; U.S. Environmental Protection Agency, *The River Basin Model*, loc. cit.

Linen—U.S. Environmental Protection Agency, *The River Basin Model*, loc. cit.; Levine, VI, loc. cit.

Silk—U.S. Environmental Protection Agency, *The River Basin Model*, loc. cit.; Levine, VI, loc. cit.

Lead smelting—Kuznetsov and L'vovich, loc. cit.; *IWP* (1967): no. 1, 17, 20-22, 55; U.S. Environmental Protection Agency, *The River Basin Model*, loc. cit.

Zinc smelting—Kuznetsov and L'vovich, loc. cit.; *IWP* (1967): no. 1, pp. 17, 20-22, 55; U.S. Environmental Protection Agency, *The River Basin Model*, loc. cit.

Sulfuric acid—Levine, VI, loc. cit.; Theodore Shabad, "News Notes," *SGRaT* (March 1972): 187; U.S. Environmental Protection Agency, *The River Basin Model*, loc. cit.

Phosphate fertilizer—U.S. Environmental Protection Agency, *The River Basin Model*, loc. cit.; and *Inorganic Fertilizer and Phosphate Mining Industries*, loc. cit.

Nitrogen fertilizer—Loiter, loc. cit.; Kuznetsov and L'vovich, loc. cit.; U.S. Environmental Protection Agency, *The River Basin Model*, loc. cit.

Synthetic rubber—Kuznetsov and L'vovich, loc. cit.; Abramov, loc. cit.; U.S. Environmental Protection Agency, *The River Basin Model*, loc. cit.; Nemerov, loc. cit.

119

per metric ton of the particular industrial product (for instance, 50 m³ of waste water/ton of oil refined). The "domestic effluent norm" refers to the average volume of waste water produced per urban resident per year.

Similarly, an "industrial BOD norm" refers to the average amount of BOD produced during the industrial processing of a given amount of product, expressed as grams or kilograms of BOD per ton of product. This norm may also be defined in terms of the average amount of BOD contained in 1 m³ of effluent produced as a result of any particular industrial process. Since in this case the "industrial effluent norm" will already have been employed, the "BOD norm" is expressed in gm/m³ of waste water. The total annual BOD load for a given region, therefore, may be expressed in kilograms. The "domestic BOD norm" is defined as the average amount of BOD produced per urban resident per year (gm/person/year). In this study, the norms for BOD have all been converted to grams per cubic meter of effluent.

"Thermal effluent norms" are composed of two coefficients. The first is simply the volume of water required for cooling per physical unit of output. More important is the quantity of heat energy, measured in kcal/m³ of water coolant, that the cooling process adds to the "thermal" effluent. For example, if during the cooling process the water temperature is raised one degree centigrade, then 1,000 kcal/m³ have been added to the cooling water. Hence, the second "thermal effluent norm" can be expressed as the seasonal average (positive) temperature deviation, in degrees centigrade, of the thermal discharge from the ambient temperature of the incoming water. Thus, to obtain an estimate of the thermal-pollution load generated by the production of one ton of steel, one simply multiplies the first thermal effluent coefficient by the second.

For this analysis, however, the second coefficient has been adjusted (if necessary) so that the total thermal load measured in kcal/yr for industry j of region i could be computed simply by multiplying the total annual effluent volume of industry j of region i by the adjusted coefficient.

Some additional comments need to be made about the thermal-pollution parameter. As Table 5.2 reveals, not every effluent-generating activity included in this analysis is a thermal polluter. Neither coal cleaning nor domestic sewage has been considered as a thermal polluter. Although fossil-fuel and nuclear power plants are by far the greatest contributors to thermal water pollution, their effluents have not been included in the derivation of "total effluent" loads by region. In Table 5.2 the row labeled "Thermal power" has both the coefficient for the volume of thermal effluent per unit of output ($1,290 \text{ m}^3 \text{kw}^{-1} \text{yr}^{-1}$) and the temperature deviation norm (7.2°C.). The former coefficient takes into account the average volume of coolant required per kilowatt of generating capacity per hour and the annual average number of actual hours of power generation. Finally, it has been assumed that the thermal-power industry does not contribute to regional BOD loads.

Data Manipulation and Generation

The data manipulation subroutines of the PSTAT statistical package were utilized to generate three new matrixes from the original 25 × 28 raw data matrix. These matrixes were named total effluent 1970, total thermal 1970, and total BOD 1970. The raw data matrixes were first modified so that the annual production output data were expressed in units equivalent to their respective effluent norms—that is, the individual variable columns were multiplied by the appropriate power of ten to convert to metric tons (per year). The textile industry variables, numbers 19-22 (see Table 5.1) were multiplied by the appropriate coefficients to convert linear meters of fabric (per year) into tons of fabric (per year).

One of these modified raw-data matrixes (1970 data) is represented on the left-hand side of Figure 5.1. Columns of variables 4 through 28 of the modified matrix were multiplied by their respective "total effluent norms" (see Table 5.2) to produce columns 4 through 28 of the "total effluent matrix." Variables 29 through 31 (Figure 5.1) were generated as follows. Columns 4-28 (excluding column 16) were totaled to obtain variable 29. The remaining two variables were obtained simply by dividing variable 29, the estimated annual effluent generated within a given region, by the total runoff and local surface flow of the region, respectively. These last two variables served as the raw input for two different univariate regionalizations (discussed below).

The data manipulation outlined above was repeated to produce the total BOD 1970. However, for reasons mentioned earlier, columns 4-28 of the "total effluent 1970" matrix were used for obtaining the "total BOD 1970" matrix. Accordingly, columns 4 through 28 of the BOD matrix were obtained by multiplying columns 4 through 28 of the "total effluent 1970" matrix by their respective BOD "effluent norms."

In each of the cases, three variables directly analogous to variables 29, 30, and 31 of the "total effluent matrix" were generated. The final matrix produced was for thermal pollution. The procedure used to generate it was essentially the same as for the two matrixes above.

From these calculations six mappable indexes of potential pollution intensity, by region, emerge directly from the three matrixes (that is, variables 30 and 31 of each matrix). These six "hydrologic" indexes represent estimated potential concentrations of effluent, BOD, and thermal wastes in the water bodies of any given region. It should be noted, however, that all are expressed in quantities per cubic meter of water per year. Thus, in the case of BOD and thermal wastes, which degrade with time, the calculated indexes are higher than one would expect at any given time.

Of these six calculated indexes, only four were selected for final mapping:

FIGURE 5.1

Raw Data Matrix Modified and Total Effluent Matrix

Regions i i = 1 → 25	Raw Data Matrix Modified Variables j for Region i j = 1 → 28				Total Effluent Matrix* Variables j for Region i j = 1 → 31				
R_1	$V_{1,1}$	$V_{1,2}$	$\ldots\ldots$	$V_{1,28}$	$E_{1,4}$	$E_{1,5}$	$\ldots\ldots$ $E_{1,28}$	$V_{1,29}$.	$V_{1,31}$
R_2	$V_{2,1}$	$V_{2,2}$	$\ldots\ldots$	$V_{2,28}$	$E_{2,4}$	$E_{2,5}$	$\ldots\ldots$ $E_{2,28}$	$V_{2,29}$.	$V_{2,31}$
$\ldots$	$\ldots$	$\ldots$	$\ldots$	$\ldots$	$\ldots$	$\ldots$	$\ldots$	$\ldots$	$\ldots$
R_i	$V_{i,1}$	$V_{i,2}$	$\ldots\ldots$	V_{ij}	$E_{i,4}$	$E_{i,5}$	$\ldots\ldots$ $E_{i,28}$	$V_{i,29}$ ..	V_{ij}

Where: $V_{i,29} = \sum\limits_{j=4}^{28} E_{ij}$ = total volume of effluent for Region i

$$V_{i,30} = \frac{V_{i,29}}{V_{i,2}} = \frac{\text{total effluent for Region i}}{\text{total runoff for Region i}}$$

$$V_{i,31} = \frac{V_{i,29}}{V_{i,3}} = \frac{\text{total effluent for Region i}}{\text{local surface flow for Region i}}$$

$E_{ij} = 0$ for j = 16

and $E_{ij} = V_{ij} \times N_j$

for i = 1 → 25

    j = 4 → 28,

and where N_j = the "total effluent norm" for variable j.

*Variables 1–3 are the same as those of the raw data matrix modified and are not illustrated here.

> effluent (1970)/total runoff
> effluent (1970)/local surface flow
> thermal (1970)/total runoff
> BOD (1970)/total runoff.

Only one of the three pollution parameters expressed in terms of local surface flow was selected for mapping because, if any of these indexes had been mapped and compared with their appropriate parameter in terms of total runoff, a consistent pattern would have emerged. Essentially, regions along the Dnieper would be placed in higher or "worse" categories in terms of local surface flow than in terms of total runoff. Because of this consistency and because total runoff seems to be a more meaningful hydrologic parameter, the other two pollutants/local surface flow indexes were not mapped.

It is now appropriate to discuss the significant spatial and quantitative aspects of the four mapped indexes of Ukrainian water-pollution potential.

MAPPED RESULTS OF THE ANALYSIS

The discussion of the four mapped indicators of estimated water pollution potential is divided into three sections, dealing in turn with effluent volume, thermal pollution, and BOD. Again it should be stressed that the mapped indexes are based upon estimates of the total pollutants prior to any treatment, although they are thought to be accurate representations of the relative intensity of actual pollution. Although it was not previously mentioned, before generating the "total effluent" matrix, oblast coal production was reduced to the fraction that receives cleaning.[16] Also, the total volume of industrial effluent in each region was reduced by 20 percent to take account of industrial waste-water recycling and pollution-abatement effects.[17] This reduction represents a refinement over previous works[18] and affects both the total effluent and BOD indexes, but not the "thermal," ones which were calculated by multiplying the appropriate thermal effluent norms by the columns of the total effluent matrix prior to the 20 percent reduction.

Total Estimated Effluent

In index for 1970 effluent volume in terms of the total runoff is represented by Map 5.2. It should be noted that this index is expressed in terms of potential concentration. Thus, values greater than 1.00 mean that the volume of effluent exceeds the annual volume of total runoff of a given region. In such situations industrial and domestic surface-water users are "recycling" their own and others' waste water.

MAP 5.2

Concentration of Effluent in Total Runoff
(m^3/m^3)

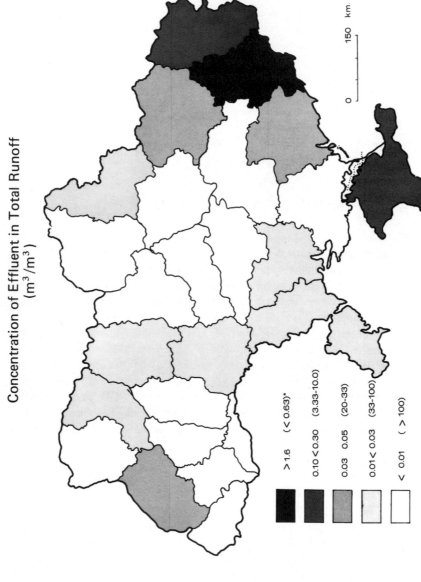

>1.6	(< 0.63)*	
0.10 < 0.30	(3.33–10.0)	
0.03 0.05	(20–33)	
0.01< 0.03	(33–100)	
< 0.01	(> 100)	

150 km.

Note: Figures in parentheses are dilution factors.

It is not very surprising that the highest value coincides with the major industrial region—Donets'k Oblast. In fact, compared with an earlier parallel study utilizing 137 regions encompassing the entire USSR, Donets'k Oblast emerged as the worst "potential" pollution region of the entire country, followed by Cheliabinsk Oblast in the Urals, Karaganda Oblast in Kazakhstan and Lipetsk Oblast in Central European Russia. All four regions have modest freshwater supplies coupled with concentrations of heavy industry. In the purely Ukrainian context, only Donets'k, Voroshylovhrad, and Crimea oblasts fall into the "very serious potential" pollution category of having less than a tenfold effluent dilution capacity (expressed in terms of the total surface flow of any given region).

A recent Soviet article indicates that the total volumes (without taking treatment into account) of effluent discharged into Ukrainian receiving waters in 1966 were 42.90 km^3 and 59.00 km^3, respectively.[19] This investigation arrives at a total effluent volume of 59.94 km^3 for 1970. Of this total quantity, thermal power coolant contributed 30.09 km^3, and other municipal and other industrial discharges 29.85 km^3, assuming a 20 percent reduction by recycling. The Soviet figures probably refer to the discharges effluent volumes after recycling has been taken into account. The same source claims that in 1966 only 14.90 km^3, and in 1973 only 13.60 km^3, of effluent were disposed of without treatment.[20] In other words, during this seven-year period, the proportion of the Ukrainian-generated sewage subjected to treatment prior to discharge increased from 65 percent to 77 percent. While these claims appear impressive, the treatment process—with a few notable exceptions—involves only primary or mechanical treatment, which is far more effective in removal of suspended solids than BOD. Thus, the previously mentioned 20 percent reduction incorporated into both the total effluent and BOD indexes mapped for this study seems quite realistic.

Furthermore, the effluent concentration values (in terms of total runoff) estimated in this study and the earlier works are consistent with the Soviet long-range perspective of estimated regional sewage dilution factors. In fact, the calculated values are considerably lower than the Soviet long-range perspectives for some watersheds.[21]

If the total estimated regional effluent volumes are expressed in terms of their potential concentration in the local surface flow, some striking changes emerge (see Map 5.3). First, all regions in the three highest categories would potentially be suffering from serious pollution levels if no "upstream" inflow were available to help dilute the local waste loads. Second, the greatly diminished assimilative capacity of the Dnieper when only local surface flow is considered places several of the regions through which it traverses in high potential pollution categories—especially Dnipropetrovs'k and Zaporizhzhia oblasts.

MAP 5.3

Concentration of Effluent in Local Surface Flow
(m^3/m^3)

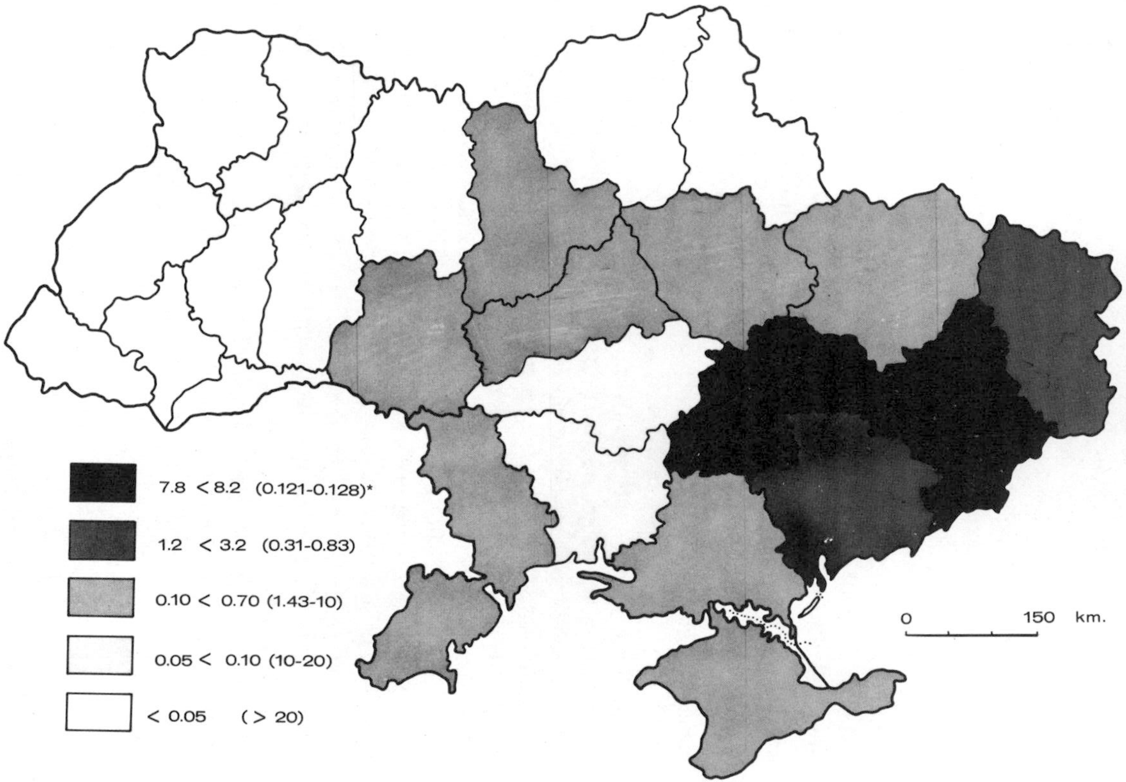

	7.8 < 8.2 (0.121-0.128)*
	1.2 < 3.2 (0.31-0.83)
	0.10 < 0.70 (1.43-10)
	0.05 < 0.10 (10-20)
	< 0.05 (> 20)

150 km.

0

Thermal Pollution Index

The thermal pollution index values represented in Map 5.4 are expressed in units equivalent to the rise in water temperature, measured in degrees centigrade, that would occur if all the thermal wastes were introduced into a given region's surface-water bodies. For example, the total estimated annual thermal waste of Donets'k Oblast would be sufficient to raise the temperature of the region's total annual volume of runoff by 23 degrees centigrade—assuming, hypothetically, that no evaporation or heat transfer to the atmosphere occurred, that the specific heat remained equal to 1.0, and that no phase changes occurred. Donets'k Oblast, in fact, has the highest regional thermal-pollution index of the entire USSR.

If all the thermal effluent were discharged directly into the Ukraine's bodies of water, serious thermal-pollution problems would probably exist within all regions in the two highest mapped classes: Donets'k, Kharkiv, Voroshylovhrad, and Crimea oblasts. The Crimea is made into a potential "hot spot" primarily as a result of its well-developed food-processing industries (such as fruit, vegetable, and fish canning) and its very low freshwater supply. The results of this investigation suggest that the southeastern Ukraine and Crimea may have serious thermal-waste problems unless wet and dry cooling towers have already been built on a massive scale.

The BOD Index

The production of BOD is highly correlated with urban population, food-processing industries, petroleum refining, paper making, and textile manufacture. At the union scale, however, the regional BOD/total runoff index values are not always strongly and positively correlated with the regions having high BOD-generating activities. For example, the European north is the major pulp-and-paper-producing area of the USSR; however, the relatively high runoff in this area damps down the BOD/total runoff values. The Volga and Dnieper rivers have a similar impact upon the food, petroleum, textile, fertilizer, and chemical industries within their respective watersheds, especially within their lower reaches. Hence, regions with major metallurgical industries and low runoff densities (total runoff of region i/area of region i) have the highest BOD/total runoff indexes. Although metallurgical industries have low BOD/m^3 of effluent concentrations, their tremendously large absolute effluent volumes result in massive absolute BOD quantities. Hence, Donets'k, Cheliabinsk, and Karaganda oblasts have the severest potential BOD contamination problems. Within the Ukraine, Crimea and Voroshylovhrad oblasts join Donets'k as potentially serious centers of biological contamination.

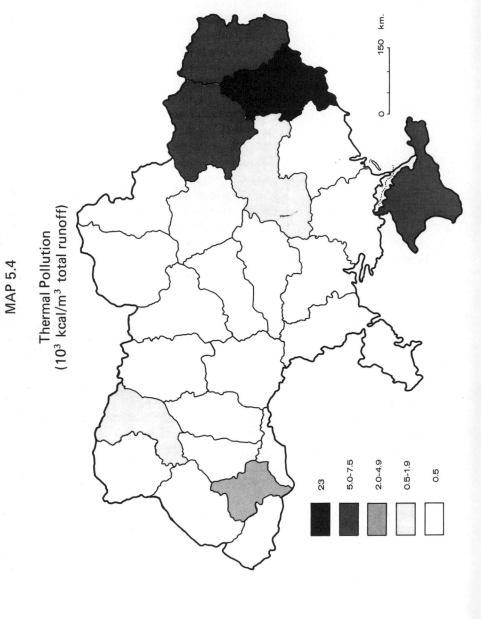

MAP 5.4

Thermal Pollution
(10^3 kcal/m^3 total runoff)

23

5.0-7.5

2.0-4.9

0.5-1.9

0.5

150 km.

0

MAP 5.5

Concentration of BOD in Total Runoff
(gm/m^3)

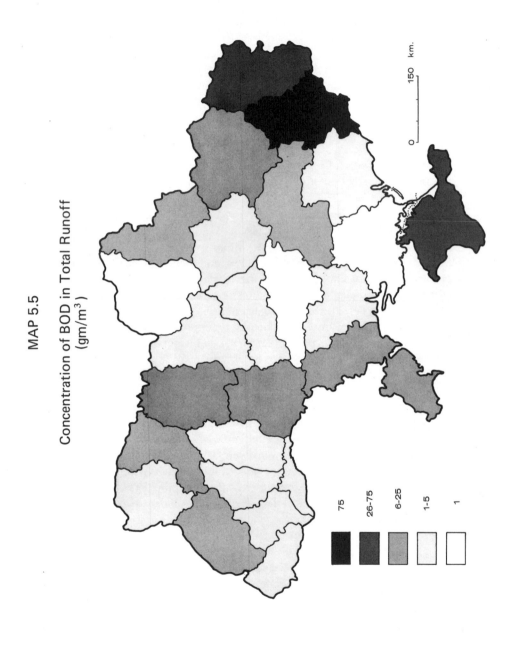

■	75
■	26-75
▨	6-25
□	1-5
□	1

150 km.

Summary of the Analysis
and Comparison of the Ukraine
with Rest of the USSR

By considering only a few industries and the Ukrainian urban population, it has been possible to arrive at several indexes and maps that illustrate fairly well an estimate of the Ukrainian water-pollution potential on a regional scale. But the question could be asked: How do these water-pollution "potential" indexes for the Ukraine compare with those of the rest of the USSR?

At the union scale, utilizing the same methodology as outlined here and 137 regions, the estimating procedure reveals six major pollution problem areas. In descending order of intensity they are the southeastern Ukraine (potentially the most intensively polluted region of the country by far); the Urals, especially Cheliabinsk Oblast; Tula, Lipetsk, and Moscow oblasts in Central European Russia; Andizhan, Fergana, Namangan, and Tashkent oblasts in Uzbekistan; Minsk, Mogilev, and Vitebsk oblasts in Belorussia; and the Kuznetsk Basin (Kemerovo Oblast).[22] These areas are those most often cited by Soviet sources as having serious pollution problems. The pollution potential is high in these six problem areas not only because of the existence of major polluting enterprises within them, but also because these regions are all rather poorly endowed with freshwater supplies. Hence, this analysis implicitly points out the general inverse geographical relationship between water supply (regardless of whether it is expressed as $m^3/km^2/yr$ or $m^3/person/yr$) and water demand. Accordingly, one can see the powerful underlying rationale for many of the Soviet Union's water management policies and practices, especially the grandiose water-diversion schemes.[23]

Thus, at the union level the four oblasts of the southeastern Ukraine— Dnipropetrovs'k, Voroshylovhrad, Zaporizhzhia, and especially Donets'k— constitute potentially the most severely polluted region of the entire country. At the same time, the remaining twenty-one Ukrainian oblasts would have to be considered as currently having low pollution potentials, with the possible exception of the Crimea, which has an intermediate position. Even here, however, the potential despoilation of the surface freshwaters of the Crimea would be rather low, since most of the pollution-generating activities probably discharge their wastes directly into the Black Sea. The numerous empirical examples of Black Sea and Azov Sea coastal pollution support this interpretation.[24]

Because, as stated previously, more than 75 percent of the total average flow of fresh water in the Ukraine originates beyond the republic's borders, another question that might be asked is whether the Ukraine, as a result of the spatial pattern of centrally planned Soviet economic development, has evolved, even inadvertently, into a "cesspool" for the industrial and municipal waste loads discharged into the "upstream" sections of rivers that eventually traverse the Ukraine. In order to evaluate the plausibility of this interpretation, the total estimated effluent volumes, BOD loads, and thermal wastes of all other Soviet regions that serve as even partial watersheds for Ukrainian rivers were totaled and added to their respective estimated quantitites for the Ukraine as a whole. These regions include the Moldavian SSR, Brest, Gomel', Minsk, Mogilev, and Vitebsk oblasts of the Belorussian SSR, and Smolensk, Briansk, Belgorod, and Kursk oblasts of the RSFSR.

The regions beyond the republic contribute only 10.2 percent of the total combined potential effluent volume, 14.0 percent of the total combined BOD load, and 22.5 percent of the total combined potential thermal discharge in terms of heat content. Because both BOD loads and thermal wastes degrade down-stream (rivers do not remain "hot" for long), the two latter percentages exagger-ate the potential organic and thermal pollution of Ukrainian bodies of water from sources external to the republic. At the same time, one of the most polluted water basins of the entire country—the Sivers'kyi Donets' Basin, receives the vast majority of its harmful contaminants from the Ukraine and discharges them into the Don River of the RSFSR. Thus, this analysis does not support the idea that the Ukraine serves as a cesspool for other regions of the USSR.

Finally, the empirical case studies referred to early in this paper indicate that in terms of actual pollution problems, Donets'k, Voroshylovhrad, and Dnipropetrovs'k oblasts are some of the worst regions, if not the worst, of the entire country. Eutrophication problems have developed within shallow bays of the Dnieper River reservoirs. In addition to several severely contaminated Don-bass rivers, other foci of serious contamination exist along sections of the Dnister, Southern Buh, Dnieper, and Inhulets' (drains the regions surrounding the iron and steel center of Kryvyi Rih) rivers. Moreover, more than 200 coastal loci of the Black Sea and Azov Sea coasts have been identified as suffering to varying degrees from the deleterious impact of municipal and industrial waste discharges. At the same time, examples of remedial and preventive actions in the Ukraine are not uncommon.[25]

CONCLUSION

This author has written elsewhere about Soviet institutional deficiencies with regard to water-quality management. An interested reader can find relevant detail there and in the work of Marshall Goldman.[26] At this time the recently discovered fact that water users, if they are not the initial withdrawer of the water, do pay a nominal fee for water use should be acknowledged. However, since the large users of water, such as major industrial firms, commonly have their own water-supply system, they may have little incentive to conserve on its use. Second, although an elaborate set of water-quality norms exist, the fines levied for violating them serve as highly ineffective pollution deterrents, com-pared with the high monetary and nonpecuniary rewards for "fulfilling the plan."

This comparison is pertinent because it is often possible to achieve plan targets at small cost by violating the weak legal sanctions against stream and lake pollution.

Furthermore, the record of enforcement of maximum permissible concentration norms has been at best inconsistent. Identifying a culprit is made difficult by the fact that the Soviet Union and the Ukraine have "instream" water-quality standards rather than qualitative and quantitative standards for the discharge of effluents.

At this juncture it seems that the Ukraine and the USSR have two important theoretical water-quality management advantages over the United States. First, the centralized control over the economy allows for the adoption of the ecologically rational basin-management concept. In fact, for water-management purposes the entire country is already divided into 102 river-basin inspectorates whose role is to monitor the quality of the water within their respective jurisdictions.[27] Second, at least in theory, the central control of the economy could, if the leadership so decided, translate itself into a crash program or campaign to improve water quality.

Given the long history of suppressed consumer demand in the USSR, however, such an allocation of scarce resources appears most improbable. On the other hand, during the 1971-75 Five-Year Plan, a total of 2.1 billion rubles was allocated for pollution-control measures in the USSR.[28] Reportedly about 1 billion rubles of this amount was invested in water-pollution control efforts in the Ukraine. In fact, between 1962 and 1972, while capital expenditures for development of the Ukrainian economy increased by 170 percent, the volume of capital investment in water-pollution control projects increased by 320 percent.[29] In 1972 the annual expenditures for treating industrial sewage in the Ukraine amounted to 269 million rubles (where operating expenditures equaled 125 million rubles), the value of treatment facilities equaled 1.2 billion rubles, and the so-called "coefficient of economic effectiveness of capital investment" equaled 0.12 (or $125 + 0.12 \times 1,200 = 269$ million rubles). At the same time, the economic benefit from these expenditures in terms of the elimination or abatement of pollution damages has been estimated to be 9.1 rubles per ruble of pollution-control expenses.[30]

Unlike the U.S. Environmental Protection Agency's 1983 zero-discharge objective, Soviet planners and engineers consider instream self-purification an economically and ecologically rational use of surface waters. Accordingly, the economic benefits of self-purification processes in the Ukraine for 1970 and 1973 have been estimated at 4.85 and 5.12 billion rubles, respectively. These "natural" benefits significantly exceed those estimated for the work of artificial sewage-treatment facilities in the same two years by 2.40 and 1.92 billion rubles.[31] Thus, to a very considerable extent nature's healing powers are still being employed in the Ukraine (and the USSR in general) to soothe the ecological wounds inflicted upon the local aqueous environment by human economic activity.

In summary, on the basis of this and previous investigations, the Soviet and Ukrainian experience with respect to water-quality management compares quite closely with what one might expect of a poor or developing nation (regardless of its institutions). This conclusion stems directly from the Soviet leadership's emphasis on rapid economic growth. Hence, the USSR—and the Ukraine within the USSR—have taken an exploitative path in developing natural resources, like that of the United States or Japan. The pilot project of the All-Union Scientific Research Institute for the Protection of Waters (VNDIVO) to develop and construct a computer-automated pollution-control system on a 75-km. stretch of the Sivers'kyi Donets' River certainly symbolizes a change in resource consciousness,[32] but perhaps a change dictated by a history of neglect of water-resource management practices. Paradoxically, it seems that only as a nation becomes richer do (or can) its priorities undergo a relative change of emphasis from production and consumption of material goods and energy to protection, enhancement, and enjoyment of the physical environment. Hope exists that the USSR has embarked on this journey toward greater ecological awareness and concern over its share of the world's free yet priceless good—clean water. Nevertheless, in the short run the average Soviet consumer seems more than willing to ingest a bit of dirty Volga or Dnieper water in order to purchase a clean new Volga (or Moskvich or Zaporozhets') automobile.

NOTES

1. J. H. Dales, "The Property Interface," in Robert Dorfman and Nancy S. Dorfman, eds., *Economics of the Environment* (New York: Norton, 1972), pp. 308-22.

2. Comparison between the Ukraine and the rest of the USSR is based upon the results of two studies by Craig ZumBrunnen, "A Spatial and Quantitative Estimate of the Water Pollution Generating Potential of the Soviet Union: A First Approximation," *Discussion Paper* no. 40 (Columbus: Department of Geography, Ohio State University, December 1973); "An Estimate of the Impact of Recent Soviet Industrial and Urban Growth upon Surface Water Quality," in W. A. Douglas Jackson, ed., *Soviet Resource Management and the Environment* (Columbus, Ohio: AAASS Press, forthcoming).

3. Craig ZumBrunnen, "Water Pollution in the Black and Azov Seas," in Frederick Singleton, ed., *Environmental Misuse in the USSR* (New York: Praeger, forthcoming); and "VNDIVO and Ukrainian Water Quality Management," *Annals of the Ukrainian Academy of Arts and Sciences in the United States* 13 (1977) (forthcoming).

4. A fuller treatment of this topic is available in Craig ZumBrunnen, "Institutional Reasons for Soviet Water Pollution Problems," *Proceedings of the Association of American Geographers* (April 1974): 105-08.

5. *Osobennosti prirodnykh i meliorativnykh uslovii zony nedostatochnogo uvlazheniia i problemy pereraspredeleniia stoka rechnykh basseinov po territorii SSSR* (Moscow, 1969), pp. 44-45.

6. M. I. L'vovich, *Mirovye vodnye resursy i ikh budushchee* (Moscow, 1974), pp. 264-70.

7. L. A. Kul'skii and V. V. Dal', *Problemy chistoi vody* (Kiev, 1974), pp. 78-79.

8. Ibid., p. 78.

9. For example, see *Osobennosti prirodnykh* (entire volume); S. P. Kovalenko, I. D. Pichakhchi, and T. T. Strel'tsova, "Printsipy korrektirovki perspektivnogo razmeshcheniia proizvoditel'nykh sil v predelakh vodnogo basseina po vodookhrannomu faktoru," *Problemy okhrany vod* (1974): no. 5, 3-12.

10. M. S. Protas'ev, ed., *Vodnye resursy i vodnyi balans territorii Sovetskogo Soiuza* (Leningrad, 1967).

11. *Pravda (P)*, March 25, 1971.

12. David Keith Todd, ed., *The Water Encyclopedia* (Port Washington, N.Y.: Water Information Center, 1970), pp. 309-10.

13. Iu. P. Belichenko, "Vsesoiuznye soveshchanie po ispol'zovaniiu i okhrane vodnykh resursov," *Gidrotekhnika i melioratsiia* (September 1968): 112.

14. ZumBrunnen, "A Spatial and Quantitative Estimate," pp. 9-14.

15. Ibid., pp. 9-21; ZumBrunnen, "An Estimate," pp. 6-28 of draft form.

16. For data on the fraction of coal receiving cleaning, see Ian F. Elliot, *The Soviet Energy Balance* (New York: Praeger, 1974), p. 172.

17. The 20 percent value for the Ukraine was provided by personnel of VNDIVO during discussions held at Kharkiv in May-July 1975.

18. ZumBrunnen, "A Spatial and Quantitative Estimate"; ZumBrunnen, "An Estimate."

19. L. Chernega, "Otsenka ekonomicheskoi effektivnosti kompleksa vodookhrannykh meropriiatii na Ukraine," *Ekonomika Sovetskoi Ukrainy (ESU)* (June 1976): no. 6, 56.

20. Ibid., pp. 54-56.

21. For a comparison with Soviet regional long-run expected sewage dilution factors, see A. I. L'vovich, "Problemy okhrany rek vodoemov ot zagriazneniia stochnymi vodami," *Izvestiia Akademii Nauk SSSR, seriia geograficheskaia* (1963): 3, 37.

22. ZumBrunnen, "A Spatial and Quantitative Estimate" (entire article); and "An Estimate"

23. V. Molchanov, "At the Project Map: Turning Northern Waters Southward," *Current Digest of the Soviet Press (CDSP)* (July 27, 1971): 12, 31-32.

24. ZumBrunnen, "Water Pollution"

25. ZumBrunnen, "VNDIVO . . . Management" (entire article); and "Water Pollution" (entire article).

26. ZumBrunnen, "Institutional Reasons," pp. 105-08; Marshall Goldman, *The Spoils of Progress* (Cambridge, Mass.: MIT Press, 1972).

27. Iu. P. Belichenko and Iu. G. Iegorov, "Ob opyte raboty organov vodnogo nadzora," *Problemy okhrany vod* (1974): no. 5, 13.

28. V. P. Lozanskii, "Okhrana vod ot zagriazneniia—vazhnaia funktsiia vodnogo khoziaistva," *Problemy okhrany vod i ispol'zovaniia vod* (1973): no. 2, 5.

29. L. Chernega and N. Kudenko, "Otsenka ekonomicheskoi effektivnosti vodookhrannykh meropriiatii," *ESU* (August 1972): no. 8, 54.

30. Ibid., pp. 55, 57.

31. Chernega, "Otsenka ekonomicheskoi," p. 56.

32. ZumBrunnen, "Ukrainian Water"

6

MANPOWER

F. Douglas Whitehouse
David W. Bronson

INTRODUCTION

> We have done and will do everything so that the national economy
> of all-union republics will grow and develop, so that their culture—
> nationalist in form, socialist in content—will flourish still further[1]
>
> Nikita Khrushchev

A basic tenet of Soviet thought is that all republics gain from their socialist union, and Soviet authorities seem intent on not publishing data that would disprove this dogma. Since manpower is fundamental to economic development, examining regional demographic data is essential in answering the question of gain or loss. Moreover, despite incompleteness, ambiguity, and distortion, the data from the all-union censuses of 1959 and 1970 provide a wealth of information on the Ukraine and Ukrainians.

As indicated above, Soviet authorities take care not to provide clear examples of regional inequalities. Moreover, the vast differences between the underdeveloped southern republics and unionwide norms are conspicuously absent in the Ukraine. Census materials for 1959 and 1970 indicate that by most broad-based demographic, educational, and labor force yardsticks, the Ukraine is near the national average. Where interrepublic differences appear, it is often difficult to ascertain the causes: tradition, natural conditions, historical accident, and local attitudes, as well as policies set in Moscow, intermingle to cause disparities in manpower growth, training, and employment.

The Muslim attitude toward the role of women, for example, has strongly influenced educational levels and labor force participation in some southern republics. These attitudes have tended to be contrary to Moscow's policy and have hindered economic development. Similarly, the demographic impact of

World War II on the Ukraine must be recognized. The Ukraine suffered disproportionately high losses during the war, particularly among men who were in their early twenties. Educational attainment, birth rates, and size of labor force have all been adversely affected by the war.

Primarily using census data, this article examines the size, structure, education, and movement of Ukrainian manpower. These data, when compared with similar information for other republics and union norms, lead to certain conclusions as to the relative strengths and weaknesses of the Ukraine. The evidence provides clues to whether manpower problems are hindering or facilitating development relative to other regions.

SIZE AND COMPOSITION OF POPULATION

In 1970, the population of the Ukraine was 47.1 million persons, nearly 20 percent of the total Soviet population (see Table 1). The Ukraine ranked second among the republics in population size, behind the RSFSR, and had 3.5 times the population of third-ranked Kazakhstan.

The first thing that appears from examining the 1970 census is that when speaking of the Ukraine, we are not speaking only of Ukrainians. Ukrainians, according to the census, numbered 40.8 million in 1970; 35.3 million of them (86.5 percent) resided in the Ukraine, 3.3 million (8.2 percent) lived in the RSFSR, and 933,000 lived in Kazakhstan.[2] The remaining 1.3 million Ukrainians are scattered among the other 12 republics.

Ukrainian development has not been impeded by serious overpopulation or—as in the case of Kazakhstan—great underpopulation. With approximately 80 persons per square kilometer, the Ukraine is the third most densely populated republic in the USSR. Its population density is more than 10 times that of the RSFSR and 15 times that of Kazakhstan.[3] The Ukraine approximates Illinois in population density.

Regional identity and development have been fostered by the long history of the Ukraine, a common language, and a dominant native population that in 1970 constituted 75 percent of the total population of the Ukraine. In contrast, Kazakhs accounted for less than 33 percent of the total population of Kazakhstan in 1970.[4] Russians, the second most important nationality group in the Ukraine, accounted for 20 percent of the population in 1970, compared with almost 19 percent in 1959. The remaining 5 percent of the population of the Ukraine is non-Ukrainian and non-Russian—a polyglot group that includes almost 800,000 Jews, nearly 400,000 Belorussians, about 300,000 Poles, more than 100,000 Greeks, a like number of Romanians, 30,000 gypsies, and a host of other nationality groups. If share of population is an indicator of Russian domination— a simplistic proposition at best—the Ukraine falls about midway between

TABLE 6.1

Distribution of the Ukraine's Population by Nationality, 1970

Nationality	Hundred Persons
Total	47,126.5
Ukrainians	35,283.9
Russians	9,126.3
Jews	777.1
Belorussians	385.8
Poles	295.1
Moldavians	265.9
Bulgarians	234.4
Hungarians	157.7
Romanians	112.1
Greeks	106.9
Tartars	76.2
Armenians	33.4
Gypsies	30.1
Yugoslavs	26.5
Others	215.1

Source: (TsSu), *Itogi vsesoiuznoi perepisi naseleniia 1970 goda* (Census), (Moscow, 1972), p. 152.

Kazakhstan, where 42 percent of the population was Russian in 1970, and Armenia, where Russians constituted less than 3 percent of the population.

URBANIZATION

Urbanization is generally considered a key indicator of development. Although the share of the Soviet population in cities has risen from less than 20 percent in 1913 to nearly 67 percent, the Soviet Union remains well behind most developed nations in the urbanization process. It was not until the 1960s that the population of the cities exceeded the rural population. The process of urbanization in the Ukraine mirrors the national trend, reflecting the transition from an agrarian economy to an industrialized state. Nevertheless, the fact that nearly 50 percent of the Ukrainian population still lives in the countryside attests to both the dependence of the USSR on the Ukraine for food and the inability of agriculture under the Soviet system to develop into a modern capital-intensive sector, as has occurred in the developed West.*

EDUCATION

Although the qualitative aspects of manpower resources have been recognized at least since Adam Smith, increasing attention has been devoted in recent years to the importance of education in the development process.[5] Indeed, herculean efforts have been made by Edward Denison and others to quantify education's contribution to economic growth.[6]

Soviet leaders have long counted on education as a key element in transforming the USSR from a backward agrarian economy into a modern industrialized state. Compulsory universal schooling has gradually extended the length of formal education. A versatile system of formal factory training and night and part-time secondary and higher education has supplemented the full-time program. The merits and deficiencies of the Soviet education process are beyond the scope of this chapter. Undeniably, education has been an important element in Soviet development, but by Western standards average educational attainment remains low.

Data on education could provide a clue to Soviet policy toward nationalities. If, for example, educational opportunities were unevenly distributed among the republics, they would tend to foster development most in republics where education was favored. The population in other republics would suffer from such discrimination. Of course, in viewing the data one must bear in mind the possible influence of ethnic attitudes toward education.

In reviewing census materials, we concentrated on higher education, since this is probably the key to development. The census provides education data on two major categories: the entire population over 10 years of age with education, and the employed population over 10 years of age with education. Since most of the adult population is employed, it seems to make little difference which concept is used when making republic comparisons or measuring trends over time.

The differences in educational attainment between the Ukraine and the RSFSR, or between the Ukraine and the national average are generally small. For example, the share of the adult population with higher education in the

---

*At the beginning of 1974, the urban population in the Ukraine accounted for 58 percent of the total, while for the USSR this percentage was 60. The Ukraine ranked fifth in this respect, after Estonia, RSFSR, Latvia, and Armenia. See *Narkhoz 1973*, pp. 10-11.

TABLE 6.2

Number of Persons with Higher Education by Age Group, 1970
(per 1,000 persons 10 years of age and older)

	Total	20-29	30-39	40-49	50-54	55-59	60+
USSR	42	50	88	62	49	31	22
RSFSR	44	52	90	62	48	32	26
Ukraine	40	41	83	61	51	29	19
Belorussia	35	49	78	52	44	23	10
Uzbekistan	36	56	86	58	46	29	12
Kazakhstan	35	49	80	54	34	20	9
Georgia	73	74	124	127	119	86	46
Azerbaidzhan	44	58	85	84	73	54	24
Lithuania	35	52	77	50	26	19	9
Moldavia	29	39	67	41	30	19	12
Latvia	46	47	96	71	52	36	21
Kirgizia	35	54	82	57	40	21	9
Tadzhikistan	29	48	69	45	31	20	8
Armenia	57	70	105	109	105	77	33
Turkmenia	33	51	81	54	32	20	8
Estonia	47	57	105	67	38	28	18

Source: Census, III, pp. 6-29.

Ukraine was 4.0 percent in 1970, compared with the national average of 4.2 percent (see Table 6.2). Among the republics, the Ukraine ranked sixth in the share of adult population with higher education.

Examining these data by age groups—the percent of each population age group with higher education—provides some interesting, but largely not unexpected, insights. As expected, the share of university-trained persons declines in the older age brackets, reflecting the postwar policy of expanding higher education opportunities. For example, in most republics the share of university-trained persons in their forties is only about 67 percent that found in the 30-39 age group. Similarly, those in their late fifties with higher education form a much smaller group than those in their early fifties—reflecting the impact of World War II on the then university-age population.

A minor mystery is the fact that although the higher educational attainment in the Ukraine is fairly representative of the nation as a whole in nearly all age groups, the Ukraine ranks next to last among the republics in the share of population 20 to 29 years of age with higher education. This occurs largely among men: only 3.3 percent of males 20 to 29 years of age had a higher education in

TABLE 6.3

Number of Persons with Higher Education by Age Group, Urban and Rural, 1970
(per 1,000 persons age 10 or older)

	Total		20-29		30-39		40-49		50-54		55-59		60+	
	Urban	Rural	Urban	Rural	Urban	Rural	Urban	Rural	Urban	Rural	Urban	Rural	Urban	Rural
USSR	62	14	61	29	123	32	91	20	74	14	52	6	42	3
RSFSR	61	14	59	31	120	31	86	19	68	12	50	6	43	3
Ukraine	63	11	53	19	123	25	95	18	83	14	53	6	41	2
Belorussia	66	12	61	29	129	28	98	16	91	16	60	14	34	1
Uzbekistan	62	18	76	38	135	50	96	28	78	16	53	8	30	2
Kazakhstan	51	17	59	34	111	41	76	25	51	15	32	7	18	2
Georgia	121	27	110	32	193	50	191	55	180	46	144	25	97	8
Azerbaidzhan	70	14	76	26	132	31	121	30	104	21	83	11	47	2
Lithuania	61	8	70	20	118	21	86	10	53	4	31	3	25	2
Moldavia	66	11	63	23	142	27	100	11	79	5	57	3	40	1
Latvia	65	14	56	25	122	39	95	21	79	8	58	6	37	4
Kirgizia	58	19	69	40	129	47	94	28	67	16	39	7	21	2
Tadzhikistan	51	14	66	33	114	35	79	19	54	11	37	5	21	1
Armenia	82	16	88	25	148	32	149	38	144	33	113	19	55	3
Turkmenia	48	17	63	35	110	46	77	26	49	11	33	5	18	1
Estonia	63	18	66	34	127	53	87	22	56	7	44	6	32	4

Source: Census, III, pp. 30-77.

1970. Only in Moldavia is the share as small. In four republics—Uzbekistan, Georgia, Azerbaidzhan, and Armenia—the share is nearly twice as high as in the Ukraine. This anomaly seems to be explained, at least in part, in the disproportionately large share of part-time students in the Ukraine. Only about 40 percent of university students there are full-time, comparted with nearly 50 percent for the USSR as a whole. Many of the part-time students in the Ukraine apparently complete schooling in their thirties rather than their twenties.

Examining the census data of those with higher education by age and type of residence—that is, urban or rural—graphically illustrates the point that Soviet sociologists have long made about the relative disadvantage of rural residents in obtaining education. For the USSR as a whole, the share of adult population with higher education is about 4.5 times higher in urban areas than in the countryside (see Table 6.3). In the Ukraine the differential is 5.5 times. The Ukraine ranks fifth among the republics in terms of share of urban population with higher education. However, it falls into a next-to-last place tie with Moldavia in terms of rural population with higher education. Only one rural adult Ukrainian in 100 had higher education in 1970. Among those 60 years of age and over, only one rural Ukrainian in 500 had a university degree.

For approximately every 10 adult males in the USSR with a higher education there are about seven females in the same category. This ratio holds in the Ukraine as well. Among the republics Ukrainian men rank seventh in terms of higher educational attainment; Ukrainian women rank fifth (see Table 6.4). The role of women in the Ukraine—in terms of education—has risen far more sharply than that of men, in comparison with other republics. The ratio of men to women with higher education tends to be much higher in the older age groups than in the younger. For example, among those over sixty years of age, the share of men with higher education is nearly four times that of women. In the 30-39 age bracket, however, the ratio is only about 1.2 men for every woman with higher education.

Examining attainment of higher education by nationality reveals differences that are masked in the data given by republic. For example, the share of Ukrainians in the USSR with higher education is only about 75 percent as large as the share of Russians.[7] The census also shows that employed persons with a higher education have a tendency to work outside their native republic. For example, employed Russians with university educations constitute about 6.5 percent of all employed Russians in the RSFSR (see Table 6.5), while Russians in the Ukraine with higher education account for almost 10 percent of all employed Russians in the Ukraine. The same holds true for Ukrainians. The share with higher education is greater for those working in the RSFSR than for those working in the Ukraine. This probably reflects little more than occupational mobility—namely, the conscious policy of promoting mixing of one nationality with others.

TABLE 6.4

Number of Persons with Higher Education by Age and Sex, 1970
(per 1,000 persons age 10 or older)

	Total		20-29		30-39		40-49		50-54		55-59		60+	
	Men	Women	Men	Women	Men	Women	Men	Women	Men	Women	Men	Women	Men	Women
USSR	48	37	41	59	93	83	76	52	74	33	56	18	43	12
RSFSR	49	39	41	63	92	89	74	53	71	34	57	19	54	14
Ukraine	47	34	33	49	90	77	75	50	78	35	53	15	38	10
Belorussia	42	30	39	59	86	71	69	39	73	26	44	11	20	5
Uzbekistan	46	27	60	51	107	65	79	50	76	27	54	14	19	6
Kazakhstan	41	30	43	56	89	72	72	38	57	19	40	9	19	4
Georgia	83	65	62	85	129	120	144	113	176	82	146	50	78	25
Azerbaidzhan	57	33	61	55	107	64	109	61	120	43	103	24	47	11
Lithuania	38	32	40	63	81	72	62	41	40	17	33	10	16	5
Moldavia	34	26	33	45	77	58	52	33	42	20	31	11	21	6
Latvia	50	43	35	59	92	99	83	62	72	38	55	23	37	12
Kirgizia	42	29	48	59	95	70	73	43	64	25	40	10	16	4
Tadzhikistan	39	20	59	38	90	49	61	30	53	15	37	8	13	4
Armenia	66	50	62	78	115	95	132	87	164	65	132	42	55	18
Turkmenia	44	23	58	43	103	58	77	33	56	16	39	8	15	4
Estonia	52	43	47	68	101	110	79	58	55	26	46	16	37	10

Source: Census, III, pp. 6-29.

144

TABLE 6.5

Higher Education by Nationality, 1970
(per 1,000 employed)

	RSFSR	Ukraine
Russians	65	98
Males	65	100
Females	65	96
Urban	82	109
Rural	24	34
Ukrainians	94	47
Males	100	51
Females	85	43
Urban	114	76
Rural	38	18

Source: Census, IV, pp. 606, 618.

In terms of republic budget expenditures, students in the Ukraine and the RSFSR get roughly equal treatment. Republic budget outlays on education in the Ukraine were 58.4 rubles per person in 1970, compared with 30.9 rubles in 1960. Per capita expenditures on education were about 10 percent higher in the RSFSR, but the share of education expenditures in national income was slightly higher in the Ukraine. Education expenditures, however, also come from a number of sources outside the republic budget. Most important are expenditures from the union budget. The end use of these expenditures by republic is not known; they could be a means of favoring educational programs in some republics at the expense of others.

Despite the enormous efforts made by central authorities to raise educational levels in the Ukraine as well as in other republics, the fact remains that educational attainment is still very low by Western standards. This has probably impeded the introduction of new technology, particularly in agriculture, where educational levels are lowest. It has also impeded the transfer of labor from farms to cities, partly because farm labor lacks the skills needed by industry. To the extent that labor-saving techniques have been introduced in agriculture, a growing group of surplus unskilled farm workers has been created. Perhaps, recognizing this, Ukrainian planners have been developing small-scale, labor-intensive industries in rural areas to absorb these displaced farm workers.

GROWTH

Wide regional differences in population increase in the USSR reflect patterns of growth that are characteristic of the development process throughout much of the world. The lowest rates of growth have occurred primarily in the western republics, where urbanization is fairly well established and per capita income is relatively high. The Ukraine ranks among the slowest-growing republics; its population is only about 33 percent larger than it was in 1913, while most of the southern republics have doubled in size and the USSR as a whole is 50 percent again as large as it was in 1913. Even measured over the shorter run—between the 1959 and 1970 censuses—the Ukraine is marked by relatively slow growth (see Table 6.6).

The low rate of population growth stems from the low rate of natural increase and the lack of significant immigration, which has been so important to the growth of other republics, such as Kazakhstan.

Adverse demographic characteristics and falling fertility have led to a plummeting rate of natural population increase in the Ukraine. Between 1960

TABLE 6.6

Population Growth by Republic, 1959-70
(percent)

Republic	Percent
Tadzhikistan	46
Uzbekistan	45
Kirgizia	42
Turkmenia	42
Armenia	41
Kazakhstan	40
Azerbaidzhan	38
Moldavia	24
USSR	16
Georgia	16
Lithuania	15
Latvia	13
Estonia	13
Ukraine	13
Belorussia	12
RSFSR	11

Source: Narodnoe Khoziaistvo SSSR (Narkhoz) 1974 (Moscow, 1975), p. 9.

TABLE 6.7

Population of Working Age, 1959-2000
(million persons)

	Total Population	Working Age	Working Age as Percent of Total
USSR			
1959	208.8	119.8	57.4
1970	241.6	130.6	54.1
1980	266.3	154.5	58.0
1990	293.6	160.7	54.7
2000	316.7	172.3	54.4
Ukraine			
1959	41.9	24.9	59.4
1970	47.1	26.2	55.6
1980	50.3	29.2	58.1
1990	52.6	29.2	55.5
2000	53.6	29.3	54.7

Source: George Baldwin, *Projections of the Population of the USSR and Eight Subdivisions, by Age and Sex: 1973 to 2000*, Series P-91, no. 24 (Washington, D.C.: U.S. Department of Commerce, 1975), p. 17.

and 1973, birth rates declined 27 percent, death rates rose 35 percent, and the rate of natural increase fell to less than 0.5 percent per year.[8] In contrast, the national average is higher for birth rates and lower for death rates. In part, the declining birth rate in the Ukraine reflects fewer women in the prime child-bearing ages (20-34 years). Between the 1959 and 1970 censuses the number of women in this age group in the Ukraine declined 10 percent, while the total population of the Ukraine increased by 13 percent. Similarly, the rising death rate reflects an increasing share of older persons.[9]

According to a U.S. Department of Commerce study, if we assume that the gross reproduction rate will remain constant at the estimated 1972 level, current trend in Ukrainian birth rates and death rates will continue until the year 2000.[10] If Ukrainian population growth occurs according to this projection, as seems likely, it portends a stagnation in the size of the able-bodied population (according to Soviet definitions of "able-bodied"—males 16 to 59 years of age, females 16 to 54). The working-age population will increase by 3 million persons during the 1970s, but there will be virtually no increase in the working-age population from 1980 to the end of the century (see Table 6.7). This may hinder development of the much-neglected services sector of the economy, which tends to be labor-intensive. With virtually all the able-bodied population either working or attending school on a full-time basis, and with most working-age women already in the labor force, raising labor-force participation rates does not appear to be a way of maintaining current labor-force growth rates.

Faced with a probability of little or no growth in the Ukrainian manpower pool after 1980, Soviet leaders must increasingly turn to labor-saving methods to achieve economic growth. This will probably require an intensification of the effort to provide basic skills to all youths, particularly rural youths. In this regard, the program to provide universal secondary education will likely receive increasing emphasis.

MIGRATION

When the contributions of natural increase to total population growth are compared with the contributions of migration, it is apparent that migration played a relatively minor role in total population growth in the Ukraine between 1959 and 1970—only 18 percent of the growth in total population was due to an influx of people from other republics.[11] Migration, however, has been the chief factor in the growth of the urban population in the Ukraine. Between 1959 and 1970, the urban population increased by 6.5 million. The migration of rural residents to urban areas accounted for 3 million and the natural increase accounted for 2.5 million. The remaining 1 million was the result of the reclassification of rural settlements as cities. Thus, migration was a significant factor in the growth and development of the Ukraine, since urbanization is certainly one of the most important aspects of population change associated with modernization.

As an index of mobility, migration statistics for the two years prior to the 1970 census show that Ukrainians ranked sixth among the 15 major nationality groups—following the Russians, Belorussians, and the three Baltic nationalities. Five percent of all Ukrainians living in the USSR changed their place of residence during this period, compared with nearly 7 percent of the much larger Russian population. More than 50 percent of these movements, however, were intrarepublic transfers, the largest share of which were from rural to urban areas. Migration flows between the Ukraine and all other republics, on the other hand, were overwhelmingly urban to urban. The only exception to this pattern was the dominant migration of rural residents of the central Chernozem region—where the economy is predominantly agricultural—to the cities of the Ukraine.

The net result of the interrepublic transfers during 1968-70 was an influx of more than 30,000 people into the Ukraine, mainly from Central Asia, Kazakhstan, and the Transcaucasus. The bulk of individual transfers, however, occurred between the Ukraine and the RSFSR (see Table 6.8). In fact, more than 75 percent

TABLE 6.8

Net Change in Migration Between the Ukraine and Other Republics, 1968-70

	Out-migration to		In-migration from		Net Change (persons)
	Persons	Percent	Persons	Percent	
RSFSR	427,730	77.4	419,660	72.0	−8,070
Belorussia	23,699	4.3	22,260	3.8	−1,439
Uzbekistan	7,036	1.3	18,419	3.2	+11,383
Kazakhstan	47,700	8.6	65,711	11.3	+18,011
Georgia	3,468	0.6	8,356	1.4	+4,888
Azerbaidzhan	2,357	0.4	6,656	1.1	+4,299
Lithuania	3,609	0.7	2,261	0.4	−1,348
Moldavia	18,253	3.3	18,090	3.1	−163
Latvia	6,267	1.1	3,474	0.6	−2,793
Kirgizia	2,049	0.4	5,194	0.9	+3,145
Tadzhikistan	1,866	0.3	4,706	0.8	+2,840
Armenia	1,277	0.2	2,022	0.3	+745
Turkmenia	3,234	0.6	3,632	0.6	+398
Estonia	4,408	0.8	2,766	0.5	−1,642
Total	552,953	100.0	583,207	100.0	+30,254

Source: Census, VII, pp. 6-7.

of out-migration from the Ukraine went to the RSFSR and more than 70 percent of the in-migration into the Ukraine came from the RSFSR. That this transfer between the Ukraine and the RSFSR has been the trend for some time is suggested by the fact that the Russian population in the Ukraine grew by some 2 million persons between 1959 and 1970.

Of the remaining republics, the largest migration flows both into and out of the Ukraine have occurred with Kazakhstan, Belorussia, Uzbekistan, and Moldavia. Most of the in-migrants from these republics settled in urban areas— notably in the highly industrialized Donets'k-Dnieper region. Indeed, between 1968 and 1970 nearly 60 percent of all in-migrants from the RSFSR settled in urban areas of the Donets'k-Dnieper region, as did more than 50 percent of in-migrants from both Kazakhstan and Belorussia.[12]

The dominance of the urban-to-urban pattern of interrepublic migration suggests that many of the migrants entering the Ukraine have been skilled laborers and professionals. Indeed, a breakdown of the professional structure of in-migration into the Ukraine given in a recent study shows that the majority of migrants from the RSFSR, Kazakhstan, Belorussia, and Moldavia consisted of those employed in the service professions (health, education, science, culture, trade) and in transportation.[13] Although a similar breakdown of the professional structure of out-migrants is not available, it seems likely that a large share of these have been skilled laborers and professionals. This view is supported both by the urban-to-urban pattern of migration and by the fact, noted earlier, that employed Ukrainians living in the RSFSR have higher education levels than employed Russians living in the RSFSR.

It is not clear whether, on balance, this interrepublic migration has been a detriment or benefit to the Ukraine. On the one hand, if the bulk of in-migration has consisted of non-Ukrainians taking skilled jobs that would otherwise be held by Ukrainians, then the development of a skilled indigenous Ukrainian labor force may have been impeded. Moreover, such a situation would force the displaced Ukrainians to take less-skilled jobs or to migrate to other republics to utilize their skills. On the other hand, if in-migration has brought professional services to the Ukraine, raising the educational and skill levels of the labor force more rapidly than otherwise would have been the case, then the economic development of the republic has been enhanced. Because of the relatively low volume of recent interrepublic migration, the economic impact of these transfers has been negligible. During earlier periods, however—when, for example, educated farm youths were sent from the Ukraine to the virgin lands during the 1950s— there undoubtedly was some loss for the Ukraine.

IMPLICATIONS FOR THE LABOR FORCE

Turning to the economic use of the population, we see from the 1970 census that the Ukraine ranks fifth among the republics in the share of the population that is economically active. In 1970, more than 80 percent of employed persons in the Ukraine worked in the branches of "material production"; nearly 33 percent of the total were in agriculture and forestry. The "nonproductive" branches—health, education, science, and art—accounted for 12.5 percent of all employment (see Table 6.9). Contrasting 1970 employment in the Ukraine with that in the RSFSR shows that the Ukraine has a smaller share of employment in the nonproductive sector; a smaller share of employment in the nonagricultural branches of the productive sector; and a much larger share of employment in agriculture.

Although these findings suggest that the Ukraine is less developed than the RSFSR, the differences have narrowed since 1959. Moreover, with the exception of collective farms, the branch structure of the nonagricultural labor force in the Ukraine is a mirror image of that in the Russian Republic. In 1970, the share of the population classified as collective farmers in the Ukraine was more than twice the share in the RSFSR (see Table 6.10). Only in three southern republics— Tadzhikistan, Turkmenia, and Uzbekistan—has the rate of decline in collective

TABLE 6.9

Distribution of Employed Population,
Ukraine and RSFSR, 1959 and 1970
(percent)

	Ukraine		RSFSR	
	1959	1970	1959	1970
Total employed	100.0	100.0	100.0	100.0
In branches of "material production"	86.7	81.3	82.6	77.1
Industry, construction, transportation, communication	32.6	43.3	44.7	50.5
Agriculture, forestry	49.3	30.8	31.8	18.9
Trade, public dining, material technical supply	4.6	6.7	5.7	7.1
In "nonproductive" branches	12.2	18.3	16.0	22.6
Education, science, art, health	8.4	12.5	10.8	15.1

Source: Census, V, pp. 295-96.

TABLE 6.10

Collective Farmers as a Share
of Population, 1970

	Percent	1970 as Percent of 1959
Moldavia	49.6	73.4
Tadzhikistan	41.1	76.8
Turkmenia	37.2	88.4
Uzbekistan	34.0	79.8
Ukraine	30.3	73.7
Kirgizia	28.4	68.1
Belorussia	28.2	58.1
Georgia	28.0	63.6
Lithuania	26.2	60.5
Azerbaidzhan	24.5	57.8
USSR	20.5	65.3
Latvia	17.6	67.4
Armenia	17.1	45.6
RSFSR	14.3	59.0
Estonia	13.1	63.6
Kazakhstan	8.2	39.6

Source: Census, V, pp. 8-15.

farm population been slower than in the Ukraine. Although the lot of collective farmers has improved greatly in recent years, the kolkhoznik still ranks at the bottom of the economic and social ladder.[14]

In 1970 the Ukraine accounted for 25 percent of the total agricultural labor force in the USSR, 33 percent of the collective farmers, but only 20 percent of the agricultural specialists with higher or secondary specialized education. Because of the Ukraine's comparative advantage in agriculture, one would expect decision makers, at both the republic and the union levels, to promote education among the farmers in order to maximize this advantage. That, apparently has not been done. As noted earlier, the rural population of the Ukraine has less higher education, on average, than the USSR as a whole. Moreover, the differences in urban-rural education levels are considerably greater in the Ukraine than in the RSFSR.

One must ask why Soviet decision makers have failed to maximize the comparative advantage of the Ukraine through conversion of more collective farms to state farms. In part, the transfer of collective farmers to the state farm system would exacerbate the displacement of many collective farm workers with no readily employable skills, thus compounding the problem of excess rural labor. Perhaps more significant may be the leadership's decision to concentrate skilled labor in manpower-deficit areas, such as the New Lands. Indeed, the fact that Ukrainians living in rural Kazakhstan have a higher educational level than those living in rural areas of the Ukraine may reflect the decision to siphon off skilled labor from the already developed agricultural base in the Ukraine. This practice reflects the high priority placed on establishing a second grain-growing region to offset the periodic failures suffered in the European portions of the USSR.

To the degree that centrally imposed decisions regarding investment, income, and manpower have hindered agricultural development, the Ukraine has borne an unequal burden in the USSR. In particular, the prolonged imposition of the collective farm system in the Ukraine has probably caused a loss in personal incomes. Indeed, the average monthly wage of Ukrainians employed on state farms has been running roughly 5 percent below the national average. Similarly, collective farmers in the Ukraine consistently have earned less than the national average from the socialized sector of the farm (see Table 6.11). Moreover, there is a greater differential in the Ukraine between the earnings of collective farmers and state farmers than in the RSFSR or in the nation as a whole.

Earnings from private plots, which account for roughly 25 percent of collective farm family income, further widen the income gap between Ukrainian farmers and national norms. For example, M. I. Sidorova reports that in 1969, average earnings of collective farm families from private plot activity in the Ukraine were 95 percent of the national average.[15] In contrast, private plot earnings in Belorussia and Moldavia—republics contiguous to the Ukraine—were 119 percent and 113 percent of the national average, respectively.[16]

TABLE 6.11

Average Agricultural Earnings per Worker,
USSR, RSFSR, Ukraine, 1960-74
(rubles per month)

	State Farmers	Collective Farmers	Collective Farmers as Percent of State Farmers
USSR			
1960	53.8	28.4	53
1965	75.0	51.5	69
1970	101.0	74.8	74
1974	124.0	90.4	73
RSFSR			
1960	54.3	30.5	56
1965	76.2	50.2	66
1970	103.6	78.0	75
1974	129.5	96.5	75
Ukraine			
1960	51.8	23.7	46
1965	71.5	49.8	70
1970	95.7	66.6	70
1974	115.7	81.5	70

Sources: USSR—collective farmers, 1960, calculated from data in *Narodnoe khoziaistvo SSSR 1970 (Narkhoz)* (Moscow, 1971), pp. 382-83; 1965, 1970, 1974, calculated from data in *Narkhoz 1974*, p. 422; state farmers, 1960, *Narkhoz 1970*, p. 519; 1965, 1970, 1974, *Narkhoz 1974*, p. 562. RSFSR—collective farmers, 1960, calculated from data in *Narkhoz RSFSR 1970*, p. 267; 1965, 1970, 1974, calculated from data in *RSFSR v tsifrakh v 1974 godu* (Moscow, 1975), p. 65; state farmers, 1960, *Narkhoz RSFSR 1970*, p. 341; 1965, 1970, 1974, *RSFSR v tsifrakh v 1974 godu* (Moscow, 1975), p. 85. Ukraine—collective farmers, 1960, calculated from data in *Narodne hospodarstvo Ukrains'koi RSR 1970 (Narhosp)* (Kiev, 1970), p. 271; 1965, 1970, 1974, calculated from data in *UkRSR v tsyfrakh 1974* (Kiev, 1975), p. 71; state farmers, 1960, *Narhosp 1970*, p. 381; 1965, 1970, 1974, *UkRSR v tsyfrakh 1974*, p. 155.

However, to the extent that conversion from the collective to the state farm system would have increased the number of unemployable farm workers, the difference in average earnings between the two institutions would exaggerate the economic loss resulting from prolonged imposition of the collective farm system. On balance, the age, sex, and educational characteristics of the Ukrainian labor force seem to show that such a trade-off between incomes and employment has been prevalent in the economic development of the Ukraine.

NOTES

1. Quoted in Jaan Pennar, Ivan I. Bakalo, and George Z. F. Bereday, *Modernization and Diversity in Soviet Education* (New York: Praeger, 1971), p. 174.

2. TsSu, *Itogi vsesoiuznoi perepisi naseleniia 1970 goda* (*Census*), IV (Moscow, 1972), p. 13.

3. *Narodnoe khoziaistvo SSSR 1973* (Moscow, 1974), (*Narkhoz*), pp. 16-21.

4. *Census*, IV, p. 13.

5. See, for example, Frederick Harbison and Charles A. Myers, *Education, Manpower, and Economic Growth: Strategies of Human Resources Development* (New York: McGraw-Hill, 1964).

6. Edward F. Denison, *Accounting for United States Economic Growth, 1929-1969* (Washington, D.C.: Brookings Institution, 1974).

7. *Census*, IV, pp. 393-94.

8. *Narodne hospodarstvo Ukrains'koi RSR 1973* (Kiev, 1974), (*Narhosp*), p. 17.

9. *Census*, II, pp. 20-21.

10. George Baldwin, *Projections of the Population of the USSR and Eight Subdivisions, by Age and Sex: 1973 to 2000*, Series P-91, no. 24 (Washington, D.C.: U.S. Department of Commerce, 1975), p. 17.

11. F. Douglas Whitehouse, "Demographic Aspects of Regional Economic Development in the USSR," in V. N. Bandera and Z. L. Melnyk, eds., *The Soviet Economy in Regional Perspective* (New York: Praeger, 1973), p. 161.

12. *Census*, VII, pp. 79-80.

13. V. V. Onikienko and V. A. Popovkin, *Kompleksnoe issledovanie migratsionnykh protsessov* (Moscow, 1973), p. 119.

14. For details on economic progress of farm families, see David W. Bronson and Constance B. Krueger, "The Revolution in Soviet Farm Household Income, 1953-1967," in James R. Millar, ed., *The Soviet Rural Community* (Urbana, Ill.: University of Illinois Press, 1971), pp. 214-58.

15. M. I. Sidorova, *Vozmeshchenie neobkhodimykh zatrat i formirovanie fonda vosproizvodstva rabochei sily v kolkhozakh* (Moscow, 1972), p. 115.

16. Ibid.

7

MINERALS AND ENERGY
Leslie Dienes

INTRODUCTION

It has been a generally accepted proposition of modern economic thought that the secular trend of economic development leads to a declining share of natural resources in the production of current income. The recent abrupt change in the terms of trade for fuels and key materials has demonstrated the easy reversibility of the process in the short run, and possibly in the much longer run as well. Very properly, however, it has also been vigorously denied that a decline in this ratio (income from the resource sector to total income) would indicate the diminishing importance of that sector and its contribution to economic growth. By definition, the increasing complexity of an economy implies the addition of other types of production to that of natural resources; and this expansion may in large part be fostered by the efficiency of the resource sector itself.*

In market economies, most regions enter the commercial stage by exploiting some natural resource. For young regions tied to metropolitan centers, the crucial role of natural resources exploited in response to exogenous demand is explicitly embodied in the export-base theory. Since the late eighteenth century, perhaps down to World War I, the economic development of much of the

---

*Conversely, a continued high ratio may simply indicate inefficient production from this sector and/or this sector's inability to foster economic development within a region. See, for example, the comment by G. H. Dales to T. W. Schultz's article, "Connections Between Natural Resources and Economic Growth," in Joseph G. Spengler, ed., *Natural Resources and Economic Growth* (Washington, D.C.: Resources for the Future, 1961), pp. 16-19.

Ukraine approximated the contours of that model.* The Soviet Ukraine continues to be an open economy within the framework of a planned spatial system, bound to an outside center of decision making. However, it has been a mature region for some time, with human and capital resources as indigenous as its soil, climate, and mineral wealth. Not only has this made it much easier to develop a broad range of products with relatively small resource content for interregional export, but the growing local market has greatly expanded the role of region-serving activities. Under the Soviet system of planned production targets and allocated factor supplies, the export-base theory is certainly inappropriate to explain the mechanism of regional development. On the other hand, important features of this model—those related to regional specialization and comparative advantage— have found expression in a large body of recent Soviet literature. The speciali- zation or "export" sectors are said "to determine the place of a region in the national and international division of labor" and are claimed to be those "that make the most efficient use of natural and economic conditions for production of a commodity for the national and international markets."[1]

It is, therefore, appropriate to ask to what extent, through what locational linkages and stages of processing, do Ukrainian natural resources enter into the spatial economic system of the USSR today? If, from a region's point of view, good resources are identified by their ability to support a stream of nationally wanted products and to stimulate the development of industrial agglomerations through extensive locationally associated production linkages,[2] Ukrainian resource endowment in the past has been more than adequate. How adequate is

---

*This is far less true of the forest-steppe zone of the Right Bank Ukraine than that of the other regions. Without Bukovyna and Habsburg Galicia, the present-day Southwest Economic Region, largely corresponding to that zone, already had a population of some 6 million and a population density of 26 per square kilometer in 1851. Since then, popu- lation growth has approximated the natural increase for the rest of the Ukraine, implying an end to in-migration. Continued net capital inflow to spur the production and processing of sugar beets, the new "export" staple, is conceivable but not very likely. In-migration con- tinued, however, albeit in a much reduced fashion, into the Black Sea steppes of the Ukraine until the end of the century. For some four decades prior to the Soviet era, large labor and capital inflows were associated with the exploitation of the region's coal and iron ore resources, and in 1908-10 more than 40 percent of the fuel and 60 percent of the metal produced was transported out of the Ukraine to other regions of the empire. (From the eastern Ukraine alone, the share of interregional export was much larger still.) Data from J. W. Leasure and R. A. Lewis, *Population Changes in Russia and the USSR: A Set of Comparable Territorial Units* (San Diego: San Diego State College Press, 1966), pp. 12, 13, 29; J. W. Leasure and R. A. Lewis, "Internal Migration in Russia in the Late Nineteenth Century," *Slavic Review* (*SR*) (September 1968): 373-85; R. S. Livshits, *Razmeshchenie chernoi metallurgii SSR* (Moscow, 1958), pp. 112-32, esp. p. 129; and R. S. Livshits, *Razmeshchenie promyshlennosti v dorevolutsionnoi Rossii* (Moscow, 1955), pp. 232-71, esp. p. 242.

it now? Given the tendencies to gradual resource depletion and to increasing cost, at least in the mineral branches; given unavoidable, though planned, changes in the national demand mix and in the technology of production, can the resources of this republic continue to support substantial and efficient "export" sectors? At what cost can they be sufficiently expanded (and/or supplemented) to supply in the future the complex agglomerations and interlocking activities they have helped to generate? Is such expansion of the resource base in fact taking place?

This chapter examines these problems in the domain of fuel-energy and mineral resources and primary processing industries dependent on them. Analysis of these sectors alone is insufficient for any conclusion regarding a net economic gain or loss accruing to the Ukraine. However, it should help to illuminate the position and functional relationship of this republic in the Soviet economic system.

RESOURCE ENDOWMENT AND COMPARATIVE ADVANTAGE OF PRIMARY INDUSTRIES IN THE UKRAINE

Until the middle of the twentieth century, Ukrainian fuel and mineral resources were admirably suited to support a wide range of products of top priority for the national economy. Even more than under Sergei Witte, the new state under the Soviets demanded metals, heavy machines, and the power to run them. Military needs, together with the way that rigid central planning hampered gradual, timely shifts in industrial processes and in input and product mixes, prolonged uncontested reign of coal, iron, and traditional mineral chemicals in the USSR. The shift in the fuel balance and the advent of petrochemicals, synthetics, exotic metals, and cybernetics were badly delayed.

It is on the basis of coal, iron, and other traditional minerals, together with the products of its soils, that the Ukraine built up its "export base" and developed its economic specialization in the Soviet spatial system. For long the largest supplier of solid fuels, ferrous metals, heavy machines, and some chemical minerals, this "export base," however, is no longer sufficiently "modern" even in an economy still dominated by the "metal eaters" and "tonnage producers." The shift to petroleum fuels and more sophisticated synthetics has worsened the Ukraine's resource endowment.

Many years of emphasis on heavy, capital-intensive, and spatially inelastic branches of industry also created serious obstacles to diversification and the improvement of geographic balance within the republic (Map 7.1). As late as 1967, in only 4 of the 25 Ukrainian oblasts did industrial fixed assets per capita exceed the mean for the republic. In 11 oblasts, accounting for 30 percent of the population, the level of industrialization did not reach 60 percent of the Ukrainian average; and about 33 percent of the Ukraine's population fell in this

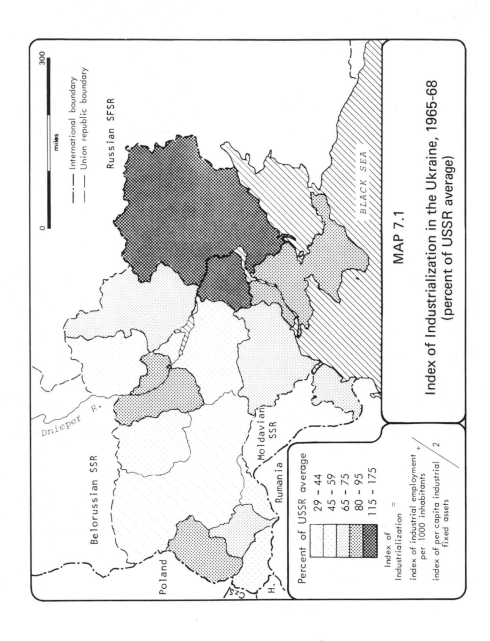

MAP 7.1

Index of Industrialization in the Ukraine, 1965-68
(percent of USSR average)

Percent of USSR average

29 – 44
45 – 59
65 – 75
80 – 95
115 – 175

$$\text{Index of Industrialization} = \dfrac{\text{index of industrial employment per 1000 inhabitants} + \text{index of per capita industrial fixed assets}}{2}$$

International boundary
Union republic boundary

Russian SFSR

BLACK SEA

Dnieper R.

Belorussian SSR

Moldavian SSR

Rumania

Poland

Czs.

H.

miles

0   300

category at the beginning of the 1960s.[3] Finally, this specialization has increased the region's fuel and energy needs to the point where its fuel output already appears insufficient to guarantee local demand and to achieve fuel autonomy. By 1970, net fuel export from the Ukraine, amounting to 18 million tons of standard fuel equivalent, or 7.3 percent of Ukrainian consumption plus inventories,[4] was composed almost entirely of coking coal and coke shipped abroad and to other regions of the USSR.* Excluding coking coal from the fuel mix, the Ukraine seems already to be a net importer of energy—and the deficit is increasing rapidly.[†]

The known mineral riches of the Ukraine, most of them exploited since tsarist times, have been well-suited to supplying the traditional products of heavy industry (Map 7.2). Though possessing but a tiny fraction of total probable coal reserves, the republic does boast 10 percent of all discovered reserves surveyed in any fashion (*zabalansovye zapasy*, or $A + B + C_1 + C_2$ categories), and 16 percent of all those in the industrial reserves category ($A + B + C_1$) whose contours, composition and quality have been determined in some detail.[5] Equally important is the fact that more than 18 percent of proved Ukrainian reserves are of prime coking quality, with another 40 percent being good gas coal, most of it suitable for coking with proper blending.[6] The Ukraine is richly endowed with ferrous ores and alloy metals. Industrial reserves ($A + B + C_1$) of iron ore, mostly in the great Kryvyi Rih-Kremenchuk Basin, account for 33 percent of all Soviet reserves. Despite many decades of exploitation, this basin also accounts for more than 20 percent of all high-grade ores (55-60 percent iron content), which require no beneficiation.[7] The Ukraine also has huge resources of refractory materials, rock salt, and by far the largest native sulfur deposits of the Soviet Union. Aside from the small Galician fields (gained after World War II), petroleum and natural gas finds are far more recent and have played but a minor

---

*International export of hard coal reached 20 million tons, and of coke, 4.2 million tons in 1970. *Vneshnaia torgovlia SSSR (VT) 1971*, pp. 27, 67, 68. Virtually all the coke comes from the Ukraine, which also accounted for 78 percent of all Soviet hard coal and 71 percent of coke export in 1970. P. V. Voloboi and V. A. Popovkin, *Problemy terytorial'noi spetsializatsii i kompleksnoho rozvytku narodnoho hospodarstva Ukrains'koi RSR* (Kiev, 1972), p. 177. Among the countries receiving hard coal from the USSR, one can easily identify those whose imports are mostly or entirely coking coal. In addition, the Ukraine was the chief supplier of coking coal to the blast furnaces of Lipetsk, with capacities reaching 4.2 million tons of pig iron in 1970. Since 0.81 tons of coke (or some 1.3 tons of coking coal) was needed to produce a ton of pig iron, the complex must have imported 5-6 million tons of Donbas coal. S. I. Detina, N. V. Obchinninskii, and O. T. Shakhovo, *Problemy razvitiia i razmeshcheniia proizvoditel'nykh sil Tsentral'no-Chernozemnogo Raiona* (Moscow, 1973), pp. 40, 84.

†According to a recent estimate of the Ukrainian Academy of Sciences, a deficit of 50 million tons of standard fuel equivalent was expected in 1975. Akademiia Nauk-Gosplan, *Ukrainskaia SSR. Ekonomicheskie raiony* (Moscow, 1972), p. 80.

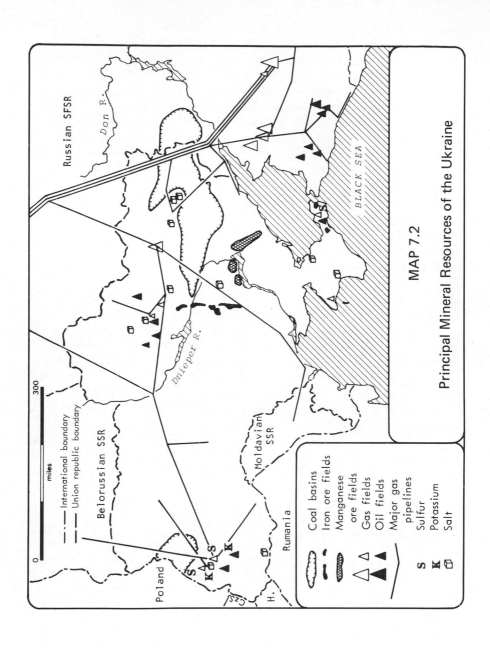

MAP 7.2

Principal Mineral Resources of the Ukraine

Coal basins
Iron ore fields
Manganese
  ore fields
Gas fields
Oil fields
Major gas
  pipelines
Sulfur
Potassium
Salt

role in the traditional specialization of the Ukraine. Their present and future significance will be treated later.

Production costs in the Ukrainian coal fields have always been high. Neither the Donbas, which accounts for 98 percent of Ukrainian reserves, nor the other small fields (opened in the 1950s) are blessed with favorable geological conditions. The seams are narrow, frequently faulted, and lit at great depth—67 percent of $A + B + C_1$ reserves (and more in the less certain categories) are found between 300 and 1,200 meters (Table 7.1). With the gradual depletion of upper seams, conditions are worsening (Table 7.2), and modernization cannot counteract the trend toward increasing cost. Because of their good location, however, the coal fields in the Ukraine have so far remained the cheapest suppliers of coal to the southwestern portion of the European USSR (south and west of the line joining Leningrad and Saratov), which contains half of the Soviet population and industry. Throughout the 1960s, Donets coal could be delivered in Moscow for the same cost as Kuzbas (Kuznetsk Basin) coal from open pits, assuming a 12.5 percent interest rate (that is, an eight-year recoupment period) on investment in production and transport. Kuzbas coal cost much more in Leningrad, the Baltic, and Belorussia; the two latter regions could also be supplied more cheaply from the small Volynian field of the western Ukraine. Varying the capital charge would change the watershed of coal delivery in the Moscow area, but would leave its basic contours essentially unchanged.*

Thanks to this locational advantage, the Ukraine long remained the largest fuel-producing region of the USSR. On the eve of World War II, its output in calorific units surpassed that of the vast RSFSR, and far outdistanced that of all other republics combined. As late as 1970, after decades of vigorous eastward push in Soviet economic development, the Ukraine still matched the share of the entire Asiatic USSR in primary energy supplies—a full 20 percent of the Soviet total. But since the early 1960s, it has fallen behind the Volga region (including Bashkiria), on which the meteoric rise of the petroleum industry conferred a probably ephemeral preeminence.[8] The Ukraine, however, still accounts for

---

*Because of much higher investment needed per ton of coal in the Ukrainian fields, Kuzbas coal has an edge in the Moscow area when higher capital charges are applied. On the other hand, increasing distance from the Kuzbas—and hence higher capital and operating cost on Kuzbas coal—more than negates this advantage west and southwest of Moscow, where Donbas coal remains considerably cheaper even with higher capital charges. Data from Akademiia Nauk SSSR, *Promyshlennost' v khoziaistvennom komplekse ekonomicheskikh raionov SSSR* (Moscow, 1964), p. 86; A. E. Probst, *Razvitie toplivnoi bazy raionov SSSR* (Moscow, 1968), p. 31; N. V. Mel'nikov, *Mineral'noe toplivo*, 2nd ed. (Moscow, 1971), pp. 175, 183.

TABLE 7.1

Distribution of Coal Reserves in the Donbas, by Depth of Seams

Range of Depth (meters)	Industrial Reserves— $A+B+C_1$ (billion tons)	Percent of Total	C_2 Reserves (billion tons)	Percent of Total	Total Surveyed Reserves (billion tons)	Percent of Total
0–300	15.0	29.8	4.8	7.6	19.8	17.4
301–600	18.6	37.0	11.0	17.3	29.6	26.0
601–1,200	14.6	29.0	28.6	45.0	43.2	38.0
1,201–1,800	2.1	4.2	19.1	30.1	21.2	18.6
Total	50.3	100.0	63.5	100.0	113.8	100.0

Source: Adapted from Akademiia Nauk SSSR, *Toplivno-energeticheskie resursy* (Moscow: Nauka, 1968), p. 70.

TABLE 7.2

Expected Distribution of Shafts and Their Output in the Ukrainian Donbas, by Depth, 1970–80

Range of Depth (meters)	1970 Percent of Shafts	1970 Percent of Coal Output	1975 Percent of Shafts	1975 Percent of Coal Output	1980 Percent of Shafts	1980 Percent of Coal Output
< 300	27.8	19.9	18.2	12.0	10.0	5.0
300–600	52.9	47.2	54.5	44.7	56.1	44.2
601–700	8.5	13.7	9.9	9.8	13.9	10.3
701–800	6.1	11.0	8.2	12.7	7.6	11.5
801–900	2.8	2.2	3.7	6.5	5.1	10.0
901–1,000	1.6	5.9	4.0	9.1	5.8	13.2
1,001–1,100	0.3	0.1	1.5	5.2	1.5	5.8
Total	100.0	100.0	100.0	100.0	100.0	100.0

Source: N. I. Ivanov et al., "Perspektivy razvitiia shakhtnogo fonda Ukrainskogo Donbassa," in Donetskii Nauchno-Issledoval'nyi Ugol'nyi Institut, *Sovershenstvovanie gornogo khoziaistva shakht Donbassa* (1968): no. 43, 5, 9.

48 percent of all Soviet production of coking coal,[9] and perhaps 90 percent of all export of this commodity.*

In contrast with the high cost of coal, unrivaled though it may be in much of the European USSR, production costs of iron ore and manganese are very favorable. Although, as elsewhere in the country, the rich iron ores at shallow depth have been worked out, the sinking of deeper shafts—and, more important, the enrichment of poorer quartzites from open pit mines—have kept Ukrainian concentrates competitive on the national and Council of Mutual Economic Assistance (CMEA) markets. The weighted average cost of dressed ore from Ukrainian mines was only 90 percent of the Soviet mean in 1970.[10] With a 12 percent interest rate on investment, Ukrainian concentrate of equivalent ferrous content, costing only 85 percent of the Soviet average, was more than 50 percent cheaper than the mean cost of concentrates in the Urals, and twice as cheap as that in western Siberia. The rich ores of the newly developed Kursk Magnetic Anomaly (KMA) fields south of Moscow show similarly low cost indexes, and, with reserves rivaling those of the Ukraine, will ease the burden on the Ukrainian deposits (Table 7.3). Still, despite strong efforts to diversify iron ore sources, the Ukraine has produced more than 50 percent of all concentrates in each year since reconstruction from World War II.[11] Its share reached 56 percent in 1973.[12] After 1962, the region ceased to be a net shipper of ore to other republics of the USSR, but it continued to account for nearly all Soviet, foreign export of ore through the 1960s (98 percent in 1967, and all of it before 1960),[13] with 30 percent of its total output crossing the USSR boundary. Similarly, the Ukraine meets more than 80 percent of Soviet manganese demand today, and contributes close to 50 percent of all manganese export as well.[14]

As important as the role of national demand for a region's natural resources is the extent of locationally associated production linkages characterizing those resources. Since coke began to be used for the smelting of iron, permitting the construction of ever larger furnaces,† ferrous metallurgy has been distinguished by its ability to generate clusters of industries linked vertically through the different stages of the production process, as well as horizontally through utilization of by-products and other complementary relationships. Until recently,

---

*An agreement with Japan to supply the latter with 104.4 million tons of coking coal from the Chul'man deposit of southern Iakutia between 1979 and 1998 will somewhat reduce the present share of the Ukraine in the export of Soviet coking coal in the near future. Moscow Narodny Bank, *Press Bulletin*, July 3, 1974, p. 12; June 12, 1974, p. 2. In 1973 Japan took 2.8 million tons of the 24.5 million tons of Soviet hard coal export, but most of the export to Japan is known to have come from the Kuzbas. *Vneshnaia torgovlia SSSR (VT) 1973*, p. 70.

†By contrast, the softness of charcoal held down the size of furnaces and, together with the large demand for wood, kept the iron industry dispersed in earlier times.

TABLE 7.3

Relative Cost of Iron per Ton of Concentrate, Soviet Regions, 1970
(percent of Soviet average)

	Percent
USSR	100.0
Northwest	92.7
Central regions	86.4
Volga regions	152.9
Ukraine	84.5
Transcaucasia	104.3
Urals	129.9
West Siberia	181.7
East Siberia	124.9
Kazakhstan	123.7

Notes: Cost = variable cost + 12 percent capital charge.
   West Siberia includes the Abakan and Teisk mines of eastern Siberia.
   Source: N. D. Leliukhina, *Ekonomicheskaia effektivnost' razmeshcheniia chernoi metallurgii* (Moscow, 1973), p. 159.

the much greater weight of inputs relative to the weight of the metal required a location near those inputs, particularly coking coal. The shipment of such heavy materials and products has also influenced the growth of transport facilities and related services.

The juxtaposition of excellent raw materials and proximity to the country's major urban centers have been instrumental in the creation of a huge complex of ferrous metallurgy, metal fabricating, heavy machinery, coke-chemical, and related industries in the eastern Ukraine. Even after the forced development of the Urals and the meteoric wartime growth of its heavy industry (a time of destruction in the Donbas), the locational and manpower advantages continued largely to cancel out the rising cost of major inputs in the Ukrainian iron and steel industry. In the early 1950s, all major Ural mills, enjoying low-cost coke from Kuzbas coal hauled at preferential freight rates, could send their products to Moscow somewhat more cheaply than their Ukrainian counterparts.[15] A decade later, only the Magnitogorsk plant could deliver pig iron and steel to Moscow and Leningrad more cheaply than the Ukrainian producers; and the latter, of course, enjoyed a still stronger locational advantage in supplying the southern regions of the European USSR, the Baltic, and Belorussia, not to mention the countries of eastern Central Europe. By the 1970s, the depletion of the uncommonly cheap high-grade ore reserves at Magnitogorsk and the gradual change-over to low-quality Kustanai supplies have eroded the formerly exceptional economic position of the Magnitogorsk steel mill, which now boasts a much smaller cost advantage vis-a-vis the eastern Ukraine (and other centers) than was true before.[16]

In the course of economic development and maturation, the Ukraine has become more self-sufficient within the Soviet regional system, a point strongly emphasized recently by Vsevolod Holubnychy.[17] Today some 80 percent of its gross output is reportedly produced and consumed within its frontiers.[18] This total, however, is not value added, and corresponds more or less to all transactions in an input-output table. Compared with final product (net output), exports and imports would account for a far larger share than 20 percent, and such a share is not unusual for so well endowed a region, which is larger than France and has almost as many people.*

The industrial structure of the Ukraine, however, is still unbalanced; it was probably much more so in earlier years. The argument I wish to present here is that while, for the most part, the present structure and specialization have been rational and economically sound from the vantage point of the whole Soviet system, they are becoming increasingly disadvantageous from a strictly Ukrainian point of view. Yet the two can perhaps remain compatible, provided two strategies are pursued:

1. An earnest effort to diversify the industrial structure of the republic, reducing its relative dependence on heavy resource-using (especially energy-demanding) sectors and accelerating the growth of light manufacturing, particularly west of the Dnieper.

2. An equally serious effort to husband local energy resources and to expand and supplement them at cost no higher than the marginal cost of Donbas coal.

---

*In the province of Ontario, which is 1965 concentrated 42 percent of all Canada's commodity-producing industries (by value added), exports accounted for 56 percent of value added, but only 19 percent of all transactions (total gross output). *Ontario Statistical Review* (1973): 36-37, 58. Although nations are "open economies" to a lesser degree than regions within nations, most West European countries and Japan enjoy a far less balanced supply of domestic resources than the Ukraine does. For the larger nations, the share of export in their GNP ranged from 10 to 20 percent during the late 1960s. *UN Statistical Yearbook 1970* (New York: United Nations, 1971), pp. 404-09, 604-05.

STRUCTURAL AND DYNAMIC PROBLEMS
OF RESOURCE-BASED SPECIALIZATION
IN THE UKRAINE

The industrial complex of the Ukraine is still heavily weighted toward the lower, resource-using stages of production. The latter have outputs far in excess of Ukrainian needs, while the higher, more complex stages are insufficiently developed to fully satisfy demand. The iron and steel industry of the republic today is much larger than that of any country in Western Europe, and probably larger than that of France and England combined.* Its engineering industries are distinguished by a far higher ratio of volume to value than those of any other Soviet region (a 52 percent higher metal consumption per ruble of output than USSR machine-building as a whole in 1965),[19] yet they could absorb only 54 percent of the pig iron and 50 percent of the rolled steel production in 1970, the rest being exported to other Soviet regions and foreign countries.[20] The value of output of Ukrainian machine building roughly equals the value of demand for machines in the republic.† Unfortunately, many of the light engineering branches are largely absent; and the Ukraine must import 45 percent of all its machinery demand while shipping out nearly 50 percent of its own products, most of which are of low value by weight.[21]

It also appears that up to 33 percent of all sulfuric acid output, and possibly more of soda output, was sent out of the republic in the mid-1960s,‡ although

---

*In the early 1970s, the production of pig iron, crude steel, and rolled steel far surpassed that in the West European states. The combined tonnage of the three products exceeded the joint output of Britain and France, although only in pig iron did the Ukraine produce more than those countries together. The ferrous metallurgy of the Ukraine is based entirely on domestic iron ore and coke, while most of the iron ore and some of the coking coal used in West Europe are imported. Even France relies on overseas ore for 25 percent of its supply. OECD, *The Iron and Steel Industry in 1972 and Trends in 1973* (Paris: OECD, 1974), esp. pp. 36, 40-41; *Narodnoe khoziaistvo SSSR 1972*, pp. 212-14.

†The ratio of production to consumption is 1.06. V. P. Evstigneev, *Effektivnost' razmeshcheniia mashinostroeniia v vostochnykh i zapadnykh raionakh SSR* (Moscow, 1972), p. 79.

‡Estimated from data about shipment to Soviet regions and abroad from Donets'k and Voroshylovhrad oblasts, which account for the bulk of sulfuric acid production in the Ukraine. Data from *Ekonomika Donbassa* (Moscow, 1971), p. 77; *Vneshnaia torgovlia SSSR 1918-66*, pp. 86-88; P. V. Voloboi and V. A. Popovkin, *Problemy terytorial'noi spetsializatsii i kompleksnoho rozvytku narodnoho hospodartsva Ukrains'koi RSR* (Kiev, 1972), p. 177; *Ukraina za p'iatdesiat rokiv (1917-1967)* (Kiev, 1967), p. 123. *Ekonomika Donbassa*, p. 77, also gives a detailed percentage breakdown of shipment of soda products and fertilizers, though no absolute figures can be estimated. However, the Ukraine in 1965 accounted for almost 33 percent, and in 1970, 25 percent, of all soda ash produced in the USSR. The first figure is much higher than the share of Ukrainian consumption. Voloboi and Popovkin, op. cit., pp. 128-29.

a huge deficit existed, and continues to exist, in the far more valuable synthetic material branches of the chemical industry. On a per capita basis, the Ukraine produced only 15 percent as much plastics, less than 50 percent as much rubber goods, and 75 percent as much man-made fibers as the Soviet average in 1967. The indexes are equally low when compared with national income or total industrial output, and were even lower in 1960.[22] A number of new petrochemical and synthetic material-producing centers are helping to round out the traditional chemical profile. The big Kalush complex, for example, is planned to account for almost 50 percent of the increment in Soviet vinyl plastic output between 1970 and 1975.[23] Still, it is fair to say that in more valuable chemicals, just as in more complex machines, the Ukraine continues to experience a large "import leakage" as part of its unfavorable trade structure.

The role of the Ukraine is particularly great in the export of Soviet minerals and heavy resource-based materials abroad. Aside from petroleum and forest products, the great bulk of such Soviet exports originated in the Ukraine throughout the 1960s, with the percentages frequently increasing. By contrast, in heavy resource-based but more sophisticated goods, such as steel pipe and ferroalloys, the share of the Ukraine was far smaller; and its contribution to the value of all Soviet machinery exports dropped below 17 percent in 1970 (Table 7.4). The dependence of the European socialist countries on the Ukraine for basic raw materials, heavy metallurgical, and semifinished goods is particularly great. These small states are seriously deficient in natural resources (even coal-rich Poland suffers from a shortage of coking coal, for example) and lack the hard-currency reserves to turn elsewhere for supplies.[24] In terms of Soviet f.o.b. prices, they imported more from the Ukraine than they exported during 1958-65 and, most probably, afterwards (14 percent more in 1965 and 21.4 percent more in 1958).[25] However, their balance of trade with the Soviet Union as a whole was much less negative.[26]

Not counting sugar, some 67 percent of which is transported out of the republic,* the "export base" of the Ukraine thus consists of high-volume, low-value primary commodities and semifinished materials. At the same time, aside from timber and oil, the "import leakage" consists of consumer goods, light and precision machinery, and synthetic products, which yield faster returns on investment and generally embody more labor skills and/or advanced technology. The lack of consumer and light engineering branches is especially serious in view of the woefully underdeveloped nature of manufacturing in the densely settled western part of the Ukraine. In the southwest economic region, with 44 percent

---

*Since there is no reason to suppose that per capita consumption of sugar in the Ukraine differs greatly from the Soviet average, local demand should approximate the share of the republic in the total Soviet population. Data for production and population from *Narodnoe khoziaistvo SSSR* (Moscow, 1974), pp. 9, 321.

TABLE 7.4

Share of the Ukraine in Total Soviet Export of Selected Products, 1965 and 1970
(percent)

	1970	1965
Hard coal	78.3	64.6
Coke	70.9	n.a.
Natural gas	100.0	100.0
Iron ore	98.1	95.7
Pig iron	80.9	74.4
Rolled steel	64.0	67.3
Pipe steel	n.a.	27.4
Ferroalloys	n.a.	29.7
Sulfuric acid	65.3	n.a.
Native sulfur	n.a.	84.3
Manganese ore	51.7	n.a.
Superphosphate	n.a.	97.0
All machines and equipment	16.8	n.a.

n.a. = data not available.

Sources: 1970—P. V. Voloboi and V. A. Popovkin, *Problemy terytorial'noi spetsializatsii i kompleksnoho rozvytku narodnoho hospodarstva Ukrains'koi RSR* (Kiev, 1972), p. 177; 1965—N. G. Klimko, ed., *Problemy razvitiia ekonomiki sotsialisticheskikh stran Evropy* (Kiev, 1968), p. 361.

of the Ukrainian population, only Kiev and L'viv can boast a developed engineering industry. In 10 of the region's 13 oblasts, the share of the engineering industries in total industrial employment remained under 33 percent of the Ukrainian average in 1967.[27]

The geographic and sectoral concentration and imbalances of investment have tended to reinforce each other. The emphasis on the spatially concentrated and highly capital-intensive heavy industrial complex most probably contributed to the undercapitalization of other sectors by making it more difficult to obtain scarce investment funds. For example, despite the general absence of light manufacturing, Ukrainian industry outside the Donets'-Dnieper area is rather undercapitalized on a per employee basis.[28] (Food processing, which is well developed, requires much capital per worker.)* Still more glaring, supplies of capital equip-

---

*Per man-year of employment, the food industries of the USSR used more fixed capital in 1966 than the machine-building group as a whole. The sugar industry, prominent

ment, mechanical power, and electricity to the agricultural labor force of the republic are far below the Soviet average; and in two of its three major economic regions they fall to or are less than the Central Asian level.[29]

The stress on low-value-producing primary industries, which face worsening of resource conditions, have also resulted in a rapid decline of capital productivity. Between 1960 and 1972, capital productivity (*fondootdacha*) in the Ukraine declined much faster than in the Soviet Union as a whole, and slightly faster even than in the Russian Republic, despite the vast scope of Siberian projects in the latter (relative to a base of 100 in 1960, the respective indexes in 1972 were 83, 92, and 84).[30] The gross return to industrial fixed capital in coal and metallurgy fell much below the Soviet mean both at the beginning and at the end of the 1960s. Despite the much higher profitability of industry in the rest of the "South," the locational and infrastructural advantages of the region, and its labor productivity indexes (at least on a par with the national mean, even when the effects of the branch structure are neutralized), low capital returns in the Dnieper-Don heavy industrial complex depressed average profitability for the whole of the Ukraine. Even after the 1968 price reform, the return to industrial capital barely reached the Soviet mean; it had been much lower before.[31]

More ominous for the future is the increasingly strained supply of energy. The situation is unquestionably aggravated by the long-standing specialization in heavy-fuel-and-power-consuming industries in the eastern Ukraine; ferrous metallurgy and power stations alone consume 60 percent of all fuel used in the republic.[32] The problem manifests itself in a relatively uneconomic energy mix, in growing physical shortages, and in high costs. Like the problem of the industrial structure in general, it also has a geographic expression, shown by the huge differences in per capita fuel and energy consumption among the Ukrainian regions, with some 50 percent of the republic having indexes below the Cental Asian level.* The question of energy supplies and their impact on economic

---

in the Ukraine, was slightly more capital-intensive than nonferrous metallurgy and 86 percent as capital-intensive as ferrous ores and metals. V. G. Treml, B. L. Kostinsky, and D. M. Gallik, "Interindustry Structure of the Soviet Economy: 1959 and 1966," in Joint Economic Committee, *Soviet Economic Prospects for the Seventies* (Washington, D.C.: U.S. Government Printing Office, 1973), pp. 266-67.

*The shares of all major economic regions in total Soviet fuel consumption are given for 1962 in Akademiia Nauk SSSR, *Zakonomernosti i faktory razvitiia ekonomicheskikh raionov SSSR* (Moscow, 1965), p. 146. The 1967 per capita electric power consumption relative to the Ukrainian mean is given in all three economic regions and all oblasts of the republic in P. Voloboi and V. Popovkin, "O pokazateliakh khoziaistvennogo urovnia raionov i oblastei," *ESU* (1968): no. 10, 59. Per capita consumption in the Ukraine was 96 percent of the Soviet average in 1970. *Elektricheskie stantsii* (1971): no. 1, 2. The latter source provides data for all Soviet republics.

development increasingly troubles Ukrainian scholars, who see the industrial growth of their republic threatened in the future.

The Ukrainian energy mix continues to be dominated by coal, which is expensive and increasingly in short supply. On a calorific basis, coal accounted for more than 60 percent of all fuel production in 1973 and more than 55 percent of consumption during the mid-1960s.[33] In electric stations, its share is more than 60 percent even today.* The republic does have big reserves of natural gas, but little oil. Thanks to a number of oil finds in the eastern Ukraine since the latter 1950s, crude production (originally based on the small Galician fields operating since the nineteenth century) climbed from a mere 2 million tons to over 13 million tons per year. Since the early 1970s, however, output has been stationary, with a decline projected for 1975.[34]

During the 1960s, a dramatic increase in natural gas production, mostly from the big Shebelynka field, pushed the Ukraine's share to 30 percent of the Soviet total by the end of that decade. Output has peaked, however, and in natural gas too the contribution of the Ukraine has begun to decline.[35] Exploratory drilling during 1966-70 was already reaching depths of 3,500-4,500 meters, and the expansion of this work to depths below 5,000 meters is considered to be an urgent task. Since the mid-1960s, additions to reserves have not kept up with output, despite 8.7 million meters of drilling. At current rates of production, industrial $(A + B + C_1)$ reserves of gas, as of the end of 1969, will last for less than a decade, and fully proven ones (A + B category) for no more than seven years.[36] Soviet prospectors expressed hope of expanding Ukrainian industrial reserves during the 1970s to guarantee output for 17 years at current or slightly reduced annual rates; but this would require the proving of nearly 50 percent of all probable reserves (*prognoznye zapasy*), an incredibly successful ratio.[37]

Even the coal supply is worrisome. In the mid-1960s, 33 percent of the Donbas collieries had less than 15 years of reserves.[38] In addition, output per 1,000 rubles of fixed investment from new collieries during 1966-70 was only 17 tons—2.5 times less than the average for the Soviet coal industry as a whole.[39] During the 1970s, the production of steam coal cannot be expanded by more than 15 to 20 million tons.[40] New capacity increases of 30 million tons are now under way,[41] but further major expansion seems to entail unacceptable risks and costs. At the end of 1972, the average depth of underground work in the Donbas reached below 500 meters;[42] by 1975, 33 percent of all coal output is to come from depths of more than 700 meters, and by 1980, 40 percent (Table 7.2). In deep mines, the methane released per ton of coal reaches 100 cubic meters,

---

*Donbas coal alone accounted for 60 percent of the fuel supply to Ukrainian power stations. V. V. Ershevich and E. A. Shteinberg, "Razvitie energosistem UkSSR," *Energetika i elektrifikatsiia* (1971): no. 5, 6.

requiring the forced injection of air 20 times the weight of coal mined; and the high temperatures necessitate expensive ventilation and cooling.[43] The shipment of Donets' steam coal to distant parts of the European USSR is being curtailed, and beyond 1975 it is to be used solely in the Ukraine and immediately adjoining provinces of the lower Volga and central Chernozem regions.[44] Ukrainian planners also urge the acceleration of construction on the Central Asia-central and western Siberia-central gas trunk-line systems in order to eliminate the export of gas to Moscow from their republic.[45]

The Ukraine must continue to furnish the great bulk of coking coal imported by the East European countries, and until the end of the 1970s it will provide most of the exports of natural gas from the Soviet Union, amounting to about 14 billion cubic meters (8.5 billion cubic meters to Eastern Europe and 5.5 billion cubic meters to Western Europe).[46] The construction of the huge Orenburg-Uzhorod pipeline, a joint CMEA undertaking for the transport of Russian gas to both Eastern Europe and Western Europe, will sharply reduce the relative share, though perhaps not the absolute volume of Ukrainian natural gas in total Soviet gas export.* Similarly, the buildup of the big new metallurgical base on the KMA will presumably account for much of the increment in the export of energy-intensive ferrous ores and metals, but is unlikely to result in any absolute reduction of the volume sent abroad from the Ukraine.

In terms of export of Soviet electric power, the demand on the Ukraine will intensify. In 1973, 9.5 billion kwh net was transmitted outside the Ukraine, all of it evidently abroad; this accounted for more than 95 percent of Soviet export.[47] Hungary, accounting for 42 percent of all Soviet electricity export, received 4.18 billion kwh in 1973. Bulgaria, Czechoslovakia, and Poland combined received almost exactly as much.[48] Presently a very high-voltage (750 kv) intertie with an ultimate transmission capacity of 2000 mw between Vinnytsia and Albertirsa, Hungary, is under construction to strengthen the existing system of interconnection. With a 75 percent capacity factor, it could transmit 17 billion kwh to the East European neighbors of the USSR and, with an 80 percent capacity factor, more than 18 billion.† Since the hydroelectric potential of the Ukraine is almost fully utilized, this export will have to come from conventional thermal plants and/or new nuclear stations. Generation of 17 billion kwh in conventional

---

*Altogether, plans for 1980 envisage the export of 21.4 billion cubic meters to CMEA countries and 28.6 billion cubic meters to Western countries. Obviously only a fraction of that export can come from the Ukraine. Moscow Narodny Bank, *Press Bulletin*, November 20, 1974, p. 10; and December 11, 1974, pp. 3, 4-5; *Energy International* (April 1973): 45.

†Although there will be some return flow of peak power, the direction will be primarily westward, since Hungary alone hopes to receive 1,350 mw by 1980 (11.5 billion kwh, assuming a 75 percent capacity factor). *Energia és atomtechnika*, June 22, 1974, p. 3.

plants will require more than 7 million tons of hard coal.* That tonnage represents more than half the projected output of the Volynia Basin.†

In view of the worsening energy supplies throughout the European USSR, recent articles have stressed the importance of investing in fuel-saving measures. Although such opportunities still exist in the Ukraine, a closer examination of the two key industries (ferrous metallurgy and power stations), which account for 60 percent of all fuel consumption, reveals strict limits to such savings. Already 97 percent of all pig iron in the republic is smelted with the help of natural gas injected into the blast furnace, and 85 percent of open-hearth steel with the application of oxygen.[49] Further expansion of such fuel-saving technologies will not be significant. Nearly 33 percent of all Ukrainian electric stations, small and obsolete for the most part, use much more fuel than the republic's average for the industry. However, these small, isolated plants serve consumers with very irregular demand. Hooking the latter into the power grid will indeed save fuel, but at the expense of reducing capital efficiency in the unified network, a trade-off no doubt rational but far from cost-free. In the big generating plants of the unified grid, heat rates are approaching thermodynamic limits and further improvements will be quite difficult. Significant economies are doubtless possible in less fuel-intensive industries, where a large portion of plants, with obsolete equipment, have fuel coefficients 30-40 percent above the branch average.[50] As in other regions of the USSR, however, most of greatest economizing steps—shifting to better fuels and dramatically more efficient technologies— have already been taken.

It is thus virtually certain that per capita energy, and particularly electricity, consumption in the Ukraine must increase significantly even with a vigorous effort to reduce the relative dependence on resource-based and energy-intensive activities. In fact, the success of economic diversification will in no small measure depend on much greater supplies of electric power to hitherto neglected economic sectors. In 1970, for example, a Ukrainian collective farmer received only 75 percent as much power for farm use as his fellow worker in the RSFSR and less than 50 percent as much as one in the Baltic republics. The provision of all mechanized power to farmers on both collective and state farms in the Ukraine reached but 55 percent of the level of mechanization in the RSFSR and did not exceed that in Central Asia.[51] Outside the Donets'-Dnieper region, fuel and electricity use during the 1960s was abnormally low in all economic sectors; and

---

*With heat rates of 340 grams of standard fuel (1 gram = 7 kilocalories) per kwh of electricity; the average 1973 heat rate at district stations of the USSR was 348 grams. *Narkhoz 1973*, p. 257.

†The 1975 output is planned to be 14 million tons, but further expansion is not feasible. Akademia Nauk-Gosplan, *Ukrainskaia SSR* (Moscow, 1972), p. 81; Akademiia Nauk SSSR, *Toplivno-Energeticheskie resursy* (Moscow, 1968), p. 85.

in the southwest, with 44 percent of the republic's population, it approximated the Tadzhikistan and Turkmenia level, below that of Uzbekistan. It is obvious that this long-neglected, populous half of the Ukraine cannot hope to increase the productivity of its labor force and approach the level of other European regions of the USSR without a significant expansion of energy, particularly electric power, supply.

Further diversification, long urged by Ukrainian economists, and to some degree noticeable during the 1960s, is receiving greater emphasis in the 1970s. At the same time, a severe curtailment of new energy-intensive industries in the Ukraine is now the accepted line of development.[52] However, the areal separation of fuel-and-energy-intensive and labor-intensive activities and production stages is not always feasible, particularly in the petrochemical and synthetic material industries.[53] Still, with a strong commitment to such a strategy, an authoritative source expects the demand for energy—specifically electric energy—in the republic as a whole to increase rapidly but at a rate somewhat below the national rate. Outside the Donets'-Dnieper region, however, power consumption during the 1980s is planned to grow faster than the average for the Ukraine or for the USSR as a whole.[54]

The favorable location and, aside from coal and oil, the geological condition of Ukrainian mineral resources have so far yielded very substantial income to the Soviet state through large rent payments. I. S. Koropeckyj has estimated the differential rent in the Ukrainian extractive industry for 1970 as 1.3 billion rubles, or 23 percent of the Soviet total.[55] This is a high share, in view of the fact that the Ukraine accounts for less than 3 percent of the country's territory, 19 percent of its population, and 18 percent of value added in Soviet industry.[56] Because it is in the fuel-energy industries that local supplies are proving inadequate, it is important to ask to what extent these crucial industries in the Ukraine have been contributing to total income, and have been able to generate their investment capital.

Since the 1967 price reform, fuel consumers in this republic are paying for Ukrainian coal, gas, and crude oil resources about 1.6 billion rubles per year in excess of the production and delivery cost of these fuels (exclusive of investment charges for prospecting and output). The excess value paid by natural gas users alone comes to some 700 million rubles.[57] Total investment in the fuel industries of the Ukraine (not counting refineries) amounted to roughly 4.5 billion rubles during the 1966-70 Five Year Plan, with 5.1 billion being earmarked for the first half of the 1970s—less than 1 billion per year.[58] Until 1975, therefore, Ukrainian fuels sold within the republic have generated an annual "surplus value" of 600 million rubles; significant surpluses have also been realized from sales outside the Ukraine. Before 1967, the coal industry of this republic was subsidized but—at least in the 1960s—much of this subsidy seems to have been equalized by the growing extra revenues received from Ukrainian natural gas. As I have shown elsewhere, only on the gas resources of the adjoining North

Caucasus in the RSFSR is such a high "surplus value" collected on fuel anywhere in the Soviet Union today.[59]

For some time, therefore, the fuel industries of the Ukraine have been generating income well above the investment capital received. In addition, very large revenues have been collected on other minerals, particularly iron ore, manganese, and sulfur. Under the impending threat of partial resource exhaustion, coupled with continued locational advantages for further manufacturing growth within the Soviet and CMEA system as a whole, equity and efficiency considerations would demand that such "surplus value" be invested in expanding and supplementing local energy reserves at reasonable cost. The problem is crucial, not only for the Ukrainian economy but, beyond that, for the entire Soviet Union; and it is highly significant for the CMEA bloc as a whole. Geographers have noted that fully 50 percent of the entire Soviet population resides within a radius of 600 miles from Kharkiv; they provide at least 50 percent of the country's industrial and agricultural output.[60] The north-central Ukraine and the adjoining black earth center of the RSFSR constitute the area from which the entire Soviet bloc market is accessible to the least total transport effort.[61] Any deceleration of economic growth here on account of an energy constraint is likely to have a greater multiplied dampening effect than in more peripheral parts of the country.

FUTURE DEMAND AND PROSPECTS FOR SUPPLEMENTING UKRAINIAN ENERGY SUPPLIES

Projections of energy demand are notoriously difficult, even in a planned economy. Although the growth of energy consumption in the long run seems closely related to economic development and the rate of technological advance, the increase in energy use does not proceed with much regularity through time. Neither does it have a systematic relationship to growth of population, gross national product (GNP), or industry in the short run. Energy is not a uniform product; it is used at grossly different degrees of efficiency even in the same economy, and the energy elasticity of any economy's output varies significantly in different stages of the economy's development. Projections of energy demand for an individual region without sovereign powers are more difficult still. Decisions concerning the fuel-energy sector are closely intertwined with questions involving the spatial dimension and structure of the economy as a whole; and the various regional alternatives of industrial expansion, resource transfer, and substitution involve exceedingly complex economic and sociopolitical issues.

During the 1960s, the growth of energy consumption in the USSR as a whole dropped from the high annual rate of 7.4 percent prevailing during the previous decade to 5.1 percent.[62] This was somewhat below the GNP growth rate, and well below the industrial growth rate (17 to 40 percent below the latter, depending on whether one accepts the official index or various Western estimates for Soviet industrial growth).[63] Lower rates for energy consumption were made possible by the shift during the 1960s to more efficient fuels and fuel-using processes, such as diesel and electric traction on the railroads, substitution of natural gas for coal in many industrial uses, and the near elimination of firewood from the household sector. In the Ukraine fuel consumption, which accounted for more than 99 percent of all gross primary energy use, increased a little more slowly, averaging 4.85 percent during the 1960s.[64] As a result, per capita demand in the Ukraine, which somewhat exceeded the Soviet mean during the 1960s, today closely approximates the average for the country as a whole.* The trend conforms to the slower growth of industry and to the gradual shift toward less energy-intensive and more labor-intensive activities.

The continuation of the latter trend will most likely keep the rate of increase in Ukrainian energy demand below that for the whole USSR and slightly below the rate for GNP. During the 1970s and early 1980s, therefore, the rate should fall somewhere between 4 and 5 percent. An annual rate below 4 percent is extremely unlikely, for most of the major energy-saving measures through fuel substitution have already been taken; at the same time, long-repressed income-elastic uses will certainly play a greater role than in the past. A planned deceleration of GNP growth in the Ukraine, resulting in a lower rate of increase in energy demand, cannot be ruled out, but is certain to be vigorously resisted by Ukrainian planners.

With a 4-5 percent annual growth rate, total energy demand in 1980 should reach 343 million-396.5 million tons of standard fuel equivalent, respectively; and by middecade it should range from nearly 420 to more than 480 million.[65] Total production of all primary sources in 1975 was to reach no more than 280 million tons, corresponding to expected demand at a 4 percent growth rate.[66] However, more than 10 percent of the 1975 output is committed to consumers outside the Ukraine and abroad, even at the most conservative estimate.[67] Almost three times as much left the republic in 1971.[68] Therefore, even if there is a cutback on all interregional and international fuel export apart from coking coal (surely an unfeasible proposition), Ukrainian fuel production would have to expand by a minimum of 80 million tons of standard fuel equivalent in 1975-80, and by at least double that amount by the mid-1980s, merely to keep today's small net energy deficit from widening. An annual growth in consumption above the minimum 4 percent level would require substantially greater increases in output.

---

*In 1965, the Ukraine contained 19.6 percent of the Soviet population, but accounted for 21.5 percent of all primary energy consumption; in 1970 the respective shares were 19.4 and 20.7 percent. *Narkhoz 1965*, p. 9, *1970*, p. 9.

Such an output increase is clearly well beyond the resources of the Ukraine. Its coal mines can at best furnish a 30-million ton increment by the turn of the 1980s,[69] its crude oil production is now declining, and its natural gas output is stationary. The water-power potentials are almost fully utilized. In recent years, hydroplants have provided only 7–8 percent of electricity output, much of it as peak power, and less than 1 percent of total primary energy production.[70] Barring the unlikely discovery of a really major oil pool or another huge gas field comparable with Shebelynka, the widening gap between energy supply and demand must be filled by nonconventional power sources and by "imports" from the Soviet East.

Nuclear Power and EHV Transmission

As in other regions of the European USSR, Soviet planners increasingly regard nuclear power as an economically attractive energy source for the Ukraine. By 1970, growing experience and improvements in technology had brought operating costs at the newest Soviet atomic plants (using pressurized, water-cooled, water-moderated reactors, termed VVER-440) to less than 0.50 kopek per kwh.[71] Although investment per kilowatt (kw) of capacity is significantly higher than at conventional thermal stations, the total cost per kwh, inclusive of interest charges, reportedly falls below that of electricity generated at conventional plants west of the Volga that burn any kind of fuel.[72] In additon to the VVER-440, Soviet scientists have developed a much larger, 1,000-megawatt channel-type uranium-graphite reactor, the RBMK-1000, for which the USSR seems to have particularly high expectations.[73] None of the 4,000-mw capacity put on stream by 1974 was yet in the Ukraine, but the first of two RBMK-1000 reactors was scheduled to go into operation at Chornobyl', near Kiev, in 1975. Two additional nuclear stations with capacities of 2,000 mw and 880 mw, respectively, are proposed for the western Ukraine in the Ivano-Frankivs'k and Rovno areas.[74] By the end of 1975, only 2.3 percent of total capacity in the southern grid (embracing the Ukraine, Moldavia, and Rostov Oblast) is to be nuclear.[75] Nevertheless, atomic stations may account for 40 percent of all incremental capacity during the 1980s.[76] However, since even today not much more than 25 percent of all energy is consumed in the form of electricity (a share forecast to reach 40 percent by 1990),[77] not even such an accelerated nuclear development can stave off dependence on imported energy from other regions.

The worsening energy shortage in the southern part of the the European Plain (Ukraine, Lower Don, and Volga areas) is stimulating proposals for long-distance, extra-high-voltage (EHV) transmission of electricity from beyond the Urals. Soviet energy planners have long regarded EHV transmission as a means of tapping the nontransportable but vast and very cheap lignite and low-grade coal reserves of the country's interior for the benefit of the energy-hungry European USSR. Even though much greater problems have been encountered in the development of this technology than anticipated, EHV transmission of power from the Asiatic USSR is still regarded as realizable in the not-too-distant future. Recently V. A. Ryl'skii and his associates made the strong, and to me convincing, recommendation that the destination of the proposed EHV trunklines (1,500 kv, DC) from the Ekibastuz coal field should be Volgograd, from which node electricity could be transmitted to both Moscow and the Ukraine through the existing, but now grossly underutilized, high-voltage network.[78]

This power would not be cheap. With a 15 percent capital charge, transmission costs alone would approach 1 kopek per kwh.[79] This is two to three times the cost of generation at the best thermal plants today.[80] At such cost, trans-Ural electricity cannot yet compete in the European USSR,[81] and certainly not in the Ukraine. In the latter, the marginal cost of electricity in the 1980s is projected to be 0.9 kopek per kwh if generated by nuclear plants, and 1.0 kopek if generated by conventional systems (using culm).[82] At any rate, one such DC trunkline, energized at 1,500 kv and with a transmission capacity of 6 million kw (able to transmit 40-42 billion kwh at a 76-80 percent load factor)[83] could save no more than 12-13 million tons of standard fuel equivalent.* That tonnage would represent some 4-5 percent of present consumption. Whatever the fate of this ambitious EHV project, it can be only a costly and minor supplement to energy resources required by the Ukraine. The Soviet East must make its major contribution to the Ukrainian energy balance via fuel rather than power.

Ukrainian Demand and the Role of Siberian Fuels

A satisfactory treatment of this problem requires attention to several major considerations. On the demand side, Ukrainian fuel needs must be seen in the context of the growing fuel shortage in the whole European USSR and, to some extent, even in the entire CMEA. On the supply side, one must look not merely at the size and production costs of Siberian fuel resources, but at their transportability and the technological lead time that controls their exploitation and delivery. Increasingly, their availability for the Ukraine (as for other regions) cannot be isolated from Soviet response to the dramatically improved export

---

*With a heat rate of 330 grams of standard fuel per kwh of electricity, the 1973 heat rate at Soviet district stations was 348 grams. *Narkhoz 1973*, p. 257. The efficiency of the best conventional thermal plants is now approaching thermodynamic limits.

opportunities for hydrocarbons, particularly oil. The Ukraine is not a sovereign state. In view of its manpower and locational advantages, its economic interests cannot be willfully ignored without injury to the whole Soviet spatial system. But there is no guarantee that, in the short and medium runs, the maximizing of benefits from new resources in the Soviet regional system as a whole would necessarily coincide with the maximization of benefits in any of its constituent parts.

Economic growth in the whole European USSR, including the Urals and Transcaucasia, increasingly hinges on massive and rapidly growing transport of fuels from the Asiatic parts of the country. Representing 80 percent of the Soviet total,* fuel consumption in the European USSR exceeded production by about 140 million tons of standard fuel in 1970.[84] Despite the severe restriction of energy-intensive activities in Western regions, even strongly pro-Siberian planners find it inconceivable that these regions could account for less than 70-72 percent of total demand by the early 1980s.[85] To keep the deficit from widening, fuel production in the European USSR would have to grow by at least 550 million tons of standard fuel equivalent.[†] This clearly is an impossible feat, and economists expect a shortfall of 350-400 million tons.[86] Nor can Soviet plans ignore the needs of Eastern Europe, which in 1973 imported about 12.5 percent of all the energy it used, including 75 percent of its oil and a growing share of its gas requirements (all of its net hydrocarbon imports coming from the USSR).[87] At a June 1975 COMECON conference, Soviet leaders promised to further increase petroleum deliveries, albeit at a much higher price,[88] and far greater growth will take place in Soviet natural gas supplies to the area. By 1980, some 120 million tons of standard fuel equivalent of petroleum and gas apparently will be committed to Eastern Europe annually,[‡] with small amounts also to other Communist countries.

---

*The 1970 share was roughly 80 percent in total fuel consumption, and 78 percent in stationary fuel consumption (boiler and furnace uses). V. Kudinov and S. Litvak, "O toplivnoenergeticheskom balanse," *Vestnik statistiki* (*VS*) (1972): no. 9, 36, 42; and Vsesoiuznyi Institut Nauchnoi i Tekhnicheskoi Informatsii, *Razrabotka neftianykh i gazovykh mestorozhdenii*, IV (Moscow, 1972), pp. 44-45.

†Consumption in 1970 reached roughly 900 million tons of standard fuel equivalent. *Narkhoz 1922-72*, p. 61. Production, therefore, amounted to about 760 million tons. Assuming total Soviet fuel consumption will increase 70 percent by 1980 (corresponding to an annual rate of 5.45 percent, while the 1970-75 plan calls for a 5.95 percent yearly increase in output), and assuming no less than 71 percent of all consumption will take place in the European parts and the Urals, the latter regions will need 1,350 million tons of standard fuel. This projection is actually lower than that given by A. E. Probst in *Voprosy razmeshcheniia sotsialisticheskoi promyshlennosti* (Moscow, 1971), pp. 218-19.

‡Plans for 1980 envisage a flow of more than 21 billion cubic meters of natural gas, equal to some 25 million tons of standard fuel. Moscow Narodny Bank, *Press Bulletin*, June 19, 1974, pp. 4-5. Since one ton of oil equals about 1.45 ton of standard fuel, even

The prospect and magnitude of fuel supply to the Ukraine from beyond the Urals, therefore, must be seen in the context of a massive westward flow of energy that may exceed what is going to Japan today.[89] It also must be seen in the context of the economic, technological, and logistic problems of optimizing this flow overland through an area that is larger than the United States and has 300 million consumers. The vast coal and hydropower resources of eastern Siberia are largely immobile, and the coals of Kazakhstan cannot be transported beyond the western slopes of the Urals. Consequently, this huge 280-290 million standard-ton equivalent flow must consist primarily of crude oil, natural gas, and the hard coal of the Kuzbas, of which only the first two are of interest for the Ukraine.

The total amount of liquid and gaseous fuels that Soviet Asia can deliver to the Urals and westward should reach a 280-290-million-standard-ton equivalent in 1975 and 460-480 million tons by 1980.* Although this flow is sufficient to cover the fuel deficit in the European USSR and most of that in Eastern Europe, it cannot, in my view, at the same time sustain the present or enlarged oil export to hard-currency areas. Neither can Soviet plans for incremental energy consumption and a rational energy mix be isolated from the comparative advantage of Soviet fuels, particularly oil, on the world market. The profit on exported crude, which almost certainly exceeds $4 per barrel ($29 per ton) at the Black Sea ports in the mid-1970s,† should have a powerful effect on

---

with the commitment of only 65 million tons of petroleum, roughly 120 million tons of standard fuel would be delivered in the form of oil and gas. Soviet oil exports to East Europe in 1974 already reached 59 million tons (*VT 1975*, passim).

*Turkmenia is to produce 50 billion cubic meters of gas by 1975 and send most of it to central Russia through a huge pipeline system now nearly complete. The Uzbekistan-Ural system has a capacity of 22 billion cubic meters per year and pipes about that much. The recently completed 48-inch Medvezhe (western Siberia)-Moscow trunkline can deliver 14.5 billion cubic meters annually once all compressor stations are completed. T. Shabad, "News Notes," *SGRaT* (September, 1974): pp. 442-43; (February 1975): 121; Akademiia Nauk SSSR and Gosplan SSSR, *Sredneaziatskii ekonomicheskii raion* (Moscow, 1972), pp. 60-61. An older line from western Siberia to the Urals has a capacity of 10 billion cubic meters. Shabad, *Basic Industrial*, p. 243. Western Siberian petroleum output in 1975 was scheduled to reach 146.5 million tons; and with only three large eastern refineries expecting to use this oil during the 1970s, it is reasonable to suppose that between 90 and 100 million tons will flow westward. *Ekonomicheskaia gazeta* (1975): no. 3, 2. Oil development in Kazakhstan has been slowed, but 1975 production should still exceed 23 million tons. *SGRaT* (May 1975): 334. The 1980 projection is based on the assumption that western Siberian petroleum production will reach 270 million tons and two more giant natural gas pipelines will be completed from the Ob estuary to the Moscow area.

†This estimate, made by Arthur W. Write, is based on the official exchange rate of $1.35:1 ruble (with the proper caveat) and is predicated on an average wellhead cost of western Siberian crude at 10 rubles per metric ton (1.40 rubles per U.S. barrel) and on a transport cost of 1 kopek per ton kilometer through large-diameter pipelines. Arthur W.

planners' decisions, provided they can obtain long-term guarantees for prices that sustain such profit.

It is thus entirely possible that, from about 1975 to 1980, the Ukraine, like some other regions, will not obtain from Soviet Asia all the fuel needed (80 million tons of oil equivalent by the end of the 1970s) to support a 4 percent growth in energy consumption along with levels of fuel exports current in the mid-1970s. Moscow planners may decide to lower the industrial growth rate or refrain from expanding energy supplies to other sectors in this republic. I am not prepared to judge the economic rationality of such a decision, I have no way of knowing whether an incremental ton of Siberian oil, whose cost in the eastern Ukraine and Moscow or the western Ukraine and Leningrad is almost identical, yields greater return in the Ukrainian or the Russian centers. The problem is larger than the optimization of energy flows per se, a simulation of which I attempted elsewhere.[90] Because of variations in labor productivity, and differences in industrial structure and past investment in fixed facilities, the same increment in energy demand does not have equal weight throughout the spatial system. Still less do I know whether $30 of profit gained from a ton of exported petroleum results in greater economic benefit to the Soviet state than an extra ton of oil consumed in the Ukraine (or elsewhere), though I suspect it does.

Beyond the early 1980s, the future is still more blurred; but it seems that constraints on energy supply from the Soviet East may be less severe. We lack data on proven reserves of Siberian oil (though further exploration could raise output to above 400 million tons),* but transport difficulties for the really massive flow of natural gas should be largely overcome by then. Soviet plans call for the piping of some 300 billion cubic meters of gas (more than 340 million tons of standard fuel equivalent) from the supergiant fields around the Ob estuary, where discovered reserves are claimed to be larger than those of North America as a whole.[91] In addition, large quantities of eastern Siberian lignite (either in the form of briquets or of electricity) should by that time reach the Urals, releasing gas and oil for regions farther west. Also, as a result of such

---

Write, "The USSR and the Energy Crisis," *Foreign Affairs* (October 1974). The average wellhead cost in western Siberia is the most uncertain part of the estimate. From recent Soviet sources, one can derive wellhead costs ranging from 6 to 9 rubles, depending on the interest charge. See N. V. Mel'nikov, *Mineral'noe toplivo* (Moscow, 1971), p. 179, and data given by Robert Campbell, "Siberian Energy Resources and the World Energy Market," in M. Yves Laulan, ed., *Exploitation of Siberia's Natural Resources* (Brussels: NATO, 1974), p. 73.

*A Soviet article claims that western Siberian oil reserves are adequate to raise annual output to 400-500 million tons. The nature of these "reserves," however, is not explained; and the statement should be regarded as an expression of faith in the region's potential rather than as a forecast. K. M. Zviagintseva, "On the Three Fuel and Energy Supply Zones of Siberia," *SGRaT* (October 1974): 497.

massive energy transfers, whatever remains of the dwindling reserves of the northern Caucasus* should all be used locally and in the eastern Ukraine.

Even through unamortized pipelines, the cost of western Siberian and Central Asian gas in the Ukraine should be somewhat lower than the marginal cost of Donets' coal, and that of fuel oil from western Siberian crude no more than 50 percent of that on an even calorific basis.[92] But the big pipeline system between the northern Caucasus, the eastern Ukraine, and Moscow, presently transporting some 52 billion cubic meters northward, is fully amortized. With the flow reversed, that amount of Siberian gas should cost little more than in the Central Region. Moreover, in order to utilize the transcontinental pipeline system at full capacity and eliminate seasonal oscillation, the exhausted Ukrainian (and northern Caucasian) reservoirs should, and no doubt will, be filled. With considerable economic justification, Ukrainian planners could then demand original prices for this gas, at least on the net amount that had been withdrawn from the republic for other regions of the USSR and for export.

Even withholding judgment on the extent of Soviet oil reserves, there is no reason why sufficient quantities of Siberian hydrocarbons could not be piped to the Ukraine to guarantee incremental fuel needs in the longer runs. For the shorter run, however, the time lag in development and pipeline construction (particularly for natural gas) and the competing demands of other regions and of export earnings (particularly for oil) must be reckoned with. A 1972 study suggested 28-33 billion cubic meters of gas "imports" into the Ukraine by 1975 (about 50 percent from Soviet Asia), with roughly the same amount to be sent out of the republic. Yet it is clear that no more than 15 billion cubic meters are received today, all from the neighboring Russian region of the northern Caucasus, where reserves are also quickly depleting, while the Ukraine pipes out almost twice as much.[93] In the future, presumably the early 1980s, the study foresees an inflow that may reach 75 billion cubic meters, but anticipates a very substantial growth of exports as well.[94]

The contradictory signals in the Soviet press regarding the future supply and surplus of oil may be politically instigated; they may also reflect genuine uncertainties in response to the growth of proven petroleum reserves. But there are no doubts about the vast size of Soviet natural gas resources; and delays notwithstanding, Soviet technology seems fully capable of making them available

---

*Of all Soviet gas reserves, those of the northern Caucasus are being depleted at the most rapid rate. Since 1970, output from the two most prolific centers of the region (Krasnodar and Stavropol's *krais*) declined by almost 60 percent. *Ekonomicheskaia gazeta* (1975): no. 17, 5. "Surplus" petroleum from the northern Caucasus now moves mostly to the Ukraine, but a decline has also begun in oil production. A. N. Markova, "Razvitie mezhraionnykh sviazei po produktam pererabotki nefti," *Voprosy geografii* (1964): no. 65, 65-66; T. Shabad, "News Notes," *SGRaT* (May 1975): 333.

to consuming areas. Nor are there reasons to believe that Soviet interest in applying tertiary recovery techniques to old reservoirs should not significantly increase the available supply of crude oil in the future.[95] In contrast with the erratic record of Western powers, one must give Soviet planners relatively high marks for the long-range, purposeful, and by and large sound development and management of their energy resources since the mid-1950s. Such purposeful, long-range planning should continue to bear fruit in the future.

It is virtually certain, however, that the gradual exhaustion of reserves in the European USSR and the increasing reliance on the eastern regions will continue to raise the cost of energy in all major consuming areas west of the Urals. Equally important, the eastward shift in fuel supplies will increase the demand on western provinces, including the Ukraine, to provide massive investment funds; but data for such capital flows are presently unavailable, and will likely remain so. In the short and even medium run, such investment flows are most unlikely to be exactly balanced by the return flow of natural resources for each and every region. The Ukraine may not receive its full fair share of eastern energy in the immediate future. Most probably it will not, and cannot, receive it at the speed at which the much more accessible Ukrainian reserves were exploited for the benefit of the republic and the Soviet Union as a whole. We may speculate about possible alternative paths of resource development in the hypothetical situation of sovereign control over mineral reserves, perhaps resulting in a slower rate of resource depletion, but the exercise will not take us very far. Energy self-sufficiency for any region and republic west of the Urals (with the possible exception of Estonia) is not a choice open to the Soviet government today.

CONCLUSION

In this chapter I hoped to highlight the influence of mineral resources on the economic development and industrial profile of the second most important Soviet republic. In the age of coal, steel, and heavy machinery, these resources were almost ideally suited to support a stream of nationally wanted products. In the eastern part of the Ukraine, they have helped to generate a massive complex of interlocking basic manufacturing activities rivaling that in the Ruhr. Given priorities of central planners, which in the Soviet context substitute for national demand, the industrial sectors that came to determine the place of the republic in the national and international (CMEA) division of labor were those based on fuel-energy production, the metallurgical cycle, and the extraction and processing of heavy chemicals. This line of development has achieved for the Ukraine an industrial might that, if measured by the output of basic capital goods, seems to exceed that of the great nation-states of Western Europe. Despite a relative decline in its previous dominance, brought about by war destruction and the conscious eastward push of Soviet economic policy, this heavy industrial complex is still the largest in the USSR today.

Given the resource base, superior location, and sectoral priorities of Soviet leadership, such specialization for the Ukraine served the goals of central planners well. It also bestowed real benefits on the Ukraine itself in the form of established production facilities, an excellent transport infrastructure, and a great economic weight within the Soviet and CMEA regional system. However, the detrimental effects of this specialization are also obvious, and have become more acute of late. The low-value resource-extractive industries and primary and semifinished manufacturing represent an increasingly unfavorable "export base," particularly in view of the shortage of oil in the republic. The dominance of hightly capital-intensive, spatially inelastic industries has resulted in a relatively low level of profitability. It has retarded dispersion and diversification, and has helped to perpetuate gross underutilization of labor and serious underdevelopment in more than 50 percent of the Ukraine. And, more ominous for the future, the continued overemphasis on heavy, primary sectors has pushed the region's energy need to the point where its fuel output is no longer sufficient to guarantee past rates of economic growth. Impending resource exhaustion has cast its shadow over this most richly endowed of all comparably sized regions of the USSR.

Greater diversification of the industrial base, with stress on labor-intensive light engineering, automotive, and consumer products, is imperative if these problems are to be alleviated. Indeed, the increasing manpower shortage in the Soviet economy outside the Muslim and Caucasian provinces is making the Ukraine's labor resources, relative to its mineral wealth, much more important for the country as a whole. At the same time, the emergence of big new ferrous ore and metallurgical centers on the Russian Plain will ease the strain placed on Ukrainian supplies by other Soviet and CMEA areas. Also, the massive flow of Siberian and Transcaspian hydrocarbon fuels to theEuropean RSFSR and westward should eliminate these regions' traditional demands for Ukrainian energy resources.

Yet, even with greater diversification and a sharp relative decrease of energy-intensive primary industries in the industrial structure and economic specialization, Ukrainian energy needs are outspacing domestic supplies, and will increasingly do so in the future. Having been a major provider of fuel for all European regions of the country since the nineteenth century, the Ukraine sees its economic growth threatened by an impending energy shortage—made all the more critical by the serious underdevelopment of its own western provinces. Like other west-of-the-Urals areas, the Ukraine must depend on nuclear power and fuels from Soviet Asia for its incremental energy needs, though it should also have an increasing claim on the remaining hydrocarbon reserves of the neighboring northern Caucasus. Nuclear development, Siberian supplies, and the worsening geological conditions of domestic reserves are certain to require greater investment and increasing lead time in development. For the rest of the 1970s, perhaps even longer, competing demands of other Soviet regions and of the CMEA countries for Siberian crude and the sharp rise in the opportunity cost of Russian oil for export will further complicate the problem of energy supply.

The future is by no means gloomy. All around, the Ukraine is still the best-endowed Soviet province, and its metallic and nonfuel mineral riches are clearly capable of further expansion. Despite real strain on its fuel economy, the growing energy deficit is far from the worst in the country's major regions, though it could become very serious by the mid-1980s. Its industrial momentum, increasingly important manpower resources, and locational advantages within a more tightly knit CMEA, will likely ensure it sufficient supplies of "imported" fuels from the Soviet East in the longer run. At what cost and actual investment contribution these will be secured are impossible to guess, but it seems that the incremental cost of this energy should be roughly in line with the most expensive domestic sources. As in other mature regions, natural resources have largely played their part in economic growth. Their role is being taken by other sectors, which now must assume the burden of supplementing and even supplanting the dwindling reserves and low-cost supplies.

NOTES

1. I. V. Nikol'skii, "The Role of Economic Sectors in the Formation of Regional Production Complexes," *Soviet Geography: Review and Translations (SGRaT)* (January 1972): 17. The author includes a detailed bibliography of Soviet works concerned with the specialization and economic base of production complexes and economic regions. Such regional comparative advantage is naturally understood within a structurally controlled system reflecting planners' goals.

2. H. S. Perloff and L. Wingo, "Natural Resource Endowment and Regional Economic Growth," in Joseph G. Spengler, ed., *Natural Resources and Economic Growth* (Washington, D.C.: Resources for the Future, 1961), p. 200. The authors' third requirement, a high induced multiplier (that is, that a substantial proportion of the returns from the export sector find its way into active demand for regionally produced goods and services) need not apply under a command economy. Under central planning, the level and composition of consumer demand are not allowed to limit production seriously.

3. Akademiia Nauk SSSR and Gosplan SSSR, *Ukrainskaia SSR, Ekonomicheskie raiony* (Moscow, 1972), p. 221; M. M. Palamarchuk, V. D. Sliusar, and I. S. Bazhan, "Rivni ekonomichnoho rozvytku raioniv UkRSR i osnovni napriamy ikh zblyzhennia," in Akademiia Nauk UkRSR, *Suchasni problemy heohrafichnoi nauky v UkRSR* (Kiev, 1966), p. 78. The level of industrialization relative to the Ukrainian average was computed as follows:

$$\frac{\text{index of industrial employment per 1,000 inhabitants} + \text{index per capita industrial fixed assets}}{2}$$

Since labor-intensive industries tend not to be highly capital-intensive, and vice versa, such an index minimizes the distortion of branch structure in the different parts of the republic.

4. *Narodne hospodarstvo Ukrains'koi RSR* 1971 (Kiev, 1972) *(Narhosp) 1971*, p. 66. The reference here is to export not compensated by import on a calorific basis. Gross "export" from the Ukraine was, of course, much larger—almost 67 million tons of standard fuel—but imports were also very large.

5. Akademiia Nauk SSSR, *Toplivno-energeticheskie resursy* (Moscow, 1968), pp. 64-66. For an explanation of the various reserve categories for solid fuels and minerals, see *Ekonomicheskaia entsiklopediia. Promyshlennost' i stroitel'stvo*, I (Moscow, 1969), pp. 502-03.

6. *Toplivno-energeticheskie resursy*, p. 67. According to Akademiia Nauk-Gosplan, *Ukrainskaia SSR*, p. 77, 38 percent of the A + B + C$_1$ reserves of the Ukrainian part of the Donbas is coking coal.

7. Akademiia Nauk Ukrains'koi RSR, *Kadastr mineral'nykh resursiv Ukrains'koi RSR* (Kiev, 1971), pp. 71, 94; Theodore Shabad, *Basic Industrial Resources of the USSR* (New York: Columbia University Press, 1969), p. 187.

8. A. E. Probst, *Razvitie toplivnoi bazy raionov SSR* (Moscow, 1968), p. 48, gives total regional shares on a calorific basis at intervals until 1965. The share of the trans-Ural regions in 1970 can be computed by converting output in physical units to calorific equivalents (1 ton of oil = 1.45 standard ton; 1,000 cubic meters of dry natural gas = 1.5 standard ton). Conversion equivalents for coals from the various fields are given by A. E. Probst, Iu. A. Sokolov, and T. E. Makarova, *Sravnitel'nye tekhniko-ekonomicheskie pokazateli po dobyche i transportu topliva po raionam SSSR* (Moscow, 1964), p. 37. Hydroelectricity can be converted as 1 kwh = 123 grams or 336 grams of standard fuel, depending on the methodology employed. Output data were taken from *Narodnoe khoziaistvo SSSR (Narkhoz) 1922-1972* (Moscow, 1973), pp. 61, 142; *Narhosp 1971*, p. 66; *Ugol'* (1972): no. 4, 69.

9. Ibid.

10. N. D. Leliukhina, *Ekonomicheskaia effektivnost' razmeshcheniia chernoi metallurgii* (Moscow, 1973), pp. 124-27, 149. For 1965, when the weighted mean cost of Ukrainian concentrate was 93 percent of the Soviet average, see R. S. Livshits, *Effektivnost' kontsentratsii proizvodstva v promyshlennosti SSSR* (Moscow, 1971), p. 271. Seventy-five percent of both the raw iron ore and the manganese mined in the Ukraine in 1970 came from open-pit operations. A decade earlier, open-pit mines accounted for less than 45 percent of undressed ores of both metals. I. A. Zaitsev, *Nauchno-tekhnicheskii progress i effektivnost' proizvodstva chernykh metallov* (Kiev, 1973), p. 73.

11. Akademiia Nauk Ukrains'koi RSR, *Kadastr mineral'nykh*, p. 71.

12. T. Shabad, "News Notes," *SGRaT* (June 1974): 377.

13. Akademiia Nauk Ukrajns'koi RSR, *Kadastr mineral'nykh*, pp. 88-90; *Vneshnaia torgovlia SSSR (VT) 1918-66*, pp. 128-29; *VT 1967*, p. 27. The rapid development of the Kursk Magnetic Anomaly will substantially reduce the share of the Ukraine in the export of Soviet iron ore. Recently a 2,500-million DM contract was signed with a West German consortium to build a combine near Kursk with an annual capacity of 5 million tons of metallic pellets and 2.7 million tons of rolled metal, with Germany purchasing 40 percent of the pellets. *Izvestia (I)*, March 28, 1974; Moscow Narodny Bank, *Press Bulletin*, March 27, 1974, pp. 4-5. East-European countries are also participating in the development of the KMA. See *Népszabadság* (Budapest), January 23, 1974, p. 10.

14. Computed from data given in T. Shabad, "News Notes," *SGRaT* (June 1974): 378.

15. Livshits, *Razmeshchenie chernoi*, pp. 226-31, 236-37, 242, 244.

16. Akademiia Nauk SSSR, *Promyshlennost' v khoziaistvennom*, insert after p. 236 and p. 242; N. D. Leliukhina, *Perspektivy razvitiia chernoi metallurgii tsentral'nykh raionov SSSR* (Moscow, 1966), p. 163.

17. Vsevolod Holubnychy, "Some Realities in the Economic Integration of East-Central Europe," *Studies for a New Central Europe*, ser. 3, nos. 3-4 (1973/74): 87-97.

18. *Ukraine: A Concise Encyclopaedia* (Toronto: Toronto University Press, 1970), II, p. 902.

19. V. P. Estigneev, *Effektivnost' razmeshcheniia mashinostroeniia v vostochnykh i zapadnykh raionakh SSSR* (Moscow, 1972), pp. 93-94.

20. Leliukhina, *Ekonomicheskaia effektivnost'*, p. 32. At the same time, 21 percent of the ferrous metals consumed (probably representing special types) had to be imported. Ibid., p. 26. Because of incomplete specialization of Ukrainian rolling mills, rolled steel imports entering the Ukraine from other republics increased in 1961-68 from 1.4 to 6 million tons. *Ukrainskaia SSR. Ekonomicheskie raiony*, p. 208.

21. Evstigneev, op. cit., p. 79.

22. P. V. Voloboi and V. A. Popovkin, *Problemy terytorial'noi spetsializatsii i kompleksnoho rozvytku narodnoho hospodartsva Ukrains'koi RSR* (Kiev, 1972), pp. 120-21. In 1960, less than 40 percent of the chemical industry's output in the Donets'k-Dnieper region was accounted for by heavy, basic chemicals. Leslie Dienes, *Locational Factors and Locational Developments in the Soviet Chemical Industry*, Department of Geography, University of Chicago, Research Paper no. 119 (1968), p. 185.

23. T. Shabad, "News Notes," *SGRaT* (March 1975): 198.

24. See the article concerning the economic interdependence of the Ukraine and the East European members of Comecon by Holubnychy, op. cit., pp. 87-97.

25. N. G. Klimov, ed., *Problemy razvitiia ekonomiki sotsialisticheskikh stran Evropy* (Kiev, 1968), p. 368.

26. *VT 1966*, pp. 63-69.

27. Voloboi and Popovkin, op. cit., pp. 226-27. Also see Akademiia Nauk UkRSR, *Rozmishchennia produktyvnykh syl Ukrains'koi RSR*, IX (Kiev, 1970), pp. 18-21, for individual cities.

28. L. N. Telepko, *Urovni ekonomicheskogo razvitiia raionov SSSR* (Moscow, 1971), p. 157.

29. Telepko, op. cit., p. 81; *Sel'skoe khoziaistvo SSSR* (Moscow, 1971), p. 408; *Narkhoz 1973*, p. 193.

30. For the Ukraine, the change in fondootdacha is given in A. Fedorishcheva, "O vzaimosviazi pokazatelei ispol'zovaniia osnovnykh fondov i proizvoditel'nosti truda," *Ekonomika Sovetskoi Ukrainy* (*ESU*) (1974): no. 5, 22. For the USSR and the RSFSR, it is computed from the growth rates of industrial fixed assets and of industrial output between 1960 and 1972. Data from *Narkhoz 1972*, pp. 60, 196; *Narkhoz RSFSR 1967*, p. 66; *Narkhoz RSFSR 1972*, p. 39.

31. Leslie Dienes, "Investment Priorities in Soviet Regions," *Annals of the Association of American Geographers* 62 (1972): 440-41.

32. M. A. Zurabov and M. Ia. Aizenberg, "Piatiletka i problemy ekonomiki topliva," *Organizatsiia i planirovanie otraslei narodnogo khoziaistva* (*OiPONKh*) (1972): no. 26-27, 79.

33. *Narhosp 1973*, p. 117; Probst, op. cit., p. 223. Probst's table includes secondary fuel resources (those transformed from primary fuel). The table was recomputed to exclude them.

34. Economist Intelligence Unit, *Soviet Oil to 1980*, QER Special, no. 14 (June 1973): 9; T. Shabad, "News Notes," *SGRaT* (May 1975): 333-34.

35. T. Shabad, "News Notes," *SGRaT* (May 1975): 333-34.

36. V. N. Kal'chenko, *Hazova promyslovist' i tekhnichnyi prohres* (Kiev, 1972), pp. 72-75, 95. Also see M. Tikhonov and S. Polevoi, "Nekotorye voprosy ratsional'nogo ispol'zovaniia toplivnykh resursov Ukrainskoi SSR," *ESU* (1974): no. 8, 9.

37. Kal'chenko, op. cit., pp. 73, 96.

38. G. B. Iakusha, *Tekhniko-ekonomicheskie osnovy razvitiia elektro-energetiki ekonomicheskikh raionov UkSSR* (Kiev, 1965), pp. 62-63.

39. *Ugol'* (1973): no. 10, 50.

40. Akademiia Nauk-Gosplan, *Ukrainskaia SSR*, p. 72.

41. N. Khudosovtsev, "Ugol'naia promyshlennost' Ukrainy v reshaiushchem godu piatiletki," *ESU* (1973): no. 8, 13. An earlier source claims capacity expansion of 55 million tons. See *ESU* (1969): no. 11, 28.

42. Tikhonov and Polevoi, op. cit., p. 7.

43. Khudosovtsev, op. cit., pp. 12-13.

44. A. S. Pavlenko and N. N. Nekrasov, eds., *Energetika SSSR v 1970-1975 godakh* (Moscow, 1972), pp. 173-74.

45. M. Aizenberg, "Ekonomicheskie problemy toplivnogo balansa Ukrainskoi SSR," *ESU* (1969): no. 11, 28.

46. *VT 1974*, passim.

47. *Narhosp 1973*, p. 113; *VT 1973*, p. 71.

48. *VT 1973*, p. 71; *Külkereskedelmi statisztikai évkönyv, 1972* (Budapest, 1973), p. 154. The value of electricity imported by Hungary from the USSR reached a full 50 percent of the value of petroleum imports from the USSR.

49. Zurabov and Aizenberg, loc. cit.

50. Ibid., pp. 79-80.

51. *Sel'skoe khoziaistvo*, p. 408; *Narkhoz 1973*, p. 193.

52. *Gosudarstvennyi piatiletnyi plan razvitiia narodnogo khoziaistva SSSR no 1971-1975 gody* (Moscow, 1972), pp. 261-62; V. A. Ryl'skii et al., *Eletroenergeticheskaia baza ekonomicheskikh raionov SSSR* (Moscow, 1974), p. 148.

53. Dienes, *Locational Factors*, pp. 118-20, 212-23, 228-33.

54. Ryl'skii, op. cit., p. 148.

55. I. S. Koropeckyj, "National Income of the Soviet Union Republics in 1970; Revision and Some Applications," in Zbigniew M. Fallenbuchl, ed., *Economic Development in the Soviet Union and Eastern Europe* (New York: Praeger, 1975).

56. *Narkhoz 1973*, p. 9; Telepko, op. cit., pp. 80, 82.

57. Price data at various consumer points are given in V. M. Gal'perin, "Novye optovye tseny v promyshlennosti," *Gazovaia promyshlennost'* (1967): no. 1, 6; V. K. Shkatov and B. B. Suponitskii, *Optovye tseny no produktsiu tiazheloi promyshlennosti* (Moscow, 1969), pp. 45, 52-58. Production and capital cost data are given in Probst et al., op. cit., pp. 30-33, 37, and Appendix; N. V. Mel'nikov, *Mineral'noe toplivo* (2nd ed.; Moscow, 1971), pp. 175-80; *Neftianaia i gazovaia promyshlennost'* (1973): no. 5, 27. All petroleum produced in the Ukraine is consumed locally; natural gas consumption in 1970 is given in Kal'chenko, op. cit., p. 52, as 47.8 billion cubic meters. With respect to coal, the separation of steam coal and coking coal consumption is essential because of the very large price difference between the two. Ukrainian coking coal output in various years is given in *Narkhoz 1973*, p. 262. Of the 80.7 billion tons produced in 1970, 20-22 million tons were exported and sent to other Soviet republics; the rest must have been consumed locally. See Akademiia Nauk SSSR, *Promyshlennost' v khoziaistvennom komplekse ekonomicheskikh raionov SSSR* (Moscow, 1964), p. 86; A. E. Probst, *Razvitie toplivnoi bazy raionov SSSR* (Moscow, 1968), p. 31; Melnikov, op. cit., pp. 175, 183. Of the 126.4 million tons of steam coal produced in 1970, 40-42 million tons was sent to other republics and abroad. Some 84-86 million tons, therefore, was consumed in the Ukraine. See above sources for coal and *Transport i sviaz' SSSR* (Moscow, 1972), pp. 50-51, for shipment of all hard coal and coke to other Soviet republics from the Ukraine.

58. P. I. Baldin and V. V. Nezhentsev, "Tempy, proportsii i uroven' razvitiia ugol'noi promyshlennosti Ukrainskoi SSR v deviatoi piatiletke," *OiPONKh* (1972): no. 26-27, 70,

72; *Neftianaia i gazovaia promyshlennost'* (1973): no. 5, 26; and Kal'chenko, op. cit., p. 97.

59. Leslie Dienes, "Issues in Soviet Energy Policy and Conflicts over Fuel Costs in Regional Development," *Soviet Studies (SS)* (July 1971): 41-42.

60. David Hooson, "The Outlook for Regional Development in the Soviet Union," *Slavic Review (SR)* (September 1972): 552.

61. Chauncy D. Harris, *Cities of the Soviet Union* (Chicago: Rand McNally, 1970), pp. 208, 220-25.

62. *Narkhoz 1922-72*, p. 61. Growth rates computed by the compound interest formula.

63. Ibid., pp. 126, 128; Rush V. Greenslade and Wade E. Robertson, "Industrial Production in the USSR," in Joint Economic Committee, op. cit., pp. 271-78; Peter G. Peterson, *U.S.-Soviet Commercial Relationships in the New Era* (Washington, D.C.: U.S. Department of Commerce, 1972), Annex A, pp. 2, 4, 11.

64. *Narhosp 1971*, p. 66; Kal'chenko, op. cit., p. 46. The former source gives fuel and primary energy balances for 1965 and 1970. The latter gives per capita fuel consumption in 1960, 1965, and 1970. Total consumption was derived by multiplying per capita figures by total population, obtained from the respective yearbooks. Because of an apparent difference in the methodology of computation, Kal'chenko's totals are lower in 1965 and 1970. The growth rate derived from Kal'chenko data may be overstated, since during 1965-70 it significantly exceeds the rate available from *Narhosp*. On the other hand, there is no reason to suspect his rate of 4.9 percent given for the first half of the decade, since energy consumption in the USSR as a whole increased 5.8 percent during this period. *Narkhoz 1922-72*, p. 61. Growth rates computed by the compound interest formula.

65. Computed by the compound interest formula.

66. Kal'chenko, op. cit., p. 38; *Gosudarstvennyi piatiletnyi plan*, p. 366. Physical units have been converted to standard fuel equivalent. The percentage of hydroelectricity in 1975 could have been no more than in 1970.

67. Kal'chenko, op. cit., pp. 39-46.

68. *Narhosp 1971*, p. 116.

69. See Khudosovtsev, op. cit., pp. 12-13; Tikhonov and Polevoi, op. cit., p. 7.

70. *Narhosp 1973*, p. 116.

71. In Iu. Iaroshevich, "Ekonomicheskie problemy razvitiia atomnoi energetiki," *Voprosy ekonomiki (VE)* (1971): no. 6, 74; S. Fel'd and V. Shul'ga, "Problemy sovershenstvovaniia toplivno-energeticheskogo balansa," *Planovoe khoziaistvo (PKh)* (1969): no. 2, 79; *Elektrichestvo* (1970): no. 6, 4.

72. Pavlenko and Nekrasov, op. cit., pp. 138-39.

73. Philip R. Pryde and Lucy T. Pryde, "Soviet Nuclear Power," *Environment* (April 1974): 28.

74. Theodore Shabad, "News Notes," *SGRaT* (October 1974): 521.

75. *Energetika i elektrifikatsiia* (1974): no. 1, 18.

76. Ryl'skii, op. cit., p. 149.

77. Pavlenko and Nekrasov, op. cit., p. 38. The share of power stations in total gross fuel-energy consumption is considerably higher, reaching 36 percent in 1970. However, thermal power stations supply not only electricity but also large quantities of heat for space heating and process steam. *Ekonomika promyshlennosti* (1972): no. 9, 42; *Teploenergetika* (1970): no. 4, 6.

78. V. A. Ryl'skii, *Ekonomika mezhraionnykh elektroenergeticheskikh sviazei v SSSR* (Moscow, 1972), pp. 76-86.

79. Ibid., pp. 81, 99.

80. A. Ia. Avrukh et al., "Nekotorye voprosy povysheniia ekonomicheskoi effektivnosti raboty," *Elektricheskie stantsii* (1971): no. 7.

81. See ibid. on power costs in Soviet electric systems in 1970.

82. Ryl'skii, *Elektroenergeticheskaia baza*, p. 149.

83. Ryl'skii, *Ekonomika*, pp. 76-86; *Elektricheskie stantsii* (1970): no. 4, 4.

84. A. E. Probst, "Puti razvitiia toplivnogo khoziaistva SSSR," *VE* (1971): no. 6, 55.

85. A. E. Probst, *Voprosy razmeshcheniia sotsialisticheskoi promyshlennosti* (Moscow, 1971), pp. 218-19.

86. Probst, "Puti razvitiia," p. 55.

87. J. R. Lee, "Petroleum Supply in Eastern Europe," in Joint Economic Committee, *Reorientation and Commercial Relations of the Economies of Eastern Europe* (Washington, D.C.: U.S. Government Printing Office, 1974), pp. 408-19. Until 1974, the modest quantities imported from the Third World and Western countries were evidently counterbalanced by the export of refined products to the West. This, however, is unlikely to continue.

88. *The Economist*, June 5, 1975, p. 123. In January 1975, the price of Soviet oil delivered to East Europe rose 133 percent, from 16 to 37 rubles. New York *Times*, January 28, 1975, p. 3. Since this price is still 33 percent below world price levels, further increases can be expected.

89. John Surrey, "Japan's Uncertain Energy Prospects: The Problem of Import Dependence," *Energy Policy* (September 1974): 216-17.

90. Dienes, "Issues in Soviet"; and "Geographical Problems of Allocation in the Soviet Fuel Supply," *Energy Policy* (June 1973): 3-20.

91. V. G. Vasil'ev, "Poiskovo-razvedochnye raboty na gaz v SSSR," *Gazovaia promyshlennost'* (1971): no. 5, 6-7; "UN Report on Natural Gas," United Nations, Economic and Social Council, ref. G/R4 (September 1973); and J. V. Licence, "Siberia in the Context of World Natural Gas Supplies," in M. Y. Laulan, ed., *Exploitation of Siberia's Natural Resources* (Brussels: NATO, 1974), pp. 168-69, 176, supply data on reserves. For plans on production and the quantities to be sent to the European USSR, see Mel'nikov, op. cit., p. 194; *Ekonomicheskaia gazeta* (*EG*) (1970): no. 16, 19; *Ekonomika RSFSR. Soiuznye respubliki v novoi piatiletke* (Moscow, 1967), p. 98; and *Gazovaia promyshlennost'* (1969): no. 11, 13-16.

92. Mel'nikov, op. cit., pp. 175-83; Probst et al., op. cit., pp. 37-38 and Appendix.

93. Kal'chenko, op. cit., p. 100; A. K. Kortunov, *Gazovaia promyshlennost SSSR* (Moscow, 1967), p. 101.

94. Kal'chenko, op. cit., p. 100. Soviet exports have risen from 2.3 billion cubic meters in 1970 to about 14 billion cubic meters in 1974, though some of this probably comes from outside the Ukraine. *VT 1973*.

95. *EG* (1974): no. 11, 7-8.

8

INPUT-OUTPUT
ANALYSIS
James W. Gillula

INTRODUCTION

The study of the productive relations of an individual Soviet republic or economic region within the rest of the USSR has long been hampered by a lack of comprehensive data covering the imports and exports of all goods produced or consumed within a region. Even with the increase in the extent of the collection and publication of regional economic statistics since its revival in the late 1950s, data collection on interregional flows has been limited to shipments of a few major commodities expressed in physical units. Although balances of the national income and gross social product produced and used reportedly have been calculated annually for republics since 1958, the consideration of external relations has entered only as a balancing element in these accounts—the net export-import balance, which (together with losses) accounts for the difference between national income produced and used. Isolated studies have been made by Soviet economists to analyze a wider range of interregional commodity flows for individual regions. These have not, however, allowed an integration of data on exports and imports with an overall balance of production and consumption.

Since the early 1960s, however, this situation is being rectified to an increasing extent with the development of regional input-output analysis in the

The author gratefully acknowledges the support of the International Research and Exchanges Board for a 10-month research stay in the Soviet Union and of the Ford Foundation for research done within the Soviet Input-Output Research Project at Duke University. Consultation with Professor Vladimir G. Treml was invaluable in the preparation of this chapter. Thanks are also due to Per Strangert for the use of his preliminary estimates of some input-output totals for the Ukraine and to Stephen Rapawy for his estimates of employment in the Ukraine, which are included as Appendix B.

Soviet Union. An input-output table is an overall balance of the production and distribution of the output of all sectors of the economy for all uses, and the construction of regional input-output tables has thus required new efforts in the direction of determining interregional flows for each sector. The compilation of regional input-output tables has provided a new source of statistical information for the analysis of many aspects of the economies of individual Soviet republics, and the data on interregional flows that they include are certainly one of their most important features.

Work on regional input-output tables in the Soviet Union began in the late 1950s with the construction of ex post tables for four subregions of the RSFSR. During the early 1960s, initial efforts at constructing input-output tables were undertaken in each of the Baltic republics, the Transcaucasian republics, and Belorussia. With the experience of work on these early tables, it was decided that in conjunction with work on the construction of the second major national ex post input-output table (for 1966), separate tables would be compiled for each republic for that year. In 1970, while these tables for all republics were being completed, a further research effort was undertaken by the Central Economic-Mathematical Institute (TsEMI) to produce ex post input-output tables for each of the 10 large economic regions of the RSFSR for 1966.

Although ex post input-output tables were constructed for all republics for 1966, the extent of the publication of data from these tables and the use of the tables for economic analysis and planning have varied widely among republics. Basic data on interindustry flows have been published in regional statistical handbooks for eight republics including the Ukraine.[1] For several republics (including three for which data did not appear in statistical handbooks) monographs have been published describing the construction of tables and extensively analyzing the structure of input-output relations. The availability of these tables has also given rise to a wide range of studies of the productive relations of individual branches, interregional flows, and other topics of particular interest for the economy of a given republic. Again in 1972 data were collected to compile input-output tables for all republics. Data from some of these tables, including that for the Ukraine,[2] have begun to appear in regional statistical handbooks. However, the construction of these 1972 tables has not yet given rise to many published studies of the economies of individual republics based on input-output data. Only a few articles based on these 1972 tables had appeared in Soviet economic journals through 1976.[3]

Although these regional input-output tables are a potentially valuable statistical source for the analysis of interregional flows and other aspects of the economies of Soviet republics, the publication of data from these tables in statistical handbooks is never complete. As with the publication of input-output tables for the USSR as a whole, data for the interindustry deliveries of some sectors may be omitted; and values of gross output, nonmaterial inputs, and deliveries for final uses usually are omitted entirely or are summarized in terms of percentage breakdowns. In order for an input-output table to be a useful analytical tool, the values of any unpublished flows must be estimated to complete it. This can be accomplished by drawing on information from studies that have used the complete input-output table and by using data published in statistical handbooks. In this chapter a 16-sector reconstructed version of the 1966 input-output table for the Ukraine is presented, and this table is used in an analysis of the external economic relations of the Ukraine.[4]

In the section below, experience with the use of input-output analysis in the Ukraine is surveyed. Some particular features of Soviet input-output tables are then summarized before discussing the data base from which the Ukrainian table was constructed and presenting the reconstructed 16-sector table. The structure of Ukrainian exports and imports and their share of republic production and consumption are then analyzed using the values of input-output flows. Finally, the matrixes of direct and full input coefficients calculated for the Ukraine are used to analyze some indirect effects of its external relations.

USE OF INPUT-OUTPUT ANALYSIS
IN THE UKRAINE

As the brief summary of the development of regional input-output analysis in the USSR indicated, the Ukraine was not involved in the initial Soviet experiments with compiling input-output tables in the early 1960s. The 1966 input-output table was the first constructed for the Ukraine.* In contrast with the experience with the use of input-output tables in many smaller republics, the use of input-output analysis in the Ukraine has been limited. Work on the construction of the 1966 table was reported in a single article.[5] Although in other republics, the publication of data from input-output tables was accompanied by articles in economic journals analyzing the overall proportions of the table, such publications did not appear in the Ukraine. Furthermore, only a few isolated uses of the data from the input-output table have been made in the analysis of individual sectors of the Ukrainian economy. This situation was altered somewhat in 1974, with the publication of a major book on the methodology of constructing the 1966 input-output table and an analysis of its basic structure.[6]

Although the types of uses of input-output tables applied extensively in other republics have been limited in the Ukraine, a research group in the Economic Scientific Research Institute (ENDI) of the Ukrainian Gosplan has done considerable work in an area of input-output analysis important for integrating

---

*However, some work was carried out in the Ukraine in the 1920s on balance of the economy in matrix form. This is described by V. Myshkis, *Khoziaistvo Ukrainy* (1927): nos. 2 and 3.

it with regularly collected statistical data and improving its applicability to economic planning. As discussed further in the next section, Soviet ex post input-output tables (both national and regional) are constructed on the basis of a sector classification that differs from the one used by TsSU (Central Statistical Administration) in its statistical accounting and by Gosplan (State Planning Committee) in formulating plans. Sectors of the economy in an input-output table are defined on a "commodity" basis (that is, each sector shows the production and distribution of a group of products, regardless of the "economic branch" or establishment in which they are produced). This difference from the TsSU and Gosplan branch classifications (which are based on the sums of the statistical reports of enterprises that may produce goods properly classified in other "economic branches") represents a major limitation on the possibility of using existing input-output tables in economic planning.

In order to integrate the input-output table with the basic economic balances that should constitute an overall balance of the economy of a republic (balances of production, capital formation, labor use), an ENDI research group constructed an input-output table for the Ukraine in terms of economic sectors as normally defined in TsSU accounting practice.[7] The primary data from the statistical survey that underlay the 1966 input-output table were used to construct an input-output table for 20-30 sectors. This provided a more detailed breakdown of the balance of the republic's economy, but its potential use for planning purposes is still hindered by the lack of studies of changes in the structure of material inputs over time (a topic widely studied in other republics).

As with other particular applications of regional input-output tables, the analysis of the external relations of the Ukraine, based on input-output data, has been less extensive than that for other republics. The construction of the 1966 input-output tables for each republic required special statistical surveys to determine the total values of interregional flows, and in most cases the values of exports (and imports) by each sector to (and from) each other republic were also surveyed. Such a survey was carried out for the Ukraine, but few of its details have been published. Although several republics (including Latvia, Estonia, Armenia, and Kirgizia) have published tables showing the distribution by republic of their imports and exports, this type of information has not been published for the Ukraine. Much of the analysis of imports and exports in this paper is drawn from an account of the methodology and some summary results of the survey of interregional flows published by ENDI.[8]

A number of factors may be cited in an attempt to explain the lagging development of the use of input-output analysis in the Ukraine. Although the construction of an input-output table for an economy as large and complex as that of the Ukraine is a major task, the Ukraine clearly has the capability to organize such an effort, since it has been in the forefront among Soviet republics in other areas of the development of methodology for regional income accounting and guidelines for formulating economic plans for republics and their subregions.[9] The relatively late publication of the 1966 table is one factor in explaining its limited use.* A more important factor, however, is the apparently limited access to the complete input-output table that economists outside the Ukrainian Gosplan ENDI have been given. The extent of the effort to avoid the publication of certain portions of the original table is shown by the fact that even the one major published study on the structure of the Ukrainian economy that is based on the 1966 table largely used data from the partially published matrix of interindustry flows.[10] This failure to widen the range of input-output studies has left the Ukraine behind other republics in what seems to be an increasingly important area of regional accounting and planning.

SOVIET INPUT-OUTPUT ACCOUNTING

Soviet input-output tables (both national and regional) reflect the basic division in Soviet statistical accounting methodology between productive and nonproviductive branches of the economy.† The first quadrant of a table shows only interindustry flows among sectors of material production. "Nonproductive" branches of the economy are included in the second quadrant as users of final output, along with personal consumption, capital accumulation, payments for depreciation and repair, exports, and other miscellaneous final uses. Third-quadrant entries in the input-output table show wages, profits, turnover tax, and other elements of value added (national income).‡ Depreciation charges are shown as a separate row between the first and third quadrants.

Imports may be treated in various ways in input-output tables. In some earlier experiments with Soviet regional input-output tables, the value of noncompetitive imports was shown as a row of inputs to purchasing sectors. Each element of this row thus represented the imports of the products of all

---

*The late appearance of the table may be accounted for in part by the size of the task involved in collecting information. It was found necessary to carry out some additional surveys in 1967, while the table was being compiled, to supplement the original information. The survey of organizations involved in interregional flows and the possible difficulty of obtaining information from union enterprises are other factors that may have extended the time needed to complete the table.

†The discussion of Soviet input-output accounting methodology in this section applies to the 1966 ex post input-output tables for the USSR and republics in general. Input-output tables for other years and individual republics have been constructed with variations of this methodology. For a more detailed discussion of these topics, see V. G. Treml et al., *The Structure of the Soviet Economy* (New York: Praeger, 1972), chs. 2-6.

‡The numbering of quadrants in Soviet input-output tables differs from that normally used in the tables of Western countries. The "northeast" (final demand) quadrant is numbered II, and the "southwest" (value added) quadrant is numbered III.

sectors used as inputs in each domestic sector can be distinguished, this row can be disaggregated to show a complete matrix of imported input coefficients. Flows in the first quadrant, with imports defined in this way, thus represent only domestically produced inputs. In the 1966 (national and regional) input-output tables, however, a single vector of imports is distinguished; each element represents the total value of the output of a given sector that is imported rather than the value of the output of all other sectors used as inputs. Each first-quadrant entry with imports defined in this way represents the total value of produced plus imported inputs used in the production of the output of a sector. This vector of imports is normally shown as a column in the second quadrant with a negative sign, although in the display of some tables, the values of imports are also shown at the bottom of the third quadrant together with an additional row showing the total supply (produced plus imported) of the products of each sector. The imports and exports shown in a regional input-output table include both interregional and international flows, and it will be in this combined sense that those terms are used here unless specific reference to foreign imports or exports is made.

Soviet ex post input-output tables are constructed to be consistent with the values of major economic aggregates in the national income and product accounts calculated annually by the TsSU. However, because of some basic methodological differences in the accounting practices used in input-output tables, the values of these totals may not be identical with those published in statistical handbooks. The two major sources of such differences are the use of a classification of sectors on a "commodity" basis, as mentioned above, and the valuation of the tables in final purchasers' prices.*

It is desirable to construct input-output tables in terms of sectors defined on a commodity basis, since the structure of inputs is not then affected by changes over time in the organizational structure of the economy. The value of the output of each sector in an input-output table thus defined is determined by first subtracting from the value of output of the economic branch (in standard national income accounting) the value of the output of products assigned to other sectors of the input-output table. This smaller total is the "profile" production for a given economic branch. The total output of the sector defined on a commodity basis is then determined by adding to its "profile" production the value of its goods produced (as "nonprofile" output) in all other economic

---

*USSR input-output tables have also been constructed in terms of producers' prices, but all 1966 tables for republics were constructed using purchasers' prices. The table for Latvia differs slightly from those of other republics in the valuation of imports and exports. See A. G. Granberg, ed., *Mezhotraslevye balansy v analize territorial'nykh proportsii SSSR* (Novosibirsk, 1975), p. 104.

branches. This adjustment of gross output totals primarily affects the relative sizes of the values of output of individual industrial sectors.

Since the data on the use of material and other inputs regularly collected by TsSU covers only broad categories of inputs and does not allow expenditures on "profile" production to be distinguished, the construction of input-output tables requires a major data-gathering effort. The structure of inputs for the "profile" production of each sector and the total value of "profile" and "non-profile" production are determined on the basis of complete or selective surveys of the enterprises in each branch. (The survey conducted for the 1966 Ukrainian table is described in the next section.)

The use of purchasers' prices in most Soviet input-output tables is dictated by the fact that the data necessary for construction of tables are obtained directly from enterprises. These enterprises know the value of inputs purchased in terms of prices they pay (that is, purchasers' prices, which include distribution charges and turnover taxes, if any). The producing enterprises, of course, also have information on the value of their output in enterprise prices. However, because of complexities of the Soviet supply and distribution system, they have little or no knowledge of the ultimate destination of their output. Thus, of necessity Soviet input-output tables are built up from columns and not from rows, and such a process necessitates the use of purchasers' prices. This is a shortcoming of Soviet input-output tables recognized by Soviet economists: changes in the pattern of distribution to its users of a given value of a sector's output (in physical units) can affect the total value of output, and direct input coefficients are subject to changes over time that are unrelated to technological factors.

As a result of the use of purchasers' prices, the value of gross social product for the economy shown in an input-output table is larger than that reported in producers' prices in statistical handbooks as the total value of output of the "Freight Transportation" and "Trade and Distribution" sectors. This double counting occurs because the value of the output of these services sectors is included both in the value of inputs of each sector and in the value of its deliveries for all uses. The structure of the gross value of output by branch as shown in the input-output table will also differ from that calculated in producers' prices because of the differential use of transportation and distribution services among sectors. A further result of the use of purchasers' prices in input-output accounting is that the rows of the "Transportation" and "Trade and Distribution" sectors show deliveries only to sectors of material production (first-quadrant flows). Deliveries by these sectors for final uses are zero by definition.

One additional difference between input-output and standard TsSU accounting practices that is relevant for the reconstruction of the Ukrainian input-output table is the treatment of national income. Although the total of produced national income as shown in statistical handbooks is unaffected by the factors discussed above, that total is adjusted in the input-output table by removing the "special income from foreign trade" included in the value of national income of the "Trade and Distribution" branch as it is reported in statistical handbooks. This "special income" arises as a result of the differences between the prices paid by the Soviet Foreign Trade Ministry to producers of exports and the prices charged foreign purchasers for these products, plus the differences between prices paid by the Foreign Trade Ministry for imports and those charged domestic consumers of imports. Since producers of exports are paid enterprise prices (excluding turnover taxes) for their products and domestic consumers of imports are charged industry prices (including turnover taxes), this difference is always positive and is substantial for the USSR as a whole.[11]

Under standard accounting practices, this special income from foreign trade is allocated among republics by TsSU USSR according to their participation in foreign trade and is included in the values of produced national income for the "Trade and Distribution" branch reported in republic statistical handbooks. Since this income is not offset by output entries for the "Trade and Distribution" branch, it must be subtracted from the value of national income for this branch and from the total value of national income produced in order to maintain a balance in the input-output table.

THE 1966 UKRAINIAN INPUT-OUTPUT TABLE

The 1966 input-output table for the Ukraine was constructed by the Ukrainian TsSU with the participation of the republic Gosplan and the Institute of Economics of the Ukrainian Academy of Sciences.[12] They followed the general methodological guidelines established by the TsSU USSR, and the particular methodological features of Soviet input-output tables described above. It was constructed in purchasers' prices on the basis of a classification of sectors in "commodity" terms. The list of sectors differs only slightly from that employed in the USSR input-output table in value terms for 1966. The USSR table was constructed for 110 branches, including 95 branches of industry, 5 of construction, and 2 of transportation, while the table for the Ukraine distinguished 105 branches, including an equal number of industry branches but only one branch each for construction and transportation.

In constructing the Ukrainian input-output table, a wide range of statistical information from the standard TsSU reporting forms was used. In addition to the use of the major totals of the national income and product accounts as control totals for the input-output table, information on the freight transportation and trade and distribution branches from enterprise reporting forms was employed. The totals drawn from national income accounts included those for major subdivisions of final output (personal and public consumption and the accumulation of fixed and working capital) and the various elements of national income (wages, social security payments, profits, turnover tax). However, in order to determine the values of each of these entries for the sectors of the input-output table defined on a commodity basis, and to gather information on the structure of material inputs, a special survey of enterprises was undertaken.

A survey for the construction of the 1966 Ukrainian input-output table covered more than 8,500 enterprises and organizations.[13] For branches with a small number of heterogeneous enterprises, the survey was often complete, while for branches composed of a large number of homogeneous enterprises, selective sampling was used. Complete surveys of all enterprises were conducted in the branches of ferrous and nonferrous metallurgy, coke products, oil extraction and refining, gas, and chemical products, and in many subbranches of machine-building and metalworking. For industry as a whole, the enterprises surveyed included 7.1 percent of all industrial enterprises; they produced 48.9 percent of the total value of output of industry, using 44.2 percent of the industrial labor force and 53.8 percent of industrial fixed capital stock.[14] In other branches of material production, 5-10 percent of enterprises were surveyed, including 939 kolkhozes and 134 sovkhozes and about 10 percent of transportation enterprises. The structure of material inputs for branches in the nonproductive sphere was determined from a survey of about 5 percent of all organizations and institutions of health, education, culture, passenger transportation, housing, and administration.

The collection of data on Ukrainian interregional and international flows also required an extensive survey of organizations involved in these external relations.[15] The primary sources of information in this survey were union-republic and republic ministries and organizations of material-technical supply and some union supply administrations located in the Ukraine. These include the Chief Administration for Material-Technical Supply UkSSR and its territorial administrations, the Ministry of Trade UkSSR, and more than 17 Ukrainian ministries for various branches of the economy. Since both production and distribution organizations were surveyed, only the exports and imports of products not handled by the Ministry of Trade and the Ministry of Supply were surveyed in production ministries, in order to avoid double counting of exports and imports. Data were collected on total supply, on total imports and exports, and on the distribution of both imports and exports among other Soviet republics and foreign countries.

To supplement the basic information from this survey, additional sources of data were used: plans for the production and delivery of machinery and equipment, a special survey of the imports and exports of the food industry and of agricultural products, an energy-fuel balance for the Ukraine, and transportation statistics for the Ukraine on the interregional flows of several basic commodities in physical units. The values of foreign exports and imports of the Ukraine were obtained from information supplied by the Ministry of Foreign Trade of the USSR, the departments for foreign trade in Gosplan USSR and UkSSR, and the Chief Administration of Material-Technical Supply UkSSR.

As the summary of input-output analysis in the Ukraine pointed out, the publication of input-output data and studies using the input-output table for analysis of the Ukrainian economy have been quite limited compared to other Soviet republics. However, available Ukrainian sources, together with a comparative study of the 1966 input-output tables for all Soviet republics,[16] have made it possible to reconstruct a 16-sector version of the 1966 Ukrainian table. Data on the interindustry flows of the Ukraine taken from the original 105-sector table were published in a 47-sector format that omits 29 of these sectors and shows the flows of many others as aggregates of two or more of the sectors in the original table.

The sectors in the original 105 sector table that have been omitted in the published table can be determined by comparison with the sector classification for the 1966 input-output table for the USSR, which was constructed for a nearly identical list of industry branches. Where sector names for aggregated branches in the published table were ambiguous as to the inclusion of sectors, key interindustry flows were examined to determine where omissions seemed likely. The single omitted "Fuels" sector is a minor one—"Other Fuels." The omission of this sector has no effect on the input structure of the aggregate "Fuels" branch, since its output is entirely imported.[17] Some minor "Wood and Paper Products" and "Construction Materials" subsectors omitted also constitute only a small share of the output of their respective branches. However, there are major omissions in the published matrix of interindustry flows for "Machine Building and Metalworking" and "Food Products." Unpublished flows for these branches represent a substantial share of the branch total. For "Machine Building and Metalworking," unpublished sectors include the major branches "Radiotechnical Machinery and Equipment (M&E)," "Electronic Products," "Repair of M&E," "Railroad Rolling Stock and Equipment," "Shipbuilding," "Cable Products," and "Other Metal Wares."* Under "Food Products," the major sector "Other Food Products" was omitted, as were "Confections," "Tobacco Products," "Cosmetics," and two unidentified sectors.

Input-output data published by TsSU also included a sample of direct and full input coefficients that are helpful in estimating the values of gross output for a number of sectors. But no data from the second or third quadrant of the Ukrainian input-output table were published.

The reconstruction of the 1966 Ukrainian input-output table was carried out in two stages. First, a complete table was reconstructed in terms of the

---

*Other omitted machine-building and metalworking sectors are "Casting M&E," "Logging and Paper M&E," "Printing M&E," "Medical Implements," "Other Products of Machine Building," "Metal Structures," and "Abrasives."

six major branches of the economy ("Industry," "Construction," "Agriculture and Forestry," "Transportation and Communications," "Trade and Distribution," and "Other Branches of Material Production"), based on the information for a complete four-sector table given by Bondarenko.[18] Subsequently, the control totals derived for "Industry" were used in conjunction with additional information on the breakdown of second-quadrant and third-quadrant totals by branches of industry to estimate a 16-sector version of the table. (The reconstruction process and the sources on which it was based are described in Appendix A.) The complete 16-sector input-output table for the Ukraine is given in Table 8.1. Matrixes of direct input coefficients and full input coefficients (the Leontief inverse $(I-A)^{-1}$) are given in Tables 8.2 and 8.3.

With the information available, it was possible to distinguish two columns of final output (quadrant II) in addition to those for exports and imports (totals of foreign plus interregional deliveries). "Consumption" (both personal and social) is shown separately, and the "Other Final Demand" column includes deliveries for capital accumulation, payments for capital depreciation and repair, losses, and other elements of final demand. In the third quadrant, the values of "National Income" for each sector (total value added) are broken down to show "Wages" and "Other Value Added." The latter includes payments to social security, profits, turnover taxes, and all other elements of national income.

Comparing the reconstructed 16-sector table with the published 47-sector table, the extent of omissions in the published data on interindustry flows can be determined. There was an omission of 18.3 percent of all flows in the first quadrant, and 27.2 percent of all flows between subbranches of "Industry" were omitted. Approximately 17.0 percent of "Industry" deliveries to the other five branches of the economy and 10.0 percent of the inputs to "Industry" from these branches were omitted.

One important aspect of the reconstruction of the Ukrainian input-output table should be noted for its use in analysis. Although good estimates for each of the 10 major sectors of industry and industry totals were possible for most elements of the table, information was often lacking on the "Industry N.E.C." sector, which served as a residual entry in the calculation of many entries. No analytical significance can thus be attached to specific estimates made for this sector.* On the other hand, any errors in the entries of the "Industry N.E.C." sector should have little total effect on such analytical exercises as the calculation and use of the Leontief inverse.

---

*Studies of the input-output relations of "Industry N.E.C." offer little insight into the Soviet economy, since this sector is composed of a very heterogeneous group of products and is subject to large changes in product mix over time.

TABLE 8.1

Input-Output Table for the Ukrainian SSR, 1966 (purchasers' prices, × 1,000 rubles)

	1 Metallurgy	2 Fuels	3 Power	4 Machine Bldg. Metalwrkg.	5 Chem. Products	6 Wood and Paper Products
1 Metallurgy	2425977	28920	5315	1309899	98573	23500
2 Fuels	860236	812962	339258	181280	72327	23780
3 Elec. and therm. power	116278	102164	329	119040	56761	12260
4 Machine bldg., metalwrkg.	240400	129000	19800	2822500	27200	19570
5 Chemical products	85471	37793	2404	385100	664821	47530
6 Wood and paper products	36750	149000	1400	127600	64900	552400
7 Construction materials	10360	12830	600	25100	1900	1950
8 Glass and porcelain	2367	410	441	21570	15547	15960
9 Textiles and apparel	30213	26026	2435	124600	57765	56600
10 Food products	6630	4500	700	33500	142300	6900
11 Industry N.E.C.	30201	20447	7183	93770	18722	9440
12 Industry total	3844883	1324051	379865	5243957	1220815	769890
13 Construction	0	0	0	0	0	0
14 Agriculture and forestry	232	334	0	140	5548	3510
15 Frt., trans., and commun.	431215	845364	1035	271700	205509	137200
16 Trade and distribution	149269	200250	0	177400	77027	83900
17 Other sectors	74400	0	100	26800	1100	5500
18 Total material inputs	4500000	2370000	381000	5720000	1510000	1000000
19 Depreciation	470000	580000	168000	430000	120000	45000
20 Mater. inputs + depr.	4970000	2900000	549000	6150000	1630000	1045000
21 Wages	700000	1239000	108000	2153000	207000	643000
22 Other nat. income	530000	-39000	381000	2602000	563000	-88000
23 National income	1230000	1200000	489000	4755000	770000	555000
24 Gross value of output	6200000	4100000	1038000	10905000	2400000	1600000

	7 Construction Materials	8 Glass and Porcelain	9 Textiles and Apparel	10 Food Products	11 Industry N.E.C.	12 Industry Total
1 Metallurgy	133520	9826	5867	43930	16151	4101476
2 Fuels	98050	13547	13492	135300	40750	2590981
3 Elec. and therm. power	37830	3233	17042	36300	9388	510625
4 Machine bldg., metalwrkg.	51100	7820	27500	36800	3510	3385199
5 Chemical products	25900	13968	153772	60700	77167	1554625
6 Wood and paper products	29200	12540	23100	125600	162530	1285019
7 Construction materials	294000	3080	1480	18200	5100	374600
8 Glass and porcelain	2960	12429	258	24800	9052	105794
9 Textiles and apparel	19600	3414	3025750	33400	45076	3424878
10 Food products	16200	310	93900	4471199	99620	4875757
11 Industry N.E.C.	26000	1448	33597	60470	8430	309708
12 Industry total	734360	81615	3395757	5046699	476774	22518656
13 Construction	0	0	0	0	0	0
14 Agriculture and forestry	140	67	433985	7526199	57700	8027855
15 Frt., trans., and commun.	773000	15861	35944	175100	32785	2924712
16 Trade and distribution	29700	12257	293813	1294199	60941	2378756
17 Other sectors	2800	200	500	7800	800	120000
18 Total material inputs	1540000	110000	4160000	14050000	629000	35970000
19 Depreciation	120000	12000	40000	190000	25000	2150000
20 Mater. inputs + depr.	1660000	122000	4200000	14240000	654000	38120000
21 Wages	427000	68000	580000	516000	183000	6824000
22 Other nat. income	513000	200000	1800000	5144000	340000	11946000
23 National income	940000	268000	2380000	5660000	523000	18770000
24 Gross value of output	2600000	390000	6580000	19900000	1177000	56890000

(continued)

205

(Table 8.1 continued)

	13 Const.	14 Agric. and Forestry	15 Frt, trans, and Commun.	16 Trade Dist.	17 Other Sectors	18 Total Mater. Deliveries
1 Metallurgy	398484	21945	20965	7126	0	4550000
2 Fuels	133131	285742	308390	65755	1000	3385000
3 Elec. and therm. power	35889	34366	56480	47640	2000	687000
4 Machine bldg., metalwrkg.	534600	342400	147100	53700	2000	4465000
5 Chemical products	115549	247820	66465	20540	5000	2010000
6 Wood and paper products	524200	94700	27800	48280	20000	2000000
7 Construction materials	1955399	35700	7100	12200	0	2385000
8 Glass and porcelain	105484	3918	1183	13621	0	230000
9 Textiles and apparel	45224	49415	28383	23099	9000	3580000
10 Food products	9340	117100	2500	45300	0	5050000
11 Industry N.E.C.	68700	140199	17695	34698	27000	598000
12 Industry total	3926000	1373304	684061	371959	66000	28940000
13 Constuction	0	0	0	0	0	0
14 Agriculture and forestry	0	4147796	1297	11047	2000	12190000
15 Frt., trans., and commun.	6999	227652	4642	18994	7000	3190000
16 Trade and distribution	0	621243	0	0	40000	3040000
17 Other sectors	94000	12000	0	2000	2000	230000
18 Total material inputs	4027000	6382000	690000	404000	117000	47590000
19 Depreciation	273000	878000	500000	226000	3000	4030000
20 Mater. inputs + depr.	4300000	7260000	1190000	630000	120000	51620000
21 Wages	1248000	4779000	1734000	1058000	679000	12829000
22 Other nat. income	2002000	7191000	266000	1352000	-169000	26080992
23 National income	3250000	11970000	2000000	2410000	510000	38910000
24 Gross value of output	7550000	19230000	3190000	3040000	630000	90530000

	19 Consump.	20 Other Fin. Dem.	21 Exports	22 Imports	23 Final Product	24 Gross Output
1 Metallurgy	60000	140000	1850000	-400000	1650000	6200000
2 Fuels	445000	200000	890000	-820000	715000	4100000
3 Elec. and therm. power	340000	0	53000	-42000	351000	1038000
4 Machine bldg., metalwrkg.	1210000	4625000	3200000	-2595000	6440000	10905000
5 Chemical products	380000	200000	650000	-840000	390000	2400000
6 Wood and paper products	620000	80000	100000	-1200000	-400000	1600000
7 Construction materials	660000	60000	25000	-530000	215000	2600000
8 Glass and porcelain	125000	14000	45000	-24000	160000	390000
9 Textiles and apparel	5530000	110000	700000	-3340000	3000000	6580000
10 Food products	10800000	930000	4500000	-1380000	14850000	19900000
11 Industry N.E.C.	0	421000	437000	-279000	579000	1177000
12 Industry total	20170000	6780000	12450000	-11450000	27950000	56890000
13 Constuction	0	7550000	0	0	7550000	7550000
14 Agriculture and forestry	5120000	1280000	950000	-310000	7040000	19230000
15 Frt., trans., and commun.	0	0	0	0	0	3190000
16 Trade and distribution	0	0	0	0	0	3040000
17 Other sectors	520000	-10000	0	-110000	400000	630000
18 Total material inputs	25810000	12600000	13400000	-11870000	42940000	90530000
19 Depreciation	1860000	0	0	0	0	0
20 Mater. inputs + depr.	26670000	0	0	0	0	0
21 Wages	0	0	0	0	0	0
22 Other nat. income	0	0	0	0	0	0
23 National income	0	0	0	0	0	0
24 Gross value of output	0	0	0	0	0	0

Note: N.E.C. = not elsewhere classified.

TABLE 8.2

Input-Output Table for the Ukrainian SSR, 1966:
Matrix of Direct Input Coefficients

		1 Metals	2 Fuels	3 Power
1	Metallurgy	0.39129	0.00705	0.00512
2	Fuels	0.13875	0.19828	0.32684
3	Elec. and therm. power	0.01875	0.02492	0.00032
4	Machine bldg., metalwrkg.	0.03877	0.03146	0.01908
5	Chemical products	0.01379	0.00922	0.00232
6	Wood and paper products	0.00593	0.03634	0.00135
7	Construction materials	0.00167	0.00313	0.00058
8	Glass and porcelain	0.00038	0.00010	0.00042
9	Textiles and apparel	0.00487	0.00635	0.00235
10	Food products	0.00107	0.00110	0.00067
11	Industry N.E.C.	0.00487	0.00499	0.00692
12	Construction	0.0	0.0	0.0
13	Agriculture and forestry	0.00004	0.00008	0.0
14	Frt., trans., and commun.	0.06955	0.20619	0.00100
15	Trade and distribution	0.02408	0.04884	0.0
16	Other sectors	0.01200	0.0	0.00010
17	Total material inputs	0.72581	0.57805	0.36705

		9 Textiles and Apparel	10 Food Prod.	11 Industry N.E.C.
1	Metallurgy	0.00089	0.00221	0.01372
2	Fuels	0.00205	0.00680	0.03462
3	Elec. and therm. power	0.00259	0.00182	0.00798
4	Machine bldg., metalwrkg.	0.00418	0.00185	0.00298
5	Chemical products	0.02337	0.00305	0.06556
6	Wood and paper products	0.00351	0.00631	0.13809
7	Construction materials	0.00022	0.00091	0.00433
8	Glass and porcelain	0.00004	0.00125	0.00769
9	Textiles and apparel	0.45984	0.00168	0.03830
10	Food products	1.01427	0.22468	0.08464
11	Industry N.E.C.	0.00511	0.00304	0.00716
12	Construction	0.0	0.0	0.0
13	Agriculture and forestry	0.06596	0.37820	0.04902
14	Frt., trans., and commun.	0.00546	0.00880	0.02785
15	Trade and distribution	0.04465	0.06504	0.05178
16	Other sectors	0.00008	0.00039	0.00068
17	Total material imputs	0.63222	0.70603	0.53441

4 Mach. Bldg., Metwrkg.	5 Chem. Prod.	6 Wood and Paper	7 Const. Mater.	8 Glass and Porc.
0.12012	0.04107	0.01469	0.05135	0.02519
0.01662	0.03014	0.01486	0.03771	0.03474
0.01092	0.02365	0.00766	0.01455	0.00829
0.25883	0.01133	0.01223	0.01965	0.02005
0.03531	0.27701	0.02971	0.00996	0.03582
0.01170	0.02704	0.34525	0.01123	0.03215
0.00230	0.00079	0.00122	0.11308	0.00790
0.00198	0.00648	0.00997	0.00114	0.03187
0.01143	0.02407	0.03537	0.00754	0.00875
0.00307	0.05929	0.00431	0.00623	0.00079
0.00860	0.00780	0.00590	0.01000	0.00371
0.0	0.0	0.0	0.0	0.0
0.00001	0.00231	0.00219	0.00005	0.00017
0.02492	0.08563	0.08575	0.29731	0.04067
0.01627	0.03209	0.05244	0.01142	0.03143
0.00246	0.00046	0.00344	0.00108	0.00051
0.52453	0.62917	0.62500	0.59231	0.28205

12 Const.	13 Agric. and Forestry	14 Frt., Tran., and Com.	15 Trade and Dist.	16 Other Sectors
0.05278	0.00114	0.00657	0.00234	0.0
0.01763	0.01486	0.09667	0.02163	0.00159
0.00475	0.00179	0.01771	0.01567	0.00317
0.07081	0.01781	0.04611	0.01766	0.00317
0.01530	0.01289	0.02084	0.00676	0.00794
0.06943	0.00492	0.00871	0.01588	0.03175
0.25899	0.00186	0.00223	0.00401	0.0
0.01397	0.00020	0.00037	0.00448	0.0
0.00599	0.00257	0.00890	0.00760	0.01429
0.00124	0.00609	0.00078	0.01490	0.0
0.00910	0.00729	0.00555	0.01141	0.04286
0.0	0.0	0.0	0.0	0.0
0.0	0.12569	0.00041	0.00363	0.00317
0.00093	0.01184	0.00146	0.00625	0.01111
0.0	0.03231	0.0	0.0	0.06349
0.01245	0.00062	0.0	0.00066	0.00317
0.53338	0.33188	0.21630	0.13289	0.18571

Note: N.E.C. = not elsewhere classified.

TABLE 8.3

Input-Output Table for the Ukrainian SSR, 1966: Matrix of Full Input Coefficients

		1	2	3
		Metals	Fuels	Power
1	Metallurgy	1.67924	0.04059	0.02809
2	Fuels	0.34341	1.31454	0.43489
3	Elec. and therm. power	0.04811	0.04257	1.01537
4	Machine bldg., metalwrkg.	0.12037	0.08150	0.05416
5	Chemical products	0.05401	0.03667	0.01827
6	Wood and paper products	0.04790	0.08508	0.03291
7	Construction materials	0.00579	0.00628	0.00291
8	Glass and porcelain	0.00236	0.00203	0.00134
9	Textiles and apparel	0.03362	0.03179	0.01684
10	Food products	0.01164	0.00925	0.00556
11	Industry N.E.C.	0.01522	0.01146	0.01129
12	Construction	0.0	0.0	0.0
13	Agriculture and forestry	0.01031	0.00884	0.00518
14	Frt., trans., and commun.	0.20298	0.28990	0.10013
15	Trade and distribution	0.06824	0.07525	0.02710
16	Other sectors	0.02078	0.00108	0.00073

		9	10	11
		Textiles and Appar.	Food Prod.	Industry N.E.C.
1	Metallurgy	0.01452	0.01551	0.04621
2	Fuels	0.02558	0.03884	0.08661
3	Elec. and therm. power	0.01039	0.00840	0.01982
4	Machine bldg., metalwrkg.	0.02274	0.02701	0.02842
5	Chemical products	0.06928	0.02369	0.11507
6	Wood and paper products	0.02235	0.02692	0.23136
7	Construction materials	0.00177	0.00364	0.00703
8	Glass and porcelain	0.00150	0.00293	0.01196
9	Textiles and apparel	1.86069	0.01413	0.09840
10	Food products	0.04464	1.30058	0.12590
11	Industry N.E.C.	0.01351	0.01117	1.01417
12	Construction	0.0	0.0	0.0
13	Agriculture and forestry	0.17958	0.62973	0.13385
14	Frt., trans. and commun.	0.02902	0.03535	0.08627
15	Trade and distribution	0.09796	0.11124	0.09165
16	Other sectors	0.00069	0.00135	0.00239

4 Mach. Bldg., Metwrkg.	5 Chem. Prod.	6 Wood and Paper	7 Const. Mater.	8 Glass and Porc.
0.28247	0.11195	0.05711	0.11942	0.06038
0.10652	0.11830	0.07674	0.13880	0.07827
0.02802	0.04427	0.02243	0.03173	0.01655
1.37883	0.04956	0.04813	0.06946	0.04358
0.08257	1.40423	0.08017	0.03920	0.06281
0.04351	0.07675	1.54612	0.04124	0.06337
0.00524	0.00335	0.00390	1.12976	0.01034
0.00436	0.01106	0.01728	0.00268	1.03445
0.04335	0.07712	0.11316	0.03272	0.02889
0.01630	0.11373	0.02109	0.01651	0.00905
0.01672	0.01655	0.01432	0.01699	0.00731
0.0	0.0	0.0	0.0	0.0
0.01325	0.06717	0.02572	0.01246	0.00811
0.09002	0.16513	0.16475	0.38331	0.07836
0.04430	0.07279	0.09854	0.03120	0.04658
0.00706	0.00255	0.00630	0.00304	0.00167

12 Const.	13 Agric. and Forestry	14 Frt., Tran. and Com.	15 Trade and Dist.	16 Other Sectors
0.14758	0.01384	0.03205	0.01378	0.00724
0.09642	0.03680	0.14639	0.04368	0.01582
0.02115	0.00622	0.02514	0.01891	0.00696
0.12901	0.03738	0.07534	0.03034	0.01106
0.04931	0.02914	0.03944	0.01642	0.02163
0.13044	0.01806	0.02787	0.03225	0.06292
0.29396	0.00338	0.00362	0.00514	0.00089
0.01713	0.00109	0.00129	0.00535	0.00155
0.03594	0.01210	0.02542	0.02007	0.03696
0.01271	0.01509	0.00654	0.02307	0.00930
0.01789	0.01131	0.00846	0.01316	0.04546
1.00000	0.0	0.0	0.0	0.0
0.01108	1.28440	0.00665	0.01847	0.01510
0.13929	0.03066	1.04334	0.02391	0.02500
0.02738	0.04837	0.01422	1.00915	0.07400
0.01543	0.00119	0.00072	0.00107	1.00362

Note: N.E.C. = Not elsewhere classified.

THE EXTERNAL ECONOMIC RELATIONS
OF THE UKRAINE

The structure of exports and imports for the Ukraine and their shares in total production and consumption as shown in the 1966 Ukrainian input-output table are given in Table 8.4. Values of "Republic Production" used in the calculation of the ratios shown in Table 8.4 are the gross values of output (GVOs) as shown in the input-output table, while the values of "Republic Consumption" used are equal to GVO less exports plus imports. Exports and imports include both interregional and international flows.

As Table 8.4 shows, about 33 percent of the total value of Ukrainian exports is products of the food industry and nearly 25 percent is products of "Machine Building and Metalworking." Machinery also accounts for more than

TABLE 8.4

Structure of Imports and Exports, Ukraine, 1966
(percent)

Aggregate Branch	Exports		Imports	
	As a Per-cent of Total Exports	As a Per-cent of Republic Production	As a Per-cent of Total Imports	As a Per-cent of Republic Consumption
Metallurgy	13.8	29.8	3.4	8.4
Fuels	6.6	21.7	6.9	20.3
Machine building and metalworking	23.9	29.3	21.9	25.2
Power	0.4	5.1	0.4	4.1
Chemical products	4.9	27.1	7.1	32.4
Wood and paper	0.7	6.3	10.1	44.4
Construction materials	0.2	0.1	4.5	17.1
Glass and porcelain	0.3	11.5	0.2	6.5
Textiles and apparel	5.2	10.6	28.1	36.2
Food products	33.6	22.6	11.6	8.2
Industry N.E.C.	3.3	37.1	2.3	27.4
Industry total	92.9	21.9	96.5	20.5
Agriculture and forestry	7.1	4.9	2.6	1.7
Other branches	0.0	0.0	0.9	14.9
Total material products	100.0	14.8	100.0	13.3

Note: N.E.C. = not elsewhere classified.

TABLE 8.5

Structure of Production and Use of Output, Ukraine, 1966
(percent)

Aggregate Branch	Gross Value of Output	Total Republic Use
Metallurgy	6.85	5.34
Fuels	4.53	4.52
Power	1.15	1.15
Machine building and metalworking	12.05	11.57
Chemical products	2.65	2.91
Wood and paper	1.77	3.03
Construction materials	2.87	3.49
Glass and porcelain	0.43	0.41
Textiles and apparel	7.27	10.36
Food products	21.98	18.85
Industry N.E.C.	1.30	1.14
Industry total	62.84	62.80
Construction	8.34	8.48
Agriculture and forestry	21.24	20.89
Transportation and communication	3.52	3.58
Trade and distribution	3.36	3.42
Other branches	0.70	0.83
Total	100.0	100.0

Note: N.E.C. = not elsewhere classified.

20 percent of all imports, but the largest share of imports is accounted for by products of the "Textiles and Apparel" sector. As would be expected, given the size of the Ukrainian economy, the shares of exports in total production and of imports in total consumption are much smaller for the republic than they are for smaller Soviet republics. For most other union republics excluding the RSFSR, these two proportions range from 20 percent to 30 percent, while for the Ukraine they are 14.8 percent and 13.3 percent, respectively.[19] For some individual sectors, however, these ratios are significantly higher. Nearly 30 percent of the total domestic output of both "Machine Building and Metalworking" and "Metallurgy" is exported, while imports account for the largest shares of total republic consumption in the "Wood and Paper Products" and "Textiles and Apparel" sectors.

The Ukraine has a positive balance of trade overall in its relations with other Soviet republics and foreign countries, exporting about 1.53 billion rubles more than it imports. As a result, its "national income used" is that much lower

TABLE 8.6

Interregional Flows and Major Commodity Groups, Ukraine, 1966
(million tons)

Commodity Group	Exports	Imports	Balance
Coal	48.30	6.41	+41.89
Oil and oil products	2.37	26.01	−23.64
Metal ores	6.98	7.12	−0.14
Wood and timber	0.03	28.05	−28.02
Cement	0.23	0.28	−0.05
Total freight shipments	136.41	101.30	+35.11

Source: Narkhoz 1967, pp. 554–67.

than produced national income.* Similarly, the total value of output consumed in the republic (in both the "productive" and "nonproductive" spheres) is less than the GVO for the republic by this amount. In the Ukraine the export-import balance represents 3.93 percent of produced national income and 1.69 percent of republic GVO.

External relations produce some significant differences in the shares of total production and total consumption within the republic for individual sectors. Table 8.5 shows the percentage breakdown of total production and total republic consumption in the Ukraine as defined for Table 8.4. For sectors not involved in external flows, the shares in total use are somewhat larger as a result of the positive export-import balance. For individual sectors with a positive export-import balance (especially "Metallurgy," "Machine Building and Metalworking," and "Food Products"), shares of total use are smaller, while for sectors with a negative export-import balance (such as "Wood and Paper Products," "Textiles and Apparel" and "Construction Materials") shares in republic use are larger.

Published values of the interregional flows of five major commodity groups for the Ukraine provide some additional detail on its external relations. The values of these flows for 1966 are given in Table 8.6.

---

*Losses must also be subtracted from produced national income to determine the value of used national income. However, it was impossible to eliminate them from the values of total use of the output of each sector in the calculations made below.

The values in this table are particularly useful for examining the balance of trade for the fuels sector. Overall, as the input-output table shows, this sector has a small positive export-import balance with large flows both into and out of the republic. As is evident from the table, this is a result of the fact that the Ukraine imports most of the oil products it consumes while exporting a large amount of coal. The Ukraine is also an important exporter of natural gas. It accounted for 100 percent of the foreign exports of natural gas of the USSR as a whole in 1966.[20]

Table 8.6 shows that the Ukraine imports and exports about an equal amount of ores in total. For ferrous metals, however, the Ukraine has a large positive export-import balance with other republics. In 1965 more than 15 million

TABLE 8.7

Structure of Machinery Imports and Exports, Ukraine, 1966
(percent)

Machinery	Imports	Exports
Energy M&E	0.4	0.2
Electrotechnical M&E	7.0	7.5
Cable products	5.0	3.7
Radiotechnical M&E	10.0	5.0
Machine tools	3.1	2.2
Forging-pressing M&E	1.0	0.0
Tools and dies	2.5	1.0
Precision instruments	5.0	2.8
Metallurgical M&E	0.0	2.0
Pumps and compressors	2.8	2.7
Chemical industry M&E	3.7	5.0
Light industry M&E	6.7	3.3
Hoisting-transporting M&E	0.0	2.3
Construction M&E	0.0	6.6
Automobiles	43.0	12.3
Tractors and agricultural M&E	0.0	5.6
Bearings	3.7	1.0
Mining M&E	0.0	1.8
Food industry M&E	1.3	2.3
Other transportation M&E	0.0	4.5
Other machine building	4.8	28.2
Total	100.0	100.0

Note: M&E = machinery and equipment.

Source: O. I. Moskvyn, A. V. Shylaeva, and S. D. Batenko, *Pytrannia vyznachennia pokaznykiv vvozu produktsii Ukrains'koi RSR* (Kiev, 1970), p. 31.

TABLE 8.8

Shares of Imports in Total Use of Wood and
Paper Products, Ukraine, 1966
(percent)

Wood and Paper Products	Percent
Sawn wood	66.5
Timber	38.0
Compressed boards	2.3
Plywood	37.0
Furniture	14.0
Paper and cardboard	56.0

Source: O. I. Moskvyn, A. V. Shylaeva, and Sh. D. Batenko, *Pytannia vyznachennia pokaznykiv vvozu produktsii Ukrains'koi RSR* (Kiev, 1970), p. 37.

tons of ferrous metals were delivered to other republics and 1.5 million tons were imported.[21] The Ukraine also occupies a leading role in the foreign export of metals and ores for the USSR as a whole, providing 95.3 percent of the iron ore, 78.0 percent of ferrous metals, 74.4 percent of cast iron, and 60.0 percent of the coke products exported by the USSR in 1966.[22]

A more detailed breakdown of the exports and imports of machinery for the Ukraine is given in Table 8.7. The largest share of machinery imports in the Ukraine is accounted for by imports of automobiles (43.0 percent). Radiotechnical, electrotechnical, and light industry machinery and equipment account for another 23.7 percent of machinery imports. The largest share of electrotechnical machinery and equipment imports (59.0 percent) is made up of electrical motors.[23] Radios and receivers constitute 90.0 percent of the imports of radiotechnical machinery.

The largest share of machinery exports is accounted for by products of the undefined category "Other Machine Building." Since only a few minor sectors of machine building are not shown separately in Table 8.7 (including electronic products, logging and paper, and printing machinery and equipment), this category may include some defense-related production. The exports of electrotechnical machinery are made up primarily of transformers (33.0 percent) and electrical motors (19.0 percent).

As indicated by the data in Table 8.6, the Ukraine imports a large amount of its wood products. The share of imports (from both other republics and foreign countries) in the total value of republic consumption of some wood and paper products are given in Table 8.8. The largest shares of the imports of sawn wood were made up of timber (52.0 percent) and construction lumber (22.0

percent).[24] In addition to importing a substantial amount of cut lumber (primarily from the Baltic republics and the RSFSR), the Ukraine exported a small share of republic production of cut lumber (1.7 percent of total production), primarily to Belorussia and Moldavia. Furthermore, despite imports of paper products that covered 56.0 percent of republic needs, 18.0 percent of republic output of paper products was exported.

The external flows of construction materials as a whole do not represent large proportions of republic consumption and production. As Table 8.6 shows, the Ukraine both imports and exports small amounts of cement. In 1966, imports of cement accounted for 4.0 percent of consumption, while exports accounted for 7.0 percent of the total production of cement.[25] For asbestos pipes, each of these proportions was 22.0 percent.

Although information on the destination of Ukrainian exports and the sources of their inputs in terms of input-output sectors for 1966 is not available, the general distribution of these flows, based on transportation statistics in 1964, is given in Table 8.9. The largest share of both imports and exports is with the European part of the RSFSR, although exports to Belorussia and the Baltic republics are also substantial. During the 1950s and early 1960s, the share of exports to the RSFSR gradually declined and was offset by an increase in deliveries to Belorussia and the Baltic republics. The major change in the pattern of imports during this period was an increase in the share of shipments from the RSFSR.[26]

TABLE 8.9

Shares of Other Republics in Exports and Imports of the Ukraine, 1964
(percent)

Other Republics	Exports	Imports
RSFSR	61.1	88.6
(European Part of RSFSR)	(59.1)	(85.8)
Belorussian SSR	15.0	2.0
Transcaucasian republics	4.7	2.5
Moldavian SSR	5.4	1.2
Kazakhstan SSR	1.3	3.2
Central Asian republics	1.4	0.5
Baltic republics	11.1	2.0
Total	100.0	100.0

Source: F. Khyliuk, "Rozvytok mizhrespublikans'kykh ekonomichnykh zv'iazkiv UkRSR," *Ekonomika Radians'koi Ukrainy* (1966): no. 12, 9.

Breaking down the columns for exports and imports in the reconstructed Ukrainian input-output table to distinguish foreign trade from flows involving other Soviet republics was impossible on the basis of available information. However, since the Ukraine plays a major role in the foreign trade of the USSR, it is important to summarize its foreign flows. Some percentages of the shares of the Ukraine in total USSR exports were given above. In addition to its importance as an exporter of ores and metals, the Ukraine provided 86.9 percent of the superphosphates, 64.4 percent of the sugar, and 18.0 percent of all machinery exported by the USSR in 1966.[27] The share of the Ukraine in the total foreign trade turnover of the Soviet Union in 1966 was reported to be 18.2 percent.[28] However, the shares of exports and imports in the total foreign trade turnover of the Ukraine could not be reliably estimated.

The basic commodity structure of Ukrainian foreign exports and imports in 1967 is presented in Table 8.10 in terms of the prices and the classification of commodities used in foreign trade statistics. While this breakdown of foreign trade for the Ukraine cannot be used in connection with the Ukrainiant input-output table, it provides a useful picture of the structure of Ukrainian foreign trade. The largest shares of Ukrainian exports are fuels, ores, and metals; the major imports are machinery and equipment, industrial goods, and foodstuffs.

The most important attribute of the input-output model is its usefulness for analyzing complex interrelationships in an economy. The main analytical

TABLE 8.10

Foreign Exports and Imports, Ukraine, 1967
(percent)

Commodity Group	Exports	Imports
Machinery and Equipment	17.2	37.2
Fuel, mineral raw materials, and metals	66.0	10.6
Chemical products, mineral fertilizer	4.0	6.4
Construction materials	0.5	0.3
Plant and animal raw materials	1.1	9.1
Raw materials for the production of foodstuffs	3.8	7.0
Foodstuffs	7.0	13.4
Industrial consumption goods	0.4	16.0
Total	100.0	100.0

Note: The data are in terms of commodity groups as defined in Soviet foreign trade statistics.

Source: Entsyklopediia narodnoho hospodarstva Ukrains'koi RSR (Kiev, 1969), I, 564; II, 156.

tool for such analyses is the Leontief inverse matrix.* The product of this matrix and any column vector of final output gives the total value of all direct and indirect material inputs necessary for the production of that vector of final output. (In the same way, the product of the matrix of direct input coefficients and a vector of final output gives total direct inputs necessary for the production of this vector.) An input-output table can thus be used to analyze the indirect requirements for the production of the vectors of exports and (competitive) imports in an economy.

For a regional input-output table constructed as the tables for Soviet republics are, however, this type of matrix multiplication, using the Leontief inverse calculated from the table, does not give a completely accurate picture of indirect effects. This is true because the columns of material inputs for all sectors include both domestically produced and imported inputs. (See "Soviet Input-Output Accounting," above.) Thus, when the Leontief inverse is calculated, some indirect effects that occur outside the region will not be considered. The appropriate tool for the analysis of such indirect effects is an interregional input-output model that is composed of matrixes of imported as well as domestic input coefficients.†

The extent of the distortions involved in this type of calculation with a one-region model should be less for a large region like the Ukraine, however, than for other Soviet republics that have more open economies. Values of the direct and full material requirements for the production of vectors of Ukrainian exports and imports that total 1,000 rubles have been calculated and are presented in Tables 8.11 and 8.12. It was not possible to distinguish "noncompetitive" imports for the Ukraine (those not produced within the republic); this introduces a further distortion in the interpretation of results, since the object of this calculation for imports is to determine the savings in total material cost by importing a given vector of output.

Given the limitations of these calculations, only the broadest results will be outlined. The "Trade and Distribution" sectors, which do not directly participate in external trade, have positive values of direct and full exports and imports because their output is employed as intermediate inputs. "Construction," however, has zero entries in these calculations becuae, by definition in Soviet input-output tables, this sector delivers no output for intermediate use.

---

*Each element of this matrix, r_{ij} (calculated as $R = (1 - A)^{-1}$, where A is the matrix of direct input coefficients), shows the total value of all direct and indirect inputs required from sector i to produce a unit of the output of sector j.

†The Soviet Regional Input-Output Research Project at Duke University, of which the author is a member, is currently working toward the construction of such a model based on reconstructed input-output tables for Soviet republics for 1966.

As Tables 8.11 and 8.12 show, the total values of social product needed for the production of 1,000 rubles of both exports and imports are essentially the same. The shares of some individual sectors in each of these four columns are quite different from their shares in actual exports and imports, however, reflecting the indirect export and import of their output. Although agricultural products account for only 7.1 percent of total exports, they make up 24.0 percent of "direct exports" and 14.6 percent of "full exports," largely as a result of agricultural output embodied in the exports of food products. Similarly, agriculture accounts for shares of direct and full imports (11.6 and 7.7 percent, respectively) that are larger than its share of actual imports because of the agricultural output embodied in the imports of "Textiles and Apparel" and some food products. The share of "Metallurgy" in full imports is also nearly twice its

TABLE 8.11

Direct and Full Exports, Ukraine, 1966
(rubles)

Aggregate Branch	Direct Exports	Full Exports
Metallurgy	87	317
Fuels	44	189
Power	9	20
Machine building and metalworking	72	368
Chemical products	30	116
Wood and paper	17	57
Construction materials	2	7
Glass and porcelain	2	7
Textiles and apparel	31	128
Food industry	83	456
Industry N.E.C.	6	46
Construction	0	0
Agriculture and forestry	147	325
Transportation and communication	40	98
Trade and distribution	41	79
Other sectors	2	5
Total	614	2,225

Note   direct exports = A · X
         full exports = (I – A)$^{-1}$ · X
where X is a vector of exports for the Ukraine with the structure of 1966 Ukrainian exports and totaling 1,000 rubles.

TABLE 8.12

Direct and Full Imports; Ukraine, 1966
(rubles)

Aggregate Branch	Direct Imports	Full Imports
Metallurgy	48	148
Fuels	31	164
Power	9	26
Machine building and metalworking	65	334
Chemical products	41	158
Wood and paper	48	196
Construction materials	6	54
Glass and porcelain	2	7
Textiles and apparel	139	559
Food industry	40	183
Industry N.E.C.	6	38
Construction	0	0
Agriculture and forestry	69	172
Transportation and communication	54	108
Trade and distribution	38	78
Other sectors	1	4
Total	596	2,227

Note: direct imports = $A \cdot M$

full imports = $(I - A)^{-1} \cdot M$

where M is a vector of imports for the Ukraine with the structure of 1966 Ukrainian imports and totaling 1,000 rubles.

share in actual imports, a situation that reflects the indirect importing of metals in the products of other branches.

Another widespread application of input-output tables for the analysis of external flows of an economy is the calculation of total capital and labor (and possibly other fixed resources) embodied in exports and imports. The overall effectiveness of the external trade of an economy can thus be evaluated. Estimates of capital stock and labor supply by sector are available for the Ukraine. However, for such an analysis to be done using Soviet input-output data, there would have to be a number of basic adjustments of the data that were impossible within the scope of this study.[29] The construction of input-output tables for the Ukraine and other Soviet republics, however, has made such analyses of their external relations an increasing possibility.

CONCLUSION

A 16-sector version of the first input-output table compiled for the Ukraine has been reconstructed here from the partially published table and from other sources on input-output analysis in the Ukraine. Values of imports and exports by sector from this table have been used to analyze the dependence of the Ukrainian economy on imported goods and the proportion of the output of each sector that is exported to other Soviet republics and to other countries. Although the use of the Ukrainian input-output table in this chapter has been limited to an analysis of the external economic relations of the Ukraine, it provides a basis for many other types of analysis of the Ukrainian economy. The estimation by Stephen Rapawy of labor inputs for the Ukraine in 1966 to correspond to the sector classification of the input-output table has further improved the analytical usefulness of the table. (See Appendix B.)

APPENDIX A

Reconstruction of the 1966 Ukrainian Input-Output Table

The four-sector Ukrainian input-output table given by V. V. Bondarenko[30] provides only the relative sizes of all entries in the original table, since it shows what the values of flows would be with the sum of gross output plus imports for the economy assumed to be exactly 100.0 billion rubles. Since this value was actually slightly higher for the Ukraine in 1966, all values given must be multiplied by a common factor. Furthermore, while "Industry," "Agriculture and Forestry," and "Transportation and Communications" are shown as individual sectors, the fourth branch, "All Other Branches," must be broken down into the sectors "Construction," "Trade and Distribution," and "Other Sectors of Material Production" to produce the standard six-sector table.

In order to determine the size of the factor by which all entries in the four-sector table are to be multiplied, the true value of one or more entries in the input-output table must be compared with the corresponding conditional value given in the four-sector table. The most reliable means for calculating the necessary adjusting factor was found to be the ratio of the actual total national income produced, as shown in the Ukrainian input-output table, to the corresponding conditional value given in the four-sector table. The value of national income was estimated at 38.91 million rubles,[31] and the value in the four-sector table is 38.0 million rubles. Thus, the factor by which all entries in the four sector table were multiplied is

$$38.91/38.0 = 1.0239 \sim 1.024.$$

In the process of reconstructing the six-sector table, several additional sources of information were used that allowed more accurate estimation than the four-sector table alone. A detailed breakdown of final product (second-quadrant entries of the input-output table) is given by Bondarenko for the major sectors of the economy.[32] This percentage breakdown was used to calculate the values of deliveries for "Consumption," "Accumulation" (both "Fixed Capital" and "Working Capital"), "Replacement of Capital and Repair," and "Exports and Losses" on a six-sector basis.

Percentage ratios of the share of total output exported (to other Soviet republics and to other countries), given by A. G. Granberg,[33] for "Industry" and "Total Material Production" were used to calculate the values of exports. Exports of "Agriculture" can be calculated as a residual, since no other branches export their output. Thus, "Exports" can be completely separated from the "Exports, Losses and Other Final Demand" sector shown by Bondarenko.

In reconstructing the first quadrant of the table, values for interindustry deliveries between "Construction," "Agriculture and Forestry," "Transportation and Communications," and "Trade and Distribution" were taken directly from the published 47-sector version of the table. Only the rows and columns of "Industry" (for which there were omitted sectors in the 47-sector table) and "Other Sectors" (which was omitted in that table) remained to be estimated.

The column of "Material Inputs" for "Trade and Distribution" was completed from a percentage breakdown of inputs given for this sector.[34] This source also gives a breakdown of material inputs to "Trade and Distribution" by branches of industry that was used in the construction of the 16-sector version of the table.

For the sectors "Construction," "Agriculture and Forestry," and "Transportation and Communications," the values of "Total Material Inputs" (excluding depreciation) were calculated from estimates of GVO and coefficients of the share of material inputs in total value of output given by Granberg.[35] For each of these three sectors (and for "Industry" as well) the relatively small inputs from "Other Sectors" were estimated on the assumption that the share of inputs from this sector in total material inputs was the same for the Ukraine as for the USSR as a whole.[36] The deliveries of "Industry" to each of these three sectors were then calculated as residuals (the difference between total material inputs and the sum of inputs from all other sectors).

The value of "Total Material Inputs" for "Other Sectors" was calculated as a residual, subtracting the sum of the estimates for "Total Material Inputs" for all other sectors from "Total Material Inputs" for the economy. The column of "Material Inputs" for "Other Sectors" was then estimated on the assumption that the structure of inputs for this sector in the Ukraine was the same as in the USSR as a whole. This assumption seems well-founded, since there apparently was no independent survey for the activities that make up this sector when the Ukrainian input-output table was being compiled.[37]

Using first-quadrant row totals for "Industry," "Agriculture and Forestry," and "Transportation and Communications" that were estimated from the four-sector table, the delivery of each of these sectors to "Industry" is estimated as the residual calculated by subtracting from it the deliveries to all other sectors. The final entries to be estimated in order to complete the reconstruction of the first quadrant are the delivery of "Trade and Distribution" to "Industry" and the first-quadrant row total for "Trade and Distribution." These are the entries in the columns for "Industry" material inputs and "Total Material Deliveries" needed to balance both columns.

Information given for the four-sector table by Bondarenko was used to calculate the third-quadrant entries for "Industry," "Agriculture and Forestry," and "Transportation and Communication." Values of GVO (equal to "Total Resources") have been calculated above for "Construction" (equal to its deliveries to "Final Demand") and "Trade and Distribution" (equal to the sum of its deliveries for material production). For "Other Sectors," GVO is estimated as the sum of all deliveries (quadrants I and II), less approximately 110 million rubles in imports, as shown in the four-sector table.

Estimates of imports for "Industry" and total imports are calculated by using coefficients of imports as a percentage of total resources given by Granberg.[38] Imports of "Agriculture and Forestry" are calculated as a residual.

The value of depreciation for "Construction" is the residual remaining after all other depreciation estimates have been figured. With total material inputs previously estimated, the value of national income for "Construction" is found by subtraction from GVO. The value of national income for "Other Sectors" is the residual remaining after national income estimates for all other sectors have been made.

In order to reconstruct the matrix of interindustry flows on a 16-sector basis, the published 47-sector data were first aggregated to the sector classification used. Some of the omitted flows were then estimated by using percentage breakdowns of the inputs and deliveries of various sectors given in several sources.[39] In the absence of complete information from which all omitted first-quadrant flows could be estimated, all remaining omissions were derived on the assumption that the structure of material inputs for these aggregate branches of the Ukrainian economy is similar to that for the USSR as a whole. Omitted material inputs for each sector were distributed among the sectors for which omissions occurred in the published data as they would have been distributed in the complete 1966 input-output table for the USSR as a whole if the same sectors were omitted from that table.* While this method of estimation limits the

---

*The 1966 input-output table for the USSR was aggregated to a sector classification which distinguished sectors published and unpublished for the Ukraine. Data for the USSR

use of the final reconstructed Ukrainian input-output table in any subsequent comparative USSR-Ukraine analysis of the structure of material inputs, the basic assumption of the similarity of the structures of the Ukrainian and USSR economies appears to be well-founded. An extensive comparative analysis of the structures of the economiies of all republics and the USSR as a whole that is based on the 1966 input-output tables shows that, of all republics excluding the RSFSR, the structure of the Ukrainian economy is the most similar to that of the USSR.[40] This is true in two senses. First, the structure of total output, both by major sectors of the economy and by subsectors within each major branch, is most similar to the USSR for the Ukraine. Secondly, for each branch the structure of material inputs is, on the average, most similar for the Ukraine.

Granberg also provides an important source of information for the reconstruction of the Ukrainian input-output table—values of the sum of all material inputs for 12 of the 16 sectors distinguished in the reconstructed table.[41] For sectors for which independent estimates of GVO could be made, the value of total material inputs could be directly calculated by using these coefficients.* Alternatively, for sectors for which no GVO estimate was otherwise possible, the value of unpublished material inputs was first estimated as described above, using the structure of the USSR table, and the resulting estimates of total material inputs were used with the coefficients given by Granberg to calculate initial estimates of GVO. A check of these estimates of GVO was possible by using a percentage breakdown of GVO for 13 sectors of the economy in producers' prices given by Granberg.[42]

With estimates of total material inputs and GVO calculated for each sector, the individual elements in the second and third quadrants for each sector of industry were estimated in the following way. The depreciation entry for each sector was calculated by multiplying published coefficients of depreciation

---

were taken from V. G. Treml et al., *The Structure of the Soviet Economy* (New York: Praeger, 1972), and from *Narkhoz 1967*, pp. 64-111, for several sectors published in the Ukrainian data but not reconstructed individually in the USSR table. The percentage breakdown of the material inputs for each sector was then calculated, and the shares of unpublished sectors in the inputs of each sector in the Ukrainian table were assumed to be equal to the shares of these sectors in the USSR.

*For two sectors, "Power" and "Glass and Porcelain," estimates of GVO were calculated from published values of individual interindustry flows and their corresponding direct input coefficients, using the relationship $GVO_j = x_{ij}/a_{ij}$. The value of total output for the "Machine Building and Metalworking" sector in the input-output table was given in A. D. Sai, "Struktura obshchestvennogo produkta Ukrainskoi SSR i sovershenstvovanie metodiki ego planirovaniia" (unpublished dissertation; Kiev: NDEI, Gosplan UkRSR, 1970), p. 185. The GVOs for "Food Products" and "Chemical Products" could also be estimated from published value data and information on the distribution of total output and total inputs.

charges as a percent of fixed capital stock for the Ukraine by estimates of the value of fixed capital stock.[43] The use of data in terms of branches as defined in statistical handbooks introduces some error into the calculation of depreciation for input-output branches. However, the effects of commodity-establishment adjustment on capital stock for the input-output table of the USSR as a whole were not large. Some of these depreciation estimates were later adjusted to ensure a balance with other second-quadrant entries for certain sectors that were estimated from particular data on the input-output relations of individual sectors.

Given estimates of GVO (X_i) total material inputs ($\Sigma_i\, X_{ij}$) and depreciation (D_i) for each sector, values of national income (NI_i) were calculated as

$$NI_i = X_i - \sum_i X_{ij} - D_i$$

Using coefficients of the ratio of national income to total resources (GVO plus imports) for each sector given by Bondarenko,[44] values of total resources by sector were calculated. Estimates of imports (interregional plus international) were then calculated as the difference between total resources and GVO for each sector. The "National Income" entry for each sector was further subdivided into "Wages" and "Other National Income," using A. Tretiakova's estimates of wages by branches of industry for the Ukraine in 1966.[45]

The "Total Final Demand" entry for each branch of industry was estimated by using ratios of final demand to total resources given by Bondarenko.[46] These values are the sum of deliveries by each branch for personal and social consumption, accumulation of fixed and working capital, replacement of capital and repair, and other final uses plus exports minus imports. Adding the previously calculated estimates of imports to "Total Final demand" for each sector gives the value of all the above deliveries for "Nonproductive" uses of output plus exports. The values of the deliveries by all branches of industry for "Consumption" (both personal and social) were subdivided from this total, using a percentage breakdown of total deliveries for consumption in the Ukrainian input-output table given by Granberg.[47]

Information that would be helpful in directly estimating the value of exports by branch of industry for the Ukraine is limited. Two sources report the approximate shares of a few major branches in total exports and imports,[48] but in some cases it is unclear whether the fractions quoted are proportions of total external flows or of industry flows only. Another source gives percentage breakdowns of Ukrainian imports and exports for 1966, but these are based on incomplete data.[49] Thus, with the exception of the major exporting branches for the Ukraine, the elements of "Total Final Demand" less "Consumption" were first estimated, and exports were calculated as a residual. These estimates were calculated by distributing deliveries for capital accumulation according to a percentage breakdown of accumulation given by Bondarenko,[50] allocating "Payments for Depreciation and Repair" to the "Machine-Building and Metalworking Branch," and allocating "Losses and Other Elements of Final Demand" proportionally by branch, according to the share of each branch in total final demand.

APPENDIX B

Distribution of Ukrainian Employment in 1966

Published data for the Ukrainian input-output table, unlike that for the USSR, do not contain labor coefficients that would permit derivation of labor expenditures by sector. To overcome this omission, annual average employment published in the statistical handbooks will be used for the 16 sectors. This is not an entirely satisfactory arrangement, since the scopes of coverage of the two sets of data differ somewhat. In theory, statistics in an input-output table should be strictly limited to the specified sector, but data reported by branch of the economy or industry will contain a share of extraneous activities.

A considerable degree of comparability is found for many sectors when the two sets of data are compared for the USSR in 1966.[51] However, significant differences are found in construction, transport and communication, and agriculture. Maximum deviation occurs in construction, where employment derived from labor coefficients is more than 50 percent higher than the reported figure. The huge discrepancy cannot be explained satisfactorily, but some factors contributing to the differences can be identified. Input-output data comprise all activities, regardless of the sector of origin. But construction is a widely diffused activity, and some employment will be reported under other sectors of the economy. The statistical handbook data further exclude collective farmers engaged in construction and private construction performed by individuals; employment of prisoners and students engaged in construction might also be excluded, either partially or completely. The reported figures for transport and communication are more than 33 percent higher than the input-output data imply. The reasons for the large discrepancy are not apparent, but the division of employment between material production and service undoubtedly is a contributing factor. The differences in agriculture seem to center on the labor inputs expended on private plots. It would seem that the input-output table includes employment in private agriculture, as reported in the statistical handbooks. But these data have been rejected by most Soviet and Western writers as understating the actual input into the sector.

Despite these discrepancies, reported employment, both for the Soviet Union and for the Ukraine, used in conjunction with the input-output data,

Prepared by Stephen Rapawy.

TABLE 8.13

Annual Average Employment, by Sector of the Economy: USSR and the Ukraine, 1966
(in thousands)

Sector	USSR (1)	Ukraine (2)	Ukraine as a Percent of USSR (3)
Total	110,600	22,909	20.7
Material production sphere, total	89,657	19,296	21.5
Industry	28,514	5,291	18.6
Construction	7,549	1,374	18.2
Forestry	409	72	17.6
Agriculture	39,785	10,059	25.3
State	8,894	1,123	12.6
Collective farm	18,600	6,003	32.3
Private	12,291	2,933	23.9
Transport and communication	6,285	1,170	18.6
Trade, public dining, material-technical supply and sales, and procurement	6,261	1,189	19.0
Other	854	141	16.5
Service sphere, total	20,943	3,613	17.3
Transport and communication	2,152	351	16.3
Housing—communal economy and personal services	2,489	426	17.1
Health services	4,427	871	19.7
Education and culture	6,895	1,228	17.8
Art	380	63	16.6
Science and scientific services	2,741	352	12.8
Credit and insurance organizations	313	54	17.3
Government administration	1,546	268	17.3

Note: Data adjusted to 1970 classification.

Sources and Methodology:

Column 1–Murray Feshback and Stephen Rapawy, "Labor Constraints in the Five-Year Plan," in Joint Economic Committee, *Soviet Economic Prospects for the Seventies* (Washington, D.C.: U.S. Government Printing Office, 1973), pp. 508–09, 520–21. Employment in transport and communications was divided between material production and service spheres by using percent distribution of service sphere employment by branch of the economy, reported in TsSU, *Strana Sovetov za 50 let* (Moscow, 1967), pp. 216–17.

Column 2–Data for forestry was obtained from TsSU, *Trud v SSSR* (Moscow, 1968), p. 45, and the remaining sectors, with the exception of construction, art, other, and private agriculture, from *Narodne hospodarstvo Ukrains'koi: RSR 1968* (Kiev, 1969) (*Narhosp*) *1968*, pp. 316, 413. Forestry employment in 1969 was derived by extrapolating the 1966 employment at 0.5 percent annually, the annual growth for the years 1960–66. *Trud v SSSR*, loc cit. Residual for 1965 and 1969 (derived from reported employment in *Narhosp 1970*, p. 377, minus forestry employment in *Trud v SSSR*, loc cit.) was interpolated linearly; the 1966 figure was split between art and other in proportion to the USSR employment for the two sectors in 1966. The differences between the sum of reported or derived employment by the sector and total reported figures for the sector was added to construction. Employment in private agriculture was estimated on the basis of 1958 labor inputs published by A. Gol'tsov, "Ispol'zovanie trudovykh resusov v kolkhozakh," *Ekonomicheskie nauki* (1961): no. 1, 46–47. When the inputs are multiplied by the total number of sown hectares in the private sector and by the respective numbers of cattle, pigs, sheep, and goats tended, they yield the number of man-days–which were converted to 280-day man-year equivalents. The estimates include noncollectivized peasantry. Data on sown acreage and livestock are given in the following sources: Sown area was estimated by taking the complement, 6.6 percent of the reported sown area in the socialized sector, given in TsSU, *Ukraina za p'iatdesiat' rokiv* (Kiev, 1967), p. 135, and multiplied by the sown area in the republic, reported in *Narhosp 1969*, pp. 188–89. The distribution of transport and communication employment was made in the manner indicated in Column 1, using percentage distribution in *Ukraina za p'iatdesiat' rokiv*, p. 58.

Column 3–Derived from the data in cols. 1 and 2.

229

TABLE 8.14

Annual Average Employment, by Branch of Industry: USSR and the Ukraine, 1966
(in thousands)

Branch	USSR (1)	Ukraine (2)	Ukraine as a Percent of USSR (3)
Total	28,514	5,291	18.6
Electric power	581	96	16.5
Metallurgy	2,001	521	26.0
Fuels	1,586	606	38.2
Machine building and metalworking	10,400	1,834	17.6
Timber, woodworking, and pulp and paper	2,827	300	10.6
Chemical	1,237	197	15.9
Construction materials	1,774	371	20.9
Glass, china, and porcelain	279	63	22.6
Light industry	4,471	649	14.5
Food industry	2,680	565	21.1
Other	678	89	13.1

Sources and Methodology:

Column 1–Stephen Rapawy, *Estimates and Projections of Labor Force and Civilian Employment in the USSR: 1950 to 1990* (Washington, D.C.: U.S. Department of Commerce, 1976). Employment in the chemical industry, given in the table, differs from Rapawy's figures by including rubber and asbestos; the estimating procedure is described in Rapawy.

Column 2–The 1966 electric power employment figure of 89,500, reported in TsSU, *Trud v SSSR* (Moscow, 1968), pp. 92–93, was increased by 7.4 percent, which represents an increase of USSR employment, adjusted for later scope in Rapawy, op. cit., over the figure reported in *Trud v SSSR*. Employment for glass, china, and porcelain is reported in *Trud v SSSR*, loc. cit. Employment for the metallurgy and chemical industries was derived by obtaining a percentage of Ukrainian to USSR GVO in the corresponding branches and applying it to the USSR's employment figure. The GVO data are given in James W. Gillula's chapter in this volume and V. G. Treml et al., *The Structure of the Soviet Economy* (New York: Praeger, 1972), p. 404. Data for the remaining branches with the exception of "Other," which is residual, are reported in *Narhosp 1970*, p. 93.

Column 3–Derived from data in cols. 1 and 2.

facilitates useful comparisons. Table 8.13 presents employment for the USSR and the Ukraine, distributed between material production and service spheres and further subdivided by sector of the economy. Input-output data exclude services, and therefore the table comprises a wider scope; it accounts for all the employment and provides for more comprehensive comparisons between the Soviet Union and the Ukraine. The Ukraine accounts for 20.7 percent of the total employment in the country; it accounts for 21.5 percent of the union's total in the material production sphere, and 17.3 percent in the services sphere. The most distinctive feature of the material production sphere is the relative importance of agriculture in the republic's economy. Approximately 25 percent of the total Soviet agricultural employment and 33 percent of the collective farm employment is in the Ukraine. Private plots also play a significant role, as can be seen from the employment figures and cultivation of land: in 1966, 6.6 percent of the cultivated land was in private agriculture, compared with 3.3 percent for the Soviet Union. Ukrainian employment in the service sphere does not show significant deviation from the union pattern, with the exception of science and scientific services, which amount to 12.8 percent of the total, a figure considerably lower than the Ukraine's share in other activities.

The Ukraine's industry employment presented in Table 8.14 and disaggregated into 10 branches shows substantial differences when compared with equivalent activities at the USSR level. Employment in industry amounts to 18.6 percent of the total, but the proportion increases considerably in metallury and fuels. The Ukraine continues to remain an important iron and coal center of the Soviet Union. It accounts for 26.0 percent of the total employment in metallurgy, with approximately 90 percent concentrated in ferrous metallurgy, compared with 63 percent for the Soviet Union—a clear indication that nonferrous metals are not abundant in the republic. The fuels sector constitutes 38.2 percent of the union total and is dominated by coal, which accounts for 95.4 percent of the branch employment. The Ukraine is a large producer of natural gas, but gas extraction is not a labor-intensive activity and exerts little influence on the total employment in the sector. On the other hand, timber, woodworking, pulp and paper, and light industry are considerably below the average of other branches of industry. Timber and related activities constitute 10.6 percent of the total employment, as is to be expected, since timber resources are limited in the Ukraine. Light industry is relatively underdeveloped, constituting only 14.5 percent of the total employment.

NOTES

1. *Narodne hospodarstvo Ukrains'koi RSR 1970* (Kiev, 1971) (*Narhosp*) *1970*, pp. 61-77.

2. *Narhosp 1974*, pp. 40-49.

3. For a more detailed survey of the use of input-output analysis in the USSR, see J. W. Gillula and D. L. Bond, "The Development of Regional Input-Output Analysis in the Soviet Union," in V. G. Treml, ed., *Studies in Soviet Input-Output Analysis* (New York: Praeger, 1977).

4. The partially published input-output tables for the USSR for 1959 and 1966 have been reconstructed in this manner. See V. G. Treml, *The 1959 Soviet Intersectoral Flow Table*, 2 vols. RAC–TP–137 (McLean, Va.: Research Analysis Corporation, 1964), and V. G. Treml et al., *The Structure of the Soviet Economy: Analysis and Reconstruction of the 1966 Soviet Input-Output Table* (New York: Praeger, 1972). The 1966 input-output tables for a number of other Soviet republics have been reconstructed by the author and others in Duke University-University of North Carolina Occasional Papers on Input-Output Analysis in the USSR, nos. 10, 14, 15, 17, 18, and 19. Work on the reconstruction and analysis of the 1972 input-output tables for the Ukraine and other republics is planned when additional Soviet studies based on these tables are published.

5. V. Krashennikov and P. Nahirniak, "Pro rozrobku pershoho mizhhaluzevoho balansu suspil'noho produktu Ukrainy," *Ekonomika Radians'koi Ukrainy (ERU)* (1968): no. 6.

6. V. V. Bondarenko, ed., *Balansovyi metod vyvchennia rozvytku narodnoho hospodarstva* (Kiev, 1974).

7. The work of this group has been published in a series of small *tirazh* (edition) books by the Ukrainian Gosplan, including O. I. Moskvyn, A. D. Sai, V. O. Bohaenko, and L. H. Vasylenko, *Metodyka obchysliuvannia suspil'noho produktu soiuznoi respubliky* (Kiev, 1969); O. I. Moskvyn, N. H. Hrebenchenko, A. H. Dereviankina, and V. D. Shorstkyi, *Udoskonalennia metodyky obchyslennia material'nykh vytrat* (Kiev, 1970); A. I. Moskvin, ed., *Problemy sovershenstvovaniia balansovogo metoda planirovaniia narodnogo khoziaistva* (Kiev, 1972).

8. O. I. Moskvyn, A. V. Shylaeva, and Sh. D. Batenko, *Pytannia vyznachennia pokaznykiv vvozu ta vyvozu produktsii Ukrains'koi RSR* (Kiev, 1970).

9. In addition to sources cited in note 7, and the pioneering effort on the calculation of the national income of the Ukraine—Akademiia Nauk UkRSR, *Natsional'nyi dokhod Ukrains'koi RSR* (Kiev, 1963)—some recent Ukrainian studies in these areas are L. M. Mushketik and V. S. Naidenova, eds., *Sovershenstvovanie metodologii territorial'nogo planirovaniia i upravleniia narodnym khoziaistvom respubliki* (Kiev, 1973); Gosplan UkSSR, *Metodicheskie ukazaniia k sostavleniu plana kompleksnogo razvitiia khoziaistva oblasti* (Kiev, 1974); and L. M. Mushketik, *Kompleksnyi territorial'nyi plan v usloviiakh otraslevogo upravleniia* (Kiev, 1974). Work has also been done on an econometric model of the Ukrainian economy. It is described in A. S. Emel'ianov and F. I. Kushnirskii, *Modelirovanie pokazatelei razvitiia ekonomiki soiuznoi respubliki* (Moscow, 1974).

10. Bondarenko, op. cit. Although some sectors of the table apparently were omitted from the published table purely because they are of minor importance for the Ukrainian economy, the major omissions are in machine-building and metalworking branches, where there is considerable defense-related production.

11. A. G. Granberg, ed., *Mezhotraslevye balansy v analize territorial'nykh proportsii SSSR* (Novosibirsk, 1975), p. 148, states that the effect of this adjustment for the USSR is to reduce total produced national income in the input-output table by about 2 percent.

12. The description of work on construction of the 1966 input-output table for the Ukraine is summarized largely from Bondarenko, op. cit., and Krashennikov and Nihirniak, op. cit.

13. According to Krashennikov and Nahirniak, op. cit., p. 7, this total included 2,159 industrial enterprises, 1,073 agricultural enterprises, and 5,200 organizations and institutions of the nonproductive sphere.

14. A. V. Mar'enko, P. Nahirniak, and L. H. Savenko, *Kil'kisne vymiriuvannia efektyvnosti promyslovoho vyrobnytstva* (Kiev, 1971), p. 41.

15. This survey of exports and imports is described in Bondarenko, op. cit., pp. 130-46, and Moskvyn, Shylaeva, and Batenko, op. cit.

16. Granberg, op. cit.

17. Bondarenko, op. cit., p. 302.

18. Ibid., p. 173.

19. A. G. Granberg, "Ekonomiko-matematicheskie issledo vaniia mezhrepublikanskikh mezhotraslevykh sviazei," *Ekonomika i matematicheskie metody* (*EiMM*) (1972): no. 6, analyzes some of the overall proportions of the exports and imports of various republics.

20. M. Getmanets and Iu. Golubushin, *Sovershenstvovanie struktury i povyshenie ekonomicheskoi effektivnosti eksportnykh postavok promyshlennoi produktsii* (Kiev, 1969), p. 9. It is not stated whether these percentages are for exports in physical units or in value terms.

21. F. Khyliuk, "Roztvytok mizhrespublikans'kykh ekonomichnykh zv'iaskiv UkRSR," *ERU* (1966): no. 12, 11.

22. Getmanets and Golubushin, op. cit., p. 9.

23. This and other percentages of the shares of imports and exports of products of each machinery sector are given in Moskvyn, Shylaeva, and Batenko, op. cit., pp. 32-33.

24. This and other data on the imports and exports of wood and paper products are from ibid., p. 37.

25. Ibid., p. 38.

26. Khyliuk, op. cit., pp. 9-10.

27. Getmanets and Golubushin, loc. cit.

28. A. V. Agaev, "Uchastie Ukrainskoi SSR vo vneshneekonomicheskikh sviazakh SSSR s razvivaiushchimsia stranami," Dissertation abstract (Kiev, 1969). This figure apparently refers to the Ukrainian share of foreign trade in foreign trade prices.

29. See S. Rosefielde, *Soviet International Trade in Heckscher-Ohlin Perspective* (Lexington, Mass.: D. C. Heath, 1973), for analysis of the factor content of the foreign trade of the Soviet Union.

30. Op. cit., p. 173.

31. Granberg, *Mezhotraslevye balansy*, p. 147, gives a table showing the relative sizes of per capita national income (based on 1966 input-output table) for each republic. Using values of national income given in sources on the 1966 input-output tables of five other republics and population data for all republics in 1966, five separate estimates of national income for the Ukraine were made. All are within 0.03 million rubles of the figure given above.

32. Op. cit., p. 338.

33. Granberg, *Mezhotraslevye balansy*, p. 227.

34. V. I. Ivanitskii, *Effektivnost' ispol'zovaniia osnovnykh fondov torgovli* (Moscow, 1974), p. 21.

35. Granberg, *Mezhotraslevye balansy*, pp. 20-21.

36. These calculations were based on the USSR input-output table as reconstructed in Treml et al., op. cit., p. 185.

37. Bondarenko, op. cit., p. 126, reports that information on the input structure of "Other Sectors" was received from TsSU USSR.

38. Granberg, *Mezhotraslevye balansy*, p. 227.

39. In addition to the breakdown of inputs to "Trade and Distribution," the following sources were used: T. F. Bezruchko, "Otraslevaia struktura i pokazateli ekonomicheskogo

rosta legkoi promyshlennosti UkSSR," *Organizatsiia i planirovanie otraslei narodnogo khoziaistva* (*OiPONKh*) (1970): no. 20, 61, gives a breakdown of the deliveries of the output of "Textiles and Apparel." A. D. Sai, "Struktura obshchestvennogo produkta Ukrainskoi SSR i sovershenstvovanie metodiki ego planirovaniia" (unpublished dissertation; Kiev: NDEI, Gosplan UkSSR, 1970), pp. 65, 69, gives a breakdown of the deliveries to major users of the output of "Chemical Products" and "Fuels." Some of the information in the analysis of the first quadrant of the input-output table in Bondarenko, op. cit., pp. 292-337, was also useful.

40. Granberg, *Mezhotraslevye balansy*, pp. 128-31, 170-84. Granberg reports coefficients of variation for several comparisons of the structure of republic input-output tables with the USSR.

41. Ibid., pp. 20-21.

42. Granberg, *Mezhotraslevye balansy*, p. 124. The gross value of output for the Ukraine in producers' prices (including turnover taxes) was estimated by using Granberg's percentage breakdown and previously estimated values of GVO for "Construction," "Transportation and Communication," and "Trade and Distribution," which are the same with both sets of prices. Values of GVO in producers' prices for eight sectors of industry could then be calculated, and estimates of transportation and distribution charges were added to these values to produce GVO estimates in purchasers' prices.

43. Depreciation charges are given in *Narhosp 1967*, p. 89. The value of fixed capital stock by branch of industry in 1966 was estimated by multiplying the growth rate for the total capital stock of industry given in *Narhosp 1960*, p. 22. The value of the capital stock of each branch of industry was then calculated, using the percentage breakdown of capital stock given in *Narhosp 1967*, p. 86.

44. Op. cit., p. 175.

45. A. Tretiakova, "Determining the Labor Force, Wage Fund, and Payments for Social Security by Branches of the Economy and Basic Branches of Industry for Union Republics of the USSR in 1966," unpublished paper, 1975.

46. Op. cit., p. 175.

47. Granberg, *Mezhotraslevye balansy*, p. 229.

48. Moskvyn, Shylaeva, and Batenko, op. cit., pp. 11, 56; Bondarenko, op. cit., p. 135.

49. T. P. Temnikova, "K voprosu metodiki i organizatsii opredeleniia mezhrespublikanskogo vvoza i vyvoza," *OiPONKh* (1970): no. 19, 48.

50. Op. cit., p. 342.

51. USSR employment derived from the input-output table is given in Treml et al., op. cit., pp. 328, 401.

9

**EXTERNAL AND
INTRAUNION TRADE
AND CAPITAL TRANSFERS**
V. N. Bandera

INTRODUCTION: THE CONCEPTUAL FRAMEWORK

Despite an original intention to confine the analysis to the Ukraine's involvement in external trade and payments of the USSR, it soon became apparent that such activity is intrinsically related to intraunion trade and transfers, and that both aspects have to be considered simultaneously. Since we are considering the spatial interaction of an economic and administrative unit within a federated entity, the analysis involves the elements found essential in the theory of economic union as formulated by J. Viner, J. E. Meade, and others.[1] We must study the interaction of the member republic with the rest of the union and with outside countries. Given this framework, the central analytic questions concerning the spatial efficiency of resource allocation and the distribution of the gains from trade can also be raised with regard to the Soviet brand of economic union; likewise, questions can be raised concerning the nature of trade balances and the related transfers of capital resources. The analysis of a Soviet republic should encompass the interaction with the union and with third countries.

The application of Western theories to the Soviet system is complicated because the coordinating mechanism for economic activities is not the market but the plan. However, although the theory of economic union has not been

The author wishes to thank Dr. M. J. Lavelle of John Carroll University and Dr. T. Baumgartner of Université du Québec for their comments on an earlier draft.

235

adequately extended to the Soviet case, its relevance for the study of the position of a republic within the union is readily apparent.*

One might ask at the outset, What should be the criteria for evaluating trade activities that involve a republic? Is it sufficient to admit only the global criteria, such as maximization of total output in the union? Or is it also necessary to consider the welfare criteria of the constituent union members, which not only produce the output but also have their preferences regarding the absorption of that output?[2] The issue was readily resolved during the formation of the European Economic Community (EEC) because, in the economic sphere, all members expected to gain from the union and they agreed that unfair outcomes would be compensated by the community as a whole; moreover, economic unification as such was not meant to override the pursuit of separate cultural, social, and political objectives by the member nations. However, since the republics are components of the union, systematic negation of their preferences undoubtedly interferes with the attainment of union objectives. This is increasingly apparent when overriding global criteria like "defense potential" and "capital formation" are extended to allow maximization of "consumer welfare" or optimization of "quality of life." In that broadened perspective, the development and even the survival of various nations constituting the republics require that their economic interests be articulated and heeded.

Although the perspectives of "political economy" are often replaced in the West by "pure economics," they are essential when confronting Soviet reality. Thus it must be recognized that the interaction of a republic with other republics, with the centralized union authorities, and with outside countries occurs in a hierarchic system of command institutions. The action capability of actors belonging to the two levels of decision making—the level of the republic and the level of the union—is more unequal in the USSR than, say, in the EEC, Czechoslovakia, or, in some respects, the Dominion of Canada. We have in mind here the action capability in the political-economic sphere that is directed inward in relation to intraunion transactions as well as outward in relation to international transactions. A conspicuous manifestation of the impaired action

---

*The Hungarian economist I. Vajda distinguishes between economic integration through the removal of trade barriers and through plurinational planning. Only the latter applies to Comecon integration, but both methods promote integration within the Soviet Union. See I. Vajda, "Integration, Economic Union, and the National State," in I. Vajda and M. Simai, eds., *Foreign Trade in a Planned Economy* (Cambridge, England: Cambridge University Press, 1971). Two survey articles on economic integration by B. Balassa and F. Machlup are not as comprehensive as they purport to be. Their discusion of integration in socialist countries is limited to interaction among the CMEA signatories, but conspicuously disregards the political economies of such unions as Czechoslovakia, Yugoslavia, and the USSR. See F. Machlup, ed., *Economic Integration Worldwide, Regional and Intersectoral* (London: Macmillan Press, 1976), ch. 1, 2.

capability of the Ukraine is its limited bargaining power in external trade, although the republic's share is as high as 25 percent of total union trade and about 30 percent of exports to Comecon countries. The meaning of unequal distribution of power as it relates to the Ukraine's intraunion and external trade will be made apparent throughout the chapter, but we will call attention to this aspect in the introduction lest the discussion of details obscure the total picture.

In short, the broad conceptual framework for our discussion involves the structure of the union as a system of political economy. Although the solution of central economic questions, such as the distribution of the gains from trade and the efficiency of specialization, relies on the mechanism of plan and command, all economic activity is subject to a potent systemic bias of unequal distribution of power between the union and the republics. Hence it will be argued later that the republic's external and intraunion trade occurs in a "system of unequal exchange," as recently conceptualized by T. Baumgartner and T. Burns.[3]

This chapter comes to grips with essential analytical issues pertaining to trade and capital movements. What determines the republic's pattern of specialization within both the narrower space of the union and the larger international arena? How efficient is that specialization, and what are the gains from trade? What are the implications of the Ukraine's perennial export surplus and the corresponding unrequited loss of capital? In pursuing these questions, of special interest to us is the largely unexplored role of the foreign trade monopoly as an intermediary between the productive entities in the republics and the transactors abroad.

SPECIALIZATION AND THE GAINS FROM TRADE

Evidence About Specialization and Trade

In recent years, the growing need to appraise the Ukraine's involvement in intraunion and external trade has elicited numerous articles and books on the subject. In order to interpret the position of the republic as a member of a union, we have to distinguish the Ukraine's intraunion trade with other republics, external trade with outside countries, and total trade that combines intraunion and external components. The published evidence on the size, geographic pattern, and commodity composition of exports and imports is extensive, albeit still poorly systematized.[4]

Extent of Trade

The magnitude of the Ukraine's trade, as shown in the balance-of-payments account in Table 9.1, can be judged in relation to its total economic activity.[5]

TABLE 9.1

Balance of Payments of the Ukrainian SSR, 1966
(million rubles)

	Credit Entries Requiring In-payments	Debit Entries Requiring Out-payments	Net Credits (+) or Debits (−)
Current account			
External trade[a]			
With socialist countries	1,701	1,217	
With capitalist developed countries	303	217	
With less developed countries	193	138	
Balance with non-Union			+625
Trade with Union			
(Union government excluded)[b]	11,200	8,817	+2,383
Transaction with Union government[c]			
Net nondefense expenditure in Ukraine			+1,651
Defense expenditure in Ukraine			+3,401
Balance on current account			+8,060
Capital account: Union taxes, loans, grants			
Transfer of taxes to Moscow[d]			
Turnover tax		4,188	
Enterprise profits (20%)		3,731	
Income tax		734	
Tax on emigrant remittances[e]		100	
Net borrowing from Gosbank[f]	1,763		
Increase in savings bank deposits[f]		882	
Emigrant cash remittances[e]	140		

Ukraine's fees to United Nations[g]   −7,737
Balance on capital account   −323
Net errors and omissions
Formal overall balance of credits minus debits   0

5

Sources and Notes:

a Figures apparently exclude trade in services and tourism. Also excluded is interest on foreign loans; the USSR is a net creditor, but the Ukraine's share of interest receipts is sequestered by the union banking monopoly. Estimates in the table are based on N. G. Klimko, ed., *Problemy razvitiia ekonomiki sotsialisticheskikh stran Evropy* (Kiev, 1968), p. 360.

b This category pertains to regular or "economic" transactions and excludes direct expenditures by government agencies. The figures assume Granberg's estimate that the Ukraine's net export balance amounts to 7.5 percent of GDP—A. G. Granberg, *(Otimizatsiia territorial'nykh proportsii narodnogo khoziaistva* (Moscow, 1973), p. 159—and that the Ukraine's "total exports" amount to 33.4 percent of GDP—A. G. Granberg, ed., *Mezhotraslevye balansy v analize territorial'nykh proportsii SSSR* (Novosibirsk, 1975), p. 230).

c The figure for net union expenditures in the republic extrapolates the estimate for 1960 in Akademiia Nauk UkRSR, *Natsional'nyi dokhod Ukrains'koi RSR* (Kiev, 1963), p. 151. This category probably includes paramilitary expenditures for secret police and defense research. The figure for defense expenditure is 19 percent of the union total, reflecting the Ukraine's share in the GNP of the USSR.

d Taxes paid into the union budget are derived from *Gosudarstvennyi biudzhet SSSR i biudzhety soiuznykh respublik, 1966–1970* (Moscow, 1972).

e According to *Ukraine: A Concise Encyclopaedia* (Toronto: University of Toronto Press, 1971), II, 999, "... Ukrainians residing in the US, Canada, and other countries have been rendering considerable aid to their relatives in the UkSSR in the form of gift packages and money remittances." Tax in foreign currency on cash gifts and packages in appropriated by Moscow. A separate estimate could be made of taxes on gifts to Jews in the Ukraine.

f Derived from *Narodnoe khoziaistvo SSSR 1967.*

g The sum represents UNESCO and other United Nations assessments. The Ukraine's contribution to the United Nations technical assistance program and the special economic aid fund in 1962 amounted to 337,500 rubles. See *Ukraina i zarubizhnyi svit* (Kiev, 1970), p. 482. The Ukraine's total payments to the United Nations in 1970 amounted to $5,716,829. *New York Times*, November 2, 1971, p. 2.

In 1966, the Ukraine's total exports amounted to 13.4 billion rubles out of its national product (according to Soviet definition) of 40.11 billion rubles. In the industrial sector alone, the republic exported 21.9 percent of its output and imported 20.7 percent of the total utilized (absorbed) product in the republic.

Seen as an open economy with about 25 percent of its national product traded, the Ukraine is comparable with Austria, Belgium, and Canada. In the planned Soviet economy, the degree of "openness" of the republics generally varies inversely with their output, just as in the economies relying on the market system; the Ukraine's "total exports" are estimated to be 33.4 percent of the republic's national product, as compared with Russia's 18.1 percent and Estonia's 56.2 percent.[6] Furthermore, as has been observed in other developing countries, the relative magnitude of the Ukraine's trade has declined perceptibly as the country has industrialized and grown since the 1950s.[7]

Geographic Pattern

The Ukraine's productive structure in linked predominantly with the European regions of the union and the neighboring Comecon countries. This pattern of integration is roughly characterized by the destination of exports and the source of imports in Table 8.9.

Under the recent five-year plans, the direction of trade has been modified by efforts to rationalize the pattern of shipments, particularly by reducing the crosshauling and the shipping distances. Thus the development of industrial centers near new sources of raw materials reflects a preference for self-contained industrial complexes. As a result of the development of primary and manufacturing industries "beyond the Urals," the Ukraine's eastward shipments of industrial inputs has declined in importance. The gradually declining share of exports to the RSFSR has been replaced by increased deliveries to Belorussia, the Baltic republics, and Moldavia. The largest share of intraunion imports continues to be from the European part of the RSFSR, constituting 86 percent of the incoming tonnage in 1964. All in all, since the 1950s trade expansion has occurred along the north-south axis and trade diversion away from the west-east axis.

The Ukraine's trade with outside countries is about 25 percent of the union total, and its exports from outside countries absorb about 5 percent of its national product. This external trade, particularly with the CMEA and underdeveloped countries, expanded during the 1960s faster than trade with other union republics.

Trade Content

Being predominantly an exporter of raw materials and a net importer of machinery, manufactures, and textiles (see Table 8.4 for details), the Ukraine appears to be a typical less-developed partner relative to Comecon and, within the USSR, relative to Russia and the Baltic republics. Thus in 1965, various ores and concentrates constituted 50.2 percent of the Ukraine's external exports, compared with 21.6 percent of USSR exports; on the other hand, machinery exports to Comecone countries were 10 percent for the Ukraine, compared with 18 percent for the USSR. Favorable endowment with natural resources and geographic proximity are usually cited as reasons why the Ukraine's exports to Comecon countries are relatively high in the union total. However, the same criterion is not applied to the Ukraine's imports from Comecon, which were only 47–70 percent of the republic's exports to Comecon during 1958–65.[8] Thus, without denying that the content, size, and direction of the Ukraine's external trade are influenced by economic factors, one also has to consider the institutional factors, particularly the role of foreign trade monopoly.

Various Moscow-sponsored trade arrangements have been incorporated into long-term plans and treaties of Comecon in ways that rigidify the reliance of the bloc on industrial inputs from the Ukraine. Around 80 percent of all metallurgical inputs in Eastern Europe are supplied by the Ukraine. This applies especially to the iron and steel industry, since Comecon countries are deficient in iron and coking coal. Poland, for instance, imports 70 percent of its iron ore and 80 percent of its manganese from the Ukraine. East Germany imports more than 50 percent of its iron ore needs from the Ukraine, and probably more for the new iron and steel combine Ost.

Similar permanent exports have been established for other resources. Natural gas is piped from the western Ukraine to Silesia, major Czechoslovak cities, and West Germany. The electric power grid "Mir" (peace) is said to be integrating the resources of Comecon countries, but actually involves a net outflow of power from the Ukraine.

The items in the engineering, chemical, and consumer goods categories that are exported and imported by the Ukraine are too numerous to be discussed here in detail. But a comment must be made about trade in machinery, so important in Soviet writing. The Ukraine's external exports of machinery, largely to Comecon and less-developed countries, amounted to 17 percent of the republic's exports in 1966 and have been increasing in relative importance. In line with the union pattern, the Ukraine's imports of industrial equipment and processed inputs, largely from Comecon countries, constitute about 67 percent of the total.[9] Such imports are especially important for the development of the consumer-oriented industry. However, the evidence suggests that Soviet imports of Western machinery, predominantly essential equipment for new industrial projects like the Kama River complex, favor the eastern regions of the union. Viewed in the context of a command system, the planned content, size, and balances of the republic's external trade have a major impact on the development of the republic. The evidence presented here provides a clue to why the development of manufacturing and, especially, of consumer industry in the

TABLE 9.2

Location Quotients of Ukrainian Industries, 1960–70

Industry	Location Quotients Based on Employment			Location Quotients Based on Population		
	1960	1966	Percent Change 1960/66	1965	1970	Percent Change 1965/70
Fuels	2.12	2.04	-3.77	1.05	0.97	-8.2
Ferrous metals	2.05	1.97	-3.66	2.11	2.08	-1.1
Electrical energy	0.87	0.89	1.96	0.85	0.84	-1.2
Chemical industries				0.71	0.71	0.0
Machine building	0.92	0.95	5.13	0.84	0.80	-5.0
Wood and paper	0.51	0.57	6.31	0.52	0.45	-5.6
Construction materials	1.23	1.16	-5.51	1.00	0.85	-7.7
Light industries	0.73	0.77	5.49	0.60	0.71	15.5
Food	1.16	1.13	-2.42	1.12	1.03	-8.7

Sources: Employment adapted from H. J. Wagener, "Rules of Location and the Concept of Rationality: The Case of the USSR," in V. N. Bandera and Z. L. Melnyk, eds., *The Soviet Economy in Regional Perspective* (New York: Praeger, 1973), pp. 90–92. Population adapted from P. B. Voloboi and V. A. Popovkin, *Problemy terytorial'noi spetsializatsii i kompleksnoho rozvytku narodnoho hospodarstva UkRSR* (Kiev, 1972), p. 135.

Ukraine has been lagging behind that in other republics and, most conspicuously so, in Russia.

Empirical Evidence in Analytical Studies

The descriptive-institutional approach underlying our discussion can well be supplemented with references to more analytical studies. Especially relevant are the recent input-output studies, most notably by the Novosibirsk group led by A. G. Aganbengian and A. G. Granberg, and the Duke University group led by V. G. Treml. The thorough chapter by J. W. Gillula in the present volume offers the ·readers the fruits of this approach. These comprehensive models of interrepublic trade flows focus on the structure of input deliveries and sectoral trade balances. The method offers certain advantages and provides a valuable tool for evaluating regional policies that govern specialization and exchange. However, input-output studies for the republics are available, so far, only for selected benchmark years, and thus provide a static view of economic structure. Hence, they should be supplemented by other evidence, such as regional capital-output ratios and location quotients for various years; Table 9.2 suggests that considerable changes have taken place in the locus of production and, hence, in the pattern of specialization and exchange since 1960.[10]

The broad conclusions regarding the position of the Ukraine as a trading partner derived by various methods reinforce each other. For instance, although Granberg's input-output models indicate the transfer of capital from the Ukraine for the benefit of Siberia, the evidence attests that such restructuring has been pursued for almost half a century; indeed, this Moscow-imposed development policy again dominates the 1976–80 five-year plan. It is still poorly understood, however, how and to what extent the Ukraine's external trade is being exploited by the foreign trade monopoly on behalf of the central government. The evidence reviewed here points to a host of fundamental questions regarding economic efficiency and equity from the standpoint of a member of the union.

Determinants and Efficiency of Trade

Recent publications in the Ukraine and abroad have raised two related analytic questions. First, to what extent do factor endowments explain the observed pattern of intraunion and external trade? And, second, how efficient are the trade pattern and the underlying allocation of resources? Although both questions are important to policy makers, the second is essential in any attempt to judge the gains from trade accruing to a member of the union and, for that matter, to the entire USSR.

Factor Endowments as a Basis for Trade

Among several attempts to apply the Heckscher-Ohlin factor proportion theory to Soviet trade, H. J. Wagener's study of interrepublic specialization is of special interest to us.[11] Although agreeing with the assertion popular among Soviet economic geographers that natural resources determine a major share of intraunion and external trade, Wagener regards the observation to be analytically trivial; to say that natural conditions are the reason for the specialization of the Donbas in coal and of Kryvyi Rih in ferrous metal is like saying that the tropics specialize in tropical fruits. It is nonetheless true that the land factor, taken in a broad sense, codetermines the "absolute cost advantages" of Soviet regions (and of the Soviet Union relative to the world), and hence governs a major portion of their trade. Wagener investigates to what extent the relative endowments with capital and labor explain the regional loci of industries.

On the one hand, this type of analysis is proper because the assumption of one technology for all regions is more appropriate here than in international trade. On the other hand, it is more difficult to determine the relative scarcity of capital and labor because the wage structure is fixed and common to, and the pricing of capital absent or nominal for, all regions. Also, the extensive interregional mobility of capital impedes the classification of regions according to relative capital abundance.

We should note, however, that Wagener does not adequately recognize the importance of land as a third factor. The production functions in the Soviet case crucially involve the natural resource inputs in addition to capital and labor. Consequently, the capital-labor scarcities should be measured in relation to land.

Although Wagener's empirical test of the factor proportions theory is inconclusive, his ingenious confrontation of statistical evidence with the theory is promising. The approach can be related conceptually to similar studies in the West, and one can undoubtedly benefit from the conclusions of similar studies applying the Heckscher-Ohlin framework to other interregional cases. Moreover, Wagener's work merges with the attempts to explain overall Soviet trade with the rest of the world through use of this theory.[12]

Comparative Costs and the Gains from Trade

Since normative questions cannot be adequately analyzed within the Heckscher-Ohlin framework, one wonders about the applicability of the time-honored theory of comparative costs in the evaluation of the republic's trade. Fortunately, a study by P. V. Voloboi and V. A. Popovkin includes the discussion of "relative effectiveness of production" as a criterion for judging the rationality of specialization of the republic, and thus affords an opportunity to review the key elements of this type of analysis as well as certain intrinsic difficulties in applying the framework of comparative cost in the Soviet context.[13]

The approach of Voloboi and Popovkin may be evaluated from the standpoint of the standard formulation of the comparative cost theory in a two-country, many-commodities model. The two-country model may be a point of departure because the republic interacts with the union under the aegis of the central authority that also is the intermediary in trade with the outside world. Let C_{ij} stand for real cost (conceptually real opportunity cost or otherwise defined real cost of inputs) in countries $i = 1, 2$, and products $j = 1 \cdots n$. Rank commodities j according to relative costs in the two countries:

$$\frac{C_{1;5}}{C_{2,5}} > \frac{C_{1,3}}{C_{2,3}} > \frac{C_{1,8}}{C_{2,8}} \ldots > \frac{C_{1,n}}{C_{2,n}}$$

Thus country 1 enjoys a rising comparative cost advantage progressively from left to right in the array, while the same holds for country 2 in the opposite direction. Assume that the criterion of economic efficiency is the maximization of output with given resources (or minimization of real cost for a given output). A normative statement can then be made that the partners should specialize and trade in accord with their respective relative cost advantages. The dividing line between exportables and importables should be where the value of exports equals the value of imports, unless a difference in capital productivity justifies a net transfer of capital embodied in the appropriate trade imbalance.

Voloboi and Popovkin are consistent with the classical theory of comparative cost in recommending that the effectiveness of specialization of the republic be judged on the basis of comparative costs for a set of goods in the republic relative to those in the union.* The study makes an effort to compare "real costs" (even though their calculation is not adequately specified) and avoids using monetary values, noting, "The observed profitability and rentability of a given production reflect a discrepancy between prices and (real) values, often to a serious degree."[14] Such discrepancy is not unusual, since in market economies relative opportunity costs do not correspond to relative prices because of market imperfections and policy-induced distortions.

The study compares relative cost data for a set of about 100 goods whose quality can readily be standardized. The costs in the republic are stated as ratios

---

*One would readily agree with the authors' contention that the evaluation of territorial specialization should consider sociopolitical as well as economic criteria. P. V. Voloboi and V. A. Popovkin, *Problemy terytorial'noi spetsializatsii i kompleksnoho rozvytku narodnoho hospodarstva UkRSR* (Kiev, 1972), p. 130. However, the logic of optimization requires that such non-economic criteria be stated explicitly, and that choices be made on the basis of rather than in spite of cost considerations.

to the union average cost and, hence, can be ranked according to comparative cost advantage.* The ranking of costs is then set against a roughly corresponding set of data on the output in the republic relative to that in the union for some 50 commodities. Thus even in the absence of a reliable system of input evaluation implicit in the cost indexes, this procedure can serve as a point of departure in an effort to evaluate and improve regional specialization and trade.

The findings of the study about the relative efficiency of production are quite interesting. The low relative cost ratios tend to include the products requiring the republic's relatively abundant natural resource endowments. Thus the low relative-cost ratios [those with $c = (C_{1j}/C_{2j}) < 1$] were found for such exportables as ferrous metallurgy, some basic industrial chemicals, basic building materials like cement and brick, and such staple food items as sugar and meat.

Certain other staples show high relative costs ($c > 1$), indicating that the republic's resources are disadvantageous for their production; some of these commodities are properly net importables, including petroleum, cellulose, cotton textiles, aminoplastics, and lumber.

However, in a number of other instances the existing net exporting appears inefficient because cost ratios show $c > 1$. Such cost ratios suggest excessive specialization in coal, natural gas, manganese ore, and sulfuric acid; the reader will recall that the Ukraine is a prominent exporter of several of these items to outside countries. On the other hand, certain cost-efficient goods with $c < 1$ that are being imported include electrical and thermal energy (simultaneously exported to Europe), textiles, clothing, and shoes. In a conspicuous case where Donbas coal is relatively expensive but overexploited for export purposes, the authors offer a dubious excuse that "the time has not arrived" to curtail such exports to European Russia and Comecon countries. The criticism of the uneconomic specialization imposed on the republic brings to mind previous reactions against irrational and arbitrary investment decisions decreed by Moscow.†

However useful, the procedure used by Voloboi and Popovkin is too crude for the evaluation of what might be called "the middle range" in the array of costs showing "c" close to unity. Yet the middle range is likely to include the increasingly important manufactures. For such producers' and consumers' goods, the real cost calculation would require a summation of a long series of

---

*Ratios of republic values to "union average" in this and similar cases are sometimes used indiscriminately in Soviet and, by imitation, Western studies. Here the procedure involves unspecified distortions because union averages include varying proportions of the republic share, and these weights are not taken into account.

†Recall, for example, the protracted opposition to overexpansion of industrial facilities and power stations in Siberia at the expense of Western regions. See V. Holubnychy, "Spatial Efficiency in the Soviet Economy," in V. N. Bandera and Z. L. Melnyk, eds., *The Soviet Economy in Regional Perspective* (New York: Praeger, 1973), pp. 9–20.

values added in the process of production. Furthermore, in this middle range, marginal (and not average) costs are crucial. This is reflected in the fact that countries hardly ever specialize completely in various manufactures but, typically, produce some output for domestic purposes and some for export, while in other instances the country might both produce and import an item. The observed small differences in relative costs, not only in the discussed study but also in Western countries, suggest that trade patterns are sensitive to transportation costs, technological innovation, and changes in demand. One can therefore understand why Voloboi and Popovkin are inconclusive in their evaluation of specialization and trade in manufactures.

Although various coefficients of "relative effectiveness of production" can be helpful in the planning of specialization, the method raises the kind of thorny problems about the meaning of real costs that have been hotly debated by East European economists for years. For instance, one wonders about the adequacy of estimated union and Ukrainian costs when wages and other input prices are fixed by the plan, rent (the opportunity cost of natural resources) is omitted, and the cost of capital is either omitted or imputed arbitrarily.

In Soviet practice, the calculation of various dimensions of real costs has not advanced very far, and the relationship between prices and opportunity costs is known to be haphazard. Yet the arbitrarily fixed prices still serve as parameters in allocative decisions. To cite a case in point, the foreign trade monopoly makes territorial production assignments for export purposes primarily on the basis of the existing money cost structure and pays the enterprises the prevailing wholesale prices. Thus, the probable increases in marginal real costs due to required additional output are disregarded. Similarly, in intraunion trade, the vertically organized ministries use conventional railroad freight rates in calculating transport costs, when real opportunity costs of transport should be used in planning the location of industries. Nonetheless, Soviet economists have some confidence with regard to cost ratios that differ significantly from unity, and planners give in to reason when relative cost is significantly affected by transport costs.

Another conceptual difficulty with the approach of this and related studies is the reliance on a two-country model (the republic vs. the union) even when third countries are crucial. Thus, the relative effectiveness of production should be analyzed not only vis-a-vis the union but also vis-a-vis the rest of the world, particularly the neighboring Comecon countries. Since the republic's share in total external trade of the union is so prominent, comparative foreign costs (as reflected in world prices) should be among the criteria of efficiency of specialization. Interestingly, there are now voices questioning the wisdom of overcommitting such exhaustible natural resources as coal, gas, and metals in long-term schemes with Comecon, since the Ukraine's own internal demand is expanding while its resources are being exploited more than in proportion to known reserves. Such concerns are similar to those encountered in other richly endowed countries, such as Canada and Venezuela. In the Soviet case, however, the trade policies formulated by the central authorities obviously supersede the special require-ments of the republics. At the present time, attractive prices for raw materials in the world markets and Moscow's determination to enlarge foreign-currency earnings dictate a policy of expansion of such exports. However, even though economic rationality requires that the evaluation of the republic's specialization explicitly consider international conditions of supply and demand, such analysis is clearly impeded by the still dominant conceptual framework that sees the republic as interacting only with the union.

And, finally, the study by Voloboi and Popovkin and related Soviet studies disregard the efficiency implications of the huge perennial export surpluses of the Ukraine in its trade with both the union and outside countries. The dynamic consequences of such uncompensated capital efflux require special attention. But also from the standpoint of present static efficiency analysis, the persistent allocative distortions connected with trade imbalances loom prominently. Thus, the Ukraine's resources are overused in producing exports and import substi-tutes. Furthermore, the republic is underconsuming (underabsorbing) the imports, and hence receives inadequate incentives in the form of imported con-sumer goods, while suffering restricted access to foreign producers goods.

Division of the Gains from Trade

Soviet sources are compelled to view the effects of specialization primarily from the standpoint of the criteria enunciated by Moscow. However, intraunion and external trade entail gains as well as losses that are apportioned to the republics in different ways. Such diverse impacts on the members of the union are of great sociopolitical significance and cannot be ignored indefinitely.

From the standpoint of the republic, what are the "gains from trade," in the sense accepted by standard Western theories? First, one should consider the republic's net barter terms of trade, defined as Px/Pm, where Px is the price index of exportables and Pm is the price index of importables; when trade is balanced, the net barter terms of trade show the amount of imports per unit of exports. Realizing that the empirical investigation of this problem is yet to be undertaken intensively, we shall venture only a few general observations.* As

---

*The hypothesis that the East European countries suffered disadvantageous terms of trade with the USSR was extensively debated in the West. The loss to the satellites is esti-mated to have been 4 billion rubles during 1959–61; see A. Kutt, *Prices and the Balance Sheet in 10 Years of Soviet-Captive Countries Trade, 1955–1964* (New York: Assembly of Captive European Nations, 1966). A similar calculation is attempted for the Ukraine in relation to the union by Z. L. Melnyk, "Regional Contribution to Capital Formation in the

will be elaborated later, the foreign trade monopoly delivers the imports to the republics at "equivalent domestic prices." Moreover, even when the republic confronts excess demand for its exports, as implied by the export surpluses, the foreign trade monopoly acquires such exports at fixed domestic wholesale prices. Thus the procedure does not allow the republic to benefit directly from advantageous export and import prices in the world markets. In other types of union, where equilibrating processes are allowed, the excess demand for exports of a member would improve its terms of trade and, hence, its gain; but this does not happen in the USSR. Thus it can be argued that the system of controlled pricing depresses the republic's net barter terms of trade and hence reduces its share of the gains.*

Another index of the benefits from trade is the gross barter terms of trade, defined as total value of imports divided by total value of exports. Such an index would also prove disadvantageous to the Ukraine because, with an export surplus, it obtains less imports per unit of exports than would be the case under balanced trade. With the possible exception of the Baltic republics, only the Ukraine has been exposed to the disadvantage of large uncompensated export surpluses with both the rest of the union and third countries.

It can be argued that the phenomenon of "unequal exchange," manifesting itself in disadvantageous net and gross barter terms of trade, is being maintained only because various institutions willfully impede the equilibration of imbalances and the required adjustment of prices. The lack of equilibration was identified by F. D. Holzman as a peculiar trait of the system that obviously injects arbitrariness and distortion into economic calculus.[15] But the problem also pertains to economic equity.

Neglecting the division of the gains from trade as it relates directly to the terms of trade and the trade imbalance, Soviet economists often recommend wrong specialization policy for the republic. D. Vovko, for instance, eagerly points out how to strengthen the Ukraine's export capability but overlooks the need for imports to attain balanced exchange. Similarly, Voloboi and Popovkin

---

USSR: The Case of the Ukrainian Republic," in V. N. Bandera and Z. L. Melnyk, eds., *The Soviet Economy in Regional Perspective* (New York: Praeger, 1973), p. 119.

*Even during the 1960s, while Soviet trade was generally balanced when measured in prices actually experienced in the world markets, the same annual accounts represented substantial export surpluses when recalculated in domestic prices applicable to enterprises. See A. G. Granberg, *Optimizatsiia territorial'nykh proportsii narodnogo khoziaistva* (Moscow, 1973), pp. 126, 177. The profit to the foreign trade monopoly (FTM) accrues mainly through domestic resale of imports at arbitrary prices. The exporting enterprises absorb at least part of the extra costs of exports, which run 10–30 percent above the cost of equivalent home-destined goods. See V. O. Suprun, *Pytannia mizhnarodnoii sotsialistychnoii spetsializatsii vyrobnytstva* (Kiev, 1973), p. 153.

recommend the expansion of certain types of production in order to substitute for potential imports from other republics, for example, in the textiles from RSFSR.[16] It may well be that such import-substituting policy would help to develop the Ukraine's backward regions, which have underemployed and unskilled populations. However, equity and efficiency criteria indicate the need to raise the republic's aggregate imports and/or to reduce the exports. Put more precisely, imports should rise relative to exports at the same time the relative prices of exports should improve.

To conclude, economic rationality requires that the plan-imposed pattern of specialization of the Ukraine take into account the welfare criteria internal to the republic and consider explicitly the internal as well as international conditions of supply and demand. However, such an approach is impeded by the prevailing conceptual framework that views the republic as interacting only with the union. At the same time, union criteria, as imposed by the foreign trade monopoly and other command institutions, are supreme and seldom challenged. The resulting losses to the republic are obvious, and to the union, incalculable.

UNREQUITED EXPORT BALANCES

The unrequited export balance, resulting from tribute, war reparations, or gifts, constitutes a direct transfer of income (that is, of product evaluated at existing prices). This type of transfer is distinct from an indirect one through a system of rigged prices. Certainly, the consequences of uncompensated trade imbalances extend beyond the immediate loss of the gains from trade, and hence we propose to investigate the problem more thoroughly. We shall first interpret recent evidence regarding the Ukraine's trade balances in the context of a comprehensive balance-of-payments framework and then indicate the significance of such imbalances in several macroeconomic models. The transfers of real capital have far-reaching consequences for economic development and hence, in turn, for the republic's long-run intraunion and external trade capability.

The study of trade imbalances and other kinds of modern macroeconomic analysis of the republic as an open economy require the use of reliable balance-of-payments statistics and similar aggregated series. Unlike the national income data for the Ukraine that are now published by the United Nations and Soviet authorities, balance-of-payments accounts have not been published since 1930. Hence our discussion has to incorporate methodological aspects of estimation as well as the interpretation of scattered empirical evidence.

The Balance-of-Payments Account and Other Evidence

The methodology of the balance-of-payments account for a republic as a member of the union and the compilation of such an account on the basis of fragmentary and sometimes indirect empirical evidence has already been published.[17] Briefly stated, the balance of payments must encompass all of the Ukraine's transactions with the union, the union government, and outside countries. Furthermore, the accounting rule requires that the net balance of real transactions in goods and services be equal to the net financial balance; thus either of the balances represents the net transfer of real output between the republic and the rest of the world.

A condensed version of the balance of payments for the Ukraine in 1966 is presented in Table 9.1. The net export balance with the union and outside countries amounted to about 3 billion rubles, or 7.5 percent of the republic national product of 40.1 billion. This is in addition to union government acquisition in the Ukraine of about 5 billion rubles' worth of output in connection with administration and defense. Hence the combined "current balance" with the outside world and the union government—whether calculated in real or in financial terms—amounted to about 20 percent of the republic's national product. These figures are consistent with other evidence about the persistent unrequited efflux of capital from the Ukraine. Accumulated historical evidence shows that the export surpluses generated by the Ukraine within the tsarist empire were continued during the New Economic Policy, persisted during the prewar five-year plans (even during the famine of 1933), and were reinstituted soon after World War II.[18]

Trade Surplus as a Shortfall in Absorption

Although the disadvantage of irrevocable losses of capital is self-evident, measurement and interpretation of such losses is by no means easy. Fortunately, modern economic analysis, be it Keynesian income analysis or the mechanistic input-output model, can elucidate the interdependence between the inward-destined and outward-destined production activity in an open economy.

The recently formulated income-absorption framework is particularly suitable for clarifying the relationship between output and its utilization within the confines of the republic.[19] On the one hand, not all production generated in the republic (its national product or income) is utilized there; on the other hand, not all absorbed goods and services (those utilized in the republic) originate on its territory. Thus, for a given year, the income and absorption aggregates may be interpreted as follows. Define Y as the value of output or product generated in the republic, so that

$$Y = C_r + I_{gross} + G_r + G_{u\,net} + X \tag{1}$$

where C_r is the production of republic-destined consumption goods, I_{gross} is republic-generated investment goods plus capital depreciation allowance, G_r is expenditures of the republic and local governments, $G_{u\ net}$ is net sales to union government exclusive of union enterprises, and X is intraunion and external exports. Absorption of all types of goods and services (expenditure on final goods and services) in the republic is

$$A = C_r + I_{gross} + G_r + G_{u\ net} + M \qquad (2)$$

where M are imports from other republics and outside countries.

The difference between income Y (equation 1) and absorption A (equation 2) is the trade balance B, as in equation (3); the estimated values of the components in billion rubles are for the year 1966 and correspond to Table 9.1.

$$B = Y - A = X - M$$
$$3.0 = 40.1 - 37.1 = 13.4 - 10.4 \qquad (3)$$

Thus the net unrequited export balance is 3.0 billion rubles, and this loss of absorption equals 7.5 percent of the national product. In that interpretation, the union government's net expenditures in the republic for administration and defense-type goods and services are not counted as part of the net export balance B in the narrower sense, even though both expenditures are financed by the taxes collected in the Ukraine and transferred to Moscow.

Conceptually, then, the unrequited loss of "real capital" in the form of net export surpluses implies the equivalent loss of absorption from annual production. Such net balances consist of all types of goods; they represent the corresponding consumption and/or investment in the republic. The pattern of these imbalances is imposed "exogenously" by the central plan in pursuit of Moscow-dictated economic goals for the union as a whole. Since the workers in the Ukraine and their representatives do not have an effective voice in establishing or even criticizing these goals, the extraction of surpluses from the republic constitutes a tribute upheld by threat. The financial mechanism instituted to extract that tribute constitutes a form of taxation without representation.

It is well recognized that the planned system of the USSR has served to accomplish massive real transfers of capital intersectorally as well as territorially. The financial aspects of such transfers have been studied extensively by Z. L. Melnyk, and his chapter is this volume contains relevant bibliography. Here, we wish to underscore the less obvious fact that, in addition to intraunion trade, the Ukraine's involvement in external trade is also part of the mechanism facilitating the net extraction of value produced in the republic. When the position of the Ukraine is properly conceived in relation to the economic union and third countries, the pattern of such unrequited transfers can be represented by a flow diagram, as in Figure 9.1. As can be seen, in 1966, the Ukraine contributed 625 million rubles, and the rest of the union 210 million rubles, to the overall USSR export surplus of 835 million rubles. Hence, the republic's substantial

FIGURE 9.1

Triangular Net Flows of Trade Between the Ukraine, the Rest of the Union, and Third Countries, 1966

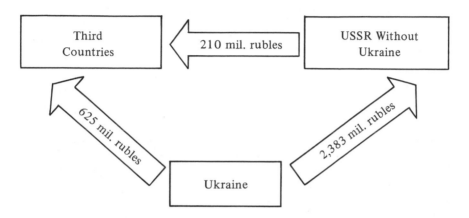

external export surplus is in addition to its huge intraunion export surplus, both representing the net unrequited transfer.

Soviet trade and credit treaties with Poland, Hungary, and other Comecon countries are intrinsically related to the suggested triangular pattern of trade balances. According to S. Prociuk, the Comecon imports from the Ukraine (formally from the USSR) are financed by Soviet long-term credits; and the repayments in equipment and machinery are channeled largely to the recently opened regions of Siberia. In that sense, the Ukraine's external exports contribute to the development of Siberia.[20]

It will be argued later that the foreign trade monopoly of the union government constitutes an integral part of the transfer mechanism.

External Balances in Econometric Studies

There is a growing interest in the Soviet Union in econometric work undertaken either from the standpoint of specific economic entities, such as the Ukraine, Georgia, the RSFSR, and the Baltic republics, or from the standpoint of the union as a whole and in investigating the interaction among all regions. Although the underlying models and computing techniques are often quite sophisticated, their authors show impatience with the inadequacy of regional statistical information. In the West, Soviet regional data suitable for econometric analysis are not readily accessible, and original econometric analysis is only starting. Here, we shall point out the relevance of Soviet econometric studies to the present argument. Of special interest are the treatment of regional balances in various models and some of those models' conclusions regarding the role of net transfers in the development of the UkSSR.

Several published econometric studies on the Ukraine as an open economy take its net trade balances into account. The model by A. Emel'ianov and F. Kushnirskii can be used to identify the impact of net exports on capital formation and, hence, economic growth of the republic. On the basis of their model it is also possible to obtain an indirect estimate of the net efflux of output during the 1960s and to hypothesize that such unrequited export balances have tended to decline both in absolute terms and relative to the GDP.[21]

A model by E. V. Detneva is of interest because it admits that the rate of capital formation in the Ukraine is not entirely assigned exogenously by the plan but is partly determined endogenously by the republic's national product.[22] And since export surpluses reduce absorption, the basis for endogenous capital formation is also curtailed. The size and persistence of the unrequited export balances are so conspicuous that their detrimental impact on the development of the republic is readily confirmed by several formal models.

Of special interest is a study by A. G. Granberg because it affords a view of the Ukraine as part of the vast and complex territorial structure of the union.[23] Granberg's report on the OMMM—the optimizing intersectoral interregional model—concentrates on the method but also discusses the empirical basis and some results of simulated experiments. The model views the union as composed of 10 regions; among these, the South (Iug) consists of the UkSSR plus tiny Moldavia and, hence, corresponds closely to the Ukraine. The model explicitly accepts the policy constraints with regard to key variables in the form of allowable "limits" and proceeds to calculate the optimal growth pattern of the 12 industries (among which is agriculture), as well as of the GDP, of each region and the USSR combined. The model not only deals explicitly with interregional balances for the sectors and the combined regions, but also takes into account external export assignments and import allocations. The study confirms the extensive capital outflows from the Ukraine and places them in the context of the territorial structure of the union.

In Granberg's study, the relation between capital flow and development process is characterized as follows:

> Regional balances of inflow and outflow of the gross output are comprehensive indicators of territorial economic interdependence. Counting external exports and imports, only the developed "South" [Ukraine plus Moldavia] and "Ural" regions make a substantive credit contribution [vklad] to the country's economy; the two regions show a credit balance in their income accounts. If external exports and imports are not counted, also "the West" [Belorussia

plus the three Baltic states] would show a credit balance in the income accounts.[24]

The reference to the credit balance in the above passage implies, in terms of Western terminology, that the Ukraine suffers a shortfall of absorption relative to the income produced in the republic. Such is the real content of the net outflow of tax revenue.

Granberg's model was used to calculate optimal regional allocation of capital and labor resources. The model accepts as given the planned development proportions and similar quantifiable revealed preferences of the policy makers, but otherwise the reported solutions seem to satisfy only the unidimensional economic objective of maximum production. Accordingly, a simulated optimal allocation of 1 million rubles of investment capital could raise the overall union product by 2.097 million rubles. To attain this result, the largest proportion of investment and the corresponding output should occur in the Ukraine (primarily in light industry, chemicals, and machine building); at the same time gross output would be curtailed mainly in the Volga region (primarily in light industry and agriculture).[25] Thus Granberg's calculations are consistent with other evidence that the productivity of capital in the Ukraine is above the union average. Furthermore, such econometric analysis supports the hypothesis, established by Western studies, that the size and direction of interregional capital transfers in the USSR have been inconsistent with the efficiency criterion of output maximization in the union as an entity.

The discussed econometric studies of the territorial aspects of resource allocation (and related works) have generated valuable results despite the official preference for a sectoral approach to planning, administration, and planometrics. But it is difficult to judge the influence of mathematically oriented and computer-assisted studies on the major policy decisions made at the center.

Capital Transfers from the Standpoint of Efficiency and Equity

Perpetuation of capital transfers of astounding magnitude raises a host of questions regarding the efficiency and equity of that process. To be sure, the answers to such questions depend on the criteria of the policy makers and of the analyst confronting historical evidence.

The perennial pattern of capital flows, with the Ukraine as the net loser, violates the fundamental economic principle that capital investments should maximize national output. Since the marginal productivity of investment is known to be higher in the Ukraine than in other regions, the net capital outflow constitutes an obvious loss to both the republic and the union. This judgment, implicit in Granberg's econometric calculations, is supported by other studies that compare territorial differences in capital-output ratios with investment patterns.[26] Although instances could be cited to show how the violation of this basic efficiency criterion has led some Soviet economists to question investment policies, the issue is being sidetracked by the official claim that other criteria— those imposed by top leadership and allegedly derived from Leninist dogma— override the pure economic calculus.

Thus, it has been maintained, particularly during the 1950s and 1960s, that investment policies and the required capital and labor movements aim to equalize economic development of the various regions. Such policy is claimed to be the Leninist solution of the nationalities problem inherited from the tsarist empire, in which peripheral regions, particularly those in Asia, were dominated by the more developed Russia proper. However, empirical evidence negates the hypothesis that the objective of regional equalization influenced the pattern of investment.[27] The interrepublic differences in development indexes have remained considerable, and regional differences in development within a major republic like the Ukraine (reflected in substantial differences in incomes and job opportunities) constitute a major unresolved problem.

Turning to still another union criterion, there is extensive evidence that policies of industrial location have been dominated by geopolitical defense objectives of the USSR as a rising military power. The keen analyst of Soviet political economy V. Holubnychy has presented extensive evidence that Soviet regionalization theories and policies have been historically subservient to geo- political military objectives of the empire.[28] But what about the economic con- sequences os such policies? It is generally agreed that the military-industrial complex in major Western countries has substantially affected the content and direction of economic development in the context of decentralized market economies. We also know that the military establishment in a centralized com- mand system interacts with the economic mechanism even more directly through the plan. Thus, when sacrosanct military objectives lay claim to the economic capacity of the country, the republics can hardly question their assigned tasks as suppliers to other regions or as trading partners with outside countries.

The reader may reflect on still another interpretation of Sovier regional development history as presented in the present volume. In Chapter 3 of this book S. H. Cohn points out that industrial development in the USSR has been spreading from the fortuitously developed "old regions" to the lagging regions, involving, in the process, the shifting of capital resources away from the former toward the latter. However, reviewing the historical evidence, one should note an important difference between the American and Soviet experiences. Whereas the westward flow of capital in the United States has taken place largely voluntarily under market incentives, the analogous eastward transfer of capital in the USSR relies on command methods and is contrary to purely economic considerations.

And, finally, the fact that the discussion of equity relating to regional economic policies is muted in Soviet publications does not mean that the problem does not exist. The issue of justice and even constitutional propriety arises in conjunction with capital transfers because, although the policies are made and enforced by Moscow, the allegedly sovereign Ukraine neither partakes effectively in the formulation of development criteria nor otherwise articulates its special interests. In Marxist theory, capital resources constitute the surplus value created by the workers and, hence, it would be normal to consider whether the conspicuous forfeiture of such surplus constitutes unwarranted exploitation. However, this aspect of the Soviet political economy cannot be discussed there openly, even from the standpoint of the otherwise propagated Marxist-Leninist theories.*

THE INWARD GRIP
OF THE FOREIGN TRADE MONOPOLY

Intraunion Structure of the Foreign Trade Monopoly

How does the system of exchange influence the action capabilities of the Ukrainian SSR? We can gain an insight into that system by asking, What is the status of the republic in the realm of foreign trade, given the preponderance of the metropolis-serving institution called the foreign trade monopoly (FTM)? A study by H. S. Levine investigates the place of external trade in the complex system of planning.[29] He points out the paradox that although the USSR has created an aura of reverence around the institution of FTM, the latter's publications are rather uncommunicative regarding the role of trade in the planning system. We propose to explore here how the FTM reaches into the republic to assign and enforce export tasks and to allocate imports.

---

*We might point out Moscow's repressive response to the recent treatise by the Kiev journalist Ivan Dziuba. The samizdat copies were circulated among Communist party functionaries, and merited several editions in the West; see the English version *Internationalism or Russification? A Study in the Soviet Nationalities Problem* (London: Weidenfeld and Nicholson, 1968). Relying on Marxist reasoning, the author exposes the economic underpinnings of linguicidal policies. He links the outflow of investable funds to the lagging development of industry in the Ukraine and the consequent emigration of native workers to other republics, where they lose their Ukrainian identity. At the same time, the centrally directed industrial expansion in Ukrainian cities encourages the immigration of Russian-speaking technicians and managers.

The problem of economic justice in connection with capital loss and related development policies relates to a much broader issue of the colonial bondage of non-Russian nationalities that has its origin in the tsarist empire. See V. Holubnychy, "Some Economic Aspects of Relations among the Soviet Republics," in E. Goldhagen, ed., *Ethnic Minorities in the Soviet Union* (New York: Praeger, 1968), pp. 55–67; and Hugh Seton-Watson, "Nationalism and Imperialism," in Royal Institute of International Affairs, *The Impact of the Russian Revolution* (London: Oxford University Press), 1967.

It is surprising that even though the Ukraine has acquired a semblance of identity in international cultural and diplomatic relations, this is hardly the case in commercial relations, be they with the Comecon, the capitalist, or the less-developed countries. To be sure, the republic, through its Ministry of Foreign Affairs (designated as a union-republic ministry), boasts of being a founding member of the United Nations, a voting member of various United Nations agencies, and a signatory to numerous international treaties.[30] Nonetheless, the Ukraine is limited to seven consular ties with the "fraternal socialist countries," and the United States consulate in Kiev was not established until 1976. Surprisingly, the UkSSR does not partake directly in the various agencies of Comecon. Although the Ukraine claimed considerable autonomy in foreign relations during the early years of the union, its foreign trade has become progressively monopolized by the metropolis.*

The term "foreign trade monopoly" as used here embraces the institutional, operational, and economic aspects of the trading system. FTM structure is pyramidal and hierarchic, with the proviso that the officials at the top can interact with the enterprises at the bottom, and can ignore or supersede republic and local administrations. The union-level Ministry of Foreign Trade oversees and coordinates the operational apparatus consisting of specialized foreign-trade combines, most of which are headquartered in Moscow. The union-level foreign-trade combines determine the export potentials and import allocations for purposes of the draft plan, and they are instrumental in implementing the centralized plans. Indeed, such combines dominate all phases of the export process other than production.

When the control figures of the plan reach the republics, and ultimately the producing enterprises, foreign demand for exportables is being communicated indirectly via the FTM. Similarly, the republic's requests for imports, when approved by central authorities, are circuitously transformed into demand for imports in the world market via appropriate union combines and their agents abroad. At least in the sphere of trade, one could hardly agree with F. E. I. Hamilton's contention that the republic and lower-level economic "actors" exercise a significant voice in the process of economic decision making.[31] Although the Ukraine's Gosplan directly plans the activity of 65 percent of industrial output and 80 percent of capital investment in the republic, it can merely "elaborate the proposals" concerning the republic-based foreign trade

---

*During its brief independence in 1918–21, the Ukraine signed economic treaties with Turkey, Russia, Germany, and several other countries. Also, the Soviet Ukraine concluded several commercial treaties during the early 1920s. The republic's considerable autonomy in foreign trade is reflected in the article "The Ukrgostorg: Its Role and Importance in the Exports of the Ukraine," in A. Troianovskii, L. Iurovskii, and M. Kaufman, eds., *Eksport, import, i kontsessii Soiuza SSR* (Moscow, 1926).

activity, which is subordinated to the union Ministry of Foreign Trade and ultimately planned by USSR Gosplan.

As can be seen, the union-level bureaus have the major share of power to determine the territorial ramifications of the planned trade. The top of the pyramid determines the allocation of capital and other resources needed for exports, as well as the allocation of imported producers' and consumers' goods. Trade is thus a policy tool used to redistribute income, technology, and capital, thereby promoting a centrally willed territorial pattern of development.

To ensure compliance with centralized plans and commands, the Ministry of Foreign Trade has traditionally relied on a tight network of "plenipotenti-aries" and other subordinated agencies in the republics. More than 1,000 enter-prises on the territory of Ukraine which participate in export production are made to comply with the assigned inflexible targets which have the highest priority.[32]

The implementation of trade commands according to centralized policies is undoubtedly facilitated by the presence in the republic of enterprises under the direct jurisdiction of union ministries or under union-republic ministries of the USSR. Such union enterprises are among the largest in the republic but are not directly planned by the republic.* They are comparable with giant Western multinationals whose management caters to the interests of the metropolis while their profitable activity escapes control by the systemically weak local governing and coordinating institutions. As important conduits of intraunion trade and net transfers of capital from the republic, the union-level enterprises perform a func-tion similar to that of the "joint companies" that operated in East Germany, Romania and other occupied countries after World War II and were subordinated to Moscow's economic interests, especially in facilitating the massive extraction of reparations. The role of union enterprises as collectors of surplus value and as instruments of territorial income redistribution invites further study. We are merely indicating their importance in the implementation of intraunion and external trade policies, especially in the exportation of key raw materials and in trade related to the military sector.

Our survey of the institutional scaffolding around the republic's foreign trade would be incomplete without mentioning several other supporting union-wide institutions. The union Ministry of Finance draws up the plans for the management of foreign currency; the State Bank of the USSR and six giant

---

*The list of enterprises under the union-republic ministries of the USSR is subject to approval by the Supreme Council of the USSR, in accordance with the constitution. The pattern and significance of control of enterprises in the republic is largely unexplored. How-ever, according to A. G. Granberg, *Optimizatsiia territorial'nykh proportsii narodnogo khoziaistva* (Moscow, 1973), p. 25, the production under the union management is growing much faster than that under union-republic and republic jurisdiction.

Soviet banks chartered abroad handle international financing and, on balance, profiteer from investing accumulated foreign reserves; the union-level Chamber of Commerce arranges trade exhibits and promotes contacts with foreign businessmen. They all enhance the power of the FTM and are hardly responsive to the republic's point of view.

The internal power of the FTM did not subside during the *sovnarkhoz* period of 1957–65, when territorial planning and administration were upgraded. In fact, the effectiveness of the FTM in extracting exports from the republic apparently was strengthened. In 1958, the Council of Ministers of the Ukraine and of several other republics had to create special commissions—composed of plenipotentiaries of the union Ministry of Foreign trade, representatives of the Gosplan, the Ministry of Finance, and the Ukraine's Economic Council—with the objective of tightening controls over export assignments in the republic.* There is no evidence that expanded territorial coordination of the Ukraine's economy during the sovnarkhoz interlude improved its bargaining power with the union FTM or gave it a larger share of the gains from international trade. On the contrary, the tightened compliance with the directives of the FTM led to an expanded share of the republic in total union exports while huge export surpluses continued to be absorbed by the rest of the union.

Operational and Behavioral Features
of the Monopoly System

The unequal action capabilities of the FTM and of the republic's enterprises and governing authorities generate rather peculiar behavior. Plant managers are by no means happy with export assignments that must meet high standards. Although the reforms increased the material incentives for managers and, nominally, for workers, the carrot is regarded as inadequate in the export sector, while the ever-threatening stick became more visible by making intentonal noncompliance with export orders a criminal offense.[33] The FTM has been extending quality specifications and control procedures to assure compliance with export standards. In recent years, the monopoly's plenipotentiaries have been stationed in strategic production centers and ports to assure high quality of export-destined machinery. Pressed by foreign competition, the FTM has spawned the State Commission for Foreign Economic Relations in order to

---

*These added regional export coordinating bureaus apparently were not dismantled when the Soviet planners reverted to branch management in 1965; see J. Quigley, *The Soviet Foreign Trade Monopoly: Institutions and Laws* (Columbus: Ohio State University Press, 1974), p. 145.

oversee the installation of exported equipment and industrial plants, mostly in the less-developed countries. Pressures for decentralization are resisted by the FTM, which prefers the entrenched command methods and maximum monopsony power in extracting export deliveries from enterprises.

Although imports of productive inputs and consumer goods are highly desirable, their assortment and territorial distribution are dependent on the criteria of the union Gosplan. The extent to which the republic Gosplan and consumer cooperatives can make suggestions on behalf of the workers and consumers is obviously limited. Although the Ministry of Foreign Trade, through its agencies abroad, is on the lookout for advanced foreign machinery and the technology that goes with it, republic administrators and enterprises cannot effectively articulate their needs because they lack contact with foreign options and avoid the inconvenience of demanding the imports during the planning process.

The inadequate motivation of enterprises in matters of trade is of particular concern to the Ukraine, which interacts extensively with the adjoining Comecon countries. One notes that reforms in Hungary have provided tangible incentives to enterprises by allowing them direct exposure to foreign export-import opportunities, by allowing decentralized decisions regarding the assortment and the method of production, and by establishing direct links between exports and imports when enterprises can utilize a portion of their currency earnings. Unlike the Soviet decentralized model of the New Economic Policy period or in present-day Hungary and Yugoslavia, the prevailing Stalinist model in the sphere of foreign trade minimizes direct contacts of Soviet enterprises with foreign customers and suppliers.* Action autonomy of decision units below the FTM is severely limited even when extensive export and import flows involve the socialist countries.

In the realm of planning, the interposition of a powerful FTM between the republic's productive apparatus and its consuming population, on the one side, and foreign markets, on the other, is more than a bureaucratic aberration. The union Gosplan devotes no more than 5 percent of its staff to territorial aspects of planning. With regard to the role of imports as a reserve against miscalculations and shortages, that benefit is hardly applicable at the level of the republic. On the other hand, the FTM is known to divert resources at will toward exports.

Criticism has been voiced in the Ukraine and the Baltic republics that production targets for interrepublic and international shipments are not

---

*The pent-up desire for foreign contacts is reflected in Soviet Ukrainian publications that proudly register the participation of Ukrainian personnel in the installation of equipment in India, Egypt, Cuba, Comecon countries, and elsewhere.

adequately specified by union plans, though they carry a high priority. Nonetheless, recent attempts to improve statistical information about the Ukraine's foreign trade have been sidetracked. As noted, experimental modeling and input-output simulations are hampered by the lack of adequate data on international and interregional trade and balances. As a result, the efforts to harness computers in the formation and implementation of plans at the level of the republics or otherwise defined economic regions are impeded.

Unlike the reformers in Eastern Europe, Soviet planners have generally failed to question the domestic economic consequences of supermonopolies like the FTM. To be sure, they deride capitalist monopolies that exploit their customers by rigging the prices and output, and they castigate the multinational corporations that disregard the interests of the weak host countries. But these same critics defy logic by claiming that Soviet supermonopolies are better because they are bigger.

Although the effects of the outward-directed power of the FTM have been experienced, and therefore studied abroad, the consequences of the inward-directed power of this and related institutions on economic efficiency and equity within the union are not well understood.[34] Certainly, the ability of the Ukraine to bargain for an equitable share of the "gains from trade" is crippled by the monopsony-monopoly powers of the FTM.

CONCLUDING REFLECTIONS ON THE STRUCTURE OF TRADE AND TRANSFERS

In the thicket of published statistical and technical details, we can discern the position of the Ukrainian republic as an entity interacting with the union and outside countries. But it is not enough to reveal the importance of the Ukraine in terms of its size, industrial potential, or geopolitical position in the USSR and Eastern Europe. One must also comprehend the observed evidence as the product of a system that shapes the process and the content of exchange.

It was suggested in the introduction and in the course of the argument that the republic's trade and transfers can be seen as being generated in a "system of unequal exchange." Thus, when the inequality in the sphere of international and interregional exchange was shown to depend crucially on the institution of foreign trade monopoly, that phenomenon should ultimately be interpreted as but one aspect of the system of planned economy that is being managed according to the objectives of the Moscow-dominated union.

The contention of the "structuralists" (as expounded by T. Baumgartner and others)—that in a system pervaded by systematic biases, the benefits and costs of production and exchange are unequally apportioned to the countries and their actors—is well borne out in the case of the Soviet Union. A disadvantageous division of the gains from trade through manipulated prices, the over-exploitation of natural resources relative to the promotion of manufacturing, the limited access to jobs in the international administrative apparatus, the loss of capital in the form of unrequited export surpluses, and the restricted access to foreign currency are all irrevocable losses with an immediate impact on the well-being of the working population and with long-run consequences for economic development. The unequal system of exchange also entails distortions in the allocation of resources and output, and there are wastes due to suboptimizations by the monopolies; although such losses to the republic and the union are not easy to measure, they are readily perceived analytically. Inasmuch as the union as a whole is making progress, the loss to the republic cannot be measured in absolute terms, but is observed as being relative to the metropolis, relative to other regions within the union, and relative to the neighboring countries.

The suggested interpretation of trade and transfers encompasses the circumstances that shape and maintain the uneven action capabilities and unequal dependency relations among the actors in the union as a system. Although Western discussions of the nature of unequal exchange largely involve the examples of periphery-metropolis relations in the context of capitalist market-oriented economies, the derived generalizations are eminently pertinent to our case. It might be argued that the inferior status of the republic and the consequent losses in welfare are so thoroughly institutionalized that they appear as normal and tolerable. But the judgment must take into account that the unequal distribution of power among the actors in the union has manifested itself in violence against dissident citizens and republic-oriented leaders.* Thus our case lends support to the conclusion of the structuralists that, in the international system, some nations are in a better position than others to structure their exchange activities so that they enhance their capabilities and interests better than their exchange partners do. Accordingly, ". . . many of the relatively less powerful countries are at a disadvantage due to internal political and social conditions—not infrequently supported or reinforced through political, economic, and cultural ties to powerful nations."[35] As can be seen, the conceptual framework of unequal exchange is not only helpful in sorting out and interpreting the published propaganda-tinted details concerning the interaction of the

---

*The suggested approach to the Soviet-type economic union fits into the "structural theory of imperialism," thus extending the Marxist-Leninist reductionist theory, which conceives of imperialism and exploitation as economic phenomena intrinsic only to monopoly-ridden market capitalism. See, for example, J. Galtung, "A Structural Theory of Imperialism," *Journal of Peace Research* (August 1971). Another keen student of the international political economy, P. D. J. Wiles, has pointed out the kinship between the capitalist and Soviet types of expansionism and exploitation, treating both in "The Economic Theory of Economic War and Imperialism," in his *Communist International Economics* (New York: Praeger, 1968).

Ukraine with the rest of the union and with third countries, but it also provides a basis for understanding the implications of such a system of exchange for the social, political, and cultural development of the Ukraine as a nation.[36]

With regard to the future, the theory of unequal exchange recognizes the likelihood of systemic changes, though perhaps not necessarily according to the Hegelian-Marxist blueprint of dialectical dynamics. The ability of those with greater power to structure exchange and development patterns favorable to themselves is never complete; other factors over which they lack control may alter action capabilities, redistribute strategic resources, and restructure patterns of dependence.

NOTES

1. The essential elements in the analysis of economic union were clarified by J. E. Meade in his classic *Problems of Economic Union* (Chicago: Chicago University Press, 1953). A historical and institutional interpretation of the USSR as a federated state is offered by R. Pipes, *The Formation of the Soviet Union: Communism and Nationalism, 1917-1923* (rev. ed.; Cambridge, Mass.: Harvard University Press, 1964); S. Olynyk, "Soviet Federalism in Theory and Practice" (Ph.D. dissertation, Georgetown University, 1965); G. Hodnett, "Debate over Soviet Federalism," *Soviet Studies (SS)* (April 1967); and D. L. Zlatopol'sky, *SSSR, federativnoe gosudarstvo* (Moscow, 1967).

2. A survey of the controversy in the Soviet literature concerning these questions as they relate to the planning process can be found in V. I. Danilov-Danilian and M. G. Zavel'skii, "Sotsial'noekonomicheskii optimum i territorial'nye problemy narodnokhoziaist-vennogo planirovaniia," *Ekonomika i matematicheskie metody (EiMM)* (1975): no. 3; also available as "The Socioeconomic Optimum and Territorial Problems of National Economic Planning," Joint Publications Research Service, Translations on USSR Economic Affairs (1975): no. 750. The authors argue that ". . . the maximization of satisfaction of material and intellectual demands of all workers" must take into account the ". . . regional differentiation of preferences and other peculiarities of an economic region as a socio-economic cell." Since an economic region has "an internal criterion of the optimum of economic activity," economic planning should be "compositional" rather than "global."

3. T. Baumgartner and T. Burns, "The Structuring of International Economic Relations," *International Studies Quarterly* (June 1975). The authors argue that economic exchange and development should be analyzed in the context of a structure in which the actors have differential control over resources and different action opportunities.

4. Essential facts and English bibliography on international economics of the Ukraine can be found in *Ukraine: A Concise Encyclopaedia*, II (Toronto: University of Toronto Press, 1971). Also see "The Ukrainian SSR on the International Scene," in M. P. Bazhan, ed., *Soviet Ukraine* (Kiev, 1969), pp. 548-61, which includes the section "Economic Ties of the UkSSR with Foreign Countries" but has no bibliography. Literature on the Ukraine's economic and cultural interaction with specific countries includes I. Kulinych, *Ekonomichni ta kulturni zv'iazky UkRSR z Nimets'koiu Demokratychnoiu Respublikoiu, 1945-1965* (Kiev, 1966); I. M. Hranchak, ed., *Ukrains'ka RSR u radians'ko-uhors'komu spivrobitnytstvi* (Kiev, 1972); Akademiia Nauk UkRSR, *Ukraina i Blyz'kyi ta Serednii Skhid* (Kiev, 1968); and V. O. Suprun and D. Vovko, eds., *Ekonomichni osnovy spivrobitnytstva z krainamy-chlenamy REV* (Kiev, 1971). For additional sources, consult S. Rapawy, "Soviet Bibliog-

raphy on the Postwar Economy of the Ukraine" and Joseph Danko, "A Bibliography of Western-Language Writings on Ukrainian Economy, 1919-1975," in *Annals of the Ukrainian Academy of Arts and Sciences in the U.S.A.* 13 (1977).

5. Estimates of the relative share of exports in the NMP of republics are found in A. G. Granberg, ed., *Mezhotraslevye balansy v analize territorial'nykh proportsii SSSR* (Novosibirsk, 1975), pp. 226-30. The quoted export shares pertain to their "full cost," derived by the input-output method, and are somewhat higher than the figures in other sources. For comparison, see a survey in English of another republic, L. Tulp, M. Vabar, and D. Rajango, *Economic Ties of the Estonian SSR* (Tallinn, 1972).

6. Granberg, op. cit., p. 230.

7. J. W. Gillula, "The 1966 Ukrainian Input-Output Table and an Analysis of the External Economic Relations of the Ukraine," Duke University and University of North Carolina, Occasional Papers on Soviet Input-Output Analysis, no. 14 (1975), pp. 45-46. Data on the rates of growth of various components of trade are also in N. G. Klimko, ed., *Problemy razvitiia ekonomiki sotsialisticheskikh stran Evropy* (Kiev, 1968), pp. 360-65.

8. Klimko, op. cit., p. 360. Estimates of the imbalance between the Ukraine's exports to and imports from Comecon and other countries are also presented by V. N. Bandera, "Interdependence Between Inreregional and International Payments: The Balance of Payments of Ukraine," in V. N. Bandera and Z. L. Melnyk, eds., *The Soviet Economy in Regional Perspective* (New York: Praeger, 1973), p. 141. V. Hobnychy's study of trade in industrial inputs contends that Soviet integration with CMEA countries involves predominantly the Ukraine and, to a lesser extent, Belorussia; see his "Trade Between Central Europe and the Soviet Union," *Studies for a New Central Europe* (1973/74): no. 3-4.

9. Gillula, op. cit., p. 39; also *Entsyklopediia narodnoho hospodarstva UkRSR* (Kiev, 1971), I, 564; and II, 156.

10. Consider also O. Zinam, "The Location Quotient Method in Soviet Regional Studies," *Annals of the Ukrainian Academy of Arts and Sciences in the U.S.A.*, 13 (1976). The locational quotient is defined as $LQ = (B_r/I_r)/(B_u/I_u)$, where B is the value of an industry and I is the value of all industries combined; r and u denote "republic" and "union," respectively. LQ greater than unity indicates specialization for export purposes. See H. W. Richardson, *Elements of Regional Economics* (London: Harmondsworth, 1969), p. 29.

11. H. J. Wagener, "Rules of Location and the Concept of Rationality: The Case of the USSR," in Bandera and Melnyk, op. cit., ch. 3.

12. Consider C. H. McMillan, "Factor Proportions and the Structure of Soviet Foreign Trade," *Association for Comparative Economic Studies Bulletin* (Spring 1973); Steven Rosefielde, *Soviet International Trade in Heckscher-Ohlin Perspective* (Lexington, Mass.: Lexington Books, 1973).

13. P. V. Voloboi and V. A. Popovkin, *Problemy terytorial'noi spetsializatsii i kompleksnoho rozvytku narodnoho hospodarstva UkRSR* (Kiev, 1972). The political economy of this problem is discussed by O. Zinam, "The Dilemma of Specialization Versus Autarky in the USSR: Issues and Solutions," in Bandera and Melnyk, op. cit., ch. 8; and his "Soviet Regional Problems: Specialization Versus Autarky," *Russian Review* (April 1972). Also see J. Wilczynski, "The Theory of Comparative Costs and Centrally Planned Economies," *Economic Journal* (March 1965).

14. Voloboi and Popovkin, op. cit., p. 132.

15. F. D. Holzman, "The Operation of Some Traditional Adjustment Mechanisms in the Foreign Trade of Centrally Planned Economies," in his *Foreign Trade Under Central Planning* (Cambridge, Mass.: Harvard University Press, 1974), ch. 4.

16. D. Vovko, *Ukraina v mizhnarodnykh ekonomichnkykh zv'iazkakh SRSR* (Kiev, 1966). Voloboi and Popovkin, op. cit., recommend curtailing the industries with high LQs and expanding those with low LQs. They essentially argue for promotion of the complex

development of the republic and reduction of instances of excessive specialization. Yet the expansion of a low-LQ industry, say textiles, would go contrary to the need to expand total imports.

17. Bandera, op. cit., pp. 134–42. The balance of payments may be compiled for a region regardless of the degree of its integration with the larger political-economic entity. An example of this is an account of Puerto Rico in W. Isard, *Methods of Regional Analysis: An Introduction to Regional Science* (New York: John Wiley, 1960), pp. 173–78. Consider also J. T. Romans, *Capital Exports and Growth Among U.S. Regions* (Middletown, Conn.: Wesleyan University Press, 1965). Soviet economists now also appreciate the value of balance-of-payments accounting; consider, for example, the survey of the estimation of exports and imports for the republic in V. V. Bondarenko, ed., *Balansovyi metod vyvchennia narodnoho hospodarstva* (Kiev, 1974), pp. 130–46.

18. See *Ukraine: A Concise Encyclopaedia*, pp. 933–46; also the chapters by W. J. Wagener, Z. L. Melnyk, and V. N. Bandera, in Bandera and Melnyk, op. cit. The accounting method and the balance-of-trade estimates for the decades preceding and following World War I are discussed in E. Glovins'kyi, "Problema rozrakhunkovoho biliansu Ukrainy," in Ukrains'kyi Naukovyi Instytut, *Suchasni problemy ekonomiky Ukrainy*, III (Warsaw, 1931). For 1926–27, the Ukraine's exports are estimated to have been 162.5 million rubles and imports 80.5 million rubles (in current prices).

19. The accounting aspects of this analysis are outlined in J. Vanek, *International Trade: Theory and Economic Policy* (Homewood, Ill.: R. D. Irwin, 1962). The logic of income-absorption is appreciated by such Soviet researchers as A. G. Granberg and V. V. Bondarenko in their cited publications.

20. S. Prociuk, "Vplyv faktora tekhnichnoho progresu na ekonomiku Ukrainy (II)," *Suchasnist'* (March 1975): 93; his article also discusses in some detail the dependence of Comecon countries on the raw materials from the Ukraine.

21. A. S. Emel'ianov and F. I. Kushnirskii, *Modelirovanie pokazatelei razvitiia ekonomiki soiuznoi respubliki* (Moscow, 1974); estimates of net capital outflow for 1960–68 were derived from that model and are presented in Bandera, op. cit., pp. 146–48.

22. E. V. Detneva, "Nekotorye perspektivnye raschety na osnove iedinoi sistemy ekonomicheskikh schetov raiona," in *Statistika narodnogo bogatstva, narodnogo dokhoda i natsional'nogo scheta* (Moscow, 1967).

23. A. G. Granberg, *Optimizatsiia territorial'nykh proportsii narodnogo khoziaistva* (Moscow, 1973).

24. Ibid., p. 156.

25. Ibid., p. 180.

26. See the review of location studies by O. Zinam, op. cit. The experience before World War II is analyzed thoroughly in I. S. Koropeckyj, *Location Problems in Soviet Industry Before World War II* (Chapel Hill: University of North Carolina Press, 1971). The evidence on capital and labor productivity in various republics is also analyzed in V. Holubnychy, "Some Economic Aspects of Relations Among the Soviet Republics," in E. Goldhagen, ed., *Ethnic Minorities in the Soviet Union* (New York: Praeger, 1968), esp. pp. 86–93; also see I. S. Koropeckyj, "Industrial Location Policy in the USSR During the Postwar Period," in Joint Economic Committee, *Economic Performance and the Military Burden in the Soviet Union* (Washington, D.C.: U.S. Government Printing Office, 1970), pp. 254–62.

27. Holubnychy, *Some Economic*, pp. 50–54, and 67–86.

28. V. Holubnychy, "Teleology of the Macroregions in Soviet Union's Long-Range Plans, 1920–90," in A. F. Burghardt, ed., *Development Regions in the Soviet Union, Eastern Europe, and Canada* (New York: Praeger, 1975). See also Koropeckyj, *Industrial Location*, pp. 262–64.

29. H. S. Levine, "The Effects of Foreign Trade on Soviet Planning Practices," in A. A. Brown and E. Neuberger, eds., *International Trade and Central Planning* (Berkeley: University of California Press, 1968).

30. K. Sawczuk, *Ukraine in the United Nations Organization: Study in Soviet Foreign Policy* (Boulder, Colo.: East European Quarterly, 1975); V. Vasilenko and I. Lukashuk, *Ukrainian SSR in Contemporary International Relations* (Kiev, 1975).

31. F. E. Ian Hamilton, "Spatial Dimensions of Soviet Economic Decision Making," in Bandera and Melnyk, op. cit., ch. 10. The assignment of export tasks by the union and union-republic branch ministry and its production associations is brought out in Levine, op. cit., p. 264. During the sovnarkhoz interlude in the early 1960s, it was hinted that trading procedures might be decentralized. A western observer prematurely claimed, "In order to encourage exports, the Soviet Government has allowed all Soviet republics to import without Ministry of Foreign Trade permission goods to a certain percentage of their export turnover. The republics, in their turn, have given this right to the regions, but with a reduced percentage. The regions have passed this right on to their export factories. . . ." A. Flegon, ed., *Soviet Foreign Trade Techniques* (London: Flegon Publishers, 1965), pp. 23–24.

32. Levine, op. cit., p. 276, cites *Ekonomicheskaia gazeta* (1966): no. 50, that among the targets still sent from the center to enterprises was the output of export goods, in physical units.

33. The formidable system of supervision by FTM is well described by J. Quigley, *The Soviet Foreign Trade Monopoly: Institutions and Laws* (Columbus: Ohio State University Press, 1974), p. 141. The broader issues connected with centralization as it relates to industrial management are discussed in S. A. Billon, "Concentration of Authority and Regional Management," in Bandera and Melnyk, op. cit., ch. 9.

34. The problem of economic misbehavior of monopolies under socialism is discussed in V. N. Bandera, "Market Orientation of State Enterprises During NEP," *SS* (July 1970): esp. 118–21.

35. T. Baumgartner, W. Buckley, and T. R. Burns, "Unequal Exchange and Uneven Development: The Structuring of Exchange and Development Patterns," paper presented at the Third International Congress of Cybernetics and Systems, Bucharest, August 1975, published in *Studies in Comparative International Development*; the quote is from the "abstract" of that paper.

36. The importance of economic factors in the restructuring of power relations in Eastern Europe since the 1920s is illuminated in V. N. Bandera, *Foreign Capital as an Instrument of National Economic Policy: A Study Based on the Experience of East European Countries Between the World Wars* (2nd ed.; The Hague: M. Nijhoff, 1968), esp. pp. 138–44. Historical parallels are also drawn between the present status of the Ukraine and that of the western Ukraine within the system of unequal exchange of interwar Poland in V. N. Bandera, "Zakhidnia Ukraina v ramkakh ekonomiky mizhvoiennoi Pol'shchi," *Ukrains'kyi Samostiinyk* (1967): no. 119–20.

10

CAPITAL FORMATION
AND FINANCIAL RELATIONS
Z. L. Melnyk

INTRODUCTION

The importance of capital formation may be stated simply: it is a major determinant of economic growth and development. The ability of an economy to generate sufficient new capital underlies its strength and vitality; only to a limited extent may domestic capital formation be supplemented by foreign funds. The continued need of the USSR to depend heavily on domestic capital, because of the traditionally limited participation of that country in the international capital markets, makes its reliance on internally generated funds that much more important. The Soviet authorities have thus exhibited considerable concern about the need to generate sufficient capital, manifested in numerous decisions regarding Soviet economic policy.

The process of allocating newly formed capital among the sectors of the economy and the criteria guiding such allocation affect the efficiency with which these resources are utilized, and determine the nature and the rate of economic development. Since capital-allocation decisions are made within the framework of economic philosophy and political climate prevailing in the society, capital allocation reflects economic, social, and political priorities of the decision makers.

In the USSR the decisions determining capital formation and its territorial and sectoral distribution are made by the central government. This dominant position of the Moscow government is reinforced by the fiscal financial system and by the organizational structure of the Soviet economy. The subordination to and direct control by the central government of those enterprises and industries that it considers essential to accomplishing its objectives enables the central government to impose its priorities and to enforce compliance with them in the fulfillment of the centrally established goals.* In doing so, the central government can, and does, redistribute income and wealth on a countrywide basis.[1] As a result, national income produced in a republic may not coincide with the income utilized in that republic,[2] and the value of net savings generated in a republic may exceed or be less than capital investments on its territory. Thus, an evaluation of capital formation in a republic must include the estimated value of capital transfers between the republic and the central government (the rest of the USSR).

Analysis of capital formation on a regional basis provides an added dimension for evaluating the USSR economy. By identifying capital-producing and capital-consuming regions, it assesses their contributions to Soviet economic development. The importance of each region in the growth of the economy and in the development of backward areas is further highlighted by an analysis of the directions and the extent of capital flows among the regions. Such an analysis also contributes to a better understanding of the complex economic relations among the Soviet republics that often involve diverse economic interests within the individual republics as well as myriad political issues.

The present study focuses on capital formation in the Ukrainian SSR, since the Ukraine is a natural focal point for such an analysis. The republic is a distinct administrative-political unit and a separate economic region of the USSR. Thus, the data are more likely to be available. Additionally, the Ukrainian SSR is a unique ethnic entity inhabited predominantly by Ukrainians.

The study summarizes the computed value of capital generated in the Ukraine in 1959-70, both by uses and by sources of capital, thus also providing an opportunity to observe the direction and the extent of intersectoral flows of investable funds in the Ukrainian SSR. An estimate of the amount of capital withdrawn from the Ukraine by the central government unilaterally and on a noncompensatory basis (mainly through the budgetary system) also is supplied. Thus, this study assesses the contribution of the Ukrainian SSR to Soviet capital formation and, therefore, the extent of the burden of Soviet economic development imposed on the population of that republic.

---

*The subordination of the industries to the various levels of government did not remain fixed. In part, the extent of the direct jurisdiction of the central government over economic enterprises—versus the subordination to republic authorities—was reflected in the shares of such bodies in the government's budget. The share of the central government in the state budget of the USSR, measured by the percent of its expenditures in the expenditures of all levels of government, was 76.8 percent in 1950, 73.9 percent in 1955, and 44.8 percent in 1959; it remained at about 41–42 percent in 1960–65, increased to 49.1 percent in 1966, and fluctuated narrowly around 52 percent in 1967–70. For details see *Gosudarstvennyi biudzhet SSSR i biudzhety soiuznykh respublik* (Moscow, 1962), p. 6; (Moscow, 1966), p. 9; (Moscow, 1972), p. 24.

The selection of the time period, especially its terminal year (1970), was constrained by the availability of the required data. Being removed from the end of World War II by more than a decade, this period is assumed to be characterized by more normal economic conditions.

ANALYTICAL APPROACH

The amount of gross capital created in a Western country may be computed by adding the value of investments in the various sectors of the economy, on the assumption that such investments represent reasonable approximations to capital accumulations in the respective industries. This assumption that sources and uses of capital parallel each other, is not justified in the case of the USSR. In the Soviet Union, the government's budget is closely linked with economic plans, investments in fixed and working capital, and the operation of economic and financial institutions as well as governmental agencies. In fact, more than 50 percent of the country's national income passes through the budgetary system* and is redistributed in accordance with the government's plan. Therefore, differences between the origins and applications of newly created capital arise at the intersectoral and geographic levels.

Two types of problems are encountered in studying Soviet capital formation. The first type encompasses a wide range of issues relating to the authenticity and validity of Soviet statistics and to the availability of specific data. These may be called "technical" problems. Problems of the second type are related to the Soviet system, and are thus "system" problems; they include conceptual definitions and measurements of economic phenomena peculiar to Soviet economic thought; the organizational scheme of the Soviet economy— including territorial, sectoral (such as agriculture, industry, finance) and intrasectoral (such as capital goods vs. consumer goods and industries, collective farms vs. state farms), and economic relations; and the administrative and political structure of the USSR.[3]

In view of these problems, the method adopted in the present study is based on an "institutional" approach.[4] This method identifies the individual sources of capital formation according to their socioeconomic attributes; it also reflects the nature of the Soviet economy and the manner in which decisions on economic and social policies are made in the USSR.

---

*During 1959–70, total revenues of the state budget of the USSR amounted to 52.9 percent of Soviet Union's national income. Computed from *Narodnoe khoziaistvo SSR (Narkhoz) 1963*, p. 501; *1970*, p. 533; *Gosudarstvennyi biudzhet SSSR i biudzhety soiuznykh respublik, 1962*, pp. 5–13, *1966*, pp. 8–16, and *1972*, pp. 10–18.

BUDGETARY REVENUES

In the Soviet budgetary system, the state budget of the USSR is a consolidated budget of all levels of government.[5] However, it is the central government's budget that is most relevant for calculating financial relations between a republic and the rest of the USSR. Unfortunately, the latter is not reported separately; it must be obtained indirectly by subtracting from the state budget the budgets of all republics (which also include local budgets). A summary of the state budget, the budgets of all republics taken together, the central government's budget, and the budget of the Ukrainian republic is presented in Tables 10.8 and 10.9, which contain, respectively, revenues and expenditures.

Since the central government does not release the data on all its receipts and expenditures by political and economic subdivisions of the USSR, such statistics—and thus financial relations between a republic or an economic region and the central government—cannot be obtained directly. They must be computed on the basis of other relevant facts and indicators.

Turnover tax is the largest single revenue item in the state budget. In 1959-70 it provided 35.9 percent of all budgetary revenues and was equal to 19 percent of Soviet national income (Soviet definition) during that period.

Turnover tax performs several functions in the Soviet economy. When it was established in 1930 as a part of the financial reform, it replaced 54 taxes and nontax levies[6] collected by the state government and various local authorities from industrial and other economic enterprises. A large part of these revenues represented indirect levies on consumers. For example, various excise taxes constituted in 1928/29 and 1929/30, respectively, 59.0 and 53.3 percent of revenues that were reclassified into turnover tax.[7] To this extent, a part of turnover tax revenues may be considered a charge on consumers—something akin to a sales and use tax. The remaining levies that were combined in the turnover tax represented rents, quasi rents, and charges on business income and agriculture that could be construed in Soviet terminology as an element of surplus value created in these sectors but realized by the state in the form of turnover tax that became a part of retail prices, mainly for consumer goods.

Traditionally prices were established in a manner that could be viewed as discriminating against capital goods and other nonconsumer industries. Prices for products of heavy and extractive industries were set at artificially low levels, sometimes even below production costs,[8] in the belief that this would encourage capital investments and industrial expansion. Even now, "Prices for means of production, as a rule, [are] below social costs of production," with the result that production costs of consumer goods are understated.[9] The differences between the actual costs of production of capital goods and their [transfer] prices are recaptured by the government as turnover tax in retail prices for consumer goods.[10] Thus, prices of consumer goods include not only production costs and profits but also an element of profit actually produced by capital goods, extractive, and other intermediate-goods industries.[11]

Turnover tax performs a similar function in agriculture. Collective farms were required to deliver a specified part of their produce to the state at prices that were far below the retail prices at which they were resold to consumers, even after allowing for processing and distribution costs. Indeed, in many instances obligatory delivery prices were below production costs on collective farms.[12] There is evidence that similar conditions existed on state farms.[13] As in the case of capital goods, the difference between government procurement prices (plus handling, processing, and distribution costs) and retail prices was collected by the government as turnover tax.[14] Such turnover tax collections, therefore, must be viewed as a part of the income of collective farms that was confiscated by the state—a tax in kind on the peasantry, a form of forced savings from agriculture.

Since turnover tax is paid by consumer-goods industries, retail organizations, and government procurement agencies, it is apparent that those republics that contribute more than their proportionate share to the output of consumer goods are net gainers; they are credited with and realize a part of income produced by republics supplying capital goods, raw materials, and products of extractive industries.[15] Similarly a part of the net income of the republics that are net suppliers of food stuffs and other agricultural commodities is shifted to the consuming republics.

The Ukrainian Soviet republic has been a major supplier of capital goods, mining products and other raw materials, semimanufactured products, and food-stuffs (Table 3.1). The value of gross output of the Ukraine's agriculture ranged in 1959-70 between 22.8 and 24.7 percent of that of the USSR.[16] The contribution of the Ukrainian SSR to the value of marketed output of Soviet agriculture in 1959, the only year for which such information was available, was 24.4 percent.[17] During the period under review (1959-70), monetary income of collective farms in the Ukraine amounted to 27.8 percent of the USSR value.[18] On the other hand, the republic imported a large amount of manufactured consumer goods[19] (on which the Ukrainian population paid turnover taxes), even though some of these products were made from raw materials and agricultural commodities produced in the Ukraine and released to plants outside the republic at the prevailing artificially reduced prices for such products.

In Soviet economic theory, surplus value is produced in both consumer-goods and capital-goods industries. Therefore, the contribution of the Ukraine to turnover tax revenues—a major component of surplus value—must reflect the share of the republic in Soviet industrial and agricultural output.[20] Yet, official data report that turnover tax collections (*Kontingent*) in the Ukrainian SSR in 1959-70 amounted to 80,010.8 million rubles,[21] or 17.8 percent of the USSR total.[22]

It follows that the amount of the portion of surplus value created in the Ukrainian economy that was represented by turnover tax must have exceeded the reported collections of this tax within the Ukrainian SSR. This difference was caused by the Soviet price system and the method of payment of the tax. As indicated, under the Soviet price structure, many nonconsumer-goods industries were required to sell their products to consumer-goods manufacturers at artificially reduced prices that did not reflect the full economic costs. This portion of surplus value created in nonconsumer-goods industries was recovered in consumer-goods prices in the form of turnover tax. However, because turnover tax was collected mainly at the point of final sale of consumer goods, the corresponding portion of surplus value created in the industries that provided consumer-goods manufacturers with fixed capital, raw materials, and semi-products was credited to consumer-goods industries. Accordingly, turnover tax revenues that were in fact created in nonconsumer goods industries and agriculture were realized in the budgets of those republics in which the final sale of consumer products occurred, and not in the republics where this portion of surplus value was created.

Thus, to obtain the true amount of the contribution of a Soviet republic to the surplus value represented by turnover tax revenues, it is necessary to compute the amount of turnover tax applicable to the output of industries subject to this tax—typically consumer goods, and to add the amount of surplus value created in nonconsumer-goods industries of that republic but realized in other republics, minus the amount of surplus value created in such industries in other republics but realized within the territory of the particular republic. In practice, such computations cannot be made because of lack of the needed data. Therefore, such estimates for the Ukraine, presented below, are based on the republic's contribution to industrial and agricultural output of the USSR as a feasible approximation.

The contribution of the Ukrainian SSR to turnover tax revenues of the USSR, presented in Table 10.1, was computed by recognizing the nature and purpose of this tax as well as the Ukraine's contribution to its value in the productive process. Taxation of consumers residing in the Ukrainian SSR was allocated to the Ukraine in proportion to the share of the republic in Soviet retail trade, excluding public catering (17.3 percent). For the entire USSR this part of turnover tax receipts was assumed to be equal to 5 percent of Soviet retail value.

The monetary equivalent of taxation in kind of agriculture could be computed as the difference between the value of its marketed output and monetary revenue or income. However, data on the value of marketed output are quite scarce, almost nonexistent, especially after 1961. The available data indicate that the value of marketed output tended to be about 1.5 to 1.7 times the monetary income of collective farms.[23] Since monetary income of Soviet

TABLE 10.1

Allocation of Turnover Tax Revenues to the Ukraine, 1959-70
(million rubles)

	USSR	Allocation Factors	Ukraine	
Sales and use tax equivalent[a]	64,103	.173	11,089.7	10.85%
Tax in kind on peasantry[b]	128,709	.238	30,632.7	29.97%
Diversion of industrial profits[c]	257,426	.235	60,495.1	59.18%
Total turnover tax	450,238[d]		102,217.5	
Paid into republic's budget			24,983.9[d]	
Turnover tax collections to central government			77,233.6	

Methodology and Sources:

[a]For lack of other data, assumed at 5 percent of retail trade, which totaled 1,282,049 million rubles in the USSR in 1959-70. Retail trade in the Ukraine for these years amounted to 224,965 million rubles (17.5 percent of the USSR total). The ratio used here, 17.3 percent, excludes the Ukraine's share in the sales of public catering. For data, see *Narodne hospodarstvo, Ukrains'koi RSR 1970* (Kiev, 1971) *Narhosp 1970*, pp. 434-35; *Narhosp 1973*, pp. 448-49; *Narodnoe khoziaistvo SSSR 1961* (Moscow, 1962) (*Narkhoz*), pp. 633-34; *Narkhoz 1970*, pp. 577-78; *Narkhoz 1973*, pp. 652-53.

[b]Statistical data through 1961, years for which the value of marketed output of Soviet agriculture is available, indicate that marketed output was approximately equal to 1.5-1.7 times monetary income of collective farms. See *Sel'skoe khoziaistvo SSSR* (Moscow, 1960), pp. 24, 64; for 1959-61, see Z. L. Melnyk, "Financial Relations Between Ukraine and Moscow in 1959-1961," *Wissenschaftliche Milleilungen* 18 (1968/1969): 37. A ratio of 1.5 times was used in the present estimates. Further, according to the available data, the Ukraine's share in the monetary income of collective farms in 1959-70 was 27.8 percent. The data on the value of marketed output in the Ukraine for 1959, the only year for which such data are available, indicate that the Ukraine's marketed output was approximately 24.5 percent of the USSR value in that year. (See ibid., p. 35.) This was within the range of the share of the Ukrainian republic in Soviet agricultural output of 22.8-24.7 percent. For this reason, in the absence of data on marketed output in the Ukraine, the midpoint of the share of the Ukrainian SSR in Soviet agricultural output, 23.8 percent, is used in these computations. (See various volumes of *Narkhoz* and *Narhosp*.)

[c]The balance of turnover tax revenues. This is assumed to represent the part of surplus value created in industry that was collected by means of turnover tax.

[d]Table 10.8.

collective farms in 1959-70 was 257,418 million rubles,[24] the equivalent of tax in kind on agriculture was estimated at 128,709-180,193 million rubles, or 28.6-40.0 percent of total turnover tax revenues. Although the upper limit appears to be somewhat high,* the lower value is conservative in relation to estimates for other time periods.[25] Nevertheless, the lower value was used in this analysis. The share of the Ukraine in this tax in kind was determined at 23.8 percent, which is approximately equal to the republic's contribution to the value of the output of Soviet agriculture.

The remainder of turnover tax revenues was assumed to be derived from industrial enterprises. (Contributions of other nonagricultural sectors of the economy were of minor importance.) Unfortunately, the data on the value of industrial output in the individual Soviet republics, needed for direct assessment of their relative contributions to the surplus value created in the industries located within each republic, are not available. However, as evident from Table 3.1, the Ukraine was a main industrial center of the USSR and a major supplier of machinery, equipment, and industrial raw materials—all of which were severely discriminated against in pricing policies. Based on this evidence, the share of the Ukrainian SSR in this part of turnover tax was estimated at 22-25 percent of the USSR amount. For convenience in presentation, the midpoint of 23.5 percent was used in Table 10.1.

These estimates reveal that turnover tax revenues created in the Ukraine in 1959-70 were 102,217.5 million rubles. The difference between this amount and the officially reported amount of 80,010.8 million rubles represents that part of the Ukraine's national income that was distributed by the central government to other republics via turnover tax and was not recognized in turnover tax receipts generated in the Ukraine.[26]

Compared with other available information, it appears that these estimates are on the low side. First, the estimated contribution of the Ukrainian SSR to Soviet turnover tax—102,218 million rubles, or 22.7 percent of the USSR total—is below the 23.9 percent estimate for 1959-61.[27] It also is almost 2 percent below the 1928-32 ratio of 25.7 percent.[28] Second, if one were to adjust correspondingly the national income of the Ukraine (475.8 billion rubles; 453.6 billion rubles plus 22.2 billion rubles adjustment) would have been equal to 20.1 percent of Soviet national income in 1959-70. Certainly this would not have been excessive—indeed, it would have been minimally reasonable—for a republic with 19.5 percent of Soviet population and a large share in Soviet industrial and agricultural output. Third, according to the existing evidence, the Ukrainian SSR

---

*This ratio is identical with the estimates of Coogan for 1935, which amounted to 39.74 percent of turnover tax revenues. James Coogan, "Bread and the Soviet Fiscal System," *Review of Economics and Statistics* (May 1953): 167.

TABLE 10.2

Computation of Central Government's Budget
in the Ukraine, 1959–70
(million rubles)

| | Central Government's Budget | | |
	Total	Allocation Factors	Ukraine
Revenues			
Turnover tax	261,469.8	[a]	77,233.6
Payments from profits	178,031.2	.235	41,837.3
Other revenues from economy	156,398.0	.200	31,279.6
Income taxes on population	42,464.4	.161	6,836.8
Government loans	4,328.5	.183	792.1
Other revenues from population	4,231.2	.195	825.1
	646,923.1		158,804.5
Expenditures			
Economy: Industry	123,164.1		
Agriculture	14,108.2		
Transportation and communication	15,969.5		
Other	75,763.9		
	229,005.3	[b]	4,080.0
Sociocultural: Education	58,172.2		
Health	5,485.1		
Collective farmers' insurance	5,021.3	.195	13,513.7
Other	622.6		
Social security	22,859.7	.178	13,185.0
Social insurance	51,213.1		
	143,374.0		26,698.7
Defense	162,999.2	.200	32,599.8
Administration	4,067.4	.200	613.5
Other	35,748.8		
Less direct aid to Kazakh, Turkmen, and Armenian Republics	12,117.5		
	23,631.3	.200	4,726.3
	575,194.7		68,718.3
Net gain to central government			90,086.2

NOTES TO TABLE 10.2

[a]See Table 10.1.

[b]Total capital investments in the Ukraine (Table 10.10)

Total capital investments in the Ukraine (Table 10.10)		100,849
Less: housing (by population)	6,368	
collective farms (internally financed)	12,086	18,454
		82,395
Financed from the republic's budget	38,367	
Less agriculture (stated separately in this presentation)	7,048	31,319
		51,076
Retained earnings	29,917	
Depreciation funds allocated for capital investments	17,079	46,996
Subsidy from the central government's budget		4,080

Retained earnings are based on the Ukraine's percentage share in deductions from profits in 1959-70. According to budgetary data presented in Table 10.8, the Ukraine contributed approximately 23.5 percent to total payments from profits. However, since enterprises in the Ukraine paid into the budget a slightly higher percentage of profits than the average in the USSR, the ratio is reduced here to 23.0 percent. (Additional analysis, by considering 1959-65 and 1966-70 separately, results in the ratio of 24.5 percent to 25.3 percent.) Thus:

Total profits in the USSR economy	535,236	million rubles
Ukraine's share (at 23.0 percent)	123,104.3	million rubles
Paid into the budgets:		
Republic	51,350.4	
Central government	41,837.3	
	93,187.7	million rubles
Retained earnings	29,916.6	million rubles

Data on profits in the USSR were obtained from *Narodnoe khoziaistvo SSR, (Narkhoz), 1961, 1963, 1965, 1968, 1969,* and *1970.* For data on payments into the budgets, also see Table 10.8.

Depreciation calculations are shown below.

Total depreciation allowances in the USSR (million rubles)		212,813
Less depreciation funds earmarked for major repairs		111,277
Depreciation funds for capital investments		101,536
Minus: Depreciation funds in agriculture	21,083	
Less: Funds earmarked for major repairs	9,436	
		11,647
Applicable depreciation funds		89,889
Ukraine's share (at 19.0 percent according to		
estimated share of the Ukraine in fixed assets		17,079

For data on depreciation allowances, see *Narkhoz 1961, 1963, 1965, 1968, 1969,* and *1970.*

Sources: Tables 10.1, 10.8, 10.9. See text for explanation of allocation factors.

contributed significantly to the interrepublic trade and showed a substantial trade surplus from these transactions. For example, in 1961 the Ukraine's net trade surplus with the rest of the USSR amounted to 1,377 million rubles and was equal to 43.7 percent of net trade surpluses in interrepublic trade.[29]

Deductions from profits (included in the analysis presented in Table 10.2) constitute another major means of redistributing income and wealth in the USSR through the budgetary system. Their role has increased since 1966 as a result of price adjustments, the method of taxing enterprises, and the reorganization of the economy, which placed a larger part of the economy under the direct control of the central government.

Deductions from profits are a function of the amount of invested capital, profitability, and schedule of payment rates. This writer was unable to compile reliable data on the value of fixed funds in the Ukraine in general, and particularly in terms of the information directly comparable with the data for the USSR. Although the Ukrainian SSR entered the era of five-year plans with 24.5 percent of fixed capital in the USSR,[30] there is evidence to support the view that fixed funds in the Ukrainian economy in 1950-70 must have been below this level. For example, the official Soviet statistics on capital investments (in comparable prices) reveal that total investments in the Ukrainian economy amounted to 19.3 percent of the USSR value during the Fourth Five-Year Plan (1946-50) and 16.5-17.0 percent in all subsequent five-year plans from 1951 to 1970. The 1946-70 weighted average ratio was 16.9 percent, and for 1961-70 it was 16.7 percent.[31]

These investments were disproportionately low in comparison with the contribution of the republic to Soviet output. Moreover, were it not for the investments of collective farms and the population from their own resources, these percentages would have been even lower. Capital investments by state and cooperative enterprises and organizations were 19.2 percent of the USSR in 1946-50 and 15.6-16.0 percent in subsequent five-year plans; 1946-70 and 1960-70 weighted average ratios were 15.7 percent and 15.3 percent, respectively. Capital investments by collective farms in the Ukraine rose steadily—from 17.3 percent in 1946-50 to 21.7 percent in 1951-55, 22.5 percent in 1956-60, 26.8 percent in 1961-65, and 26.4 percent in 1966-70; the weighted averages were 24.8 percent in 1946-70 and 26.5 in 1960-70. Capital investments by the republic's population, although fluctuating more widely, reached 28.4 percent of such USSR investments in 1966-70, with weighted average ratios of 24.3 percent and 27.7 percent in 1946-70 and 1960-70, respectively.[32]

Such low investments in the Ukrainian economy by the Soviet government must have had a particularly depressing effect on the economic development of the republic in view of the heavy losses suffered by the Ukraine in World War II. According to official Soviet information, the Ukraine accounted for 42 percent of the USSR's war losses.[33] Specifically, the Ukraine's losses represented the following percentages of the USSR losses: 42 percent of completely or partially destroyed cities and towns and 40 percent of villages; 31 percent of destroyed industrial enterprises; 40 percent of the Soviet population that became homeless as a result of the war.[34] As for the Ukraine's economy, these losses were devastating—the entire economy lay in ruins, including 90 percent of the industry, almost all collective and state farms and machine tractor stations; and at least 27 percent of the Ukraine's population was homeless.[35]

As indicated, despite such staggering losses, investments in the Ukrainian SSR to restore and rehabilitate the economy were disappointingly low, especially when compared with the republic's share in the USSR's output. The Ukrainian population, which suffered most during the war, was required to carry a disproportionately heavy burden in rebuilding its economy. Thus, while government investments in the agriculture of the USSR in 1946-70 provided 56.2 percent of such funds, in the Ukraine the ratio was only 35.4 percent; government investments in the Ukraine's agriculture were only 9.9 percent of such investments in the USSR.[36] Similarly, state and cooperative enterprises (excluding collective farms) financed 77.3 percent of housing construction in the USSR and 65.1 percent in the Ukraine.[37] Moreover, capital assets removed en masse during the war from the Ukraine into the eastern parts of the USSR were not returned to the republic. On the other hand, fiscal and financial relations in the republic indicate that the Ukraine paid for most, if not all, capital assets acquired subsequently from other republics, despite substantial war reparations received by the USSR.[38]

While the above suggests that the Ukraine's present share in the USSR fixed capital should be relatively low, there is conflicting evidence, perhaps equally credible, that does not quite support this conclusion. For example, the value of fixed funds in collective farms of the Ukraine amounted to 26.8 percent of the USSR value as of January 1, 1962,[39] and 29.5 percent in 1970. When the fixed capital of state farms is included, the 1970 ratio for all agriculture of the Ukraine becomes almost 21 percent;[40] the data for other years reveal that during the period under consideration this ratio tended to range between 20.8 and 21.5 percent. Although the information on fixed capital in other sectors of the republic's economy is very scarce, a test based on the data on profits and profitability rates (profit/fixed and working capital) indicates that the share of the Ukraine in fixed assets of Soviet industry, weighted by annual values, was equal in 1965-70 to 18.8 percent, varying between 18.5 percent and 18.9 percent.[41] Also, the Ukraine tended to dominate in capital-intensive industries, characterized by longer-life assets. Finally, according to data in Table 10.8, fixed-fund payments into the budget of the Ukrainian republic constituted 33.6 percent of such payments into the budgets of all republics. Since these payments are determined at fixed, uniform percentages of invested capital, this ratio provides additional evidence that fixed funds of the Ukraine probably exceeded 19 percent by some margin. (It is recognized that this ratio may have been influenced somewhat by regional differences in the transition of enterprises to the new system of taxation and accountability and by certain exemptions from this tax.)

Profitability of Ukrainian enterprises in those industries in which the Ukraine contributed significant shares of the USSR output was higher than, or at least equal to, the average USSR performance (light and food industries, machine building and metalworking, chemicals and petrochemicals, ferrous metals, coal, electric energy—see Table 10.10). Therefore, the Ukraine's contribution to profits must have been somewhat greater than its share in fixed assets. Additionally, available data reveal that profits of Ukrainian agriculture in 1964–70 were equal to 28.1 percent of the comparable USSR value.[42]

In view of these facts, it may not be unreasonable to assume that the contribution of the Ukrainian republic to total profits and profit taxes of the Soviet Union was close to the ratio of deductions from profits into the Ukraine's budget relative to such deductions into the budgets of all republics. This ratio in 1959–70, including payments by *sovnarkhozes*, was 23.5 percent. That figure was used in the present analysis.

Other revenues from the economy were allocated to the Ukraine in Table 10.2 at 20 percent.

Income taxes paid by the population and revenues from government bonds were allocated to the Ukraine (Table 10.2) in proportion to such payments into the budget of the republic relative to similar payments into the budgets of all Soviet republics. The contribution of the Ukraine to other revenues from the population was assumed to be equal to the weight of the republic's population in the population of the USSR, 19.5 percent.

BUDGETARY EXPENDITURES

Expenditures from the central government's budget on the Ukraine's economy were estimated at 4,080 million rubles during 1959–70. A fundamental assumption was made in these computations regarding priorities in terms of the sources of financing. These assumed priorities were generally consistent with the methods and sources of financing capital investments in the USSR.[43] However, since it was not possible to trace interregional redistribution of resources (working capital, depreciation funds, profits) among enterprises subject to control by the same ministries, a simplified hierarchy of funding was assumed, as explained in footnote b of Table 10.2. Specifically, the following order of "drawing" on financial resources was assumed: retained earnings, depreciation funds not reserved for major capital repairs, capital expenditure subsidies from the budget of the republic, and allocations (subsidies) from the central government's budget.

In estimating retained earnings in the Ukrainian economy, the share of the republic in profits of the USSR was assumed at 23.0 percent (as opposed to 23.5 percent used to allocate budgetary revenue from deductions from profits). This reduction in the share of the Ukraine in retained earnings was based on the observation that the effective rate of deductions from profits in the Ukraine was somewhat higher than in the USSR on the average, typically by 2-3 percent. Accordingly, profits in the Ukraine were estimated at 123,104.3 million rubles. By subtracting from this figure the amount of taxes paid into the republic's budget (Table 10.8) and into the central government's budget (at 23.5 percent in Table 10.2), the amount of retained earnings available for capital investments became 29,916.6 million rubles. The amount of depreciation funds available for investments in the Ukraine was obtained by applying 19 percent—the estimated share of the Ukrainian SSR in fixed capital—to the difference between total depreciation allowances in the USSR and such allowances earmarked for capital repairs. This portion of depreciation funds was estimated at 17,079 million rubles. Thus, total internal sources amounted to 46,996 million rubles.

During this period, financing of capital expenditures from the budget of the Ukrainian SSR totaled 38,367 million rubles.[44] Because of the separate treatment of agriculture in this analysis, investment outlays of 7,048 million rubles[45] were subtracted from budgetary expenditures, netting 31,319 million rubles. Thus, total resources within the Ukraine amounted to 78,315 million rubles (46,996 plus 31,319).

Investments subject to financing from these sources were equal to total capital investments, or 100,849 million rubles, less investments by collective farms and investments in housing by population (respectively 12,086 and 6,368,[46] a total of 18,454 million rubles, or 82,395 million rubles. Since 78,315 million rubles' worth of investments was financed by resources generated within the republic, the subsidy from the central government's budget was estimated at 4,080 million rubles.

Expenditures on sociocultural undertakings were divided into two parts. Expenditures on education, health, and insurance or collective farm members were assumed to be equal to the Ukraine's share in Soviet population. Expenditures on social security and social insurance were assumed to be related both to population and to the population's income. Thus, the average of the share of the Ukraine in Soviet population (19.5 percent) and in the republic's weight in income tax on population (16.1 percent—Table 10.8), 17.8 percent, was used to impute to the Ukraine the expenditures on social and cultural undertakings from the central government's budget.

In allocating to the Ukraine expenditures from the central government's budget on defense and administration, it was assumed that the main purpose of these activities was the protection of life, property, and productive capacity.

Since both the Ukraine's weight in Soviet population and its share in fixed funds were close to 20 percent, this ratio was used as the allocation factor.

The ratio of 20 percent also was applied to other expenditures. However, to obtain the amount appropriate for such allocation, the amount of direct subsidies to the Kazakh, Turkmen, and Armenian republics—12,117.5 million rubles in total—was subtracted from 35,748.8 million rubles of "other" expenditures.[47]

SUMMARY OF FINANCIAL RELATIONS WITH THE USSR

According to Table 10.2, in 1959-70 the central government retained for its purposes 90,086.2 million rubles of the revenues it collected in the Ukraine. (It amounts to $120.7 billion or $67.6 billion at the official or estimated purchasing-power exchange rate, respectively, during the mid-1970s.) This withdrawal of capital from the Ukrainian republic constituted 56.7 percent of the central government's revenues in the Ukraine and 33.6 percent of all budgetary revenues in the republic [90,086.2/(158,804.5 + 109,250.9)]. This was a marked increase from 1928-32, when the central government retained 29.8 percent of its revenues and 23.2 percent of all budgetary revenues in the republic.[48] This amount does not include the central government's gains from the participation of the republic in Soviet foreign trade. The latter were not insignificant, since the Ukraine provided some 25-30 percent of the Soviet foreign trade volume.[49] Based on the data for 1960-65, it has been estimated that without the significant trade surpluses of the Ukrainian SSR, the USSR would have had substantial foreign trade deficits not only with the rest of the world but also with Comecon.[50] An evaluation of statistics for 1963-66 revealed that the central government's net gain from exporting the Ukraine's products was 1.2-1.4 billion rubes annually.[51] With increasing Soviet exports over the years, this gain must have kept pace. Thus, it is not unreasonable to assume that during 1959-70 the central government derived a gain of some 14-17 billion rubles from trading Ukrainian products in foreign markets.

CAPITAL FORMATION IN THE UKRAINE

As indicated at the beginning of this chapter, capital formation may be stated in terms of uses of new capital as well as according to sources of its creation. Table 10.3 provides an estimate of capital formation in the Ukraine by uses—that is, by investments in the Ukraine plus net withdrawal of funds from the republic.

No doubt this is an approximate value of capital created in the Ukraine in 1959-70. The computations presented in this study, it will be recalled, had

TABLE 10.3

Capital Formation in the Ukraine by Uses, 1959–70
(actual prices)

	Million Rubles	Percent of Total
Capital investments in the Ukraine		
Industry and construction	36,632.0	20.76
Agriculture: By state	7,048.0	3.69
By collective farms	12,086.0	6.33
Total	19,134.0	10.02
Transportation and communication	10,535.0	5.52
Housing: By state	10,807.0	5.66
By population	6,368.0	3.34
Total	17,175.0	9.00
Other	14,373.0	7.53
Total capital investments in the Ukraine	100,849.0	52.82
Capital withdrawn from the Ukraine	90,086.2	47.18
Total	190,935.2	100.00

Note: Since the breakdown of investments by sectors of the economy in actual prices was not available for 1959 and 1960, the amounts in this table were computed for these two years from the data available in "comparable prices."

Sources: Narhosp 1968, pp. 377, 382, 386; *Narhosp 1970*, p. 360; *Narkhoz 1969*, pp. 509, 511.

to be based on certain assumptions; thus, they should be viewed as "best approximations." Also, the computed value of net capital withdrawal does not include a number of "leakages," such as transfers of surpluses of state insurance agencies, surplus resources of the banking system, and transfers of funds of trade organizations. However, the evidence indicates that these leakages were not significant in relation to the total value of capital formed in the Ukraine.

To obtain a breakdown of capital formation by sources, it is necessary to regroup all budgetary revenues and expenditures netted out in the process of arriving at the value of net capital withdrawn from the Ukraine. This is accomplished in Table 10.4, where individual items in the central government's budget have been reassigned to their original sources or their beneficiaries, and then regrouped by adjusting reversal entries. (All reallocation entries are identified for the reader's convenience.)

The information developed in Table 10.3 was combined with the information in Table 10.4 to obtain capital formation by sources. This step is presented in Table 10.5. A comparison of this table with similar information for

TABLE 10.4

Allocation of Capital Withdrawn from the Ukraine to Original Sources of Capital Formation, 1959–70 (million rubles)

	Central Government's Budget in Ukraine	Reallocation to Original Sources		Capital Formation	Subsidies
		Revenues	Expend.		
Revenues					
Turnover tax	102,217.5				
Less turnover tax paid into republic's budget	24,983.9				
	77,233.6[a]**				
Profit tax and deductions	41,837.3[b]*				
Other receipts from the economy	31,279.6[f]				
Taxation of population	6,836.8[c]				
Government loans	792.1[d]				
Other collections from population	825.1[e]				
Total	158,804.5				
Expenditures					
Defense and administration	33,213.3[g]				
Socio-cultural	26,698.7[h]				
Population		8,379.9[a]	33,213.3[g]	2,628.7	
		45,706.8[a]	26,698.7[h]		
		6,836.8[c]			
		792.1[d]			
		825.1[e]			
Economy, except agriculture and housing	4,080.0[i]		4,080.0[i]		4,080.0
Profit		41,720.5[b]*	4,726.3[j]	68,273.8	
		31,279.6[f]			
Agriculture		23,146.9[a]		23,263.7	
		116.8[b]*			
Other	4,726.3[j]				4,080.0
Capital withdrawn from the Ukraine	90,086.2				90,086.2
Total	158,804.5	158,804.5	68,718.3	94,166.2	94,166.2

Source: Table 10.2.

Note: Letter superscripts identify reallocation entries—they are *not* footnote references.

*Central government's revenue from profit taxes on agriculture was 415.7 million rubles. Profits of the Ukraine's agriculture relative to such profits in the USSR were 28.1 percent. This factor was used to allocate the Ukraine's share in the central government's receipts from this tax.

**Turnover tax revenue of the central government's budget in the Ukraine was allocated to agriculture at 29.97 percent and the balance (10.85 percent plus 59.18 percent) to population. The ratios were developed in Table 10.1.

TABLE 10.5

Capital Formation in the Ukraine by Uses and Sources, 1959–70
(million rubles; actual prices)

	Capital Formation by Uses (1)	Sources of Capital Withdrawn from Ukraine (2)	Adjustments (3)	Capital Formation by Sources (mil. rubles) (4)	Capital Formation by Sources (percent)
Industry, incl. profits and depreciation	39.632.0	58,874.8[c]		98,506.8	51.59
Subsidy from central government		(4,080.0)[c]		(4,080.0)	(2.14)
				94.426.8	49.45
Transportation and communication	10,535.0	9,399.0[c]**		19,934.0	10.44
Agriculture					
State	7,048.0[b]	23,263.7	7,487.7[b]*	42,837.4	22.44
Collective farms	12,086.0				
	19,134.0				
Housing					
State	10,807.0[b]				
Population	6,368.0[a]				
	17,175.0				
Other	14,373.0[b]				
Capital withdrawn from Ukraine	90,086.2				
Population		2,628.7	6,368.0[a] } 17,496.2[b]* }	26,492.9	13.88
Unallocated			7,244.1[b]*	7,244.1	3.79
Total	190.935.2	90,086.2		190,935.2	100.00

*Investments by the government in agriculture, housing and "other" amounted to 32,228 million rubles. It is assumed that 24,983.9 million rubles of this was financed from turnover tax collections by the republic's budget (Table 10.8). The balance (7,244.1 million rubles) was assumed to be paid from various other revenues of the republic's budget, and is shown here as unallocated. The assumed coverage of investments from the republic's turnover tax revenues (24,983.9 million rubles) is allocated to agriculture at 29.97 percent (see Table 10.1) and the balance to population as the ultimate payer of this tax.

**The Ukraine's share in "payments from profits" into the central government's budget (Table 10.8), computed at 20 percent.

Note: Letter superscripts identify reallocation entries—they are *not* footnote references.

Sources: Column 1—Table 10.3; Column 2—Table 10.4.

TABLE 10.6

Net Capital Outflow from the Ukraine in Comparison with the Ukraine's Economy, 1928–32, 1959–70

	1928–32	1959–61	1959–70
1. Net capital outflow from Ukraine (million rubles)	4,999.4	14,103.8	90,086.2
2. Capital investments in Ukraine (million rubles)	9,389.0	18,884.5	100,849.0
3. Net capital outflow from Ukraine as percent of capital investments in Ukrainian economy	53.3	75.2	89.3
4. Capital investments in Ukrainian industry (million rubles)	5,401.0	7,282.0	39,632.0*
5. Capital outflow from Ukraine as percent of capital investments in Ukraine's industry	92.7	193.7	227.3
6. National income of Ukraine as reported (million rubles)	n.a.	82,357.0	453,600.0
7. Capital outflow from Ukraine as percent of reported national income of Ukraine	9–12	17.1	19.9

*Includes construction.

n.a. = data not available.

Sources: 1928–32 from Z. L. Melnyk, *Soviet Capital Formation: Ukraine, 1928/29–32* (Munich: Ukrainian Free University Press, 1965). 1959–61 from Z. L. Melnyk, "Regional Contribution to Capital Formation in the USSR: The Case of the Ukrainian Republic," in V. N. Bandera and Z. L. Melnyk, eds., *The Soviet Economy in Regional Perspective* (New York: Praeger, 1973), p. 121. 1959–70 from tables 10.3 and 10.4 and various issues of *Narhosp.*

1928–32 reveals a much smaller reliance on agriculture (22.4 percent vs. 39.6 percent) and population (13.9 percent vs. 29.9 percent) in providing investable funds (aggregate savings). Also, it shows a substantial increase in the withdrawal of capital from the Ukraine—34.75 percent of capital formation in 1928–32, compared with 47.18 percent in 1959–70.[52] Tables 10.6 and 10.7 provide a perspective for the interpretation of the burden carried by the Ukraine's economy and population as a result of this substantial noncompensatory withdrawal of wealth from the Ukrainian SSSR.

SUMMARY AND CONCLUSIONS

The net capital outflow from the Ukraine may be viewed in a "global" way—that is, strictly from the point of view of the central government regardless of the "local" interests of the individual republics. The USSR is not a monolithic country, but a multinational state held together by political forces dominated by the Russians. Contrary to Soviet political doctrine, recent history has demonstrated that nationalistic attitudes in foreign economic relations, as well as clashing national interests within various countries, are not inherent exclusively to capitalist societies. Indeed, under the pressure of events, the Soviet government admitted in 1956 that it had violated the principle of equality of socialist states in dealing with its satellites and that the USSR derived excessive profits from trading with its Communist partners.[53] Western studies confirmed these charges against the USSR by its satellites.[54]

Comprehensive evidence was developed and presented by some Soviet economists on what they called economic exploitation of the Ukraine within the USSR[55] (much more guardedly in recent years). Also, some such estimates were prepared by Western students of the USSR.[56]

The present analysis indicates that the Soviet Union's central government derived substantial benefits from the Ukraine in 1959–70. As in other time periods (Tables 10.6 and 10.7), capital funds were transferred from the Ukraine to other parts of the USSR in very large amounts—in fact at levels unprecedented in international economic relations. Since these funds were redistributed by the central government according to its own plans on a noncompensatory basis, they constituted an irrevocable loss to the Ukraine, their producer. The Ukrainian population was forced to bear a disproportionate burden in supporting the Soviet economy and the central government's activities by having to suffer a lower standard of living than otherwise would have been the case. Although a surplus in the balance of payments is eagerly sought under normal circumstances, these diversions of Ukrainian capital, for which the Ukraine was not compensated and to which it retained no claim, were detrimental to its

TABLE 10.7

Estimates of Net Capital Outflows from the Ukraine, 1925–70 (net gain of central government and rest of USSR)

Researcher	Period Covered	Net Loss of Ukraine in Percent of	
		Total Receipts of Budgetary System in Ukraine	Reported National Income of Ukraine
1. M. Volobuiev	1925–27	20.0	n.a.
2. A. Richyts'kyi	1925–27	8.0–14.0	n.a.
3. Z. L. Melnyk	1928–32	23.2	9.0–12.0
4. V. Holubnychy	1940	6.3	n.a.
5. Ukrainian Academy of Sciences, Kiev	1959–61	31.1	14.2
6. Z. L. Melnyk	1959–61	37.4a	17.1
7. V. N. Bandera	1960b	30.0c–35.2d	14.4c–16.9d
	1960e	37.6	18.0
8. H. J. Wagener	1965	n.a.	9.9
9. Z. L. Melnyk	1959–70	33.6f	19.9f

n.a. = data not available.

aOr 31.1 percent of adjusted budgetary revenues.

bOn current account.

cExcluding net gains of the central government from the Ukraine's participation in Soviet foreign trade.

dIncluding net gains of the central government from the Ukraine's participation in Soviet foreign trade.

eOn capital account.

fUtilizing the low and high allocation factors in Table 10.1 (22.8–24.7 percent for tax in kind on agriculture, and 22.0–25.0 percent for diversion of industrial profits) to compute the share of the Ukrainiang SSR in turnover tax revenues results in net capital withdrawals from the republic of 84,937.8 million rubles and 95,106.1 million rubles, respectively. Correspondingly, the ratios in this table, reflecting the loss of the Ukraine, become 32.3–34.8 percent of total receipts of the budgetary system in the republic and 18.7–21.0 percent of reported national income of the Ukraine.

Sources: Lines 1 through 8 from Z. L. Melnyk, "Ukraine and Soviet Economic Development," *Ukrainian Quarterly* 29, no. 1 (Spring 1973); line 9 from the computations in this essay.

economy.* Decisions to export capital from the Ukraine were made without consultation or representation of the wishes of the Ukrainian population.

The study also reveals extensive differences between sources and applications of newly created capital. Further research is indicated on the effects of such massive intersectoral distribution of capital on economic development and living standards in the Ukraine.

APPENDIX TO CHAPTER 10

---

*Leslie Dienes has shown that the various regions of the Ukraine reveal unusually high disparities in economic development—industry, agriculture, transportation, and so on. For example, even though the Ukraine produces a very large share of agricultural equipment, ". . . the supply of capital equipment to the *agricultural* labor force of the Ukraine is far below the Soviet average, and in two of the three major Economic Regions of the Republic, the degree of capitalization per agricultural worker falls to the Central Asian, Transcaucasian or Belorussian level." The supply of electric power to the Ukraine also is alarmingly low: "Per capita electricity consumption was well under two-fifths of the Soviet mean even in 1967, and in the Southwest, with 44 percent of the Republic's population, it approximated the Tadzhik and Turkmen level, below that of Uzbekistan."

TABLE 10.8

Budget Summary: Revenues, 1959–70

	State Budget		
	1959–70	1959–65	1966–70
Total	1253866.7	602837.3	651029.4
I. Economy	1143664.5	549850.8	593813.7
1. Turnover tax	450237.8	236145.0	214092.8
2. Payments from profits	392176.6	164502.5	227674.1
a. By source: Indus. and con-			
struction	246801.1	97024.9	149776.2
Agriculture	19909.0	10269.0	9640.0
Transp. and communication	64659.7	29026.9	35632.8
Utilities	11731.8	5472.6	6259.2
Trade	10625.0	5423.4	5201.6
Other	38450.0	17285.7	21164.3
b. By type: Payment for funds	38205.6	—	38205.6
"Residual profits"	70547.5	—	70547.5
Fixed payments	8497.6	—	8497.6
Profit tax and other	274925.9	164502.5	110423.4
c. Payments by *sovnarkhozy*	—	—	—
3. Income tax from enterprises			
and organ.,	16508.0	10574.7	5933.3
including collective farms,	11026.3	7562.3	3464.0
cooperatives, and public organ.	5481.7	3012.4	2469.3
4. Resources of social insurance	66531.1	31031.0	35500.1
5. Income from forestry	3926.9	1748.1	2178.8
6. Diff. in prices on agr. eqt. and parts	—	—	—
7. Rental income from local soviets	—	—	—
8. Inc. from MTS and spec. statns.	—	—	—
9. Local levies and fees	—	—	—
10. Balance	214284.1	105849.5	108434.6
II. Population	110202.2	52986.5	57215.7
1. Taxes	96317.0	43710.6	52606.4
Incl. income tax on population	84679.1	37168.3	47510.8
Agricultural tax	4353.4	2649.8	1703.6
Tax on single citizens and sm. fam.	7261.8	3869.8	3392.0
Discrepancy	22.7	22.7	—
2. Government loans	7437.9	5980.0	1457.9
Directly to population	2141.1	683.2	1457.9
Through savings associations	5296.8	5296.8	—
3. Lottery income	2223.7	1033.0	1190.7
4. Other	4223.6	2262.9	1960.7
Other income	—	—	—
Balance of budgetary resources to cover expenditures	—	—	—

Republic Budgets			Central Government Budget		
1959–70	1959–65	1966–70	1959–70	1959–65	1966–70
606943.6	309158.8	297784.8	646923.1	293678.5	353244.6
518170.9	267160.1	251010.8	625493.6	282690.7	342802.9
188768.0	94893.3	93874.7	261469.8	141251.7	120218.1
214145.4	108169.4	105976.0	178031.2	56333.1	121698.1
151346.4	87955.1	63391.3	95454.7	9069.8	86384.9
19493.3	10132.6	9360.7	415.7	136.4	279.3
17664.8	7860.4	9804.4	46994.9	21166.5	25828.4
11731.8	5472.6	6259.2	–	–	–
9790.1	5009.4	4780.7	834.9	414.0	420.9
27253.0	14873.3	12379.7	11197.0	2412.4	8784.6
9818.5	–	9818.5	28387.1	–	28387.1
32775.8	–	32775.8	37771.7	–	37771.7
2827.2	–	2827.2	5670.4	–	5670.4
214145.4	108169.4	60554.5	178031.2	56333.1	49868.9
23134.0	23134.0	n.a.	–	–	–
16171.1	10430.0	5741.1	336.9	144.7	192.2
11026.3	7562.3	3464.0	–	–	–
5144.8	2867.7	2277.1	336.9	144.7	192.2
74955.7	36267.2	38688.5	(8424.6)	(5236.2)	(3188.4)
3926.9	1748.1	2178.8	–	–	–
9309.4	9309.4	–	(9309.4)	(9309.4)	–
1317.4	897.6	419.8	(1317.4)	(897.6)	(419.8)
181.7	181.7	–	(181.7)	(181.7)	–
9395.3	5263.4	4131.9	(9395.3)	(5263.4)	(4131.9)
–	–	–	214284.1	105849.5	108434.6
59178.1	28302.4	30875.7	51024.1	24684.1	26340.0
53845.0	24888.8	28956.2	42472.0	18821.8	23650.2
42214.7	18354.1	23860.6	42464.4	18814.2	23650.2
4353.4	2649.8	1703.6	–	–	–
7261.8	3869.8	3392.0	–	–	–
15.1	15.1	–	7.6	7.6	–
3109.4	2380.6	728.8	4328.5	3599.4	729.1
1070.8	342.0	728.8	1070.3	341.2	729.1
2038.6	2038.6	–	3258.2	3258.2	–
2223.7	1033.0	1190.7	–	–	–
–	–	–	4223.6	2262.9	1960.7
20523.2	9958.8	10564.4	(20523.2)	(9958.8)	(10564.4)
9071.4	3737.5	5333.9	(9071.4)	(3737.5)	(5333.9)

TABLE 10.8 (Continued)

	Ukr. SSR Budget		
	1959–70	1959–65	1966–70
Total	109250.9	54193.4	55057.5
I. Economy	93941.8	47007.1	46934.7
1. Turnover tax	24983.9	12401.0	12582.9
2. Payments from profits	51350.4	23334.6	28015.8
a. By source: Indus. and con-			
struction	39428.8	19714.6	19714.2
Agriculture	3616.8	1702.8	1914.0
Transp. and communication	3492.8	1618.8	1874.0
Utilities	2077.8	952.9	1124.9
Trade	1952.9	1056.5	896.4
Other	5271.3	2779.0	2492.3
b. By type: Payment for funds	3301.9	–	3301.9
"Residual profits"	8303.6	–	8303.6
Fixed payments	351.5	–	351.5
Profit tax and other	39393.4	23334.6	16058.8
c. Payments by *sovnarkhozy*	4940.0	4940.0	n.a.
3. Income tax from enterprises			
and organ.,	4143.7	2764.4	1379.3
including collective farms,	3090.8	2156.1	934.7
cooperatives, and public organ.	1052.9	608.3	444.6
4. Resources of social insurance	10054.6	6153.2	3901.4
5. Income from forestry	267.7	148.1	119.6
6. Diff. in prices on ag. eqt. and parts	929.2	929.2	–
7. Rental income from local soviets	193.6	139.5	54.1
8. Inc. from MTS and spec. statns.	42.3	42.3	–
9. Local levies and fees	1976.4	1094.8	881.6
10. Balance	–	–	–
II. Population	10363.5	5057.6	5305.9
1. Taxes	9399.3	4457.8	4941.5
Incl. income tax on population	6804.6	2961.4	3843.2
Agricultural tax	1361.2	835.3	525.9
Tax on single citizens and sm. fam.	1232.5	660.1	572.4
Discrepancy	1.0	1.0	–
2. Government loans	567.5	424.9	142.6
Directly to population	202.9	60.3	142.6
Through savings associations	364.6	364.6	–
3. Lottery income	396.7	174.9	221.8
4. Other	–	–	–
Other income	3652.6	1582.7	2069.9
Balance of budgetary resources to			
cover expenditures	1293.0	546.0	747.0

n.a. = not available.

Sources: Gosudarstvennyi biudzhet SSSR i biudzhety soiuznykh respublik (Moscow, 1962), pp. 5-13, 66-70, 106-08; (Moscow, 1966), pp. 8-16, 69-72, 108-10; (Moscow, 1972), pp. 10-18, 75-78, 116-17.

TABLE 10.9

Budget Summary: Expenditures, 1959-70

	State Budget			Republic Budgets		
	1959-70	1959-65	1966-70	1959-70	1959-65	1966-70
Total expenditures	1225347.4	582839.3	642508.1	650152.7	338409.8	311742.9
I. Economy	553205.7	259603.4	293602.3	324200.4	181848.4	142352.0
Incl. industry and construction	242744.9	118795.6	123949.3	119580.8	83988.0	35592.8
Agr., Procurements and MTS	90390.5	44626.0	45764.5	76282.3	41589.0	34693.3
Trade	43072.5	16527.4	26545.1	n.a.	n.a.	n.a.
Transportation	30335.4	17849.0	12486.4	17151.5	8814.1	7822.2
Communication	2785.6	1393.1	1392.5			515.2
Housing and utilities	52625.1	25463.3	27161.8	52625.5	25463.7	27161.8
Other	91251.7	34949.0	56302.7	58560.3	21993.6	36566.7
II. Social-cultural undertakings	447006.6	206653.2	240353.4	303632.6	144256.9	159375.7
Incl. education	198571.7	89821.2	81138.9	135133.3	65177.8	69955.5
Science			27611.6	5266.2	2465.9	2800.3
Health	76666.5	36464.5	40202.0	71181.4	33346.3	34835.1
Physical education	684.3	360.9	323.4	561.6	302.1	259.5
Social security	109266.8	53139.2	56126.9	86407.1	40108.1	46299.0
Incl. from resources of soc. ins.	78297.0	36214.8	42082.2	78297.0	36214.8	42082.2
Social insurance	51213.1	23072.8	28140.3	n.a.	n.a.	n.a.
Family assistance	5582.9	3356.6	2226.3	5083.0	2856.7	2226.3
Resources transferrable into coll. farmers' insurance	5021.3	437.3	4584.0	—	—	—
III. Defense	162999.2	82839.9	80159.3	—	—	—
IV. Administration	15777.9	7860.2	7917.7	11710.5	5999.7	5710.8
V. Other	46358.0	25882.6	20475.4	10609.2	6304.8	4304.4

TABLE 10.9 (Continued)

	Central Government Budget			Ukr. SSR Budget		
	1959-70	1959-65	1966-70	1959-70	1959-65	1966-70
Total expenditures	575194.7	244429.5	330765.2	113505.3	57337.9	56167.4
I. Economy	229005.3	77755.0	151250.3	56637.4	30052.3	26585.1
Incl. industry and construction	123164.1	34807.6	88356.5	26848.9	16943.2	9905.7
Agr., Procurements and MTS	14108.2	3037.0	11071.2	7472.7	3823.8	3648.9
Trade	n.a.	n.a.	n.a.	n.a.	n.a.	n.a.
Transportation	} 15969.5	} 10428.0	4664.2	} 2353.7	} 1162.5	} 1191.2
Communication			877.3			
Housing and utilities	—	—	—	9160.6	4703.4	4457.2
Other	75763.9	29482.8	46281.1	10801.5	3419.4	7382.1
II. Social-cultural undertakings	143374.0	62396.3	80977.7	53251.4	25328.8	27922.6
Inc. education	} 58172.2	} 22177.5	11183.4	} 24778.0	} 11905.0	12323.8
Science			24811.3			549.2
Health	5485.1	3118.2	2366.9	13276.9	6289.2	6987.7
Physical education	122.7	58.8	63.9	63.6	35.3	28.3
Social security	22859.7	13031.8	9827.9	14664.8	6803.2	7861.6
Incl. from resources of soc. ins.	—	—	—	13247.2	6146.8	7100.4
Social insurance	51213.1	23072.8	28140.3	—	—	—
Family assistance	499.9	499.9	—	468.1	296.1	172.0
Resources transferrable into coll. farmers' insurance	5021.3	437.3	4584.0	—	—	—
III. Defense	162999.2	82839.9	80159.3	—	—	—
IV. Administration	4067.4	1860.5	2206.9	1984.7	1012.2	972.5
V. Other	35748.8	19577.8	16171.0	1631.8	944.6	687.2

n.a. = data not available.

Source: Gosudarstvennyi biudzhet SSSR i biudzhety soiuznykh respublik (Moscow, 1962), pp. 18-19, 71-75,109-10; (Moscow, 1966), pp. 20-21, 73-75, 111-12; (Moscow, 1972), pp. 23-25, 79-81, 118-19.

TABLE 10.10

Profitability of Industries in the Ukraine and USSR, 1965–70
(profits divided by fixed funds plus working capital; in percent)

	1965		1966		1967	
	Ukr.	USSR	Ukr.	USSR	Ukr.	USSR
All industrial enterprises	12.9	13.0	12.6	13.3	17.2	17.1
Electric energy	8.5	4.6	6.6	4.3	8.6	7.2
Petroleum	27.3'	10.4	35.2	11.1	33.8	18.6
Coal	(18.2)	(17.0)	(19.2)	(18.0)	(5.7)	(5.3)
Ferrous metals	7.4	8.6	8.1	9.2	13.6	14.2
Chemical	18.4	14.6	20.3	15.8	18.9	16.0
Petrochemicals	16.2	23.7	19.9	23.5	23.9	27.1
Machine-building and metalworking	20.7	16.7	22.7	19.3	23.5	20.1
Forestry products and paper	18.6	6.9	18.9	6.1	23.3	13.6
Building materials	11.4	5.4	12.0	6.6	13.9	10.8
Light industry	43.4	29.9	44.5	31.4	52.4	38.3
Food industry	29.1	24.4	19.9	19.2	23.6	21.0
Transportation: Railroad	n.a.	13.3	13.1	13.8	13.3	14.4
River	n.a.	8.5	1.8	9.7	7.4	12.0
Automotive	n.a.	24.6	32.4	29.3	36.6	33.8
Communications	n.a.	11.3	19.4	11.7	19.1	12.8

TABLE 10.10 (Continued)

	1968 Ukr.	1968 USSR	1969 Ukr.	1969 USSR	1970 Ukr.	1970 USSR
All industrial enterprises	20.4	20.1	20.7	20.5	21.8	21.5
Electric energy	9.9	10.6	10.6	11.0	10.8	10.9
Petroleum	35.4	25.5	30.8	25.2	29.4	25.9
Coal	8.8	8.2	8.2	8.0	7.2	7.3
Ferrous metals	18.4	19.2	17.7	18.2	17.5	17.2
Chemical	17.9	16.2	17.8	17.1	17.1	17.4
Petrochemicals	31.0	30.3	26.3	29.8	27.2	31.5
Machine building and metalworking	23.3	21.2	23.8	21.5	24.6	22.5
Forestry products and paper	31.2	20.1	30.8	19.6	34.6	20.0
Building materials	15.8	14.2	14.9	12.8	14.0	12.2
Light industry	56.9	39.6	59.2	41.1	62.5	42.5
Food industry	22.4	22.4	23.1	24.2	29.0	27.6
Transportation: Railroad	15.3	14.5	13.4	14.4	13.0	14.0
River	7.1	13.3	7.8	13.3	8.0	12.8
Automotive	39.5	34.9	37.7	33.2	35.6	32.5
Communications	23.3	13.3	18.3	13.8	17.2	13.8

n.a. = data not available.

Sources: Ukraine—*Narhosp 1970*, pp. 526–28; USSR—*Narkhoz 1965*, p. 760; *1968*, pp. 746–47; *1969*, pp. 744–45; *1970*, pp. 706–07.

NOTES

1. Akademiia Nauk Ukrains'koi RSR, *Natsional'nyi dokhod Ukrains'koi RSR* (Kiev, 1963), pp. 128–31; S. D. Tsypkin, *Dokhody gosudarstvennogo biudzheta SSSR* (Moscow, 1973), pp. 10–11; M. A. Binder, *Gosudarstvenno-pravovye problemy vzaimopomoshchi sovetskikh narodov* (Alma-Ata, 1967), pp. 228–30.

2. *Ekonomika Radians'koi Ukrainy (ERU)* (1964): no. 2, p. 115.

3. Z. Lew Melnyk, "Regional Contribution to Capital Formation in the USSR," in V. N. Bandera and Z. Lew Melnyk, eds., *The Soviet Economy in Regional Perspective* (New York: Praeger, 1973), p. 105.

4. For a description of this and some alternative approaches, see Z. Lew Melnyk, *Soviet Capital Formation: Ukraine, 1928/29–1932* (Munich: Ukrainian Free University Press, 1965), esp. pp. 12–17.

5. For a historical perspective see, for example, R. W. Davies, *The Development of the Soviet Budgetary System* (Cambridge: Cambridge University Press, 1958); Daniel Gallik, Cestmir Jesina, and Stephen Rapawy, *The Soviet Financial System* (Washington, D.C.: U.S. Department of Commerce, 1968); F. D. Holzman, *Soviet Taxation* (Cambridge, Mass.: Harvard University Press, 1955); K. N. Plotnikov, *Ocherki istorii biudzheta sovetskogo gosudarstva* (Moscow, 1954). More recent publications providing detailed background include *Gosudarstvennyi biudzhet SSSR* (2nd ed.; Moscow, 1969); S. D. Tsypkin, op. cit.; *50 let sovetskikh finansov* (Moscow, 1967); A. G. Zverev, *Natsional'nyi dokhod i finansy SSSR* (Moscow, 1970).

6. Plotnikov, op. cit., p. 111.

7. Computed from data in *Sotsialisticheskoe stroitel'stvo SSSR* (Moscow, 1934), p. 493.

8. See, for examples, Akademiia Nauk, op. cit., pp. 132, 200–01, 208–09; D. Kondrashev, "Tsena, rentabel'nost' i khoziaistvennyi raschet," *Voprosy ekonomiki (VE)* (1960): no. 11, 108–09; Zverev, op. cit., pp. 100, 105, 107, 171.

9. S. M. Miroshchenko, *Gosudarstvennye dokhody* (Moscow, 1972), p. 14.

10. Akademiia Nauk, op. cit., pp. 196–97; Miroshchenko, loc. cit.

11. Zverev, op. cit., pp. 170–71.

12. See, for example, L. Klets'kyi, "Prybutok kolhospiv UkRSR i shliakhy ioho zbil'shennia," *ERU* (1964): no. 4, 61; F. Iu. Zakrevs'kyi, "Do pytannia rozpodilu kilhospnykh dokhodiv," *Problemy politychnoi ekonomii (PPE)* (1967): no. 34, 83–84. Even in 1968, after several rounds of increases in delivery prices, there were 226 collective farms in the Ukraine (out of 9,480 such farms) with an average deficit amounting to 3.9 percent of invested capital. Moreover, 60.9 percent (5,775) of collective farms in the Ukraine were not generating a 12 percent return on invested capital, a minimum level of return on investment that was considered necessary to provide for adequate growth in output. Indeed, "Normal conditions for economic development exist only in the farms included in the group having economically necessary and maximum levels of profitability," and this group contained only 20.3 percent (1,921) of collective farms in the republic. The average return on invested capital for all (9,480) collective farms in the Ukraine was in 1968 only 11.4 percent. Akademiia Nauk Ukrains'koi RSR, Instytut Ekonomiky, *Efektyvnist' sil's'kohospodars'koho vyrobnystva* (Kiev, 1971), pp. 119–22. This average rate of return on invested capital of collective farms in the Ukraine declined drastically in subsequent years— to 8.6 percent in 1974 and only 6.4 percent in 1975. A. Hosh, "Ob'iektyvni osnovy formuvannia chystoho produktu i valovoho dokhodu kolhospiv," *ERU* (1976): no. 11, 34.

13. L. N. Sineva, *Rentabel'nost' sovkhoznogo proizvodstva* (Moscow, 1973), passim.

14. Holzman, op. cit., p. 82; V. Bachurin, *Pribyl' i nalog s oborota v SSSR* (Moscow, 1955), pp. 24, 43; V. P. Borodatyi, "Norma rentabel'nosti kolhospnoho vyrobnytstva," *PPE* (1967): no. 34, 68; Zverev, op. cit., p. 107.

15. A. Zverev, "Voprosy metodologii ischisleniia norodnogo dokhoda," *VE* (1960): no. 11, 48; Zverev, *Natsional'nyi*, pp. 74 ff.

16. Computed from data in the various volumes of *Narodnoe khoziaistvo SSR* (*Narkhoz*) and *Narodne hosposarstvo Ukrains'koi RSR* (*Narhosp*).

17. For details see Melnyk, "Regional Contribution," Table 4.12, p. 124.

18. Computed from data in *Narhsop, 1963, 1964, 1966, 1970; Narkhoz, 1961, 1968, 1969, 1970;* TsSU, *Strana Sovetov za 50 let* (Moscow, 1967), p. 124.

19. Akademiia Nauk, *Natsional'nyi dokhod*, p. 254.

20. See, for example, sources cited in notes 14 and 18.

21. *Gosudarstvennyi biudzhet SSSR i biudzhety soiuznykh respublik, 1966*, p. 15; *1972*, p. 17; Akademiia Nauk, *Natsional'nyi dokhod*, p. 139.

22. Ibid.

23. Computed from data in *Sel'skoe khoziaistvo SSSR* (Moscow, 1960), pp. 24, 64; *Narkhoz 1961*, pp. 296, 536.

24. *Gosudarstvennyi biudzhet SSSR i biudzhety soiuznykh respublik, 1966*, p. 15; *1972*, p. 17; Akademiia Nauk, *Natsional'nyi dokhod*, p. 139.

25. In *Soviet Capital Formation*, pp. 31–42, Melnyk estimated that agriculture provided 35–37 percent of turnover tax receipts through agricultural procurements and other means during the First Five-Year Plan. Estimates for 1959–61 yielded a ratio of 32.8 percent. Z. L. Melnyk, "Financial Relations Between Ukraine and Moscow in 1959–1961," *Wissenschaftliche Mitteilungen* 18 (1968/1969): 33–39.

26. Akademiia Nauk, *Natsional'nyi dokhod*, pp. 152–53.

27. Melnyk, "Regional Contribution," p. 116.

28. Computed from data in Melnyk, *Soviet Capital Formation*, p. 38.

29. Akademiia Nauk Belorusskoi SSR, *Bratskoi sotrudnichestvo Belorusskoi SSR s soiuznymi respublikami* (Minsk, 1974), p. 118.

30. See Melnyk, *Soviet Capital Formation*, pp. 50–53.

31. Computed from *Narhosp 1970*, p. 349; *Narkhoz 1970*, pp. 479–82.

32. Ibid.

33. *Strana Sovetov*, p. 32; T. Derev'iankin, "Pisliavoienna vidbudova sotsialistychnoi industrii Ukrainy," *ERU* (1966): no. 3, 6; V. Burlin, "Radians'ka Ukraina za 30 pisliavoiennykh rokiv," *ERU* (1975): no. 5, 13.

34. These percentages were computed from data in *Strana Sovetov*, p. 32; F. Khyliuk, "Rozvytok mizhrespublikans'kykh ekonomichnykh zv'iazkiv Ukrains'koi RSR," *ERU* (1966): no. 12, 6; Konstantyn S. Kononenko, *Ukraina i Rosiia* (Munich, 1965), p. 431; and P. Rozenko, "Slavnyi shliakh borot'by i zavershen'," *ERU* (1967): no. 11, 2.

35. Kononenko, loc. cit.; Rozenko, loc. cit.; Population figure based on January 1, 1970 population. After accounting for the Ukraine's losses in population during the war, the percentage undoubtedly was significantly higher. For more details see Melnyk, "Financial Relations," pp. 27–30.

36. *Narhosp 1970*, p. 364; *Narkhoz 1970*, p. 485.

37. *Narhosp 1970*, pp. 349, 360, 362; *Narkhoz 1970*, pp. 470, 480–83.

38. Michael Maul, *Sieger und Besiegte* (Seebrück am Chiemsee: Herring-Verlag, 1948), pp. 61–75, 169.

39. Computed from V. Burlin, M. Darahan, and Ie. Dolhopolov, "Pereotsinka osnovnykh fondiv u kolhospakh UkRSR," *ERU* (1962): no. 5, 46–52; and *Narkhoz 1961*, p. 420.

40. *Narkhoz 1970*, pp. 288–89.

41. For specific data see *Narhosp 1970*, pp. 526–29; *Narkhoz 1968*, pp. 706, 709; *1970*, pp. 746, 749.

42. *Narhosp 1966*, p. 609; *1970*, p. 525; *Narkhoz 1968*, p. 743; *1969*, p. 741; *1973*, p. 763.

43. See Ihor Gordijew, "Sources of Investible Funds in Soviet Industry, 1961–1970" (doctoral diss., University of New South Wales, 1975), esp. chs. 5–8.

44. *Gosudarstvennyi biudzhet SSSR i biudzhety soiuznykh respublik 1962*, p. 110; *1966*, p. 112; *1972*, p. 119.

45. Computed from *Narhosp 1968*, pp. 360, 377, 382; *1971*, p. 360; *Narkhoz 1971*, pp. 509, 511.

46. Ibid.

47. *Gosudarstvennyi biudzhet SSSR i biudzhety soiuznykh respublik 1966*, p. 72; *1972*, p. 78.

48. Melnyk, *Soviet Capital Formation*, p. 90.

49. V. Serheev, "Tempy i faktory rozvytku mizhnarodnoho sotsialistychnoho rynku," *ERU* (1968): no. 4, 82; V. O. Suprun and D. Ia. Vovko, eds., *Ekonomichni osnovy spivrobitnytstva UkRSR z krainamy-chlenamy REV* (Kiev, 1971), p. 115; Rozenko, op. cit., p. 6; T. I. Derev'iankin, S. V. Kul'chyts'kyi, *Ekonomichnyi rozvytok Radians'koi Ukrainy, 1917–1970* (Kiev, 1970), p. 113.

50. For a summary and sources, see Z. L. Melnyk, "Ukraine and Soviet Economic Development," *Ukrainian Quarterly* 29, no. 1 (Spring 1973): 45–49.

51. For details see Melnyk, "Financial Relations," pp. 49–50.

52. For 1928–32 data, see Melnyk, *Soviet Capital Formation*, pp. 99–102.

53. See V. Holubnychy, "Some Economic Aspects of Relations Among the Soviet Republics," in Erich Goldhagen, ed., *Ethnic Minorities in the Soviet Union* (New York: Praeger, 1968), pp. 56–57.

54. Aleksander Kutt, *Price Changes and Price Discrimination in Soviet-Captive Countries Trade in 1965–1966* (New York: Assembly of Captive European Nations, 1968) and his other studies published by the same institution; Alfred Zauberman, *Economic Imperialism: The Lessons of Eastern Europe* (London: Ampersand, 1955); Horst Mendershausen, "Terms of Trade Between the Soviet Union and Communist Countries, 1955–1957," *Review of Economics and Statistics* (May 1959): 106–18.

55. M. Volubuiev, "Do problemy Ukrains'koi ekonomiky," *Bil'shovyk Ukrainy* (1928): no. 2, 46–72, and (1929): no. 3, 42–63; V. Dobrogaev, "Problema finansovogo balansa Ukrainy," *Khoziaistvo Ukrainy* (1927): no. 2; A. Richyts'kyi, "Do problemy likvidatsii perezhytkiv kolonial'-nosty ta natsionalizmu," *Bil'shovyk Ukrainy* (1928): no. 2, 73–93, and (1928): no. 3, 64–84; Akademiia Nauk, *Natsional'nyi dokhod*.

56. Melnyk, *Soviet Capital Formation*; Melnyk, "Financial Relations"; V. Holubnychy, in *Ukraine: A Concise Encyclopedia*, II (Toronto: University of Toronto Press, 1971), 722; V. N. Bandera, "Interdependence Between Interregional and International Payments: The Balance of Payments of Ukraine," in Bandera and Melnyk, op. cit., pp. 132–53; Hans-Jurgen Wagener, "Rules of Location and the Concept of Rationality: The Case of the USSR," ibid., Table 3.12, p. 99.

11

COMPARISON WITH
SOME ALTERNATIVES
Peter Wiles

POSSIBLE ALTERNATIVES

How rich and how well developed* would the Ukraine have been without Soviet rule? This is indeed a "might-have-been." Yet in some sense all questions about efficiency and justice compare what is with what might be, and this does not prevent us from asking them. The particular question posed is of passionate interest to Ukrainians wherever they live. It is therefore worth our while to invest a little thought in it. Not surprisingly, the answer must be achieved by statistical guesswork, a sort of bad cliometrics. But, unlike the inventor of cliometrics,[1] I do not believe sufficiently in the premises of my guesses to think any elaborate exercise worthwhile.

Let us first set out four plausible political assumptions.

1. The tsar won World War I, and his undiminished empire developed into a capitalist parliamentary democracy.

2. The Ukraine became an independent capitalist country in 1917, and underwent an experience like that of Poland, Czechoslovakia or Hungary; but Russia became Communist and had a very Soviet-type history.

3. The Ukraine became an independent Communist country in 1921, and adopted and retained a New Economic Policy type of economy.

4. The Ukraine was declared independent by Hitler in 1941, an action that saved him from eventual defeat. The Soviet-Nazi peace treaty of 1945 preserved

---

*In resource-rich countries with low population, these are not the same thing. In the Ukraine we perhaps need not emphasize the distinction.

an independent Ukraine occupied by neither party and hostile to both (like the Baltic States and Poland). But Hitler had left (as indeed he did) the Stalinist economic system more or less in being, and the Communist party of the Ukraine reestablished its hold on power, confirming that economic system.

There are many other possibilities, but I am unable to summon an interest in politically impossible cases.

In cases 1 and 2 the Ukraine borrowed heavily for development purposes in the 1920s. It was equally successful in either case, because (1) the tsar's credit stood behind it (the tsar had made a composition with his creditors in respect of his wartime borrowings) or (2) many Western governments supported its bond issues on sentimental grounds (which is what happened to Poland and Georgia). But, in both cases, the Ukraine suffered the slump of the 1930s, with the same violence as Eastern Europe. Instead of growing, it went backward.

Hitler's war took place all the same. In case 1 Empress Olga won the war, for her dynasty had always favored heavy industry and armaments since the time of Count Sergei Witte, and her sturdy *kulaks* (especially those of Ukrainian origin) made excellent troops who did not surrender in droves, as if they had been *kolkhozniks*.[2] After victory the still-subject Ukraine became a middle-class nation and an internal capital exporter. Many individual Ukrainian investors made killings in other parts of the empire, but St. Petersburg remained the financial center and took its share. These gains were quite unequally spread among the Ukrainian population, for the new constitutional tsarism was still very corrupt and made no serious attempt to equalize incomes. However, it did somehow raise enough taxes to expand its welfare provisions very sharply. The basis of the welfare state had of course been laid before World War I, but it was now expanded to backward areas like Central Asia and to peasants everywhere. There were also vast unprofitable state investments in infrastructure and even industry in backward areas. For all this the comparatively rich Ukraine paid more than its share of tax, though to be fair the same must be said of the Baltic states and the areas around the two capitals. The path-breaking 1963 symposium, edited by O. O. Nesterenko and I. S. Koropeckyj, on the Ukrainian national income and the imperial budget, was much criticized for neglecting these other sufferers.

Case 1 is not altogether unhappy, especially on an individual level. But growth was not as great in any period as it was under Soviet rule, except during 1918–21 and 1929–32.

From the late 1930s case 2 diverges, and poses further political problems. The Ukraine was of course heavily infiltrated by Germany, and was included in Schacht's bilateral system. But then we have to decide whether in 1941 Hitler invaded the capitalist Ukraine(2_a) or the Communist RSFSR(2_b). If the latter, the Ukraine was certainly neutral, Hitler won the war,* and we have to consider a permanently fascist Ukraine. We must refrain from speculation on the economic performance of a successful *Neue Ordnung* in Europe; the performance might have been brilliant, but the question is uninteresting. We should only note that Hitler always had a particular interest in colonizing the Ukraine, and he might well have used his Russian victory to do that. In the surely more probable case 2_a we have to decide what the RSFSR did and how the war ended. This is a political question of such complexity that a piece of "reverse economic history," seeking only crude, instant, superficial political hypotheses, should not find space for it. My inclination is to say that in case 2_a Hitler invaded the RSFSR afterward, but that Ukrainian guerrillas and the Russian army held out; he therefore lost—and the RSFSR either annexed the Ukraine or turned it into an East European satellite. If so, 2_a is uninteresting because it requires no separate treatment from case 4.

We have already arrived at an important elimination: an independent capitalist Ukraine would not have survived between Hitler and Stalin. This elimination places the Ukraine on a par with other East European countries: it is left as a Nazi colony or a Soviet satellite. However, should the independent Ukraine have allied itself closely with other East European countries, most likely all of them might have been able to defend themselves against both aggressors, Germany and Soviet Russia.

As to case 3, we may assume that in the antisocialist 1920s a Communist but independent Ukraine would have received very little foreign capital and would have made a very slow recovery. But it would have been spared Stalinism, collectivization, the command plan, and the *Yezhovshchina*. So far as can be seen, the New Economic Policy would have continued to be a successful economic order and to be capable of further growth if agricultural prices and procurement methods were tolerable.[3] Certainly, since Stalin was unique, the Ukrainian New Economic Policy would have gone on indefinitely. But our main question is whether this economic order would have been so nearly immune to the world slump as Stalin's was, especially in a country that, with 40 million people, was trading extensively with foreigners.

One is tempted to point to present-day Hungary as having a quasi-market economy and performing very well against a background of world slump and deteriorating terms of trade. It differs, however, in having only 10 million people and a system planned in more detail than the New Economic Policy. It exports about 15 percent of the national product to market economies, which perhaps

---

*That is, Ukrainian resources were available to the invaders, and they pressed successfully on to Vladivostok. Also, the V-2 rocket was developed earlier, and Britain was defeated. The United States made a settlement and did not use atomic weapons in Europe.

would have been below the Ukrainian figure in a world with only one other Communist country. With this example in mind, it seems plausible that the Ukraine would have done very well under case 3. Had it survived World War II and been able to continue as it had, the same would have held.

Case 3, then, is a rather happy one: it avoids the twin disasters of slump and Stalinism in the 1930s and ensures high growth in the 1950s and 1960s. This growth differed from the historical growth in several ways. It was lower because it was sought less obsessively, investment was smaller, and social discipline more lax. It was higher because there was no "drain" to Moscow. It was higher again because quality was not sacrificed and the consumer-cum-worker found the system more satisfactory.

Case 4 yields a Ukrainian development identical to the historical one down to 1941, plus an East European (say Polish) development since 1945. This is rather like the historical one in style, but presupposes the cessation of the internal "drain." For this reason, as well as for a much greater freedom in the internal economic decision making, the development of the Ukraine should be more successful.

THE NATURE OF INTERREGIONAL
FINANCIAL TRANSFERS

Let us now turn to this drain, and to a question only slightly less speculative: Is it fair for the Ukraine to make the financial transfers it does, in the unrequited way it does? To pose this question at all is to arrive at an apparently neglected basic proposition about socialism in all its versions: interterritorial transfers are like interpersonal transfers, and strongly disfavor the rich. They are totally of the nature of a tax, and are requited by neither amortization nor interest. It follows that richer territories would be better off, *pro tanto*, under capitalism, which even in today's welfare states makes possible some form of lending at interest. By parity of reasoning, poor countries should arrange to be annexed by the USSR!*

The Ukraine would be better off, too, as an independent socialist state, since there are certainly no such enormous financial transfers between CMEA members as those given by the richer Soviet regions. From the late 1950s the only substantial financial transfers (as opposed to terms of trade movements)

---

*They would have to be much poorer, since the great period of Soviet regional redistribution seems to have come to an end shortly after the war. Since then, the rate of current redistribution has sufficed only to keep the republics all growing at approximately the same rate.

known to me are long-term investments by other CMEA members in Soviet raw material extraction. These are repayable, and there is no system of supranational taxation; the smaller countries act as virtual sovereigns vis-a-vis the USSR. Indeed, some of the biggest transfers were made by the USSR, in the mid-1950s, though largely as an act of penitence for the reparations exacted after the war.

Within the CMEA its members enjoy more or less the same terms of trade as with the rest of the world, although there is reason to believe that East Germany and Czechoslovakia are somewhat exploited on the price side in this respect by the poorest partners, Bulgaria and Romania (USSR remained in the middle).[4] In addition to prices, however, there is the neglected aspect of costs.[5] The ordinary terms-of-trade analysis tacitly assumes that costs never exceed prices except by a formal subsidy. But the Soviet-type economy may at any moment accept a contract to sell at a world price something it can produce only far more expensively. This applies especially to satellites under political pressure. We have no data for the errors and the deliberate exploitation arising from this unusual feature; indeed, our data for price exploitation are poor, and those for capital transactions still worse.

We have no knowledge of the Ukraine's terms of trade inside the USSR (though possibly sufficient data could be extracted from a multiregional input table). The one certain thing is that the Ukraine exports intermediate goods free of turnover tax while importing consumer goods that have paid it. This particular disadvantage is discussed at length below, and by Melnyk. (See Chapter 10.) There is, of course, every reason to believe that interrepublic transfer prices reflect costs very inaccurately, but presumably in a random way only. Whatever we may think of the accuracy of our Ukrainian estimates, the transfers implied are very much bigger than those between CMEA members—since East German reparations ceased. They are also totally unrequited and only go one way. Probably, however, the situation is still more extreme in the Baltic.

Ten percent of national inome, unrequited, is a surprisingly large proportion. But how many capitalist, or Communist, comparisons have we? Does Slovakia receive, or Slovenia give, a smaller proportion on a similar reckoning? We do not know. But neither do we know about capitalism. Here the fiscal arrangements are extremely different, but they might well have comparable results. First and foremost there is a large progressive income tax. No doubt people's gross incomes, or at least their gross earnings, expand under the pressure of the market to offset this tax—in part. But for the most part it is obviously a genuine redistributor of very substantial sums; and if from rich people, then of course from rich areas. The capitalist social services operate like Communist ones, and so of course convey transfers to poor areas. In addition, poor local authorities get special subsidies, as do Central Asian republics. Investment by local authorities in road, schools, and hospitals is doubtless spent, and often financed, in ways as directly redistributive from rich to poor regions as in the USSR. In all these matters a capitalist Ukraine in a modernized tsarist Russia might find itself mulcted of about the same sum as—I guess—southeast England is mulcted within the United Kingdom.

But investment in the market sector (which in Great Britain includes most nationalized industries) eventually yields a private income to someone somewhere and we face the concept of private drain. This person is likely to live in a region where wages are also high, though perhaps not in a microregion of that kind—say in Bournemouth, not West London. As he buys the municipal bond, company share or other investment, the money flows from his residence to the place of the investment project; but as the security pays off, the money flows back and the drain is reversed. Therefore, interregional drains are smaller.

Insofar as this flow is bond amortization, it presents little theoretical difficulty, though it must surely be a statistician's nightmare. It is the interest and dividends that are the real perplexity, for the factor activity of capital occurs in one place but its earnings in another, which cannot be the case for labor.* In many cases, then, there is actually a reverse transfer, which we shall or shall not call "drain," according to ideological view of unearned income.

ADJUSTMENT OF ESTIMATED
TURNOVER TAX TRANSFERS

We now turn to more technical matters. First a note of warning. Inter-republic and republic-Moscow financial transfers should not be called, as Melnyk does, "capital." They surely depress consumption more than capital, for the consumption/income ratio is lower in the Ukraine than in any capitalist country. They are transfers of money; they more likely restrict domestic consumption than domestic investment, such being the Soviet system.

Melnyk's main contribution is to estimate the "drain" on the Ukraine. He rightly draws attention to the fact that the Ukraine, paying little turnover tax because it produces few final consumption goods, is made by orthodox Soviet accountancy to appear unproductive in comparison with other republics. The latter, making more final and fewer intermediate, extractive, or capital goods, have more turnover tax imputed to them in relation to genuine value added. The orthodox accountancy also eschews factor cost in the Western sense, since the turnover "tax" is part of socialist surplus value, and so part of "value," which is sacred. This surplus value is indeed created, say the Marxists, in the

---

*Labor can move away in order to spend, but so can capital—in both cases they leave their normal site. This is irrelevant. The regional accounts that concern us are those for income, not expenditure. If the latter are also drawn up, there must of course be adjustments for tourism.

Ukraine; but it is realized somewhere else. They too feel this to be unfair; but they are ideologically compelled to reallocate it, not abolish it (that is, go for factor cost). Melnyk was not so bound, and should not automatically have followed suit.

The situation is unfair, but hardly in a fiscal sense. It is an almost purely statistical distortion, leading to hardly any extra drain at all. The practice simply constitutes the other republics as tax gatherers for the center on certain Ukrainian goods. The tax would have been paid anyhow.

Thus, in Table 10.1, 102,217.5 million rubles is Melnyk's reasonable estimate of the turnover tax that should be imputed to the Ukraine in view of its exports of untaxed goods. But it is not what was levied: that is, as he very honestly tells us, 80,010.8 million rubles. The Ukrainian government itself did levy and did retain 24,983.9 million rubles (see Table 10.8). Therefore, the central government did levy 55,026.9, not 77,233.6, million rubles (as stated in Tables 10.1 and 10.4). The excess of 22,206.7 million rubles (102,217.5 − 80,010.8), which was never levied by anyone on Ukrainian territory, is a plausible measure of the understatement of productivity at market prices through structural distortion, but it figures neither in the republic nor the central budget. It is, however, a sum of actual rubles drained, in the sense that other republics collected this tax on behalf of Moscow.

If the Ukraine had had imputed to it, and had been taxed by, this excess amount, it would have sold intermediate goods at prices higher by the same excess: its national income at Western "factor cost" would not have changed. But by parity of reasoning, other republics would have bought intermediate goods at higher prices, been taxed less, and sold at the same prices. Thus their factor cost income would not have changed either; but their turnover tax yield, both central and republic, would have shrunk by the same total of 22,206.7 million rubles.

But the Ukraine would surely have retained some part of the excess in its republic budget; under assumption of the same retention ratio, it would be 24,983.9/80,010.8 × 22,206.7 = 6,934.2 million rubles. The other republics would have retained less according to their republic retention ratios, which differ. Thus the total drain from all the republics to the center would have varied slightly, and something like 6,934.2 million rubles would have been transferred to the Ukraine's "republic disposable income" from other republics. (Republic disposable income is the disposable income of people plus the taxes directly allocated to the republic.)

The "excess," 22,206.7 million rubles, is not a small sum. It makes a large but not overwhelming difference to Melnyk's Tables 10.2, 10.4, and 10.6. My correction of 6,934.2 million rubles is, however, a small sum. It also is a drain to the other republics, although imposed by the physical plan and the pricing procedures of the central government. It will suffice here to adjust Tables 10.4 and 10.6.

ADJUSTED TABLE 10.4:

Central Government's Budget in Ukraine, 1959-70
(million rubles)

Revenues		
Turnover tax directly levied	80,010.8	
Less turnover tax retained in Ukraine's budget	24,983.9	
Central government's actual take		55,026.9
Turnover tax indirectly levied by other republics on Ukrainian exports, less counterpart[b]	22,206.7	
Less transfer to other republics, or turnover tax that would have been retained in Ukraine	6,934.2	
		15,272.5
Central government's take		70,299.4
Total revenues		151,870.3
Sum[a] withdrawn from Ukraine		83,152.0

[a]"Sum" is preferable to "capital."
[b]This is the tax levied indirectly by the Ukraine on exports to it by other republics.

ADJUSTED TABLE 10.6

1. Sum[a] withdrawn from Ukraine	90,086.2[b]
6. National income of Ukraine as reported	453,600.0
7. (1) as percentage of (6)	19.9
8. National income plus indirectly levied turnover tax	475,806.7
9. (1) as percentage of (8)	18.9

[a]"Sum" is better than "capital."
[b]The 6,934.2 must now be added back to the 83,152.0 million rubles.

SOME GENERALIZATIONS

In other words, the tax adjustments that recommend themselves from a regional point of view would not have affected the Western "factor incomes" concept, which already correctly (or as correctly as possible under Soviet conditions) measures Ukrainian productivity and its relation to that of the rest of the Soviet Union. But the adjustments would have raised, not lowered, the direct drain, since they would have rendered a range of Ukrainian products taxable without any compensating adjustment in the tax rate.

We show this algebraically.

First, we admit the principle of taxing the means of production, if only in order to tax them as they enter into interrepublic exchange; this is the essence of the "Ukrainian correction" to which all this work points.

Second, we reject any solution that might raise retail prices anywhere, and we keep the national tax constant.

Third, we reject any excessively ad hoc solution, such as a tax on intermediate goods only when they enter interrepublic trade. We choose instead the simplest way: we convert the turnover tax into value-added tax (VAT).

Fourth, we assume constant average union rates of turnover tax and VAT, equally applied to all republics.

Thus the production account of the Ukraine was

$$X_s + V_u + T_u = P_u = R_u + W_u + X_u \tag{1}$$

where

P is the final value of all goods sold or transferred
X is the exports of intermediate goods by any area
V is wage bill and profits
T is turnover tax
R is consumption goods produced at home and retailed at home
W is the exports of consumption goods by any area
u is Ukraine
s is rest of Soviet Union.

The tax was levied at the rate

$$t = \frac{T_u}{R_u + W_u - T_u} \tag{2}$$

(We must express the tax as a rate on factor cost, whereas the Soviet economists prefer to express it as a rate on sales price because, to them, it is part of value added.)

After the change the Ukrainian production account is

$$X_s(1 + t') + V_u(1 + t') = R_u + W_u + X_u(1 + t');93) \tag{3}$$

where t' is the new VAT rate but the union tax take is constant:

$$t'(V_u + V_s) = T_u + T_s = t(V_u + V_s). \tag{4}$$

Retail prices, then, are undisturbed, by assumption (2). Thus the old rate is the same as the new $(t = t')$.

But in accordance with the rule that tax is formally incident on the territory where the taxed article is produced, tX_s is paid in area s and tX_u in the Ukraine. Thus the Ukrainian tax bill is

$$T'_u = t'V_u = t'(R_u + W_u + X_u - T_u) \tag{5}$$

and the rest of the union pays

$$T'_s = t'V_s = t'(R_s + W_s + X_s - X_u - T_s) \tag{6}$$

But $X_u > X_s$; this is the whole burden of the structural imbalance behind the "Ukrainian correction." This imbalance corresponds to a deficit in consumer goods: $W_u < W_s$, to which we return.

The old tax rate (2) can be rewritten as

$$t = \frac{T_u}{X_s - X_u + V_u} \tag{7}$$

so that the new bill minus the old bill is

$$(t' - t)V_u + t(X_u - X_s). \tag{8}$$

But with $t' = t$ this equation boils down to an excess payment by the Ukraine under the new system,

$$t(X_u - X_s) \tag{9}$$

and an equal saving to the other republics.

If we keep the rate of republic retention of tax constant at r, we have a "republic disposable national income at market prices" of

$$Y_u = V_u + rT_u$$

and a drain of

$$D_u = (1 - r)T_u$$

plus all the other items that Melnyk puts in his drain. With the new tax yield these become

$$Y'_u = V_u + rT_u$$

and

$$D'_u = (1 - r)T'_u$$

The drain as a rate on republic disposable income moves from

$$\frac{(1 - r)T_u}{V_u + rT_u}$$

to

$$\frac{(1 - r)T'_u}{V_u + rT'_u}$$

where the LHS $<$ RHS, since these simplify to

$$T_u V_u < T'_u V_u$$

So with a tax that operated rationally and a constant rate of republic retention of tax, everything would go up: republic disposable income, the drain, and the rate of the drain upon disposable income—though at different rates.

The drain is not the same as the interrepublic balance of trade. It is the Ukraine's financial balance with the central government (which produces nothing), whereas its balance of trade with other republics is not merely a fiscal matter, though taxes influence it. In the initial situation, with an orthodox turnover tax the balance of trade is

$$W_u + X_u - W_s - X_s \tag{10}$$

where the X items are untaxed, $X_u > X_s$, $W_u < W_s$. The turnover tax is already included in the W items, and their prices are constant ex hypothesi when we go over to VAT. The new balance is

$$W_u - W_s + (1 + t') (X_u - X_s) \tag{11}$$

a clear improvement for the Ukraine.

But the new balance minus the old balance (11 - 10) is exactly equal to the increased tax take (10), so the Ukraine gains nothing either way, except that if its tax retention ratio remains unchanged, it can now add $rt'(X_u - X_s)$ to republic disposable income.

None of this throws any direct light on Melnyk's "excess" discussed above, which was obtained very indirectly. But it is the same concept as (10) or (11), and it would be worthwhile to put arithmetical flesh upon my algebra by the use of a multiregional input-output table.

CONCLUSIONS

Let me end with a word of impertinent advice. Ukrainians all over the world, even Communist Ukrainians, think very ill of the Soviet Union and of the Russians who, essentially, run it. There is no room in it for spiritual values, even for Russian ones; no room for civil liberties; no room for Ukrainian culture; still less for Ukrainian nationalism—or even nationhood. Such a superstructure should surely rest upon a similar economic base, marked.by inefficiency, personal inequality, and regional exploitation. But such an inference is a form of Marxism and so, for the most part, wrong.

In terms of sheer growth, the Ukraine has done very well. This includes the growth of consumption, for the investment proportion is constant in a Soviet-type economy, as elsewhere. But in terms of the size of that proportion, of con-sumer sovereignty, quality of life, and such aspects of efficiency, the country has clearly suffered: such faults are the obverse of the virtues of the Soviet system.[6]

No system produces greater inequalities of power than the Soviet does. But economic inequality is not a necessary part of the system. Communist Eastern Europe has never suffered the USSR's economic inequality, and the latter has virtually abandoned it.[7] A non-Stalinist but Communist Ukraine would have had an East European experience—that is, there would have been much more equality than in a capitalist Ukraine.

It is the extent of regional exploitation, of the "drain," that must make anybody, let alone a Ukrainian, pause. Our figures are not very reliable, but put it at 10 percent of national income, all totally unrequited. This is a perpetual reparation greater in the long run than that paid by East Germany (25 percent of national income in 1947-53). It is the essence of socialism that such sums be neither repayable nor interest-bearing: they have the same moral status as the capitalist progressive income tax—or, rather, they would have if the Ukrainian people had ever been democratically consulted about them.

This drain does not go exclusively to the expansion of Soviet military power. It also goes to the build-up that has taken place in Central Asia. In that region it is not only Russian (and Ukrainian) immigrants who have benefited from new medical and educational services, but the native peasantry as well.* Nevertheless, it is the extent of regional exploitation, of the "drain" that must make anybody, let alone a Ukrainian, pause. Estimated at 10 percent of national income, this perpetual reparation will eventually exceed that paid by East Germany (25 percent of national income between 1947 and 1953). As is usual under socialism, these sums are neither repayable nor interest-bearing. They have the same moral status as the progressive income tax in capitalist countries, except that the Ukrainian people are never consulted. In the Soviet Union these decisions are, of course, not made on a democratic basis as in the West.

---

*Broadly speaking, Central Asian industry and urban life are on a Russian level, with Russians in senior posts; but rural productivity is very low. Central Asian poverty is mainly a matter of the vast number of young children, and does not betoken a very low level of productivity.

NOTES

1. See Robert W. Fogel, *Railroads and American Economic Growth* (Baltimore: Johns Hopkins University Press, 1964).

2. Alexander Dallin, *German Rule in Russia* (London: Macmillan, 1957), pp. 63–67.

3. See Peter Wiles, "On the Importance of Being Djugashvili," *Problems of Communism* (April 1963); Alec Nove, *An Economic History of the USSR* (London: Allen Lane, 1969), ch. 7.

4. See Peter Wiles, *Communist International Economics* (New York: Praeger, 1968), ch. 9 for the terms of trade, ch. 14 for capital transactions.

5. Ibid.

6. See Peter Wiles, *Political Economy of Communism* (Cambridge, Mass.: Harvard University Press, 1962), ch. 11.

7. See Peter Wiles, *Distribution of Income: East and West* (Amsterdam: North-Holland Press, 1974), lec. II; and A. B. Atkinson, ed., *The Personal Distribution of Incomes* (London: Allen and Unwin, 1976).

ABOUT THE EDITOR AND CONTRIBUTORS

V. N. Bandera, Professor of Economics, Temple University

David W. Bronson, Senior Research Economist, Central Intelligence Agency

Stanley H. Cohn, Professor of Economics, SUNY at Binghamton

Leslie Dienes, Associate Professor of Geography, University of Kansas

James W. Gillula, Research Associate, Duke University

Holland Hunter, Professor of Economics, Haverford College

I. S. Koropeckyj, Professor of Economics, Temple University

Z. L. Melnyk, Professor of Finance, University of Cincinnati

Stephen Rapawy, Research Analyst, U.S. Department of Commerce

Gertrude E. Schroeder, Professor of Economics, University of Virginia

F. Douglas Whitehouse, Senior Research Economist, Central Intelligence Agency

Peter Wiles, Professor of Economics, London School of Economics

Craig ZumBrunnen, Assistant Professor of Geography, University of Washington

RELATED TITLES
Published by
Praeger Special Studies

DEMOGRAPHIC DEVELOPMENTS IN THE SOVIET UNION
AND EASTERN EUROPE
edited by Leszek A. Kosinski

ENVIRONMENTAL MISUSE IN THE SOVIET UNION
edited by Fred Singleton

THE SOVIET WEST: Interplay Between Nationality
and Social Organization
edited by Ralph S. Clem

STUDIES IN SOVIET INPUT-OUTPUT ANALYSIS
edited by Vladimir G. Treml